Can Green Sustain Growth?

D1714870

INNOVATION *and* TECHNOLOGY *in the* WORLD ECONOMY

MARTIN KENNEY, *Editor*
University of California, Davis and Berkeley Roundtable
on the International Economy

Other titles in the series:

DAVID C. MOWERY, RICHARD P. NELSON, BHAVEN N. SAMPAT, AND ARVIDS A. SIEDONIS
Ivory Tower and Industrial Innovation: University-Industry Technology Transfer Before and After the Bayh-Doyle Act in the United States

MARTIN KENNEY AND RICHARD FLORIDA, EDS.
Locating Global Advantage: Industry Dynamics in the International Economy

GARY FIELDS
Territories of Profit: Communications, Capitalist Development, and the Innovative Enterprises of G.F. Swift and Dell Computer

URS VON BURG
The Triumph of Ethernet: Technological Communities and the Battle for the LAN Standard

Can Green Sustain Growth?

From the Religion to the Reality of Sustainable Prosperity

EDITED BY JOHN ZYSMAN *and* MARK HUBERTY

Stanford Business Books
An Imprint of Stanford University Press
Stanford, California

Stanford University Press
Stanford, California

Special discounts for bulk quantities of Stanford Business Books
are available to corporations, professional associations, and
other organizations. For details and discount information, con-
tact the special sales department of Stanford University Press.
Tel: (650) 736-1782, Fax: (650) 736-1784

Printed in the United States of America on acid-free, archival-
quality paper

Library of Congress Cataloging-in-Publication Data

Can green sustain growth? : from the religion to the reality of sustainable prosperity / edited by John Zysman and Mark Huberty.
     pages cm — (Innovation and technology in the world
economy)
     Includes bibliographical references and index.
     ISBN 978-0-8047-8525-9 (cloth : alk. paper) —
ISBN 978-0-8047-8857-1 (electronic)
     1. Clean energy industries—Government policy—Case stud-
ies.   2. Energy policy—Environmental aspects—Case studies.
3. Energy development—Environmental aspects—Government
policy—Case studies.   4. Sustainable development—Government policy—Case studies.   I. Zysman, John, editor of compilation.   II. Huberty, Mark, editor of compilation.   III. Series:
Innovation and technology in the world economy.
     HD9502.5.C542C36 2013
     338.9'27—dc23
                                                    2013032078

Typeset by Newgen in 10/12.5 Electra

We dedicate this book to the memory of Dr. Gary Baldwin and Per Meilstrup. Their support made this book possible, and their encouragement and enthusiasm improved it immensely. We miss them both.

Contents

Preface

The Argument in Brief

Mark Huberty and John Zysman

A simple question motivates this book: Can "green" sustain growth? The notion of "green growth" emerged as a justification for investments and policies intended to address the challenge of climate change. In that conflicted political environment, green growth was a powerful temptation: if climate policy can generate the jobs and productivity growth necessary to sustain rising incomes, then sustaining political support becomes much easier. We could act regardless of whether we agreed on bigger questions about the threat of climate change, the size of the damages it threatens, or the urgency of action.

To some, the answer to this question seems obvious: build the emissions-free windmills and solar energy systems, and in one stroke we reduce carbon emissions and create jobs. But the reality is more complicated. Building out a new green energy system may provide temporary stimulus, but it is not immediately evident that it is the source of sustained growth. For now, "green" energy — energy that entirely eliminates or substantively reduces carbon emissions from energy production — usually costs more than traditional energy sources. This both annoys consumers and raises costs for producers, requiring them to adapt to new energy sources that otherwise offer them few advantages. Similarly, arguments that green energy sources generate more jobs than traditional sources per, for example, kilowatt-hour of electricity also imply that those jobs are less productive, requiring more workers to accomplish the same thing. There is, then, an economic price for green energy in the short term. Whether green can overcome these short-term costs to create growth is thus at present unclear. The present enthusiasm for it thus appears more religion — taken on faith — than reality.

Can we move green growth from religion to reality? Part I of the book grounds the answer to this question in the idea of energy systems transformation. Taking emissions out of the energy system will require a radical recasting of the energy system. Consider electricity. Green energy sources like wind or solar power fluctuate with the natural cycles of the wind and sun they depend on. Experience has shown that this intermittency risks destabilizing existing power systems as the share of green energy rises. Hence, there are limits to how much of today's electricity generation we can replace before we have to look elsewhere. That elsewhere poses similar problems. We could, for instance, smooth these fluctuations by storing excess power on very windy days for use on calm ones. But for now, storage remains exceedingly expensive. To take another example, today's power grid is designed to bring power from big, centralized power plants to small, diffused consumers. But wind, solar, and other renewable sources will likely be diffuse themselves and located wherever natural conditions are most favorable. Hence, we will eventually need to rethink today's grid infrastructure as well. Finally, even more comprehensive solutions, like the "electrify everything, decarbonize electricity" proposals from Williams et al. (2012) and others, require still broader changes encompassing transport as well.

Part I of the book argues that green growth, if it is to help sustain the political consensus for climate policy, must find ways to exploit this wholesale transformation of the energy system for economic gain. Historically, radical changes in energy systems, whether in shifting from wood to coal, shifting from coal to oil, or electrification, all supported dramatic economic gains by changing what we could think of producing and how fast or cheaply we could produce it. More generally, technology systems transformations, such as the sequence of communications revolutions running from the telegraph to the Internet, can generate an entire universe of unanticipated opportunities throughout the economy that sustain growth. In the same sense, a low-emissions energy systems transformation may hold significant opportunities. But the economic possibilities of a transformed energy system—and the political support those possibilities may generate—will only become clear as we pursue the transformation itself. Consequently, the costs will remain evident, while the gains are murky and in the future.

Part II of the book takes up the political question posed by the present uncertainty surrounding green growth. If green growth proved to be a reality, its economic potential would generate powerful support for climate policy. But that potential will only become clear in the process of pursuing a low-emissions energy systems transformation. That transformation will, in the short term, generate higher costs and political opposition from those it displaces.

So far, that opposition—from powerful, organized industrial interests—has
effectively resisted efforts to rapidly reduce emissions, even when those efforts garnered broad public support. Hence, how can the political support for systems transformation be sustained long enough to discover the economic potential that can sustain political support for it over the long term?

We frame our answer to the question arguing that countries successfully pursuing green policy share a particular political dynamic: a green spiral. At its core, we argue in Chapter 5, the green spiral reflects a process of mutually reinforcing feedback between climate policy and industrial interests, in which the development of new infrastructure and energy approaches creates new economic clienteles who then become advocates for further action. This self-reinforcing process helps explain how market-driven, profit-oriented constituencies for climate action can emerge. These green industrial interests help stabilize policies in place and push for new policies, offsetting opposition from interests tied to the preexisting system.

The countries profiled in Part II illustrate the different nature of the green spiral for developing and developed countries. For the advanced countries, the task is reconstituting around green existing and successful energy systems. For the emerging markets, the task is not only how to provide green but how to expand the energy system itself rapidly enough to sustain economic growth. In all cases, although the outcomes differ, the particular policies adopted are shaped by the existing energy system. The existing system sets up both the economic possibilities and political fights surrounding emissions reduction.

In particular, these cases illustrate how contingent a green spiral can be. Among the rich countries, successful green growth strategies have all built a green spiral atop incremental policy steps often unrelated to the actual climate problem. The Danish case demonstrates how a strategic concern about energy security triggered an energy system development that today has culminated in broad political and industrial support for completely removing fossil fuels from Denmark's energy system. In the European Union more broadly, new concerns about energy security interacted with long-standing industrial prowess in green technology to generate policy opportunities for using climate policy to solve challenges and promote new markets. Korea's green growth strategy represented under the Lee administration an opportunity to mobilize industrial interests to confront obstacles to the next phase of growth in the Korean economy.

In contrast, countries with weak or nonexistent green growth strategy have failed to translate small tasks to big ambitions. In the United States, policy experimentation at the local level has proved successful, but that success has yet to overcome gridlocked national politics. Instead, green coalitions and policy experimentation in the United States have emerged principally at the level of the individual states such as California and Colorado. Most evidently, in the California case, acute problems of smog and a concern with the risks of nuclear power provoked specific policies that, over time, became the foundation for new action on climate change. But local success in the United States has made little difference at the national level, where the balance of policy constitutes a significant subsidy for fossil fuel and nuclear power and what isolated efforts at energy systems transformation exist remain mired in political controversy. Meanwhile, Japan decoupled pollution from economic growth and became the paragon of energy efficiency. Yet, energy policy has been dominated by brown interests, principally those who support and defend the current fossil fuel–intensive energy system, and their allies in the nuclear sector. It remains to be seen whether the Fukushima crisis will become a critical juncture in the emergence of a green growth strategy.

The chapters on emerging markets illustrate a very different policy dynamic: how a green spiral might reconcile the competing objectives of rapid development and sustainable development. While Brazil and China arguably remain "brown" countries, they have both shown leadership in major areas of green technology: biofuels for Brazil and solar electricity for China. Furthermore, as the chapter on India suggests, both distributed renewable energy and energy efficiency may provide superior solutions to energy poverty when bureaucracies and politics make expanding the traditional energy system difficult.

In short, moving green growth from religion to reality is as much a political task as a technical or economic one. We reach that conclusion by addressing three questions in the next chapters: Where might the growth potential of low-emissions technologies come from? What would allow economies to discover and maximize this potential? What do ongoing national experiences tell us about the politics of green growth? We suggest that green might well offer new sources of productivity improvements and new forms of production. But exactly how remains an open question. Addressing climate change and answering that question will require a systemic transformation of today's fossil fuel energy systems. Initiating and sustaining that transformation will, we conclude, require policy makers to find immediate material gains from transformation that can sustain the search for broad growth opportunities capable of supporting our long-term goals for the economy, the environment, and the planet at large.

Acknowledgments

This book represents the culmination of several years of work on issues surrounding technological change, emissions reduction, and economic growth. During its incubation, this work has been supported by funding from Mandag Morgen, the Danish think tank and magazine, the Alfred P. Sloan Foundation, and the University of California, Berkeley's Center for Information Technology Research in the Interest of Society (CITRIS).

Prior to the 2009 COP-15 Climate meeting, Mandag Morgen formed the Copenhagen Climate Council as a vehicle for businesspeople, scientists, and policy analysts to provide input to drive the negotiation process. We worked with the Council to hold three separate meetings on issues related to technological innovation, economic growth, and climate change. The University of California, Berkeley, provided critical financial support and leadership for the first meeting, held in May 2008. Shankar Sastry, dean of engineering; Paul Wright, director of the Center for Information Technology Research in the Interest of Society (CITRIS); and the late Dr. Gary Baldwin, director of special projects at CITRIS, deserve special acknowledgment for their contributions.

Mandag Morgen continued to sponsor the studies on green growth that form the core of this book. The cases in this book emerged from a collaboration with the Green Growth Leaders forum, a group of industrial and academic leaders formed by Mandag Morgen to press for climate action and green growth solutions in the aftermath of COP-15. Throughout our collaboration with Mandag Morgen, we have benefited enormously from the support, input, insight, and feedback we've received from founder and publisher Erik Rasmussen and from Per Meilstrup, head of the climate projects group.

Finally, the ideas in this book have improved enormously through the chance to present them to academic and policy audiences alike. We would particularly like to thank the organizers and participants of the Brussels Economic Forum 2010; the European Council Internal Competitiveness Discussion under the 2010 Belgian presidency; the Green Korea 2010 and 2012 conferences; the 2011 Council for European Studies conference; and the 2012 Tianjin Binhai Eco-Cities Forum. In addition, we've received ongoing feedback and insight from Jim Rogers, Laura Tyson, Martin Kenney, and numerous other colleagues at UC Berkeley and beyond.

Several specific acknowledgments deserve mention. Mark Huberty's research for this book was also supported by the Fulbright Foundation, the U.S. Environmental Protection Agency STAR Fellowship, and Bruegel. Ben Allen's research on Brazil received support from the SSRC International Dissertation Research Fellowship and the Instituto de Pesquisa Economica Aplicada. Brian Woodall's research was supported by a Faculty Foundation Grant from the Ivan Allen College and the Georgia Tech Foundation.

The substantive and administrative support through this project from Kate Goldman, Juliana Mandell, and Danielle Boudreau has been essential.

Can Green Sustain Growth?

I. FRAMING THE DEBATE: GREEN GROWTH AND THE TRANSFORMATION OF THE ENERGY SYSTEMS

1

FROM RELIGION TO REALITY

Energy Systems Transformation for Sustainable Prosperity

Mark Huberty and John Zysman

"Green growth" has arrived at a critical time. Progress on emissions reduction has lagged far behind our understanding of the damage potential of unchecked climate change, and this is unlikely to change anytime soon. International climate negotiations have faltered, and it remains unclear how a deal sufficiently ambitious to address the emissions problem can be enforced. Domestically, the 2008 financial crisis reduced nations' willingness and ability to pay for emissions mitigation at home. With austerity in vogue, rich countries have also lost what little enthusiasm they had to pay for ambitious emissions reductions in emerging markets abroad. As the effects of the recession have slowly faded, emissions have resumed their upward trajectory, aided by rapid development in the emerging markets.

These difficulties make the newfound popularity of green growth unsurprising. The notion of green growth suggests that the investments required to mitigate the worst effects of climate change could become sources of sustained economic growth rather than burdens. Were green growth to become a reality, it would bypass the myriad problems of climate change mitigation: who should pay, how much, and when. If green growth were possible then, as with large-scale technological transformations of the past, the shift to a low-emissions economy might catalyze a wave of investment, innovation, and job creation that could sustain and pay for itself. Rich countries could base renewed economic competitiveness on an array of new "green" industries, while emerging markets could support their ongoing development on a foundation of new low-emissions technology.

Unfortunately, green growth today remains more "religion" than "reality." Most arguments for green growth today take on faith the link between investment

4   in low-emissions technology and the creation of durable economic growth. Moving green growth beyond faith, however, appears difficult. In isolation, the gains from any specific investment in green energy are likely to be limited and short term. Instead, with some exceptions, green growth has to date functioned largely as a justification for changes to energy systems we might want to take for other reasons, such as emissions reduction or energy security.

This book looks beyond near-term investment to long-term sources of growth. We believe that translating the array of isolated investments required for emissions reduction into sustained economic growth may occur only if those investments can catalyze systemic changes in the energy system itself. Such a low-emissions energy systems transformation may then reveal new sources of employment, goods, services, and productivity growth inaccessible in today's fossil fuel–based, high-emissions energy systems.

We begin by asking two questions about the potential sources of green growth: first, *where* might this growth potential of low-emissions technologies come from, and second, *what* would allow economies to discover and maximize this potential. In this chapter and in Chapter 2, we argue that effective emissions reduction will require, in effect, a transformation of modern energy systems. That transformation will require parallel and complementary changes to the technological, economic, and political determinants of how we produce, distribute, and use energy in modern industrial societies. Most green growth arguments anticipate that this transformation will lead to durable economic growth. Inventing new energy technologies, deploying new energy infrastructure, and improving energy efficiency will, of course, require investment from, and generate employment in, sectors ranging from capital-intensive manufacturing to construction. The transition may provide, for the near term, new economic opportunities that can partially offset the cost of a transition necessary for mitigating climate change.

But whether that transition can support sustained economic growth is a separate and more difficult argument. Conceived solely in terms of jobs and investment from renewable energy, the scope and duration of opportunity are very narrow. As Chapter 3 shows, most low-emissions-related investment and employment will substitute for, rather than add to, employment in fossil fuel industries. Moreover, at least in the near future, low-emissions energy will probably cost more than equivalent fossil fuel capacity, potentially crowding out other potentially productive investment. Nor should we place broad hopes on export-led growth either. There will, of course, be countries that capture comparative advantage in green technologies and exploit those advantages to grow through exports abroad. But comparative advantage in green technologies will likely cluster in countries with specific industrial and innovative capacities that other countries will find expensive to replicate (Huberty and Zachmann 2011). Such green growth will thus not be widely shared. Of equal concern, the notion of export-led green growth threatens a new "green mercantilism" born of a perceived zero-sum game for control of green export markets.

Obtaining the technologies required for a low-emissions energy systems transformation poses equally difficult problems. Virtually no one disputes the idea that such a transformation will require an array of innovation in new and existing technologies and their widespread commercial adoption. Who will make the investments in developing these technologies remains controversial. Venture capital has been entangled with and supported other technological systems transformations, most notably the Silicon Valley brand of information technology. Countries around the world, and particularly the United States, have perhaps understandably hoped that venture capital could drive the creation of green energy technologies.

But as Kenney and Hargadon argue in Chapter 4, venture capital will likely fall short of repeating its earlier success. Energy technologies for the most part lack the rapid growth, high turnover, and low capital costs that underpinned the huge returns enjoyed by venture capital investments in ICT. Rather, the energy sector remains focused on capital-intensive, highly reliable technologies capable of integrating with preexisting, complex, economically vital systems. These characteristics run contrary to the needs of successful venture capital–financed green industry. Historically, venture capital has made an array of small investments in fast-growing sectors in the hope that one will become a massive payoff like Google. Here, however, they must make a series of much larger investments in slow-moving, capital-intensive industries, with the knowledge that more than one might become a Solyndra — a massive loss with little upside spillover. Given these incentives, the venture capital model is unlikely, on its own, to drive the innovations required for low-emissions energy systems transformation.

In light of these difficulties, we argue that enduring green growth will have to come from the potential created by a low-carbon energy systems transformation for the economy at large. Past transformations — whether in energy, as in the electrification of cities and factories in the early nineteenth century, or elsewhere, as in the ICT revolution — of course generated investment and employment in their own narrow sectors. But the explosive growth we associate with those earlier transformations derived mostly from how they changed what was possible in the broader economy. The impact of computers went well beyond replacing adding machines, and that of electrification went well beyond simply replacing gaslight. They initiated, among other changes, the radical restructuring of assembly lines and the long-distance transmission of

6   information. These transformations became sources of growth and productivity with far greater scope and impact than the narrow electrical or semiconductor sectors themselves.

We cannot know, of course, whether the low-emissions technology revolution will deliver a similar array of changes. But we emphasize that the growth opportunities of earlier transformations were not always obvious either. History is replete with failed prognostication by even the most sophisticated technologists, often about their own technologies.

Instead, moving green growth from religion to reality will require creating the economic and market space in which firms and consumers can discover the growth potential in this transformation. That, we argue, suggests a role for governments that goes beyond the limited role of setting emissions prices and supporting basic research and development. Indeed, earlier transformations demonstrated that the state has regularly played a more expansive role, even in revolutions that, like ICT, have since been heralded as triumphs of free-market innovation. Determining, then, how to repeat these past successes while avoiding the obvious risks of distortion and capture — either by today's fossil fuel industry or tomorrow's clean-technology sector — remains the primary challenge for green growth policy makers.

Transforming the energy system will, though, require making difficult choices amidst serious political conflicts. The transition we consider in the first part of the book requires a process of technical, economic, and regulatory experimentation. The experimentation, in turn requires sustained political support to survive the inevitable failures, setbacks, and misdirection. But the process of energy systems transformation will create numerous opportunities for conflict and endless reformulation of the policy environment. Even accepting the common threat of climate change, the transformation of today's fossil fuel–based economies will force difficult choices. Even if one can imagine that an energy systems transformation might be able to support green growth, it will invariably benefit some and impose costs on others. Abandoning otherwise functional fossil fuel–based energy assets will of course bring opposition from their owners, who will undoubtedly claim they made their investments in good faith to satisfy an energy-hungry society.

Rebuilding the systems of energy transmission and distribution will require state interventions in land use planning, capital investment, and regulation of monopolistic markets. Transforming energy efficiency will touch every business and household. Each of these goals, moreover, will be weighed against an array of other priorities for investment dollars. The political task of managing the conflicts about how we structure the transition and manage its costs and benefits thus becomes as important as the economic task of structuring a smooth, efficient, and cost-effective transformation. The second half of the book examines how a variety of countries — from small, rich states in Northern Europe, to giant emerging markets in Asia — have approached these technical and political challenges.

Green growth simultaneously represents enormous promise and real challenges. A low-emissions energy systems transformation that delivers broad economic growth would remove many of the roadblocks to effective climate change mitigation. But, as we endeavor to show in this book, the obvious sources of that growth are limited and finite, and the sources of transformative growth are unclear. At present, then, green growth provides a valuable creed for policy makers who desire to make progress on climate change in times of austerity. But sustaining progress over the long term will require moving green growth from political religion to economic reality.

A FIRST STEP TOWARD REALITY: GREEN GROWTH AND ENERGY SYSTEMS TRANSFORMATION

The discussion of green growth first requires that we clearly define the terms used in the book. We define *green growth* as the use of climate policy to create economic opportunity.[1] This definition, however, departs from those implied in today's debate. That debate covers at least three different concepts of green growth, all shorthand for myriad policies with diverse, and at times contradictory, goals:

1. The use of climate change mitigation policy to create jobs and other forms of economic opportunity
2. The changes required to make economic growth compatible with environmental sustainability
3. The restructuring of capitalist production to resolve both perceived inherent instability and social and ecological injustices in the system

We also depart from most analysts in how we identify the sources of growth and the tasks required to achieve it. Contrary to most green growth arguments, we find little reason to believe that the jobs and investment required for emissions reduction alone can generate significant long-term economic growth. Rather, we argue, growth can only come, if at all, through what a low-emissions energy system makes possible for the broader economy.

Making green growth a reality will therefore require exploiting the opportunities of a broad shift from today's high-emissions energy systems to low-emissions alternatives. Assessing whether this is possible requires that we first consider the unique challenges posed by this transformation. As Chapter 2 discusses at length, widespread adoption of renewable energy will introduce

8   energy sources with fundamentally different physical characteristics from to-day's fossil fuels. Maintaining the reliability of a system built around the be-havior of fossil fuels will thus require a range of technological changes that go well beyond just switching energy sources.

Physically, fossil fuels offer energy-dense, geographically centralized, con-stant supplies of power. Each successive generation of fossil fuels — coal, oil, and gas — provided denser, more easily stored, and more easily transported fuel sources. The ability to store ever-larger amounts of energy in the same place has encouraged more concentrated, centralized electricity generation. These highly centralized production systems serve diffuse households and businesses via a distribution grid designed to move geographically dense production to diffuse consumers. Finally, the system permits precise control of power gen-eration as long as fossil fuel supplies are available. This precise control permits the system to supply consumers, who operate in markets that provide little information and few incentives for flexibility, with highly reliable power.

A switch to renewable energy sources, which deliver little or no net emis-sions over their entire life cycle, poses at least three technical challenges. First, the geographic dispersion of renewable energy sources will require downstream changes to best incorporate low-emissions energy into the power system. The best locations for wind, sun, geothermal, and other renewable en-ergy sources are often located far from existing power plants, and they have far lower generation capacity per unit area. Widespread adoption of renewable energy will therefore require significant changes to a power grid designed to move power from centralized, concentrated producers to diffuse consumers. Instead, the grid will need to evolve to concentrate and redistribute power from low-density, dispersed renewable energy generation. This constitutes a major restructuring of critical infrastructure.

These changes to the grid must also confront a second challenge: intermit-tency. Renewable energy sources — particularly wind and solar electricity — depend on flows of sun and wind that vary minute by minute, seasonally, and over a period of many years. This variation leads to intermittency: fluctuations in the power available from renewable energy sources. This intermittency stands opposed to the assumption of constant and precisely controlled power supplies that underpins the stability of the rest of the energy system. Conse-quently, at sufficiently high shares of renewable energy,[2] this intermittency can destabilize the balance of supply and demand critical to the operation of the electric grid. Maintaining the stability of the energy system in the face of intermittency will require substantial changes to systems of energy transmis-sion and distribution. Expanding the grid's geographic coverage can help level out the peaks and valleys of power supply across regions. Energy storage can

provide similar services by capturing excess power at peak production periods 9
for use during supply lulls. Demand-smoothing innovations can help support
these supply-smoothing changes. "Intelligent" grids may be able to prioritize
and adjust energy consumption in parallel with supply fluctuations, enabling
significantly more efficient energy consumption. Regardless of which of these
options proves feasible, though, any of them will require an array of new innovations and substantial capital investment to adapt the power transmission and
distribution system to the new properties of energy supply. The transformation
thus goes well beyond the simple adoption of renewable energy.

Third and finally, accommodating variable generation will become much
easier if energy users can understand and respond to fluctuations in energy
supply. Today, however, both the markets for energy and the technologies that
consume it bury that information and inhibit consumer responsiveness. Improving this situation will necessitate a series of innovations that permit more
efficient and responsive use of energy. The reach of these innovations promises to be very wide — from relatively centralized solutions like smart meters to
diverse changes in appliances and consumer electronics.

These technological transformations must go hand in hand with a set of
structural changes in the markets, business models, and regulatory structures
that provide the framework in which these technical systems operate. As the
country cases and the discussion of EU energy policy in particular make clear,
the regulatory and market structures that worked for highly centralized and
vertically integrated electricity markets will likely prove suboptimal for more
decentralized and responsive low-emissions markets. Bringing an array of
new energy technologies into the network may require changes in ownership
and in control of networks, as well as the obligations of network operators.
Demand-response pricing of energy will require significant changes to the
pricing structures used in many energy systems, where users have come to
expect constant prices over time. Funding the investments required for a new
energy system will require changes to electric utilities' rate and capital investment structures. Finally, new "smart" grids will bring with them an array of
new concerns about the use of the information derived from grid intelligence.
Each of these changes will challenge firms and policy makers alike to reconfigure legacy structures to better exploit the opportunities and contain the
dangers of new technological systems.

Despite the magnitude of the change implied by a low-emissions energy
systems transformation, we should be cautious, if not skeptical, about its ability
to drive a surge in economic growth. If this transformation proves enormously
successful, it will result in an energy system that proves as capable, as reliable,
and as economical as today's. But, apart from lower emissions, that system will

offer few obvious advantages over the high-emissions system it replaced. In these terms, a low-emissions energy systems transformation offers few obvious material advantages to the broader economy. That reality raises real questions as to whether an energy sector, on its own, will become a catalyst for growth as well as a solution to climate change.

Green growth, if it is to become reality, will thus need to look beyond the obvious, but problematic, near-term investments a transformation will require. Instead, we should ask whether it is possible for such a transformation to provide opportunities for the broader economy on a scale that will represent significant returns on the investments that the transition will require. Other systems transformations have provided new opportunities for economic activity that were surprising in either their scope or magnitude. Those opportunities, in turn, became the engines that sustained transformations despite their costs. Whether green growth can do the same remains unexplored.

SYSTEMIC TRANSFORMATIONS AND ECONOMIC GROWTH

To better understand how systems transformation might catalyze broad opportunities for growth, we turn, by analogy, to an earlier instance of transformative economic growth driven by technological systems transformation. We observe that the network itself, rather than the technologies at either end, proved the transformative influence in shifting the trajectory of economic and technological systems. This result suggests that the power grid may provide opportunities to use energy systems transformation to catalyze growth. But these transformations also suggest caution in predicting that a low-emissions energy systems transformation will repeat their successes. As the following section details, low-emissions energy solutions may lack the technical and market conditions that contributed to the creation of economic growth in earlier periods.

We focus on the information technology revolution as a powerful example of how a transformative technology emerging in one sector of the economy can change goods and services and production throughout the economy, create new options and possibilities, and, in so doing, generate widespread growth. We might, of course, have chosen from an array of other instances of similarly catalytic technologies: the adoption of coal (Nef 1932; Sieferle 2001), electrification (Hughes 1979, 1983), or intermodal shipping (Levinson 2008). As with these alternatives, the history of ICT provides three important lessons for the transformation of energy systems: first, the network proved to be a significant enabling technology; second, the growth opportunities generated by the transformation came as much from the possibilities it created in the broader economy as they did from the IT sector itself; and third, regulatory intervention and public support played a co-equal role with private ingenuity in initiating and driving the transformation.

The transformation wrought by digital technology has proceeded rapidly since the 1940s, impacting an array of sectors from insurance and banking to manufacturing and international logistics. But the consolidation of the digital age only truly arrived with pervasive networking. Throughout, the speed of the ICT transformation has been remarkable. Since 1940, computing power has increased by roughly 50 percent per year on average (Nordhaus 2007). More recently, the growth in networks has complemented this exponential growth in computational power. In 1991, the U.S. National Science Foundation opened to commercial activity the internal, distributed information network it had inherited from the Department of Defense. By 2000, this "internet" accounted for at least $100 billion in annual commerce and 2.5 million jobs in the United States alone, launched several firms in the Fortune 500, and laid the foundations for a second wave of innovation in social media, communications, and logistics that continue to this day. Thus, within 20 years of its commercialization, the internet had radically transformed not just information technology but the economy at large, generating significant economic growth and productivity improvements.

The speed and apparent smoothness of the ICT revolution derive, we argue, from two transformative phases—first in hardware and then in communications. These phases shared an important set of characteristics. Both merged private investment and innovation with public sector market formation and rule making. Neither proceeded out of some grand design but rather drew on general public support for innovation and investment and regulatory structures that encouraged early experimentation, policed monopolies, and sponsored network openness. Network openness, in turn, enabled rapid private sector experimentation both within and on top of these networks. This experimentation in turn drove a symbiosis between innovation and demand. Rapid improvements in technical capabilities supported widening demand for products, which in turn supported ongoing investment and innovation in the next generation of technology. That symbiosis between the ICT sector and the broader economy made the revolution self-sustaining.

The first phase of this revolution, which we might call the hardware phase, lasted from the invention of the transistor in 1947 to the introduction of the personal computer in the early 1980s. These years saw private sector innovation, buttressed by public support for research and development and strong military demand for new technologies. Innovation also benefitted from public sector antitrust restrictions on the ability of dominant market players to restrict the diffusion of new technologies. Much of this innovation originated in the laboratories of giants like AT&T and IBM. Left to their own devices, both firms might have used control of these technologies to generate rents, constrain market competition, and compete on the basis of access rather than features. Instead, both firms found themselves at the center of massive antitrust investigations that constrained their ability to pursue monopoly control of new technology. As a result, the transistors that came out of Bell Labs in the 1950s quickly diffused into the broader market. AT&T was also denied the opportunity to use its control of the communications network to limit access to competitors experimenting with the possibilities of emerging digital technology. Likewise, IBM was constrained by ongoing investigations into anticompetitive activity that spanned the formative years of the PC industry.

The second phase of the ICT revolution built on this hardware legacy and coupled information technology to communications. Here again, public action — this time in the role of standards-setter — played a vital role in the growth opportunities that evolved from the network at the heart of the revolution. Rapid growth in ICT depended on the predictable interoperability of a range of devices. Absent common standards, the large, positive network externalities of the internet might not have materialized. Indeed, had a network model along the lines of firms like America Online or Compuserve succeeded, competition might have come to focus on network access rather than end-user innovations. Instead, the emphasis, by both the Defense Advanced Projects Research Agency (DARPA) and the National Science Foundation, on open, redundant, standards-based communication networks provided the support for the open TCP/IP communications protocols that became the Internet. Coupled to antitrust restrictions on the control of telecommunications networks, those standards enabled a range of new competitors — from Cisco and Microsoft to Google and Facebook — to build entirely new markets atop networks otherwise dominated by legacy companies like AT&T. In time, innovation in those markets destabilized old competitors and provided opportunities for transformative growth.

While the ICT revolution and the development of Silicon Valley are held up as icons of entrepreneurial capitalism and venture finance, the ICT revolution itself rested on and was supported by public policy. Antitrust policy, as noted above, assured space for such venture-backed firms as Intel and AMD in semiconductors. Early innovations benefitted from substantial public sector demand that supported firms until private markets became robust enough. In particular, the American aerospace and defense programs presented the nascent ICT sector of the 1950s and 1960s with bottomless budgets and bleeding-edge performance demands. These public sector customers made large purchases at high prices and enormous margins that underwrote waves of early innovation and experimentation among what later became ICT sector leaders. These purchases, moreover, followed on enormous public support for computational research during and after World War II. Hence, the foundation for the private sector ICT revolution, driven by ever-cheaper computers operating at ever-higher performance levels, found its roots in government sponsorship of both basic research and market formation.

The implications for green growth are clear. ICT's largest contributions to economic growth came in what it enabled rather than in the ICT sector alone. For instance, the radical transformation of finance, insurance, and media; the decomposition of production; and the emergence of global supply networks all grew from, and were unimaginable without, the capabilities created by the ICT revolution. Most recently, a new era of goods and services has opened, built on the organization of information and relationships by giants like Google and Facebook. Those innovations depend on the Internet, which grew out of the scientific research at DARPA and built upon the foundations of semiconductor innovation. In each generation, the value and productivity gains were generated by the *use* and *application* of ICT innovations, not just the innovations themselves. This symbiosis between ICT sector innovation and growth in the broader economy drove a virtuous cycle of innovation, demand, and investment that sustained repeated and ongoing waves of broadbased economic growth.

Moreover, while the transformative power of ICT appears obvious in retrospect, we should not forget the early doubts about its economic potential. In the early years of the hardware revolution, IBM, so the story goes, thought it would only sell a handful of its new mainframe computers.[3] The enormous utility of the mainframe and its successors only became apparent through experimentation in the market. Microprocessors followed a similar pattern. Intel had to invest heavily in explaining to potential customers the possibilities of this new device. Indeed, its marketing manager at the time had a Ph.D. in electrical engineering—a qualification Intel considered necessary for articulating the potential of this new technology for tangible economic benefits even to product developers in electronics firms.[4] Last but not least, the commercial power of the Internet was hardly obvious at the beginning. Whatever the power of systemic transformations for the creation of economic growth, the specific opportunities from any given transformation are often obscured at the outset.

We can distill six lessons from the transformative growth catalyzed by the ICT revolution:

1. Growth came from the transformation of existing industries as well as the creation of new ones.

14

2. Growth benefitted from substantial public as well as private support for research, development, and deployment of new technology.
3. Growth depended on supportive regulatory regimes focused on openness and competition.
4. Growth emerged from both the networks and the new opportunities created by network capabilities.
5. Growth and technological change became self-sustaining both by making existing tasks cheaper and easier and by making it possible to envision new tasks and forms of value creation.
6. Growth was not a foregone conclusion at the outset of the transformation. Rather, it required significant experimentation to discover the possibilities for growth that transformation created.

Thus, the ICT revolution was predominately a systems transformation, in two senses. First, it required a transformation of both the technologies for computation and communication, and the broader regulatory and market context that determined how firms and consumers adopted those technologies. Second, it generated massive spillover benefits by transforming the possibilities for economic activity in the broader economy. The economic growth generated by the ICT revolution was thus split between growth in the ICT sector itself, and ICT's impact in the economy writ large (van Ark, Inklaar, and McGuckin 2002). Achieving this kind of transformative growth required both private investments in new technologies and business models and public support for open, competitive, standards-based markets in which those investments could thrive. Finally, and perhaps most critically for green growth, creating growth through the information revolution required a long period of experimentation before the full potential of the systems transformation became clear. In the same sense, we should expect a period of experimentation with "green tech" before its potential becomes clear.

CHALLENGES TO GREEN GROWTH: EMPLOYMENT, MERCANTILISM, AND THE LIMITS TO SYSTEMS TRANSFORMATION

Advocates of green growth frequently argue that a low-emissions energy systems transformation can drive the same kind of innovation-led growth that has characterized the ICT revolution and its predecessors. To date, however, few policy makers or policy analysts have paid attention to whether the conditions that made ICT a revolutionary technology hold for the transformation to low-emissions energy systems. Instead, as the review of green growth arguments in Chapter 3 shows, most of the emphasis has concentrated on near-term benefits from job creation or capture of export markets in "green" goods.

The disconnect between arguments for green growth and the nature of growth-enabling systems transformations poses an array of risks for climate and energy policy. First, given the differences between prior transformations and a low-emissions energy systems transformation, there are good reasons to believe that green growth will be very difficult to achieve. Second, to the extent that green growth policies emphasize near-term benefits, advocates of these policies risk overpromising and underdelivering, to the detriment of support for long-term policy. Third, the treatment of green growth as a series of zero-sum competitions among nations for job creation and control of export markets risks a new era of "green mercantilism" that will threaten other forms of international cooperation on climate, energy, and trade policy.

NOT ICT: LOW-EMISSIONS ENERGY SYSTEMS TRANSFORMATION IN HISTORICAL PERSPECTIVE

Earlier systems transformations, like the ICT example considered above, shared a series of characteristics that made them capable of catalyzing growth both within their own narrow sectors and throughout the economy as a whole. A low-emissions energy systems transformation, however, displays relatively few of these characteristics. These differences, we argue, pose specific and difficult barriers to the use of climate investment to drive durable economic growth.

We point out at least five differences with the ICT example in particular that undermine a direct analogy between a low-emissions energy systems transformation and green growth. Unlike ICT:

1. The energy system in the advanced countries is fully built out, and new capacity will only be added slowly. Consequently, new approaches to energy must be implemented by retrofitting the existing system.
2. The energy system retrofit cannot occur in new, parallel networks. Instead, energy systems transformation must change the infrastructure of energy generation and distribution even as economies continue to rely on that same infrastructure.
3. Given the scale of the system, new investments are small relative to the system as a whole.
4. Long investment horizons do not support rapid adoption or iterated innovation in the way that ICT's very short depreciation cycles did.[5]
5. Renewable energy does not, in most cases, offer immediate competitive advantage to early adopters the way ICT investments did.

These differences raise real questions as to whether "clean energy" generates pervasive opportunity in the same way the ICT transformation and its

16 predecessors did. Spectacular success in adding renewable energy to the energy system will mean that energy users will notice no difference between electrons generated by coal and those generated by wind or solar. All the investment in storage, the smart grid, and new energy sources will go toward ensuring that today's patterns of energy use remain viable. In contrast to the first era of electrification, it will do little to enable a new era of energy uses. Appliances, lighting, heating, and motors will behave no differently after these changes than they did before. Even the invention of a whole new class of automobiles still only strives to produce a personal transportation device that is as good as the automobiles available today. Meanwhile, achieving these ends will require substantial public and private investment over decades.

This does not mean, of course, that innovations in energy technology provide no new benefits. They may, for instance, reduce energy costs, improve public health by reducing pollution, or limit damage from extreme weather events related to climate change. But these benefits are largely about cost savings or damage prevention. These technologies do not, as of yet, promise a radically different, more productive energy system that could in itself drive diverse forms of economic value creation.[6] Thus, green growth and the energy systems transformation on which it depends remain very different from these earlier epochs of transformative technological change.

In the face of these challenges to green growth, it is perhaps unsurprising that policy makers have turned to narrower arguments. Those arguments, as Chapter 3 shows, emphasize job creation and export-led growth in energy sector jobs and technologies alone, rather than the intrinsic growth-generating dynamics of low-emissions technology itself. We summarize those narrower arguments here to differentiate them from the possibility that emissions reduction may drive growth through a broader energy systems transformation. If investments in emissions reduction fail to generate near-term job and export growth, we remain concerned that longer-term possibilities will be discounted, eroding support for the long-term transformation critical to durable emissions reductions and effective climate change mitigation.

MISTAKING SHORT-TERM JOBS FOR LONG-TERM GROWTH

In the aftermath of the 2007–2009 financial crisis, the "green jobs" variant of the green growth argument gained currency across the industrial world. United States President Barack Obama, the European Union, several American states, and some European and East Asian countries have all sought to tie green energy investment to job creation.[7] This led to a significant quantity of economic stimulus funds directed to energy efficiency, renewable energy, and energy-related research and development (Barbier 2011). Support for these activities was buttressed by fears that insufficient domestic energy investment would lead to permanent disadvantages in a new green technology frontier, particularly vis-à-vis new economic powerhouses like China.[8]

This emphasis on jobs as such should raise immediate concerns on two fronts. First, a focus on job creation in the green energy sector alone cannot form the basis of sustained economic growth in advanced industrial societies. If those jobs result from Keynesian demand stimulus, as they did in 2007–2009, their viability will necessarily fade as the economy returns to full employment. In Keynes's original terms, paying people to dig holes in the ground only generates growth when it works to prime the demand pump of an economy in recession. At full employment, digging holes — or building wind turbines — might detract from more productive uses of labor elsewhere. The long-term opportunities for employment growth in the energy sector are similarly limited. Advanced industrial societies have fully built-out energy systems and relatively modest growth in energy demand. Green jobs will thus often replace "brown jobs" in operation of the energy system, and the new green jobs created for the period of system retrofitting will necessarily be short-lived, lasting only as long as the retrofit itself. Finally, those green jobs will have limited impact on the overall employment picture, as they emphasize the energy sector alone rather than the economy as a whole.[9] Thus, even if the investment in systems retrofits will lead to near-term job creation, the timeframe and scope of those jobs appears limited.

Second, the quality of those jobs is also open to question. Some have argued that an investment in green electricity generates more jobs per unit installed capacity than an investment in equivalent brown energy capacity.[10] But this implicitly suggests that the green energy industry achieves, at present, lower labor productivity than the fossil fuel power sector. If the goal is pure Keynesian job creation to employ idle labor, then this justification may make sense.[11] But in broader terms, earlier periods of systems transformation offset higher labor intensity with the intrinsic advantages of the new technologies themselves, advantages that low-emissions technology appears to lack. Thus, as a long-term employment strategy, the deployment of a low-emissions energy system appears to have limited capacity to sustain high wages in advanced industrial economies.

EXPORT-LED GROWTH AND THE NEW GREEN MERCANTILISM

Export-led growth in new green technology provides a second growth channel commonly cited in popular green growth arguments. Countries now openly express concerns that the failure to create domestic markets in green energy

18   will lead to a loss of global competitiveness, particularly to the developing world. But, as in other sectors, comparative advantage in "green" technologies will likely accrue in countries whose industrial clusters already contain closely related forms of industrial and innovative expertise.[12] Thus, the connection between green growth and domestic investment will be highly variable and will offer poor justification for low-emissions investments in many countries. Moreover, empirical evidence from Dechezleprêtre and Glachant (2011) suggests that investment in energy systems decarbonization will generate significant spillover effects that benefit foreign as well as domestic firms. This spillover also implies that countries that invest in the core technologies and intellectual property for new low-emissions goods may find the benefits from building and selling those goods going abroad. Recent trade conflicts with China over solar technologies point to these concerns. Finally, while smaller economies have generated substantial income from expertise in particular sectors, it is by no means clear that broad support for climate policies can emerge from the same sectors in much larger economies and more diversified like the United States.

Using domestic low-emissions investment to drive comparative advantage abroad also poses an array of political risks. Our primary concern lies in a view of green growth as a zero-sum game for control of international export markets. China and the U.S. area are already engaged in a series of fights in the World Trade Organization over subsidies to renewable energy technologies and renewable energy deployment.[13] Given the lack of obvious channels for green growth beyond command of export markets, this conflict was perhaps inevitable. But these pressures to integrate domestic environmental policy with international economic policy sometimes echo the mercantilism of the sixteenth to eighteenth centuries or the import substitution period of development strategies in the mid-twentieth century. There, countries also saw competitiveness as a zero-sum game among countries, justifying an array of restrictive economic policies at home and the aggressive political pursuit of markets abroad. Both periods proved particularly damaging to domestic growth and international stability alike, and they led to attempts to stabilize the international trade system through institutions like the World Trade Organization. Returning to those earlier periods in the name of justifying low-emissions energy policy appears unwise.

BEYOND JOBS AND EXPORTS: SEARCHING FOR THE OPPORTUNITIES IN SYSTEMS TRANSFORMATION

The shortcomings of popular arguments for green growth do not, of course, condemn the concept of green growth. We have argued that at present, low-emissions technologies offer few obvious benefits to the economy beyond their contributions to climate change mitigation. As long as this remains true, it would appear to limit the growth potential from a low-emissions energy systems transformation, and with it the political support that economic growth would provide long-term climate policy.

However, the economic significance of radical systems changes often comes in disguise. The advantages of a new energy system may not be evident immediately. As with IBM at the start of the ICT revolution, the marketplace may yet discover real advantages to green tech not obvious to us now. But the very different nature of this transformation, and the very large investments it will require, behooves the participants — private and public sector alike — to proactively identify the conditions that would support the process of experimentation that discovery will require. That discussion will prove a necessary precursor to policy that can go beyond merely driving the development and adoption of green energy to enable the broader adaptation in the economy as a whole.

THE POLICY CHALLENGE: ENERGY SYSTEMS TRANSFORMATION AND GREEN GROWTH

This problem should be addressed in three stages. First, we need to ask what goals policy must accomplish in order to achieve a successful energy systems transformation. Second, we need to determine what policy instruments may best achieve these goals and whether the conventional approach to climate policy is consistent with the conclusions about policies to achieve the energy system transformation. Third, if a self-sustaining, growth-inducing energy systems transformation is the ultimate goal, then we should consider how these policy instruments might be best deployed to achieve it.

Goals

Renewable energy–focused policy usually expresses a single goal: to reduce emissions via altering the dependence of industrial economies on fossil fuels. But as we saw earlier in the chapter, that goal really requires an energy systems transformation.[14] That transformation, in turn, requires parallel and complementary changes to energy production, distribution, and use in order to adapt to the different technical and economic properties of renewable energy.

The near-term goal for policy in this context cannot be the completion of the transformation itself. The scale and degree of investment required make such an outcome improbable in the near term. Rather, the real goal should be to shift the energy system onto a new and self-sustaining development trajectory. The nature of today's energy system provides large incentives to innovate within its constraints. The scale of the network means that such innovations immediately enjoy large markets and easy compatibility. These network effects pose serious problems for any attempt to transition out of the present equilibrium. But it likewise suggests that a self-sustaining process of investment and innovation in favor of a low-carbon energy system is possible, if only we can find the right policy levers to achieve the initial shift in the trajectory of the system as a whole.

Such an achievement may provide the best opportunity for green growth. As with past technological systems transformations, growth via a low-carbon energy systems transformation requires a self-sustaining pattern of innovation and investment in both the energy sector and the broader economy. At present, it remains unclear whether renewable energy can promise this kind of innovation. But it most certainly cannot if it continues to operate under the constraints of an energy system designed predominately around fossil fuels. As long as those constraints hold, firms will always face powerful incentives to seek growth-generating opportunities that draw on the economic and technological qualities of fossil fuel–based production. Even with policies to impose high carbon prices, firms will still face powerful nonprice barriers to remaining inside the present system. Instead, policy should aim to change the nature of these constraints — not just in terms of relative prices but in terms of the material choices that the energy system presents to firms and investors.

Instruments

Climate change mitigation confronts policy makers with a wide range of choices in service of both green growth and a low-carbon energy systems transformation. The most vibrant policy debates today concern the role that four different policy instruments should play:

1. Carbon pricing to incentivize both technological development and low-emissions energy adoption
2. Technology policy to support research and development
3. Regulatory policy to change market rules to favor new forms of energy production, distribution, and use[15]
4. Direct state action for public infrastructure investment and industrial policy

Conventional policy wisdom for carbon emissions mitigation argues in favor of a credible, sustainable, and high carbon price, perhaps supplemented with subsidies to basic research and development for new energy technologies (Nordhaus 2010). Such policy, its advocates argue, will allow the economy to discover the most efficient way of reducing emissions. In contrast, other options — such as industrial policy, subsidy of renewable energy sources, or mandates for energy efficiency — are seen as inefficient meddling in the market that will ultimately cost more than a policy reliant on price alone.

We can debate whether a price-based approach would suffice if the only goal were emissions reduction. But the conventional policy wisdom falls short if we hope to exploit the possibilities of energy systems transformation for economic growth. Three shortcomings in particular stand out:

1. The self-identified preconditions for a successful carbon pricing policy — a universal, sustainable, high carbon price — appear politically impossible either domestically or internationally.
2. It is by no means clear that the efficient carbon price, equal to the marginal cost of emissions, is high enough to overcome the substantial network externalities present in the energy system.
3. The carbon price offers little support for the coordination and market reform issues that will play a critical role in the viability of future energy innovations.

Politically, carbon pricing faces serious challenges. Raising carbon prices will raise energy prices, harming energy firms, energy-intensive industries, and households. The opposition this harm will create will be hard to resist. By their very nature, carbon prices create very diffuse benefits: they target no specific new energy technology and provide no specific advantage to one group of firms over another. The interests motivated by these incentives are likewise diffuse. In the face of highly motivated, acutely harmed firms and consumers, the green coalition behind carbon prices will be weak and poorly motivated. This problem worsens with higher, more punitive carbon prices. Thus, "high" undermines both "universal" and "sustainable." Together, the viability of a price-driven energy systems transformation appears in doubt.

The demand for complementary changes to achieve an energy systems transformation poses the second obstacle to a purely price-driven strategy. This approach has emerged out of a line of economic argument that treats emissions as a market failure. By this analysis, we underproduce what we need for a low-emissions energy system, falling short because of the mismatch between private and social costs. Correcting the relative prices of high- and low-emissions goods should, by this analysis, rebalance the private and social cost of emissions, generating demands for more low-emissions innovations and resolving the shortfall. As Hanemann (2009) showed, this was more or less what occurred in the highly successful use of prices to lower acid rain emissions in the United States. There, a price on sulfur and nitrogen emissions provided strong incentives to adopt existing, but higher-cost, emissions-reducing technologies, bringing down emissions rapidly and at very low prices (EPA 2005).

22   But the energy systems transformation we have outlined suggests that the present market is locked into a trajectory in which it *doesn't* produce the elements needed for a low-emissions energy system. As a system dominated by network technologies that favor fossil fuels in their current configuration, the existence of the system itself provides large incentives not to invest in alternative technologies and business models.[16] In a scenario where we have a reasonably good idea of the broad outlines of what that alternative looks like — a low-emissions energy system capable of supporting the needs of industrial society — these large barriers to entry impede progress, absent very strong incentives to the contrary. Those incentives face an additional challenge to generate not just a set of changes but a set of complementary changes across all three domains of the system: production, distribution, and use. Given the size, scale, and complexity of modern energy systems, it is reasonable to argue that the barriers to coordinated change might be very high, such that absent more directed state intervention in the markets, new innovations might not emerge or be adopted at scale.[17]

Price-based emissions policy thus has two significant limitations. It will, we contend, drive toward innovation within the current energy system rather than the generation of a new system altogether. Moreover, prices high enough to matter to any innovation and transformation will be difficult to establish and sustain. Instead, we argue that an energy systems transformation will require multi-instrument approaches blending prices, technology strategies, regulatory reform, and infrastructure investment. Each of these policy tools has a role to play. But none constitutes a comprehensive solution on its own. Moreover, we emphasize that national variation in the regulation of the energy sector, the ownership structure of its firms, and the dynamics of finance create opportunities and constraints that will affect each of these three policy tools differently. Hence, we should expect, and find ways to accommodate, distinct national solutions to systems transformation.

POINTS OF LEVERAGE IN A GREEN ENERGY SYSTEMS TRANSFORMATION

Given the complexity of these systems, policy makers face difficult choices about where to apply these policy tools in diverse regional and national contexts. With limited resources, policy makers have little choice but to seek points in the energy system where limited interventions can change the trajectory of development by altering the choices of actors throughout the system. Do similar levers exist for energy, which if pulled would induce broad private investment to capture the diverse advantages of the new system?

We define a lever to be a change or set of changes to part of the system that, if carried out, will induce or enable complementary changes in the rest of the energy system. Certainly there must be a debate about the existence and form these levers might take. For the case of the energy system, the power grid provides an excellent example of such a lever. The grid is central to choices about how to produce, distribute, and use energy; changes in the grid alter options in all three dimensions of the energy system.

Consequently, the grid provides significant leverage for policies intent on accomplishing energy systems transformation. Energy policy should use tightly focused technological innovation, coupled to regulatory reform and standards-setting processes, to develop and deploy a power grid capable of handling significant change to technologies for production and use. For example, the introduction of a "smart" grid — the integration of digital intelligence and power transmission — can support not only more efficient transmission but also more and different forms of renewable energy and improved energy efficiency. Standardization of the networks may also enable the grid to operate as a platform for further private sector innovation. That innovation, in turn, can drive both the technological advances required for the adoption of new energy sources and the investment and employment required for green growth.

CONCLUSION: GOVERNMENTS, MARKETS, AND GREEN GROWTH

Today, green growth remains largely religion. Governments pursuing it have done so in large part on the basis of faith in green growth as part of a new approach to industrial development. But sustaining emissions reduction over the long term will require that green growth be more than simply faith. Moving green growth from religion to reality, we have argued, requires rooting it in the concept of an energy systems transformation. As with past transformations, a green energy–led systems transformation may catalyze broader opportunities for growth by altering the possibilities for economic production and productivity growth. But discovering these possibilities will require active policy to induce and sustain the complementary series of technological, economic, and regulatory changes that we refer to as an *energy systems transformation*. Green growth will require policy focused on this array of activities, rather than some broader appeal to economic efficiency.

Our argument has three significant implications:

- First, with limited resources, policy makers should seek points in the energy system where limited interventions can change the trajectory of development by altering the choices of actors throughout the system. We defined such a lever to be "a change or set of changes to part of the system that, if carried out, will induce or enable complementary changes in the rest of the system."

- Second, enduring economic and political success at a green energy–led systems transformation can only come from the possibilities it would create for the broader economy. Emissions reduction is principally motivated by the need to avoid the damaging consequences of the existing energy system. But achieving emissions reduction presently provides few immediate benefits. "Green" electrons differ from "brown" electrons largely by being more expensive and requiring the expensive replacement of an effective and profitable infrastructure. Green jobs will often simply replace brown jobs. The acute costs and diffuse benefits of emissions reduction pose serious challenges to sustained progress. Consequently, policy discussion must also focus on the advantages of a low-emissions energy system. Those advantages, if they exist, will come from enabling the broader economy to discover and express the presently unknown — and often unknowable — opportunities that such a new system may create.
- Third, achieving this transformation will require a complex set of offsetting deals that often compensate those discomfited or disadvantaged, while allowing market incentives to induce the enormous private investments that will be required. Governments will need to play a role: setting technology standards and market rules, balancing losers from the transition, and investing in technology development and often in the deployment of critical infrastructure.

In the second half of the book, we consider where and how states have begun implementing these and similar policies in an attempt to overcome the barriers to green growth. Denmark has committed to a fossil fuel–free economy by 2040. The South Korean government has embarked on the development of a broadly rooted growth strategy intended to reorient the Korean economy around green technology, public transport innovation, and efficiency-improving uses of information and communications technology. And perhaps the Fukushima crisis will impel Japan to belatedly realize its enormous green growth promise. Despite the broader American inertia, California and Colorado have both embarked on economic growth strategies that emphasize the link between action on climate change mitigation and new economic opportunities. We suggest that the most successful of these attempts have built the foundations of a "green policy spiral" in which early, marginal changes in how countries organize their energy systems can lay the technological and political foundations for long-term transformation.

At such an early juncture, we cannot know — and this book does not presume to know — whether a green growth reality that builds on these small successes will emerge. We can, however, identify the shortcomings of today's faith-based arguments for green growth and anticipate what a durable green growth strategy would require of firms, consumers, and governments. Moving green growth from religion to reality will, we argue, require a technological and economic transformation akin to those of the emergence of steam, rail, or information technology. That transformation will not come through a focus on one technology or another, reliance on short-term job creation, or abstract appeals to economic efficiency. Rather, it will require attention to the restructuring of the energy system as a whole, the opportunities present in the transformation for widespread economic activity, and the role that policy must play in structuring and facilitating that systems transformation.

2

MOTIVATING GREEN GROWTH

*The Political Economy of Energy Systems
Transformation*

Mark Huberty

INTRODUCTION

As we argued in Chapter 1, green growth is inseparable from energy systems transformation. Efforts to achieve durable economic returns from low-
emissions investment must focus on how those investments enable new forms
of value creation in the economy at large. Whether this systems transformation holds such potential remains, of course, unclear. But satisfying both the
needs of long-term emissions reduction and economic growth will require
dynamics similar to earlier transformations, in which technological developments in one sector acted as a catalyst for broad-based economic growth.

This chapter makes three arguments about energy systems transformation,
the political barriers to it, and the role of policy in overcoming those barriers. First, it develops the concept of an energy systems transformation and its
consequences for the politics of green growth. Systems transformation is first
and foremost a technical problem: how to tear out and replace the energy
foundations of modern industrial society while leaving the economic superstructure untouched, vibrant, and growing. Doing so will require retiring
existing energy infrastructure; inventing suites of complementary, interoperable replacement technologies; and coordinating their deployment to ensure
a stable, affordable energy foundation for industrial society. This process is
complicated by the physics of the energy system, which requires a precise balance between energy supply and demand to maintain its operating stability.
Accomplishing this complex transformation would prove challenging enough
on its own. But effective climate change mitigation also requires that it happen on an accelerated timeline.

Second, it shows that this pattern of changes implies an array of political conflicts that will create powerful barriers to progress on climate change mitigation. Those who own and operate today's fossil fuel system will see their assets lose value. Owners of fossil fuels themselves will be forced to leave their otherwise valuable energy assets in the ground indefinitely. These groups may, justifiably, claim compensation for the lost value of investments they originally made to satisfy society's high demand for energy. Finally, energy consumers will likely see price increases that reflect the actual cost of pollution and the expense of building out a new energy system. All of these groups will be resistant to the cost of energy systems transformation and will thus have powerful incentives to oppose rapid action on climate change mitigation.

Finally, the chapter concludes by arguing for a climate policy approach that prioritizes political sustainability as well as cost and economic efficiency. Given the need for a long-term, continuous, irreversible move to a low-emissions energy system, policy must simultaneously support the technical tasks required for systems transformation and build a strong political foundation for sustained climate policy. But many mainstream climate policy proposals do not do so and thus risk exacerbating the very politics they seek to overcome.

The concept of green growth suggests one possible way forward.[1] Were a green growth "reality" possible — if the investments required for emissions reduction actually could support broad economic growth — it could, we argue, help to build the durable coalition of economic interests required to sustain long-term climate policy. It would also offer economic upsides to a low-emissions energy systems transformation, giving private actors incentives to continue the transformation even when policy weakens. But in its present form, green growth cannot, as Chapters 3 and 4 show, carry that burden. As the following chapters discuss in detail, this will require moving beyond the standard policy narratives that inform climate policy and green growth strategies today. Doing so, however, will require an altogether different political strategy. Part II suggests what such strategies would look like and shows how their politics are currently playing out across a diverse range of countries, economies, and energy systems.

SETTING UP THE TASK AHEAD: PHYSICS, STABILITY, AND CHANGE

Understanding the problem of energy systems transformation requires a brief foray into physics. We use the electricity system to illustrate the particular difficulty of a low-emissions energy systems transformation.[2] Other large-scale technological transformations have often proceeded in haphazard fashion.

28   But the properties of the electricity system limit the ability to do so this time around. The organization of energy production, distribution, and use — both its technologies and its business models and regulatory structures — is inordinately dependent on the physical properties of fossil fuels. Replacing fossil fuels in the energy system thus implies a cascading set of changes to accommodate the very different properties of renewable energy. Maintaining the ability of the electricity system to power industrial society, even as it undergoes transformation from within, will require a parallel and coordinated set of changes to technologies, business models, and regulatory structures. Doing otherwise risks the stability of the energy system, and with it the system's ability to power industrial prosperity.

The physics of electricity require careful, constant balancing of supply and demand. Electricity can't, at present, be stored at scale for any length of time. Consequently, supply and demand must be monitored and tuned in real time to maintain the stability of the power grid and ensure the reliability of the electricity supply. But as we hinted in Chapter 1, this means that in practice the system depends on precise control of supply alone. Unlike many markets, most electricity customers have little up-to-date information about how much energy they consume or the actual cost of generating that energy. All but the largest energy consumers pay for electricity based on regulated prices. Those prices don't vary as demand for electricity rises and falls throughout the day. Thus, customers have little information at any given point about the true availability of electricity or how much it actually costs. Whether they run their dishwashers after dinner like most people do or wait until 3 a.m. when electricity is plentiful and cheap, it has little impact on how well the dishwasher cleans dishes or what they pay for the electricity to run it. Finally, in the rare instances where customers do experience the consequences of too much demand, it's usually far too late to do anything about it: the blackouts on a hot afternoon due to many people running their air conditioners at the same time come too late for one individual to keep the system running by changing his or her behavior.

Fossil fuels provide the crucial abilities required to maintain the stability of a system where demand can't be effectively controlled. Successive generations of fossil fuels have delivered more energy per unit weight, in more easily transported forms, that could be more easily stored (Smil 2011). Coal was twice as energy-dense as wood; oil and natural gas were denser still. Easy shipping and storage of fossil fuels supported the development of highly specialized power plants that can be easily ramped up to meet spikes in demand and then backed off as demand weakens. Energy density also contributed to geographic density. Power plants have grown in capacity over time, generating both more energy per generator and packing more generators into individual plants. This put more tools at the disposal of operators tasked with maintaining the stability of supply and demand through precise control of generation.

These trends toward concentrated energy generation spilled over into energy transmission and distribution. Today's power grids are adapted to move power long distances from highly concentrated generators to diffuse homes and businesses. The grid also provide lots of information to system operators about the state of the system but almost no tools to energy consumers to help them understand their consumption patterns. Thus, the physical capabilities of fossil fuels permitted the stable operation of a system that demanded careful balance of supply and demand. A set of complementary technologies and infrastructure grew up around these characteristics. What emerged from this system-building process was a tightly interlinked system of energy production, distribution, and use.

Market design and regulation complement and reflect the tight technological interoperability of the electricity system. Long-term wholesale markets help stabilize energy supplies across seasonal trends in power consumption. Short-term spot markets serve the hour-by-hour need to satisfy fluctuating demand within those trends. Institutionalized, regulated capacity planning helps ensure that the capacity to generate electricity evolves with long-run growth in demand. These and other market and regulatory innovations support the stable operation of a technological system whose products can't easily be stored, whose consumers are opaque and unresponsive, and in which minor imbalances can lead to cascading and disruptive system-wide failures. But they depend on the fact that fossil fuels permit precise control of electricity production in response to fluctuating demand.

Altering the Foundations of the System:
Renewable Energy and Intermittency

Renewable energy looks little like fossil fuels. Renewable energy depends, of course, on natural energy flows like those from wind or sun. Most of these flows fluctuate over the course of the day, between days, and across seasons. At present, neither they nor the electricity they generate can be easily stored. Thus, systems operators can't depend on precise control of renewable energy generators because they can't predict precisely how much wind or solar energy will be available at any given time. Nor can they store excess power from intensely sunny or windy days for later use.[3] Renewable energy thus deprives systems operators of the basic physical properties they rely on today to manage a system that depends on a precise balance between supply and demand but does not permit active control over demand itself.

30   Left unaddressed, the mismatch between an energy system optimized around fossil fuels and new energy sources with fundamentally different capabilities will interfere with the stability of energy supplies and their ability to serve energy demand. Experience and theory both confirm the potential difficulties of introducing renewable energy without altering the rest of the system. Wind-rich regions like western Denmark or Texas, where power demand is low and renewable energy production is high, have had problems with grid overloading on windy days. Without sufficient transmission capacity to move excess power to other regions, wind-generated electricity has gone unused. In the common Scandinavian Nordpool market, negative power prices are now used to encourage wind farms to shut down rather than destabilize the power grid with excess supply (Nord Pool Spot 2009). Texas has experienced regular periods of negative market-clearing power prices in the wind-rich western region.[4] These real-world experiences confirm estimates suggesting that renewable energy shares above 20 percent of electricity generation can destabilize power grids absent accommodating changes elsewhere in the energy system (Integration of Variable Generation Task Force 2009).

Reconciling Stability and Change

The physical mismatch between fossil fuels and renewable energy poses three complex tasks for an energy systems transformation:

1. Replacing the technical infrastructure of energy production, distribution, and use
2. Inventing new technological capabilities to improve the efficiency and stability of a renewable energy-based system
3. Reforming the market structures and regulations that help manage the technical operation of the system

The Technical Problem

The technical task, replacing the physical infrastructure of the energy system, implies a set of parallel changes to preserve the technical interoperability across evolving domains of energy production, distribution, and use. While the focus of a low-emissions transformation remains on major changes to energy production, sustaining technical interoperability also implies a demand for complementary downstream technological innovations.

      A range of technical solutions have been proposed to accommodate intermittent power generation in an evolving electricity transmission system. "Smart grids" may help give system operators more information about and control over energy demand. Better control over demand would provide operators with new tools to maintain balance in the system, even as they lose some control over energy production. More extensive connection between geographically dispersed markets can help operators take advantage of the fact that variations in renewable energy flows are often uncorrelated across different regions, and thus balance can be maintained by moving power from energy-rich to energy-poor areas. Finally, better energy storage technologies can allow operators to store excess production at peak periods for use at times when demand exceeds generation capacity. Regardless of which of these solutions proves optimal, each contributes to the broader technical stability of the energy system amidst a substantial change to the basic properties that underpin it.

The Innovation Problem

The need for interoperable systems evolution begs the question of where these innovations will come from. Here we note two problems. First, as the American Energy Innovation Council (2010) has shown, the electricity sector itself has typically eschewed innovation for technical stability. Their historical research and development investment ranks at the bottom of capital-intensive industry. Hence, innovation will require not only repurposing existing patterns of investment but also building entirely new innovative capabilities in a sector that has often, and understandably, prized stability over novelty.

Second, innovation around the electricity network faces real uncertainty about how the network itself will evolve. This includes both the development of radically new systems — like large-scale energy storage, where technological uncertainty rules — and the adoption of network-level improvements like the smart grid, where regulatory and market uncertainty about standards-setting dominates. In confronting these uncertainties around how the system will evolve, innovators face real unknowns about how their creations might work in some future (Perez 1983). Resolving this uncertainty is a critical task for achieving a smooth systems transformation. Studies of network technologies suggest that new technological systems require sponsors — public or private — willing to bear the cost of coordinating the plethora of innovations required to bring the new system into being (Katz and Shapiro 1985, 1986). That can occur through a variety of means (Zachmann et al. 2012), whether by internalizing all of the choices inside one company, as with Thomas Edison's original electricity system (Hughes 1979, 1983); by standardizing key network components to reduce technical uncertainty; or by mandating the adoption of common core technologies.

Reducing network uncertainty in this case will require a diversity of approaches. More exclusively, technical problems—such as advances in power storage capacity—may favor more and more stable support for technological research and development. In contrast, where the technical options are clearer but standards remain unsettled, as with some aspects of "intelligent" grids, the traditional coordinating role of government in moving disparate grid operators in a single direction may prove the most effective. Regardless of how this is done, however, the potential for widespread innovation and competition over network optimization depends, in part, on the stability of the underlying network designs themselves.

The Market and Regulatory Problem

The organization of today's technological infrastructure for energy production, distribution, and use also depends on supportive market and regulatory frameworks. But as we've seen, those frameworks assume and exploit the properties of fossil fuels. A renewable energy system will thus require complementary changes to ensure that regulators and markets continue to provide the information and incentives to public and private actors that allow them to optimize and maintain stable, viable energy systems.

We could consider a wide range of potential changes, but three examples will suffice to illustrate the point. First, fossil fuels have permitted the energy system to treat consumer demand as something outside the control of the system. Instead, energy firms and regulators have evolved highly sophisticated markets to identify and respond to fluctuations in energy demand and to handle long- and short-term changes to consumption. Asking consumers to use smart meters and other technologies to improve their own efficiency will require an array of new technologies that both give consumers better information about their energy use and enable more optimal choices. But moving to a world of flexible demand will require more than just new technology. Incorporating responsive consumer demand will require us to adapt markets to better manage more flexible demand structures. It will also require those markets to reward consumers for their flexibility—either with lower power prices or compensation for flexibility, among other ways.

A similar form of market evolution will need to serve the management of intermittent supply. Today's markets assume that operators have substantial control over production and will choose whether to produce based on prevailing power prices. But since renewable energy producers face very low marginal costs—the wind or sun are free, and the capital is a sunk cost—they have little reason not to generate whenever conditions allow. This can easily overwhelm the stability of power markets. For instance, the Nord Pool energy market had experienced some systems instability on very windy days, when Danish generators would overwhelm the system with large amounts of intermittent electricity. Finding a solution required introducing negative power prices as a disincentive to generate under these and similarly unfavorable conditions (Nord Pool Spot 2009). Adapting the rest of the system to the new properties of the energy supply will require these and similar innovations.

Finally, successful low-emissions energy systems of the future will still require highly controllable energy sources for those periods when demand is exceptionally strong or when renewable energy production is weak. Markets that today provide incentives to build power generation assets for constant use may function poorly as tools to ensure backup capacity. Europe, for instance, has been so successful at deploying renewable energy in many markets that it has made fossil fuel investments uneconomical.[5] Markets and regulators now face the challenge of ensuring that some of that investment continues as insurance against extended periods of underproduction. Compensating those who build energy production assets that are only rarely used may require new forms of markets and business models that fund capacity rather than use.[6]

From Tasks to Process: Seeing the Transition through to the End

The complexity of the technical, economic, and regulatory changes required for a low-emissions energy systems transformation tells us a lot about the transformation process itself. As Smil (2011) has shown, earlier transformations were hardly smooth processes. Instead, they were protracted, often indirect affairs characterized by a slow accumulation of the factors required for successfully building a new energy system. The English transition from wood to coal took perhaps 200 years (Nef 1932; Warde 2007); the widespread adoption of oil for transport another 75; and the adoption of electricity another 60 to 80 years. Information technology, as discussed in Chapter 1, required 50 years to translate the invention of the transistor into the era of the Internet.

Along the way, each of these transitions left behind a trail of technological, economic, and regulatory missteps. We forget the failed promise of coal-fired steam cars, direct current electricity distribution, token-ring communications networks, and a litany of other technological cul-de-sacs. Likewise, time has obscured regulatory failures as well. London today doesn't betray the failures of nineteenth-century British electrification, caused largely by the harmful — but unintentional — failure of British regulators to structure the initial regulatory framework for electricity correctly (Hughes 1962). And we ignore the rank

34 corruption that has often driven changes to utility regulation in the United States (Troesken 1996). These and other mistakes should remind us that the process of transition is rarely smooth, nor are the correct choices obvious at the start.

FROM PROCESS TO POLITICS: COSTS, BENEFITS, AND INTERESTS

With the technical details of the problem in hand, we now turn to the second argument in this chapter: how the technical problem of transition will shape the political problem of initiating and sustaining it. We argue that the political conflicts implicit in a low-emissions energy systems transformation presently stand directly opposed to its success. The benefits of transformation as we currently understand them are poor candidates for pulling the transformation along on their own. The environmental advantages of a low-emissions energy system are real but are too diffuse and far off to motivate strong support. By the time they do become immediate and painful, it will be too late to act. And the economic benefits at present are, as we detail in the next chapter, uncertain and weak.

Absent acute benefits, initiating and sustaining a low-emissions energy systems transformation will depend on policies to directly or indirectly drive change. But the costs those policies stand to impose, and the interest groups that will bear those costs, appear likely to generate intense and durable opposition to such a transformation. Nor will passing policy into law neuter that opposition; rather, it stands to survive, and strengthen, as the costs of emissions reduction become more acute. Overcoming this unfavorable cost-benefit structure will pose major challenges to policy. But, as we will argue at the end of this chapter, present policies are likely to exacerbate rather than resolve the political tensions that confront emissions reduction today.

The Unfavorable Politics of Change

To summarize our earlier discussion, building a low-emissions energy system requires that we retire existing, profitable, useful fossil fuel energy infrastructure; make substantial investments in renewable energy sources that offer few obvious benefits over the sources they replace; and make additional changes to energy transmission and use to ensure the continued operation and stability of the energy system. This process will impose large costs on powerful economic interests, while offering few material benefits in exchange. And it will take a long time, during which, history suggests, it will be prone to missteps and redirection and open to stalling and reversal.

This set of conditions is highly unfavorable to successful climate change mitigation. Climate change mitigation offers real, long-term environmental benefits. The potential costs of unchecked climate change are real and substantial. But they are a classic public good: the benefits will accrue to everyone, regardless of who pays for emissions reduction. Most of those benefits will arrive in the distant future, long after we make the first investments in emissions reduction. When they arrive, they will count largely as costs avoided rather than improvements gained. Asking powerful economic interests to adopt long-term and expensive changes in pursuit of distant and diffuse public goods with few material benefits is hardly a recipe for enthusiastic support.

In the absence of support, building a successful policy regime will prove difficult. Effective climate policy requires long-run credibility. Investors must have confidence that building a more expensive low-emissions infrastructure today will pay off in the energy system of the future, and they must have some idea of the long-run demand for new low-emissions technologies. Consumers must believe that buying into more efficient homes, appliances, or automobiles today will pay off over time. But the political uncertainty implied by the politics of a low-emissions energy systems transformation undermines policy credibility. These and other choices about how to structure investment, behavior, and social life are usually made, as Unruh (2000, 2002) shows, in light of long-run expectations about the broad direction of energy policy. Shifting that direction — toward a low-emissions, high-efficiency trajectory — is the prime function of the policies that generate so much opposition.

Overcoming Political Myopia: Lessons from Historical Success

Thus, the political conflict generated by a low-emissions energy systems transformation stands directly opposed to the tasks that transformation requires. Of course, climate change is not the first policy regime to face this problem. Many of the most vital economic and social reforms have overcome similar barriers in pursuit of long-term benefits. Political science research (Patashnik 2003, 2008) has provided evidence that successful reforms of big, complex markets have survived by doing three things:

1. Destroying or rendering harmless the beneficiaries of the current system
2. Eliminating or neutering the bureaucracies that regulated and monitored the current system
3. Building new and powerful interests in favor of sustaining and extending reform

36   The first of these ensures that those who would stall or reverse reforms have limited ability to do so. The second deprives them of allies in government. And the third generates new interest groups in favor of reform that can sustain the same level of intensity as their opponents.

Unfortunately, the tasks required for a low-emissions energy systems transformation do not, on their own, accomplish any of these. Utility companies and their suppliers will remain in business throughout the transition, simply because the old energy system can't be easily shut down. As they survive, however, systems transformation will require these firms to retire otherwise economically viable assets, abandon in the ground valuable fossil fuel deposits, and make significant new investments in the absence of obvious economic benefit. These firms' opposition to rapid emissions reduction is understandable, if frustrating and short-sighted. Furthermore, their claims on compensation for the lost value of current assets have merit, given that they made those investments to serve the demands of an energy-hungry society. And while we may want to demonize the operators of today's fossil fuel energy systems, their active participation and expertise will be vital to effecting the systems transformation and maintaining the stability of the energy system along the way.

Likewise, the lack of acute, widespread material benefits from renewable energy and climate change mitigation limits the potential for new, powerful, economically motivated advocates for policy continuity. A few sectors, like renewable energy capital goods or energy-efficiency services, are natural supporters of policy simply because their businesses have limited opportunity without it. But the broad-based support for the transitions to coal, oil, or electricity arose primarily because of how they generated very broad opportunities throughout the economy.[7] These benefits created a natural constituency, both within the energy sector and beyond it, that favored ongoing progress. As we have argued, a low-emissions energy systems transformation presently lacks this advantage. Without it, building powerful interest groups in favor of long-term policy stability will prove difficult.

MAINSTREAM CLIMATE POLICY AND BEYOND: CAN POLICY SUPPORT POLITICS?

This leaves an unpromising landscape for long-term climate policy. Attempts to limit emissions will generate strong opposition to the adoption of regulation. The ongoing cost of emissions reduction, and the need to progressively tighten emissions limits over time, will maintain and exacerbate opposition. The lack of obvious economic advantages from low-emissions alternatives dilutes interest in the new system and deprives the systems transformation of the tailwinds enjoyed by its predecessors. Together, these characteristics combine to make policy hard to pass and harder to sustain and strengthen over time.

Given the need for ongoing, regular, permanent progress in taking emissions out of the energy system, these dynamics will require policy to look beyond a narrow focus on the technical problem of transformation alone. Rather, a successful transformation will likely require a concerted effort to use policy to build the durable political base that a low-emissions energy systems transformation currently lacks.

Creating that base will require choosing policies that implicitly or explicitly build and reinforce a political constituency for long-term emissions reduction. To date, mainstream climate policy has often focused elsewhere. In particular, policy has emphasized cost effectiveness and economic efficiency, sometimes under the assumption that low costs would help ensure long-term policy viability. But the history of large-scale policy reform suggests that this approach is insufficient. Traditionally, policy has created its own politics in one of three ways: by imposing a policy direction that traps and then undermines the opposing interests;[8] by creating durable coalitions of supportive interests; or by building institutions capable of pursuing long-term objectives regardless of short-term political opposition. Any of these three options might work for the task of energy systems transformation. But we emphasize that inattention to the political implications of policy risks heightening the political tensions that have hindered progress to date.

Efficiency Is Not Sustainability: Emissions Pricing and the Politics of Prices

The politics of emissions pricing provides an example of how policy design can exacerbate the political difficulties facing climate change mitigation. Mainstream approaches to climate policy have often emphasized economic efficiency and cost rather than political viability. Emissions pricing is one such example. By raising the price of pollution, it provides incentives for finding least-cost strategies to reduce emissions. It also relieves policy makers of the problem of "picking winners" in the new system; instead, they can simply set a price and let the process of market competition choose the optimum technological, economic, and social changes in response. Nordhaus (2010), among the more ardent supporters of price-based emissions policy, regards the use of climate pricing, perhaps coupled to support for basic research and development, as a sufficient incentive on its own for structuring a long-term systems transformation. Those who are less enthusiastic (e.g., Hansen 2009) worry about the political difficulty of imposing new costs on society. But even

38   they suggest only minor modifications, such as rebates of tax revenues to the firms and consumers that paid them.

Economic efficiency does little, however, to ensure the political stability of climate change policy. In seeking efficiency, emissions pricing imposes relatively acute costs — in the form of direct taxes — on legacy energy interests, exacerbating distributional conflict over the right to pollute. Those taxes also flow through as higher prices to the rest of the economy. By intentionally *not* "picking winners" in the new system, price-based policy regimes generate only diffuse beneficiaries, who may be poorly prepared to advocate for long-term policy stability.[9] Prices alone also do little to change incentives for incumbent bureaucracies and regulators, or to transform their incentives to support long-term energy systems transformation. Instead, emissions pricing reverses the equation: they assume some support for emissions reduction and then set out to accomplish it at the lowest cost possible.

There's little evidence that economic efficiency provides a strong foundation for such political support.[10] Patashnik (2008) points out, for example, that efficiency also motivated the 1986 U.S. tax reforms. There, the goal was a simpler tax code capable of generating equivalent revenues at lower rates by closing a wide array of tax loopholes. Economists thought that greater simplicity would reduce the cost of tax compliance, improve the efficiency of the tax system, and free up money spent on compliance and auditing for more productive use elsewhere. Initially, they were right. But loopholes quickly crept back in, and the American tax code today is more complicated than ever. Efficiency, it turned out, benefited everyone and thus no one. Loopholes, though, all had favored constituencies who ensured their return even at the cost of tax simplicity.

Emissions pricing will likely share these problems. Imposing acute costs on large and powerful industries provides those industries strong incentives to lobby for weakening or eliminating those costs. Attempting to head off these challenges through loopholes or other forms of compensation may do little to dilute these incentives, just as broadly lower taxes did little to discourage lobbying for renewed tax loopholes. In the face of such opposition, emissions pricing creates few equally powerful supporting interests. This balance of motivated opponents and weak advocates undermines credible commitment to stable and increasing emissions prices that effective policy requires. Hence, even if emissions pricing could pass into law, the political turmoil that would accompany attempts at tightening emissions controls would promote stasis. "Zombie" policies might be the outcome — policies that, while still in effect, do not generate the increasingly strict incentives needed to invent, develop, and deploy a new energy system.

These problems are borne out in practice. The few major emissions pricing regimes in place today — chiefly the European Union emissions trading scheme and the forthcoming Australian carbon tax — are filled with loopholes, exceptions, rebates, and carve-outs. All these accommodations to political opposition have received intense criticism from both climate activists and advocates and environmental economists. But despite these accommodations, none of these policies have succeeded in imposing a high emissions price. And while the European Union scheme appears durable (though for very particular reasons, as Chapter 6 describes), the Australian political opposition has sworn a "blood oath" against the carbon tax. These are hardly promising conditions for the "ubiquitous, credible, high" carbon prices that Nordhaus (2010) and others view as necessary for effective emissions reduction.

Absent the ability to build its own coalition of interests, however, carbon pricing might still turn to institutions for support. Helm, Hepburn, and Mash (2004) propose just this, suggesting that the political problem of maintaining stable emissions prices might look a lot like the challenge of managing stable prices and guarding against inflation. The risks there are similar: short-term politics favor easy money, while long-term economic growth prefers relatively stable prices. Most industrial economies have solved this by empowering central banks to ensuring price stability while insulating them from short-term political pressures. Helm, Hepburn, and Mash suggest a similar carbon central bank, charged with managing emissions prices to achieve long-term emissions reduction and insulated from the short-term opposition to higher energy costs. But the institutional solution finds almost no support anywhere in the industrialized world. The lack of either a supporting coalition for high, credible, ubiquitous emissions prices or institutions that would implement these prices in spite of political opposition suggests the limits of a carbon price as a politically viable emissions management tool.[11]

Toward Policy in Support of Politics: Possible Ways Forward

The argument to this point leaves climate policy in a dilemma. The politics of a low-emissions energy systems transformation undermine the policy stability that transformation requires. Policy designs that focus on the technical tasks of emissions reduction to the exclusion of this political reality risk exacerbating this problem. How should policy respond? We argue instead that a transformation requires policy regimes that treat political sustainability as a co-equal with the technical problem of achieving a low-cost, viable technical transition. Doing so, we suggest, would require a policy regime that embedded at least three qualities:[12]

1. Sustainability: we would have some confidence that policy was setting in motion a long-term, durable direction for energy systems transformation.
2. Resilience: the policy regime would have the capacity to endure the inevitable failures and missteps that transformation entails.
3. Responsiveness: the policy regime would have the capacity to adapt to both failures and new opportunities and to respond to new information about the pace, timing, and outcomes of systems transformation.

Sustainable, resilient, responsive policy would support a long-term trajectory toward a low-emissions energy system and a willingness and ability to recognize and correct that trajectory as we learn from experience.

We suggest that green growth provides an example of what such a policy regime would need to accomplish. If it proved possible, green growth could provide the material benefits required to build sustainable, resilient, responsive policies capable of overcoming the unfavorable political economy of emissions reduction and energy systems transformation. If green growth could move from "religion" to "reality," it would allow a low-emissions energy systems transformation to generate near-term, material benefits to the economy. The firms and workers that enjoyed those benefits would have strong reasons to support the ongoing transition to low-emissions energy. That support would help offset the opposition from those who would prefer to preserve today's fossil fuel–based energy systems. Furthermore, by generating economic growth and surplus, green growth would provide the means of compensating losers from the transformation, helping to mute their opposition.

As the following chapters discuss in detail, however, today's proposals for green growth fall far short of what this policy strategy would require. We remain uncertain as to exactly how we can use a low-emissions energy systems transformation to drive green growth. It's thus equally unclear when, or if, we should expect green growth to stabilize the politics of emissions reduction.

CONCLUSION: POLITICS, POLICY EXPERIMENTATION, AND THE GREEN SPIRAL

Discovering whether green growth can help stabilize the politics of systems transformation thus require a politics of green growth —a political context broadly supportive of discovering where and how we might exploit the transition to a low-carbon economy for broad economic growth. Moving toward a politics of green growth will thus require two separate tasks. *First*, we need to initiate an energy systems transformation to begin the process of inventing, deploying, and optimizing the low-emissions energy system of the future. And *second*, we must discover where in that process of transformation the potential for green growth exists. The first task implies the need to build, for the near term, political space in which experimentation around green growth can occur. And the second will require finding the right policies and policy instruments — policy levers, we might call them — that help open up the possibilities of growth and innovation.

We turn to these tasks in reverse order. The next two chapters review popular proposals for fueling green growth. Chapter 3 surveys the most common approaches favored by policy analysts. But it shows that their proposals, while individually of merit, lack broad applicability. Moreover, none of them explicitly addresses how the technological transformation of modern energy systems might fuel economic growth in the economy as a whole. Building on this general overview, Martin Kenney and Andrew Hargadon then consider, in Chapter 4, one of the more popular proposals for fueling growth from private sector investments in green technology. The success of venture capital in supporting the information technology revolution has given its supporters hope that it could do the same for clean technology. But as Kenney and Hargadon show, cleantech lacks the conditions that enabled venture capital success in information technology. Thus, the promise of a venture capital–driven clean-technology revolution is weak at best. These conclusions echo Zysman and Huberty (2010), who caution against facile attempts to repurpose old technology policy for the climate challenge.

If we can't repurpose what worked in the past, then we must experiment with what will work in the future. Experimentation implies some political space where we can try, fail, and succeed at different policy models. The second half of the book provides a wide range of case studies around how countries have embarked on this process of experimentation. As Kelsey, Zysman, and Huberty discuss in the introduction to Part II of the book, the case studies suggest a huge diversity of policies aimed at green growth. But the green spirals they identify share a common theme: by generating near-term benefits from energy systems transformation, they help build supportive coalitions of environmental and economic interests in favor of policy continuity. At this early stage, of course, we cannot know which of these will prove more or less successful. But together they point to the potential for using policy to help stabilize the near-term politics of energy systems transformation so the long-term opportunities for green growth might emerge.

3

The Green Growth Landscape

*Promise and Peril for Green Growth
Policy Proposals*

Mark Huberty and John Zysman

GREEN GROWTH: CHALLENGE OR DISTRACTION
FOR THE CLIMATE CHALLENGE?

Chapter 1 argues that green growth is politically compelling but economically
uncertain. This position stands in sharp contrast to the popular enthusiasm for
green growth. We take the position that successful green growth will require a
far more systemic approach to energy systems transformation and that present
green growth proposals will fall far short of their goals. To back up this strong
claim, this chapter reviews the debates over green growth to date. It addresses
two questions: what have politicians and policy advocates claimed is possible
with green growth; and does empirical evidence *support* these claims or offer
evidence they would work elsewhere? While we find some instances of successful green growth policies, they all have two shortcomings: none generate
growth through the raw advantages of green technology itself, and all of them
depend on supportive climate policies either at home or abroad. Most green
growth proposals thus leave the political and technological challenges raised
in the first two chapters of this book unaddressed.

The resulting dissonance between the broad ambitions of green growth
and the narrow conception of the policies proposed to achieve it makes green
growth policy vulnerable. Long-run, stable commitments to climate action
cannot be assumed. In making that assumption, current green growth policy
ignores the two crucial issues presented in the preceding chapters: whether
and how low-emissions energy systems will maintain and improve the long-
run growth potential of the economy; and whether a politics of green growth
exists that can generate the political space to discover how this might occur.

"Green Growth": Definitions, Concepts, and Perspectives

To date, no standard definition of *green growth* has emerged from the public and policy debate. Popular definitions range from narrow attempts to reconcile emissions reduction and economic growth, to comprehensive plans to improve the resource efficiency and environmental sustainability of the capitalist system.[1] For the purposes of this chapter, we define green growth as "job creation or GDP growth compatible with or driven by actions to reduce greenhouse gasses." This more limited definition makes no claim about the importance of the more ambitious definitions of green growth. Instead, it reflects the overwhelming interest in providing answers to the climate change problem that can also provide jobs and sustain growth in the coming years.[2]

Proposals for how to achieve these ends vary in both ambitions and approaches. Three categories of arguments have attempted to tie emissions reduction to economic growth. The first, and most modest, argues that emissions reduction was at the least cost-neutral for an economy and as such represented little threat to economic performance.[3] The second, responding to the widespread unemployment that followed on the 2008–2009 financial crisis, sought to use investment in low-emissions technology and infrastructure to create jobs in the medium term. Finally, a third, more ambitious version of green growth envisions the innovation and investment required for emissions reduction as the precursor to a new industrial revolution that would bring rapid income and GDP growth.

Each of these visions of green growth makes very different assumptions about the origins of job creation and growth, and each suggests a different strategy for economic policy. This essay outlines the debates over these policy prescriptions, documents disagreements over their chances for success, and assesses each against empirical research on the effectiveness of each policy. As we shall see, while some green growth arguments have merit and empirical support, each remains highly contingent on particular circumstances, and thus of limited scope. A broadly applicable, long-term vision of green growth will need to look beyond these measures, a topic we take up later in this chapter.

MAKING EMISSIONS REDUCTIONS COMPATIBLE WITH GROWTH

The question of cost versus benefit has dominated the climate debate since its inception. Emissions reductions are seen to require substantial investments in new technology and infrastructure. These investments are usually justified on the basis of the high cost of inaction — the price of unchecked climate change. But the cost of inaction is diffuse and uncertain, while the higher energy prices and opportunity costs of emissions reduction are immediate and obvious to both firms and consumers. Hence, the calculation of the consequences of a future disaster does not provide much support for the immediate task of passing and sustaining long-range economic policy. The distant, diffuse, uncertain benefits of avoided climate change provide weak motivation for firms and citizens to act in the face of the immediate and acute costs of higher energy prices, lost sales, or expensive investments in lower-emissions alternatives.

If cost alone presents the primary barrier to climate action, then green growth may succeed if it merely minimizes the cost of, and thus the barriers to, a transformation to a low-carbon economy. To achieve this definition of green growth — minimizing the cost of a transition to a low-carbon economy — the popular and policy debate has emphasized the preeminent role of an emissions price, possibly accompanied by subsidies for research and development of new technology and the removal of fossil fuel energy subsidies. It has also emphasized the immediate economic benefit of lowered exposure to volatile and uncertain fossil fuel prices.

Pricing Carbon: Market Mechanisms for Minimizing Transition Costs

Economists have argued that arm's-length regulation via market mechanisms will provide the most efficient, lowest-cost method of greenhouse gas emissions reduction.[4] A policy of setting a price on carbon — whether via a tax or a cap-and-trade system — can, they argue, offer greater flexibility to firms and households, ensure that emission reduction happens where the cost is lowest, and generate a clear market incentive for innovation in low-carbon technologies (CBO 2009a; Nordhaus 2010; Pooley 2010; NAS 2011).

How much will that price on carbon cost? Some estimates find that emissions prices alone can achieve emissions reduction at minimal cost to GDP compared to no action at all. The landmark *Stern Review on the Economics of Climate Change* claimed that the cost of emissions reduction policies may vary from a net gain of 3.7 percent of global GDP to a net loss of 3.4 percent, depending on how additional cost-saving mechanisms interact with the emissions price (Stern 2006). Separately, the U.S. Congressional Budget Office estimates that a national emissions pricing policy would likely reduce annual GDP growth in the United States by only 0.03 percent to 0.09 percent per annum between 2010 and 2050, against an estimated 2.4 percent average annual growth rate (CBO 2009a, 13). Both studies do suggest temporary but real increases in unemployment as labor markets adjust to the decline of high-emissions sectors and the introduction of low-emissions technology. Furthermore, other efforts, such as intensified public support for basic research in low-carbon technologies or the removal of fossil fuel subsidies, improve the cost-benefit picture when deployed alongside the carbon price.[5]

Emissions pricing advocates have substantial theoretical and empirical support for their claim that price-based policies are the cheapest way to achieve emission targets. Fischer and Newell's (2008, 158) theoretical model concludes that carbon tax and tradable emission permits are the cheapest policies to achieve emission reduction goals in the context of American power plants; in comparison, subsidies for renewable energy cost 2.47 times more than a carbon tax to achieve the same emission reduction goal. Stavins's (2003) comprehensive review of past market-based environmental policies around the world also concludes that market-based mechanisms enjoy proven success in reducing pollution at low overall cost. Finally, the American acid rain control system used a tax on sulfur dioxide — the principal cause of acid rain — to rapidly reduce acid rain–causing emissions at a fraction of the original cost estimate and with no perceptible cost to U.S. economic growth (EPA 2005). The program also generated benefits via improved recreational services and public health valued at 40 times the cost of emissions control.

Despite these relatively modest cost estimates, the potential side effects of emissions pricing have raised four concerns:

1. Increased consumer energy prices will disproportionately affect poorer people.
2. Increased energy prices will impose high costs on industry and lead to lost competitiveness, significantly increasing the cost of emissions reduction.
3. The process of permit allocation under cap-and-trade systems is open to abuses and corruption that will necessarily increase the program's cost.
4. A carbon price may be politically unfeasible in certain national contexts, delaying emission reduction efforts.

Consequently, even if successfully implemented, emissions pricing is not a panacea. Critics point to the European Union's Emissions Trading Scheme (ETS) as a case in point. Detractors attribute to the ETS Europe-wide increases in household and industrial energy costs and the labor protests that followed (Mufson 2007). The theft of carbon permits worth €30 million corroborated arguments that emissions pricing is not immune to abuse and corruption (Chaffin 2011). Furthermore, opponents contend that the EU cap has not succeeded in lowering emissions (Mufson 2007), though Duggan (2009) points out that these critiques were made while the ETS was still in an early, experimental stage. However, the 2008–2009 recession, and not the ETS, has

46   arguably been the most effective emissions reduction tool in Europe over the last decade. Nordhaus and Shellenberger (2007) anticipated these critiques in their argument that carbon cap-and-trade is politically impossible within the American political context, noting pervasive interest group and party opposition. Focus on such efforts, they argue, will derail any real action; instead, they propose massive public investment in renewable energy as the best means to achieve emissions reductions amidst a hostile political climate. Estimates in the American context (Krupnick et al. 2010) suggest that these alternatives may incur only minor additional costs, compared to a cap-and-trade strategy, in exchange for their political advantages of providing direct immediate gains and benefits.

Furthermore, cap-and-trade's successes to date may hold fewer lessons for climate policy than its advocates claim. Hanemann (2009) notes two fundamental differences between the American success with acid rain control and the climate problem, with significant implications for cost. First, the sulfur dioxide emissions in question originated from a limited number of highly centralized emissions sources. In contrast, greenhouse gas emissions arise from a large number of diffuse sources, ranging from power plants to automobiles. Market designs that worked well with a small number of well-informed participants may fail when faced with millions. Second, American power plant operators could turn to readily available and relatively inexpensive solutions for sulfur dioxide emissions reduction, such as flue scrubbers and low-sulfur coal. In contrast, most low-emissions solutions for greenhouse gasses do not yet exist, or exist only at substantial cost. In the face of these challenges, emissions pricing may impose large monetary burdens on a good that has few substitutes, raising costs in the near term without offering any alternative choices.

Eliminating Barriers to Growth: Fossil Fuel Subsidies and Corrective Taxation

Elimination of fossil fuel subsidies, by exposing consumers to the true cost of fossil fuel production, could, some argue, provide another low-cost route toward emissions reduction. The International Energy Agency estimates that global elimination of fossil fuel subsidies would simultaneously promote emissions reduction and cost savings from energy efficiency, reducing CO_2 emissions by 6.9 percent and global energy demand by 5.8 percent by 2020 (IEA 2009, 5–7).

Subsidy elimination would also free up funds for other uses. The question of what to do with those savings opens up other political fights. Green growth advocates argue for reallocating the savings from subsidy reduction to either offset the higher cost of fuels for low-income populations or invest in long-run economic growth (OECD/IEA 2010). Higher fuel prices may generate distributive conflict, such as the recent protests in India over subsidy reform, that forces the return of subsidies (Reddy 2010). To address these political concerns, proponents of subsidy reform suggest using some of the savings to compensate low-income households (Center for American Progress 2008). Improving equity has little impact on economic growth, but it can make policies more politically appealing and thus sustainable over the long term. Alternatively, the OECD (2010) suggests that recovered subsidy costs should fund tax reforms that would improve economic conditions more broadly.

Empirically, exactly how much investment could be funded this way depends, of course, on how subsidies are defined and measured and whether the subsidies, if removed, could be redirected. Using only the difference between global and domestic prices as a subsidy measure, Larsen and Shah (1992, 5) estimate that the world as a whole spent $230 billion on fossil fuel subsidies in 1991, paid mostly by middle-income and developing economies. At the other extreme, a broader and more controversial definition, including the cost of roads, highways, and the navies that secure shipping routes, valued oil subsidies for the United States alone at between $500 and $1,700 billion (ICTA 1998). Regardless of these disagreements, however, an array of studies all confirm that subsidy removal would improve economic welfare and reduce emissions, even when taking into account the losses incurred by fossil fuel producers (Larsen and Shah 1992; Koplow and Dernbach 2001; Moor 2001).

Finally, subsidy removal may also offset the cost of emissions reduction by improving energy security. For countries dependent on imported fossil fuels, exposure to volatile energy prices has adverse impacts on competitiveness via both the cost of energy and through the exchange rate channel. High and volatile energy prices raise production costs, and firms incur hedging costs when attempting to insulate themselves from volatility. Both high and volatile prices put pressure on exchange rates as import costs increase, affecting the national balance of payments and exchange rate stability. Offsetting these costs and risks may justify the higher costs of renewable energy and energy infrastructure (Keohane 2008). Senior Danish, American, and Korean policy makers have specifically cited these benefits as motivations for pursuing green energy strategies (Chang 2009; IEA 2009; Zichal 2010).

Environmental Tax Reform: Exchanging Goods for Bads

Environmental tax reform is closely related to the idea of subsidy reform. It proposes to fund tax *reductions* on labor and capital with revenues from new

48   taxes on emissions. Its advocates contend that these changes will simultaneously improve tax efficiency and reduce emissions. The resulting "double dividend" — economic growth and emissions reduction — from environmental tax reform promises both job creation and GDP growth even as emissions fall. Empirically, however, green growth from this kind of tax reform appears more likely to encourage job creation than to promote overall GDP growth. Furthermore, achieving both sides of the double dividend depends on starting from a tax code that imposes particularly high burdens on labor or capital. In countries with more efficient tax codes, green tax reform can still achieve emissions reductions but will deliver fewer economic benefits.

The research literature disputes the size, but not the concept, of economic gains from green tax reform. The most aggressive form of the double-dividend theory claims that the efficiency gains from a better tax code far outweigh whatever costs the carbon tax imposes. For this to occur, however, green tax reform must yield an increase in nonenvironmental welfare. Most studies reviewed by Goulder (1995) show that this will occur only when the taxation system is already highly inefficient. Manresa and Sancho (2005) model the Spanish CO_2 tax and show that recycling carbon tax revenue into tax reductions elsewhere can reduce emissions, make the tax system more efficient, and increase employment. But this "triple-dividend," as they call it, only came about because the Spanish tax system had placed a very high, and very inefficient, tax burden on labor. Hoerner and Bosquet's (2001) analysis of the experience of environmental tax reform in eight European countries also shows that recycling tax revenues can increase employment. Net impacts on GDP appear to be smaller: across 44 studies, the overall change in GDP growth rates before and after tax reform ranged between −0.5 percent and 0.5 percent.

Thus, environmental tax reform can support emissions reductions by raising the cost of greenhouse gas emissions and may, in some cases, improve economic efficiency and help generate *employment* growth. But it appears to have a relatively small impact on economic growth itself, and its effects are highly dependent on the structure of the original tax system. Thus, hopes that environmental tax reform funded by emissions pricing can generate net benefits from emissions taxation appear limited to specific cases; the best outcome possible in most cases appears to generate emissions reductions at little to no cost.

In sum, it may be possible to green present patterns of economic growth, reducing emissions at relatively minimal cost. Advocates of this view of green growth contend that a sensible carbon price, coupled with savings from reduced exposure to energy prices, fewer supply risks, and reduced carbon fuel subsidy costs, could drive transition costs to a minimum. But this argument remains both publicly and politically contentious, and it requires a range of choices — to impose taxes and reduce subsidies — that stand to create real opposition. Moreover, this approach as a whole offers little immediate benefit, even as it also suggests little actual pain.

BEYOND BREAKING EVEN: THE ALLURE OF GREEN JOBS

In the face of high unemployment following the 2008 financial crisis, a second, more ambitious argument for green growth emerged in the public debate. If investments in renewable energy or energy efficiency could create jobs rather than just impose costs, it could create the basis of a new green employment market. In the subsequent debate, three different versions of the green jobs argument emerged:

1. That Keynesian demand stimulus at times of recession should be used to create jobs and invest in needed improvements to the energy infrastructure.
2. That green jobs should come from the sponsorship of new green industries, whose demand for labor would offset job losses in older, "brown" sectors.
3. That cost savings from energy efficiency improvements could be recycled into consumption from more labor-intense industries, generating net job gains even as the relative demand for labor in the energy sector falls.

These arguments, while not mutually exclusive, take three very different views of how green jobs can be created, how quickly they can be created, and how long we can expect them to last.

Green Stimulus and the Keynesian Logic of Job Creation

Deficit spending by governments during recessions may, under certain circumstances, compensate for lost demand and help buffer the return to full employment. Taken a step further, advocates of emissions reduction argue that this spending should be targeted at renewable energy and energy efficiency investments that both create jobs and lay the groundwork for a lower-carbon economy (Jones 2008). These arguments found traction in response to the 2008–2009 global recession. Almost every OECD country, and some non-OECD countries, included so-called "green" spending in their economic stimulus packages. By the end of 2009, China had pledged one-third of its stimulus package, a total of $218.8 billion, to green spending and investment. The United States pledged 12 percent, or $117.8 billion, and the European Union pledged approximately 60 percent, or $23 billion. South Korea was a major outlier, committing nearly 79 percent of its stimulus package to a comprehensive green growth strategy (Barbier 2011).

50 Green Keynesianism thus implies two arguments: whether government stimulus works to promote economic growth and, in that case, whether we should use stimulus funds for green projects. The second question, of course, is a political choice. But whether that choice will successfully generate both economic growth and emissions reduction depends on the answer to the first question: whether *any* Keynesian investment generates growth. The answer depends on the scale of the Keynesian multiplier — the relationship between a dollar of spending and the scale of additional consumption or investment it promotes. This remains hotly contested among macroeconomists.[6] Whether green Keynesianism stimulus fulfilled its goals after the 2008–2009 financial crisis and recession similarly remains under evaluation. Barbier (2011) found that U.S. programs did deliver on their goal of creating 500,000 new jobs by 2012. The OECD (2010, 27) found that similar measures in South Korea added 960,000 new jobs. Houser, Mohan, and Heilmayr (2009, 2–5) found that green stimulus performed as well or better than traditional stimulus, creating 20 percent more jobs than traditional infrastructure spending and contributing to emissions reduction and energy savings. But these positive effects will very likely fade as the economy returns to full employment and opportunities to use idle resources for green energy investments disappear.

*Green Industrial Policy: Reindustrialization and
the Demand for Highly Skilled Labor*

The rationale for Keynesian job creation fades as economies return to normal growth patterns. Over the longer term, enthusiasts for a transition to green employment argue that emissions reduction targets can support a new wave of green industries, bringing it high-quality jobs, and that reallocating savings from energy efficiency investments to other sectors can expand demand across the economy as a whole.

This optimism for green capital goods like renewable energy appeals to industrial economies battered by deindustrialization and international competition (Jones 2008). Because many of these jobs are location-specific, they may be less vulnerable to offshoring than other manufacturing sectors. Constructing and maintaining wind farms or solar generators, or manufacturing very large wind turbines, requires skilled on-site workers, many in sectors that have suffered from intense competition from emerging economies (Friedman 2007). Moreover, because these industries, as Engel and Kammen (2009) argued, are more labor intensive than the sectors they replace, the green economy has the potential to become a net employment generator.

Spain green job creation has generated a great deal of interest given its emphasis on green energy as an economic development strategy (Buffa 2009). Studies of the region around Navarre, where wind turbine maker Gamesa has a significant presence, generally show positive employment effects. Faulin et al. (2006) argued that achieving a renewable electricity consumption rate of 12 percent in that region would have net positive employment effects. Moreno and Lopez (2008) found similar effects of renewable energy mandates in the Spanish region of Asturias. In this case in particular, the employment effects appear to originate from reallocating energy demand from Asturias's fossil fuel sector, which has low labor intensity compared with the manufacture, installation, operation, and maintenance of renewable energy capacity.

These results are also apparent outside Spain. In the United States, Barkenbus et al. (2006) found that biomass energy investments could complement Tennessee's preexisting expertise in agriculture and create net new jobs. Lehr et al. (2008, 117) predicted that German renewable energy firms could provide 400,000 new jobs by 2030. Most of those jobs, however, depend on the assumption that Germany will continue to excel in global export markets and that other countries will continue to demand German goods. This suggests the importance of export-led growth to green growth arguments.

Despite these results, however, we should not assume that green energy investments reliably generate net employment growth. While empirical research shows that investing in renewable energy markets can generate net employment gains, the outcome appears highly contingent on the characteristics of particular locations: labor-intensive industry in Spain, specific agricultural capacities in Tennessee, and highly competitive exporters in Germany. It remains unclear whether every region can find similar success in its own green niche. Nor are these green jobs necessarily immune to global competition. China has made major inroads into renewable energy goods, suggesting that green jobs in high-productivity manufacturing remain vulnerable to outsourcing (Glaeser 2011). Ironically, the lack of environmental regulation and resulting lower production costs may give China the opportunity to become the export leader in a variety of low-emissions goods (Dreyfuss 2010).[7] Furthermore, Sharan (2010, 2) uses the history of technological innovation to argue that renewable energy might prove *less*, not more, labor intensive than today's energy sector, leading to net job losses. Even if this didn't come to pass, however, green employment that results from higher labor intensity — by requiring more workers to achieve the same output that fossil fuel firms obtain with fewer employees — would represent a step backward for productivity growth.

More Productivity, Less Energy: Energy Efficiency
as an Employment Generator

The effort to improve energy efficiency can generate manufacturing and services employment and produce net cost savings that can go to support employment in the broader economy. Programs such as building retrofitting and weatherization are labor intensive and require on-site work that does not compete with cheaper overseas labor (Friedman 2007; Jones 2008). Thus, efficiency programs can create net employment, particularly when using labor that would otherwise sit idle during economic downturns.

Energy efficiency improvements, some argue, can also promote long-term gains through both consumer savings and improved firm productivity. As efficiency lowers energy services costs, households may spend their energy savings on other goods or services. If those goods or services are more labor intensive than energy, this expenditure switching could lead to increased employment (Roland-Holst 2008). Energy savings would also entail a net productivity gain from firms who could produce the same value with fewer inputs. Finally, proponents of the growth-generating effects of energy efficiency suggest energy efficiency investments could become self-sustaining by reinvesting a portion of the savings in the next round of improvements. Such iterated investment could create self-sustaining employment opportunities independent of government investment. The European Commission estimates that its Ecodesign Directive building efficiency measures will save 340 TWh of electricity, worth €51 billion at average electricity rates (European Commission 2011, 7; Europe's Energy Portal 2011), and Jones (2008) has made similar arguments for the United States.

Empirical studies of the employment effects of energy efficiency investments support the job creation argument. Input-output modeling of American building energy efficiency programs concluded that the program will create nearly half a million jobs, increase wages by $7.8 billion, and save $207 million worth of energy capital goods between 2005 and 2030 (Scott et al. 2008, 2283). David Roland-Holst (2008) provides evidence that between 1972 and 2006 in California, a total household energy savings of $56 billion was redirected toward other more labor-intensive goods and services, creating 1.5 million jobs with a total payroll of $45 billion over this 34-year period. Bernstein et al. (2000, 57) estimated that between 1977 and 1993, decreasing industrial and commercial energy intensity contributed to a 2.74 percent increase in per capita GDP.

However, energy efficiency jobs may be less green than they first appear. If energy efficiency improvements expand demand for energy-intensive goods, some or all of the emissions gains may be offset by growth in overall energy demand. Empirical evidence for the size of this offset remains mixed.

Schipper and Grubb's (2000, 386) empirical study of energy use in IEA countries between 1970 and 1990 revealed no significant rebound effects either
at the household or economy level. Jenkins, Nordhaus, and Shellenberger
(2011) reviewed a range of studies in developed economies that estimated the
rebound effect as positive but small—perhaps 10 to 30 percent of the savings gained by the energy efficiency investments themselves. But this result is
contradicted by the few macroeconomic studies of energy efficiency effects,
which suggest overall rebound effects on the order of 60 percent. Effects in
developing economies, where the marginal value of energy consumption is
much higher, may be even larger. Herring (2006) provides evidence that British energy demand for street lighting increased 30-fold during the Industrial
Revolution, even as lighting efficiency improved 20-fold. Jin (2007) found
more modest rebound effects, on the order of 30 to 40 percent, for residential
energy use in South Korea after the 1970 energy crises. Dimitropolous (2008)
found relatively few studies of developing economies and a very wide range of
estimates for the rebound effect in those countries, ranging from 44 percent
on the low end to 77 percent or higher. Nevertheless, this range of estimates
would suggest that at least some energy savings persist, and only a few studies
found that 100 percent of energy gains were lost to increased economic activity.

EMISSIONS REDUCTION AS A DRIVER OF GDP GROWTH: THE MOST AMBITIOUS CONTENTION

The final, and most ambitious, green growth argument proposes that emissions reduction measures can drive GDP growth. In contrast to arguments for
green employment growth, which focus on the specific job creation effects of
climate policy, proponents of green GDP growth believe that emission reductions can drive growth in aggregate output by either promoting comparative
advantage in green sectors or increasing productivity through innovation. But
the emphasis on export-led growth in many of these arguments makes them
vulnerable to two critiques: first, that export-led growth as a model has limited
applicability, and second, that it encourages a zero-sum view of the green
growth economy, promoting a new green mercantilism that could make international competition more damaging than beneficial.

Export Promotion: Winners and Losers in the Battle for Global Cleantech Markets

Global adoption of renewable energy—whether for climate or other reasons—creates a huge new market for energy technology. As this market grows,

capturing it for increased exports from domestic firms becomes an attractive growth strategy. Denmark, Korea, and China all showcase government attempts to help domestic firms acquire global market dominance through expansion of domestic markets for the same goods, support for innovation and R&D, and other policies that help lower production costs. The Danish strategy seeks to maintain Denmark's internationally competitive position in the wind industry as a key growth objective (Danish Government 2009). The Koreans focus on manufacturing green technologies such as solar and hydrogen fuel cells for export, leveraging previous high-tech manufacturing skills in semiconductor and shipbuilding (UNESCAP 2010). The Chinese have invested heavily into wind and solar production in a bid to serve domestic markets hungry for energy (Bradsher 2010a, 2010b). Finally, the European Union as a whole has explicitly targeted global competitiveness in new energy technology as one rationale for its aggressive goals for renewable energy technology development and deployment.

Using domestic markets to improve firm competitiveness in global markets has a long-standing pedigree. Most models point to the "Learning by Doing" concept to explain why. The LBD model assumes that the cost of technology decreases with cumulative output. With significant investment during a technology's infant phase, its price can decrease rapidly. If true, that would reinforce the assumption, made by both the cost minimization and GDP growth schools, that renewable energy can quickly become competitive against conventional energy. Matthias Heymann (1998) showed evidence that the Danish wind industry developed successfully as a result of a bottom-up approach that emphasized incremental innovation based on knowledge gained through building and deploying successively more advanced turbines. Grübler, Nakicenovic, and Victor (1999) provided many examples of cost reduction as a result of increased output in nascent technologies. In the United States, photovoltaic cells, wind turbines, and gas turbines all saw their cost per kilowatt capacity drop significantly as total capacity expanded (Grübler, Nakicenovic, and Victor 1999, 254).

In these and some other cases, domestic market growth has helped the pursuit of export competitiveness. Foreign markets account for 50 percent of the output of the Danish wind energy industry, which in turn accounts for 20 percent of the employment in the Danish energy sector and nearly 10 percent of all Danish exports (DWIA 2009). Siemens in Germany, Gamesa in Spain, and Vestas in Denmark have all become major international players in renewable energy, with significant employment and investment footprints at home. International competitiveness may also keep domestic investment at home. The lack of domestic capacity in the United States allowed China to capture as much as 90 percent of the California solar market's economic stimulus investments after 2007. More stable domestic investment in renewable energy might have supported the domestic capacity to keep the stimulus dollars in the United States.

Export-led green growth, however, has two vulnerabilities. First, it may not be a viable strategy everywhere. As Hidalgo et al. (2007) and Hausmann and Hidalgo (2010) show, comparative advantage in particular kinds of goods tends, in general, to grow out of similar capacities — skills, capital, knowledge, and institutions — in related sectors. Thus, even viable green export strategies face certain limits. As Huberty and Zachmann (2011) proposed, Danish and German excellence in wind turbines appears to derive from a preexisting foundation of expertise in high-precision machine tools and related goods. Nations like the United States, which may lack some of these precursors, may find export-led strategies of limited utility. Other green sectors will have different and diverse precursors. The viability of export-led strategies for any country depends heavily on which sectors, and which capabilities, a country has decided to target.

Export-led green growth also raises a second concern: that governments' reliance on export markets to repay green investments will encourage a "new green mercantilism." For example, China's preferential treatment of Chinese renewable energy firms, and aggressive intellectual property transfer requirements for foreign firms hoping to supply Chinese energy demand, has come in for heavy criticism from China's international trade partners (Bradsher 2010a, 2010b). The United Steelworkers union recently filed a WTO complaint against China, alleging that these practices constitute a violation of the WTO rules on state aid and free trade (Daily, Steitz, and Walet 2011). The Chinese counter that many countries are currently involved in subsidizing the development of renewable energy. Of course, the hope is that the rise of green sectors would give way to intraindustry trade that benefitted a wide range of sectors, rather than mere competition for control of a handful of sectors.

Empirically, the case for export-led growth is mixed. Japan, Singapore, South Korea, Taiwan, and now China usually lead the list of countries that have used export markets to successfully drive domestic development, whereas Latin America failed when it pursued related policies for import substitution. Lewer and Van den Berg (2003, 363) reviewed 53 empirical studies, examining countries from all regions of the world over time. They concluded that export growth and economic growth are positively correlated: for every 1 percentage point increase in export growth, they found a statistically significant 0.2 percentage point increase in economic growth. But whether this correlation is causal is unclear: Giles and Williams's review (2001) of 150 empirical research papers showed that even papers that attempted to estimate causality had difficulty establishing the direction of a causal link in the export-growth relationship. In other words, even if exports and economic growth are causally related, it remains unclear whether exports drive growth or vice-versa. Thus, claims that exports drive growth always and everywhere and that green goods can follow the same path should be viewed with caution.

Thus, relying on exports of renewable energy or low-emissions products to drive GDP and jobs growth remains a green growth strategy with limited applicability. Those nations that gained from first-mover advantage—Denmark and Germany in particular—did so on the basis of preexisting national competencies. Second-stage countries now face intense global competition from developing and developed countries alike, and they may lack the foundations for moving into those products. Finally, overemphasis on exports as a growth strategy may undermine both growth and emissions reduction by distorting domestic investment, denying countries the benefits of trade in green energy industries, and raising the costs of emissions reduction and renewable energy goods.

Inventing Success: Technology Breakthroughs as Foundations for Green Growth

Regardless of whether one subscribes to any green growth argument, serious reductions in greenhouse gas emissions will require substantial innovation in alternative energy technologies. Past economic successes with policy-led innovation have become models for public investment in green technology innovation. Nordhaus and Shellenberger (2007) point out that publicly supported research and development in information and computer technologies laid the foundations of the Internet and communications boom and the substantial private investment, job creation, and income growth that accompanied it. Public support for innovation is seen to play a particularly important role in reducing production costs for early-phase technologies. For renewable energy, where the cost of the actual energy source is near zero, falling production costs could lead to energy sources substantially cheaper than today's fossil fuels. Jones (2008) argues that this outcome represents the next potential industrial revolution. However, this literature continues to disagree on the appropriate model for public sponsorship of low-carbon research and development. Indeed, as Huberty and Zysman (2010) argued, it may well be that *none* of the prior models—even as different as the Manhattan Project and the Defense Advanced Research Projects Agency (DARPA) were—provide sound guidance on how to structure public investment in low-emissions technology.

Public R&D support has waxed and waned. More recently, private investors, and in particular venture capitalists, have shown increasing enthusiasm for green innovation. John Doerr of Silicon Valley fame notes that a green energy venture market that captured even a sliver of the $5 trillion global energy market would rival the Internet boom for size (Doerr 2007; Mitchell 2007). This echoes an early enthusiasm by venture capitalists for firms supplying the most cutting-edge clean technologies to meet rising demand for alternative energy (Green 2009).

Venture capital, however, faces an array of challenges. It usually prefers many small investments to a few large ones, and prefers commercialization of technology to developing it from scratch. As LaMonica (2009) pointed out, however, the slow-moving, capital-intensive, technologically conservative energy sector is poorly suited to these preferences. These characteristics have led venture capitalists away from support of new green innovation and toward support for commercialization of late-stage technologies. But as Kenney and Hargadon argue in Chapter 4, this doesn't resolve the entire problem. Achieving the necessary returns on investment for the venture capital model to work relies, in part, on rapidly growing markets in which revenues scale faster than costs. But energy markets, particularly in the developed world, face slowly growing demand and large fixed capital costs that scale with the size of deployment in the face of fixed and highly regulated revenue flows. These issues cast doubt on whether venture capital can play a role in a low-emissions energy systems transformation analogous to its success with information technology.

Finally, Porter and van der Linde (1995) proposed a very different argument—the so-called "Porter Hypothesis"—for using regulation to drive growth. They argued that forced adaptation to environmental regulation may spur growth by driving technological innovation toward outcomes that both save money and reduce emissions. But empirical support for the Porter Hypothesis remains mixed. Palmer and Oates (1995, 120) objected to Porter's assumption that firms can discover cleaner, more efficient production processes without incurring any added costs. Empirically, American firms report that, as of 1992, their pollution abatement costs and expenditures (PACE) still exceed the cost savings of regulation-induced innovation by $100 billion (Palmer and Oates 1995, 128). In contrast, while Wagner (2003, 31) found theoretical support for the concept of regulation-induced competitiveness, he also found that costs and benefits vary significantly across firms and industries, suggesting that this result may not be widely applicable. Furthermore, many of the assumed preconditions—efficient regulation, widespread demand for environmentally differentiated goods, and a reserve of cost-effective but unused technology options—often aren't present. That implies that we may face an extended

58 period of investment in new technologies and development of consumer demand before the Porter Hypothesis conditions are realized. If so, that would imply substantially higher transition costs and less favorable conditions for regulation-driven, emissions-reduction-led growth.

CONCLUSION: BEYOND EMISSIONS AND ENERGY—ENERGY SYSTEMS TRANSFORMATION AND THE CREATION OF ECONOMIC OPPORTUNITY

Despite very strong ambitions, most green growth arguments, as this chapter should make clear, have relatively modest horizons. Green growth, heralded as a coming "third industrial revolution," has been proposed as a tool to reflate economies and a means of revitalizing moribund industrial sectors. Yet, the policy proposals reviewed here have focused almost entirely on retrofitting the means by which we produce, distribute, and use energy. Most of them assume a broad desire for climate change mitigation and seek to identify immediate material benefits from having pursued it. With the exception of very near-term proposals for Keynesian spending, the arguments reviewed in this chapter do not propose mechanisms that are well aligned to prevailing theories of economic growth. They have little concept of how new renewable energy goods contribute to a superior capital stock; how green human capital would make workers or firms more productive; or how demand for green goods can become self-sustaining by enhancing productivity or providing new opportunities for goods and services.

Thus, most green growth arguments do not directly confront the problems introduced in the initial chapters of this book. They neither contemplate a full-throated transformation of the energy system nor do they envision how that transformation might, on its own, become an engine of durable economic growth. This conclusion reinforces the argument advanced in Chapter 1 that we require a great deal more experimentation to discover where and how green growth might prove possible. Part II of this book turns to how we might build the political consensus required to make that experimentation possible in the years to come.

4

Venture Capital and Clean Technology

Martin Kenney and Andrew Hargadon

INTRODUCTION

The threat of climate change has focused considerable attention on the need for reducing anthropogenic carbon emissions, predominately by reducing fossil fuel usage. That attention has brought equally considerable human and financial capital to bear on generating innovations in what has become known as the clean-technology (cleantech) industry. However, changing the existing energy infrastructure, including both coal- and gas-fired power plants and diesel- and gasoline-powered engines, represents a monumental undertaking. In addressing climate change, three options are generally recognized: mitigation of emissions, adaptation to changing environmental conditions, or suffering the consequences of deterioration. Innovation has become the primary means, in the public eye and in public policy, for pursuing both mitigation and, increasingly, adaptation. Indeed, the recent and dramatic innovations driving the information technology revolution have placed the entrepreneur and his or her financier, the venture capitalist, at the center of new policies for driving innovation. This chapter considers the wisdom of such a placement, focusing particularly on the applicability of venture capital to fostering innovation in cleantech.

Energy systems are literally at the core of all political economies and are thoroughly integrated into our everyday lives. Whether the steam engine and its relationship to the industrial revolution or the petroleum industry and the mass-consumption society, energy production, delivery, and use have played central roles in their respective historical epochs. Due to its impact on the global ecosystem, more questions have arisen during the last decade about

60   whether the current energy regime is sustainable and the possibility of transitioning to a new energy regime that is less dependent on fossil fuels. Those advocating a transition to clean technology believe this can only be accomplished by the discovery and commercialization of technological innovations. What are the mechanisms and who are the agents for financing this hoped-for transition? For a number of reasons, many believe that venture capital is ideal for financing such a transition (Wüstenhagen and Teppo 2006; for an alternative perspective, see Kenney 2010; Lange et al. 2011; Hargadon and Kenney 2012).

Advocates of venture capital as the financing mechanism draw upon the centrality of venture capitalists in financing the information technology revolution (e.g., Perez 2002). Venture capitalism coevolved with the emergence and growth of entrepreneurial activity in the information and communications industry, particularly in regions such as Silicon Valley (Kenney 2011a). The success venture capitalists experienced in funding the development of ICT giants like Apple, Cisco, Intel, Oracle, and many more firms also formed the basis of what many, perhaps euphemistically, have termed a New Economy (Gordon 2000). This remarkable record of success in ICT, combined with the modest but significant success in the biomedical fields, is attractive. And yet these advocates rarely consider the other sectors in which venture capitalists initially invested but soon abandoned due to a lack of returns. This chapter identifies the boundary conditions for successful venture capital investment and compares these conditions with the characteristics of clean technology in general, and the solar industry in particular, to establish the viability of innovation driven by venture capital investment success.

Some believe the existing energy system can only be overturned by a process of Schumpeterian creative destruction initiated by entrepreneurs. Given the sheer scope of change required, the momentum of the existing energy system, and the power of entrenched interests; given the recent emphasis in many nations upon austerity; and given the faltering confidence in the ability of governments to invest in long-term public projects, direct government action appears unlikely. In this environment, the prospect of a self-financing clean-technology revolution is appealing. Schumpeterian creative destruction—the virtuous cycle of successful innovations emerging, attracting new human and financial capital, and propagating further innovation and investment that opens new economic spaces—appears an attractive alternative for action at the scale required. Given venture capital's prominent role in the last such wave of destruction—the information technology industry—policy makers are turning to the venture capital model as a means for funding new firms whose success could affect an energy transition and thereby possibly unleashing a new and similar wave of economic and employment growth.

Utilizing an appreciative model of the boundary conditions for successful venture capital investment developed in Hargadon and Kenney (2012), we consider the possibilities for investing in clean technologies and the likelihood of venture capital–backed firms replacing today's energy system, or at least important parts of it. In this exploration, we pose the question of whether Schumpeterian creative destruction will be the dominant mode for the clean-technology change process. In particular, we pose three questions: Is clean technology an industry and, if so, how? What are the boundary conditions for venture capital's investment success, a critical component of opening new economic spaces? Where in cleantech might these conditions hold (with a deeper exploration of one area, solar power)?

IS CLEAN TECHNOLOGY AN INDUSTRY?

To investigate the potential role of venture capital in cleantech, building upon other chapters in this book, we ask whether clean technology is a coherent industry, or set of industries, joined by some unifying principle and whether this principle, like digitization was for the information and communication technologies or molecular biology was for biotechnologies, is sufficiently powerful to provide large numbers of opportunities for venture investing. This is important because all of the previous long-wave expansions were based on a group of emerging industries and technologies, and invariably one of these new technologies was a new energy source or production system.

While the media, many observers, and government policy makers refer to cleantech as a single industry, determining whether this is, in fact, the case is important analytically. The difficulty with considering cleantech as a single industry or technology is immediately apparent by the fact that the definitions of clean technologies themselves are both broad and vague. Patel (2006), as an extreme, goes so far as to suggest that cleantech, as a term, is simply a creation of the venture capitalists and has little merit beyond this. More pragmatically, Philip Cooke (2008) examines a variety of definitions before accepting Joel Makower's definition of cleantech as "a diverse range of products, services, and processes that harness renewable materials and energy sources and substantially reduce the use of all resources and dramatically cut or eliminate emissions and waste." If this definition is accepted, the sheer breadth of technologies, markets, and production processes violates the earlier definitions of an industry as a group of firms competing in a market or sharing similar knowledge bases, labor pools, and other linkages.

This diversity is illustrated in Table 4.1, which catalogues industries that are considered by the Cleantech Group, a cleantech investment consultancy, as

62 being part of clean technology. The sheer diversity of markets and knowledge bases involved in cleantech is remarkable. Using a broad definition, Chapple et al. (2011, 8) identify 194 different 8-digit SIC codes as part of the cleantech economy. To be certain, the firms in these SIC codes do not consider themselves as part of a single industry, do not compete in similar markets, and do not share technologies, labor markets, or suppliers. In the absence of a clear definition, even establishing the number of cleantech firms is difficult. For example, Chapple et al. include existing firms in industries as diverse as environmental consulting and waste recycling, including automotive recycling facilities. The inclusionary approach is not without justification because some of the greatest benefits for energy conservation and environmental protection can be expected from improving existing activities, which Chapple et al. and others refer to as "process" improvements — in other words, undertaking existing activities either more efficiently or with less effect on the environment. But it is not without its problems either; we must be very careful making generalized claims about industry attributes without a clear definition of what designates an industry.

Defining industries and their boundaries has attracted much attention in economics, management, and sociology, much of which has considered the problem of firms that span industrial boundaries (e.g., McKendrick and

TABLE 4.1

Industry segments according to the Cleantech Group

Energy Generation	Energy Storage	Energy Infrastructure	Energy Efficiency
Wind	Fuel cells	Management	Lighting
Solar	Advanced batteries	Transmission	Buildings
Hydro/marine	Hybrid systems		Glass
Biofuels			Other
Geothermal			
Other			
Transportation	Water and Wastewater	Air and Environment	Materials
Vehicles	Water treatment	Cleanup/safety	Nano
Logistics	Water conservation	Emissions control	Bio
Structures	Wastewater treatment	Monitoring/compliance	Chemical
Fuels		Trading and offsets	Other
Manufacturing/ Industrial	Agriculture	Recycling and Waste	
Advanced packaging	Natural pesticides	Recycling	
Monitoring and control	Land management	Waste treatment	
Smart production	Aquaculture		

Carroll 2001; Ruef and Patterson 2009). Sociologists have generally treated industrial boundaries as socially defined; in other words, who do the participants or significant outsiders such as financial intermediaries define as their competitors or members of their industry (see, e.g., Porac et al. 1995)? In this sense, in some of the sociological literature, the creation of industry categories has a somewhat voluntaristic cast. If key internal members (for instance, through forming trade associations) or external audiences label a set of firms as an industry, this is sufficient to make it legitimate (DiMaggio 1988). The reasons for a set of organizations becoming an industry can vary. For example, the government agencies can, in effect, mandate groups of firms as being an industry by regulating them through a common entity. To illustrate, Russo (2001) documents the emergence of an independent power generation industry that was enabled by government policy requiring that existing utilities purchase power from independents. In this illustration, the independent power industry is contiguous with independent firms selling power to the utilities. In this case, common knowledge base, supplier relations, or labor forces have no bearing on industry membership; it is defined by the work product. Since the other dimensions such as power generation technologies were not part of the definition, they may vary considerably, though their output is undifferentiated electrons. Here, the market and industry are synonymous, but the activities and even the organizational forms—for example, for-profit firms, nonprofit firms, cooperatives, and so forth—by which the electrons are produced can vary dramatically.

In economics, a more standard definition of an industry is a group of firms sharing similar technologies and producing a roughly similar product. For example, an industry could consist of firms producing a somewhat differentiated product—say, semiconductors—but selling to different customers. Thus, the firms might be somewhat different markets, but they would be members of the same industry. Here, the industry is determined by having a similar product and technologies. Such definitions of industries suggest a certain coherence in terms of activities and products. In contrast, while both bus and railroad firms provide transportation services, they are considered to be in different industries even though they compete. The relatedness of cleantech firms and sectors can also be measured through product-space analysis, a technique determining the relationship between related inputs and finished products in terms of SIC codes. Using this technique, and as discussed in earlier chapters, Mark Huberty and Georg Zachmann (2011) found that for six cleantech products, solar photovoltaic, wind turbines, nuclear power plants, nuclear reactor parts, electric meters, and electric meter parts, the respective value chains were almost entirely unrelated. The implications of the lack of

64   common suppliers are that there are likely to be few general synergies and probably relatively little knowledge-sharing between the sectors, despite the fact
that all six products are related to the electric grid and three of them generate
electricity.

While the previous paragraphs suggested that technology synergies are
likely to be limited, undoubtedly some cleantech companies participate in
the same value chains. To illustrate the significance of this observation from
the venture capital industry's perspective, successful investments in the personal computer industry created demand for related products that could be
provided by start-ups, including small magnetic storage devices (e.g., Seagate,
Shugart Associates, Tandon), software (Borland Software Corporation, Lotus
Development Corporation, Microsoft, WordPerfect), data communications
devices and software (Novell, Synoptics, 3Com), and many more. It is this con-
catenating process, evidenced in the PC industry that drives powerful waves
of creative destruction. Yet, we believe there will be far fewer opportunities
in cleantech to fund the creation of entirely new value networks composed of
new firms because fewer entirely new industries composed of new firms are
likely to emerge. If the all-electric automobile were to become the dominant
personal transportation vehicle, for example, would a process similar to what
occurred with PCs be triggered? In certain limited respects, this may be what
is happening. Venture capitalists have invested in electric automobile start-
ups such as Tesla and Fisker and firms such as A123 Systems, a battery maker.
At a macro-level, if the only new firm–to–new firm relationships are between
assemblers and battery makers, then the new value network is quite truncated.
The lack of Schumpeterian creative destruction potential is further illustrated
when we consider that only a few contracts between the new assemblers and
battery makers have emerged. So, for example, in 2010, A123 Systems signed
a contract to supply Fisker Automotive with battery packs, but for its S series
roadster, Tesla adopted lithium-ion cells produced by Japanese electronics giant Panasonic Corp., which also has a strong relationship with Toyota, which
is beginning to make electric cars. Of course, here the largest obstacle is that
existing auto and battery producers are competing in exactly the same economic spaces, and they have enormous complementary assets. While, from an
analytical perspective, the success of a movement to an all-electrical vehicle
economy would be a major technical transformation and offer business opportunities to all types of suppliers. Whether start-ups can build their productive
capacity fast enough to outflank incumbent firms in adjacent industries is unclear. It will most likely depend on how quickly it gets done, the incumbents'
ability to internalize the shift, and the types of technological developments
necessary. For Zysman and Huberty (2010b), the firms most likely to drive new

economic growth are those providing new goods and services, and it is among
them that venture capitalists search for investment opportunities. However,
here once again, the firms must display the characteristics venture capitalists
desire for justifying investment.

Ultimately, one must acknowledge that both public perception and policy
are directing human and financial capital toward cleantech, and these factors
alone warrant some defining characteristics. For the purposes of this analysis,
we use the nature of the innovation challenge as the common attribute of the
cleantech industry. In all cases, companies differing by technology, by market,
or by production processes are identifiably engaged in a similar effort to displace extant fossil fuel–based technologies and practices with lower carbon alternatives. This definition does not resolve the major concerns we have about
the ill-defined bundling of so many diverse firms, technologies, and markets
into a singular category so much as it recognizes the singularly common characteristic among them. As we'll discuss later, it is this singular commonality
that also challenges the potential role of venture capital investing.

VENTURE CAPITAL INVESTMENTS AND OUTCOMES

Successful venture capital investing is predicated upon selling previous investments to others and achieving a significant capital gain (Zider 1998). These
gains are the key to the venture capitalist's compensation and their ability to
continue raising capital. The key skills for a venture capitalist are discovering, investing in, and helping an entrepreneur or team of entrepreneurs to
organize a firm capable of exploiting a newly emerging market or an existing
market on the verge of being disrupted. The risks of making venture capital
investments are many, and, in fact, the dominant condition for them is uncertainty. There are many vectors of uncertainty. It is possible that the emerging technology does not work, that the investee firm is ill-suited to exploiting
the opportunity, or a market never appears or it fails to grow sufficiently fast.
Another vector of uncertainty is related to the entrepreneurial team and its
management capabilities. Economists have proposed understanding venture
capital investment decisions through agency theory where presumably the
investor — the principal — cannot be sure about the commitment of the agent —
the entrepreneur (Lerner 1995). It is more likely that the various vectors of
uncertainty are of greater significance to the investment's outcome than any
agency-related contractual problems. In case of negative outcomes, it is more
likely that the venture falls victim to what Stinchcombe (1965) termed the "liability of newness," which refers to the problems new firms face at their inception. In fact, the practice of venture capital investment has evolved routines,

66 norms, and even contracts to cope with this generalized uncertainty and high mortality rates (on contracts, see Suchman and Cahill 1996).

The high mortality rates among young firms with concomitant large losses mean that venture capitalists must be extremely selective in their investment choices. To build a new firm capable of the rapid growth that will increase its value sufficiently to offset the losses, venture capitalists must commit significant tranches of capital with little prospect of recovery should the firm fail. Because of the nature of the venture capital business, they must push their portfolio firms to grow extremely rapidly; long-term (slow) growth is an undesirable investment outcome. The dilemma every venture capitalist faces is that it is unwise to invest in firms that will fail or have minimal success. But venture capitalists also must take care not to miss the firms that have the potential to grow extremely rapidly, although, of course, the result is unknown ex ante. Given these conditions, venture capitalists undertake a due diligence process before deciding which firms to invest in (Tyebjee and Bruno 1984). Because the diligence process is itself iterative, entrepreneurs continually hone their business plans and, in conjunction with venture capitalists, develop a collective vision of how the firm should evolve (von Burg and Kenney 2000). Even after agreeing to invest, fund disbursement is staged. Thus, as more information emerges, the venture capitalists can gradually recalibrate their investment as they discover more about the technology, the market, and the management team.

Once the investment is made, the venture capitalists become partners in the venture and are expected to commit significant time to each portfolio firm by serving on its board of directors, making introductions, helping craft overall strategies, assisting in the recruitment of members of the management team, and monitoring the growth of the firm (Florida and Kenney 1988; Gompers and Lerner 2001; Kaplan and Strömberg 2004). Because seasoned venture capitalists have been involved in a number of start-ups, they can provide valuable advice on how to avoid the myriad pitfalls a rapidly growing firm can experience. However, because the venture capitalists' goal is to profitably liquidate their investment and their first loyalty is to their capital, their goals and interests can clash with those of the founder.

The particular economic conditions of markets, in addition to differences among individual ventures, determine the success of venture capital–backed ventures. In other words, not all markets are susceptible to transformation by small firms. In one study that examined which firms developed the most important innovations of the twentieth century, new firms contributed almost half of the innovations. These contributions, however, were greatest in immature industries where new entrants could expand in a relatively uncontested fashion (Acs and Audretsch 1988). As Lerner (2009, 60) argues, venture capital has had "relatively little impact on those [industries] dominated by mature companies. . . . Venture investors' mission is to capitalize on revolutionary changes in an industry, and the well-developed sectors often have a relatively low propensity for disruptive innovation." While these observations are useful, in the energy sector, the more relevant question is whether incumbents in neighboring sectors have the complementary assets and sufficient time to enter the emerging sector.

Ultimately, when judging whether a financial vehicle can support a particular genre of organizations, the question is whether the organizations and their markets have the characteristics necessary to meet a set of criteria. The key factors for a venture capital investment can be reduced to three interdependent criteria: rapidly growing markets, scalable technologies and ventures, and large and rapid payoffs. When these criteria are not sufficiently satisfied, then those investment opportunities are unlikely to receive venture capital. Finally, because venture capital is risk capital, it is entirely possible for venture capitalists to initiate investing in a particular sector, but evidence validating the initial investment must accumulate during the investment life cycle. If information emerges suggesting that the returns will not be as great as expected, the flow of capital to particular firms or an entire sector can be cut off. Though it is certainly possible to initially receive venture capital investment, particularly if there is significant public attention, ensuring continued investment is more difficult. We briefly expand upon these criteria below and then apply them to a few of the most salient clean technologies.

Large and Rapidly Growing Markets

Venture capitalists aim to invest in markets that are on the verge of creation (or disruption) that will allow their portfolio firms to grow rapidly by attracting customers. This growth depends on (1) the particular value proposition of the portfolio firm that is sufficiently compelling that customers rapidly adopt its new service or product or willingly migrate from incumbent technologies and competitors, and (2) market conditions that enable such new adoption or migration. In the former case, the particular offerings (and their value propositions) vary across competing firms in any given market, and it falls to the venture capital investors to discern the differences when investing in a particular industry. The latter case, however, derives from market and technology conditions and thus remains largely constant across all new and existing firms competing in a particular industry. For example, early internet firms such as Netscape, Yahoo!, Excite, and Amazon benefited from the rapid arrival of new users to the Internet, a new platform upon which they could offer their

68   services (and one where there were quite literally no competing incumbents). Such moments may also occur in existing markets, when a technological or other discontinuity is sufficiently large enough, occurs rapidly enough, or is legally protected in ways preventing incumbents' reactions.

For early-stage ventures, a market must have the promise of growth in ways that allow new ventures to scale that, in turn, justifies valuations permitting outsized returns to investors. The returns on venture capital investments depend on the market value of a new company (via initial public stock offering [IPO] or acquisition), and in new ventures, such valuations are typically multiples of revenues (rather than earnings) that reflect the anticipation of continued rapid growth. For this reason, investments have concentrated in particular industries or in industry subsegments undergoing rapid transformation or growth or experiencing massive discontinuities. These sectors naturally change over time. Ultimately, the success of venture capital is predicated upon having investment opportunities with large enough potential markets and concomitant returns to compensate for the risks.

The recent burst of venture capital investment in clean technologies was based on the expectation of rapid and widespread adoption in existing markets. This rush to invest was remarkable because since World War II, with the exception of the biomedical fields, outside the information technologies, such transformational growth has been the exception rather than the rule. Because, during the last decade, growth in the OECD energy markets has stagnated (0.14 percent annual growth rate), the adoption of clean technologies is predicated on the rapid replacement of existing technologies. While some clean technologies have experienced rapid growth in deployment in global terms, wind and solar (photovoltaic) technologies still contribute just 0.23 percent and 0.01 percent of total power generation, respectively.

A number of obstacles limit the growth rate of cleantech firms: the long life cycles of existing energy systems limit the number of customers turning over in a given year; the high capital costs limit the risk-tolerance of those customers; and the shared infrastructure and economies of scale enjoyed by existing systems make it extremely difficult for new technologies to compete on cost. In many cases, to make significant inroads in these markets, clean-technology ventures must displace entrenched competitors with a relatively undifferentiated product — watts of electricity or joules of power. The cleantech advantage, its differentiation, is that clean technologies do not produce global climate change gasses. However, if the cost of the externality is not internalized into the price, then most clean technologies are more expensive compared to existing power generation, which competes at its variable costs. Much of the current growth in cleantech deployment is because governments have mandated favorable feed-in tariffs for clean technologies, but due to the global economic crisis, many nations are decreasing the tariffs, thereby changing the relative cost of the energy generated by clean technologies. Simply put, the markets in which cleantech ventures hope to compete are large on an absolute scale, but the *relative* arrival of new customers (or churn of old customers) willing to adopt is small, limiting the growth and diffusion of emerging technologies and thus limiting the growth of the new ventures promoting them.

Scalability

Should new ventures have the good fortune of experiencing rapid growth in customer demand, a second boundary condition emerges. Frequent turnover in customers through new arrivals (a growing market), technological obsolescence (a churning market), or radical change in market structure (e.g., deregulation) creates the conditions for ventures to grow rapidly. Two dimensions of scalability then become important. First, the new venture and its underlying production technologies must be able to scale as fast as or faster than the market growth so that it can outpace later-arriving new entrants or slower-reacting incumbents. Unless new companies can emerge and become dominant players by scaling faster than competitors (new ventures and incumbents), there is little advantage to investing significant venture capital in them. In markets such as the information and biomedical technologies, the returns on equity are relatively decoupled from returns on assets. In other words, the value of a company (and its growth) is exponentially larger than its capital requirements to achieve that growth. Thus, scalability is a dominant feature of the information technology sector, and for successful venture capital investing, it is a prerequisite.

Second and related, ideally the new ventures must be able to provision the rapidly growing market without a correspondingly growing need for capital investment; this scalability is a function of both the venture and the technical and market conditions. For example, software, along with internet services, can increase production of goods and services without a corresponding increase in capital assets. The online retailer Amazon.com illustrates how financial assistance can enable a company to scale with a rapidly growing market. Amazon.com's infrastructure, though at times strained, was able to scale with the growth of internet shoppers, leaving little room for later ventures or major retailers to enter that particular segment. It is this type of growth for which venture investing is optimized. To displace incumbent systems on which markets currently depend, emerging clean technologies must be able to scale in terms of both capacity and quality. Even if a new technology does have the potential to scale in this way, the costs of achieving this scale in clean technologies rarely reflect the same ratios of investment to growth as historically seen in the information and communication technologies. Energy supply technologies, such as solar, wind, or biofuels, find that investments in R&D, while equivalent to similar investments in information and biomedical technologies, are considerably smaller than the investments needed to commercialize those technologies. Biotechnology firms solved the scaling problem by licensing their technologies, usually proprietary patented drugs, to incumbent pharmaceutical firms that had the requisite financial prowess to conduct expensive clinical trials, scale production, and manage distribution. This model worked because patents ensured that pharmaceutical firms would pay enormous sums for the rights to a candidate drug or would acquire the entire firm at an enormous premium. Most technologies in cleantech, in general, do not have the same intellectual property protection as pharmaceuticals but have similar scale-up costs.

The costs of scaling production, distribution, and installation for clean technologies like wind, solar, or biofuels often run to ten times the costs of initially developing the technology. Similarly, achieving even a fraction of the production volumes needed for additional low-carbon technology capacity requires large-scale construction or reallocation of manufacturing capacity. And because the energy sector is both heavily regulated and central to the provision of other goods and services, new technologies must meet very stringent cost, quality, and reliability expectations before they can enter (let alone scale rapidly) to serve the mass market. Indeed, both purchasing and financing decisions demand performance histories of not only the technologies under consideration but also the companies supplying those technologies and guaranteeing their performance. Most importantly, those costs grow relatively linearly with the revenue growth of the company. For example, Russ Landon, a managing director at the investment bank Canaccord Adams in Boston, compared cleantech start-ups to IT start-ups: "The capital requirements for energy start-ups are huge" (Kirsner 2010). While $25 million may develop a new biofuel production process, an additional $250 million is needed to create a production plant (and each new plant requires equivalent asset investments). In terms of pools of money, even the largest venture capital funds are relatively small (less than $1 billion per fund and, say, $3.5 billion under management). Even with syndication, opportunities requiring over $500 million are rarely attractive because the potential losses are too great. The Solyndra case, which went into bankruptcy after nearly $1 billion in private venture capital and $500 million in additional federal loan fund guarantees, provides a useful illustration. Similar high up-front capital costs are also one reason that venture capitalists will not invest in firms intending to manufacture semiconductors or build state-of-the-art data centers.

Scalability (and sheer size of the required investment), like market growth, is thus a critical factor in the ability of venture capital–backed ventures to create new economic spaces sustaining rapid industrial transformation. By growing rapidly (and relatively cheaply) in pace with growing markets, scalable ventures can provide extremely high returns to early investors. Not all technologies or firms (or their industries) are capable of scaling rapidly, nor do all technologies and ventures necessarily experience dramatically decreasing unit costs as they scale. Absent these advantages, early investors risk the high likelihood of being diluted or even washed out as the company grows.

Rapid and Large Value Creation

As noted before, the valuation of new firms, and thus the returns for the venture capital investors who backed them, requires not only a growing firm but also the promise of a growing market that will allow the new venture to scale with it. The returns on venture capital investments, in other words, depend on the market value of a new company (via IPO or acquisition), and in new ventures such valuations are typically multiples of revenues (rather than earnings) that reflect the anticipation of continued rapid growth. The high growth rates of markets and relatively low costs of scaling up thus typically differentiate the industries attracting venture capital. Contrast this with the relatively slow change and enormous scale-up costs in most energy markets, and it is difficult to envision more than a few cleantech companies generating the growth in revenues and market share, and corresponding growth in equity value, sufficient to reward venture capital investors. Of course, a mania associated with cleantech may be sufficient to ensure capital gains for the venture investors able to reach an IPO or positive trade sale for their portfolio firms, but, thus far, the IPOs have had lackluster results. For example, A123 Batteries, a venture capital–backed company, went public in September 2009 priced at $13.00 per share, with investors at that price suffering an immediate dilution of $8.37 per share. After the 180-day lockup period, when insiders were able to sell, the stock dropped. As of June 2012, following a spate of production problems associated with scaling up, the company now trades at $0.91. The now bankrupt A123 proved to be a marginal investment for the venture capitalists and a particularly bad investment for the public. Similarly, the electric car manufacturer Tesla went public in June 2010 at $17 per share, and by June 2012, it had risen to $27.90 per share, despite accelerating losses and sales of under 2,000 total automobiles in six years of operation. Many of these firms are unprofitable, and revenues are growing at less than 15 percent per year. The incumbent photovoltaic firms are experiencing revenue and profit growth rates of 20 percent, but they are no longer dependent on venture capitalists.

In sum, the interplay of these three interdependent characteristics of markets — growth, scalability, and rapid payoffs — determines whether venture capital financing can successfully open new economic spaces by funding early-stage ventures in particular sectors and at particular moments. Absent a favorable constellation of characteristics, it is difficult for individual ventures to effectively transform markets by growing sufficiently in size and valuation to validate previous venture investments and attract the ones necessary to create a self-sustaining industrial transformation. Worse, because venture capitalists use these criteria not only to identify new ventures but also to shape their strategies, augmenting venture capitalism's role when these criteria are absent can be counterproductive. Driving high-growth strategies in low-growth markets; rapidly scaling when the cost of growth outpaces the resulting equity value; or attempting to exit quickly in sectors where valuations recognize low growth and low scalability may hinder the success of individual firms. In markets with these conditions, using public monies to amplify individual venture investments may equally amplify the negative effects and destroy a promising venture.

CLEANTECH MARKETS ANALYZED

Innovation in clean technologies poses challenges that may be fundamentally different from those challenges that venture capital–backed start-ups are best suited to overcome. In developed nations, cleantech innovations must penetrate existing markets and displace incumbent energy systems or find small niches within which they can patiently develop footholds. In existing markets, there is an installed capital stock that incumbents can treat as a sunk cost, making competition economically difficult for emerging ventures and technologies that must compete with the variable cost of the continuing operation of existing plants. Alternatively, conquering niche markets, which is a frequent path for new technology adoption, may not permit sufficiently rapid growth to justify venture capital investment, particularly since neither success in the niche markets nor successfully breaking out from them is guaranteed. Given these constraints, how well does a venture capital–driven model of innovation fit with aspirations for a cleantech revolution?

As of 2012, venture capital funds continued to invest in the various clean technologies. But the number of deals was declining significantly, not only in the United States but globally as well. In the case of the United States, in the second quarter of 2012, the amount invested — $1 billion — had decreased by 11 percent, but the number of deals had dropped by 42 percent, suggesting that early-stage and follow-on deals were becoming scarcer. Moreover, four of the deals were in excess of $60 million. All this indicates that venture capitalists were concentrating their investments — again suggesting that the sector was experiencing difficulties (PricewaterhouseCoopers 2012). Given the disappointing performance of cleantech firms in achieving IPOs, after IPO performance, or being acquired at good multiples, venture capital investment will almost certainly wane unless performance on these dimensions improves. Given that the stock market by 2012 was near decade-long highs and government subsidies for clean technologies were beginning to decline, but cleantech IPOs and positive mergers were becoming less frequent, the forecast for clean technology appears cloudy. Investment in clean technology will continue for the duration of the existing funds. The reckoning will come when the cleantech venture capital firms seek to raise new funds. This is likely to be difficult.

To illustrate the structural reasons for the low returns, this section introduces a methodology for assessing the relative fit of particular markets and technologies to the boundary conditions identified in the previous section. Table 4.2 illustrates such an examination. Note that the evaluations apply to new ventures in these sectors and not the deployment of established technologies, which are typically funded with project financing. In other words, the installation of wind energy, reflecting the installation of wind turbines, reflects the growth of incumbent firms funded by project (or debt) financing and thus does not reflect the conditions for start-up ventures in wind. For reasons of

TABLE 4.2

Cleantech energy sector compared on the basis of criteria for venture capital investment

Industrial Sector	Large and Rapidly Growing Markets	Scalability	Large and Rapid Payoffs
Solar photovoltaics	0	0	–
Solar central thermal	0	–	–
Solar facility installation	–	–	–
Wind energy	–	–	–
Biofuels/ethanol	–	–	–
Geothermal	–	–	–
Advanced lighting (LED)	0	0	0
Energy management (SW/HW)	0	+	0
Energy storage	0	–	–
Transportation	–	–	–
Recycling	0	0	0
Smart grid (T&D, metering)	+	–	0

space, the evaluations of individual sectors are not presented in detail. Rather, Table 4.2 serves as an illustration of evaluating the general sectors of cleantech and the potential value of venture capital investing in each and notes when (and why) particular niche technologies or markets may make such investment viable and effective. We then evaluate one sector — solar power — as an example.

Solar Photovoltaics

According to one report, the market for solar photovoltaics globally, while having slowed down in 2011, grew 139 percent from 2009 to 2010 (Solarbuzz 2011). Even if markets slow significantly, the large and rapid growth criteria are being met, though the large number of competitors in the market means that recent solar start-ups are competing with existing firms, some of whom are incumbents. The scalability criterion is more problematic as solar photovoltaic technology requires large capital-intensive fabrication facilities that can cost hundreds of millions of dollars each. For example, Solyndra, which went bankrupt in August 2011, received a $525 million loan guarantee from the federal government to build one fabrication facility. As another example, the established firm First Solar recently completed a fabrication facility in Germany that cost $282 million (Whitmore 2011). Moreover, if demand increases sufficiently, First Solar would have to build another facility at roughly the same cost. In other words, costs of production increase roughly in line with demand, though there are likely some learning and scale economies in the production process.

From 2005 to 2007, at the height of a global warming frenzy in the media, some venture capital–backed photovoltaic firms made public stock offerings. Two successful photovoltaic IPOs were Sunpower and First Solar. Sunpower was established in 1984, had a number of owners, and went public in 2005. First Solar was established in 1990, was purchased by a venture capital firm in 1999, and then had stock sold to the public in 2006 (First Solar 2006). In 2007, GT Solar Technologies, a photovoltaic production equipment maker founded in 1984, was able to make its IPO, but in 2011, it changed its name to GT Advanced Technologies (ElectroIQ 2011). One remarkable feature of these successes is that on average it took two decades until the firms were able to undertake their IPOs. Though they are now industry leaders, these "gestation" periods are longer than the life of venture capital's funds and thus unprofitable. In terms of IPOs, the criteria of large and rapid payoffs have been unmet not only in terms of rapidity, but also only a few photovoltaic firms have been able to make initial public stock offerings. For the other exit path — trade sales — only a few sales have taken place, and the returns to investors from such sales have been marginal (Lange et al. 2011).

In 2011, a glut of solar modules on the global market drove down prices and also made the competitive environment more difficult for fledgling firms. The result was a number of bankruptcies. The situation was further compounded by the turbulent stock markets in 2011, which meant the ability for any firms, particularly those that appeared to be uncompetitive, to raise public monies was virtually nil.

CONCLUSION: ONE MODEL DOES NOT FIT ALL OPPORTUNITIES

This chapter identifies a set of structural causes as a result of economic conditions that explain both the success and limitations of venture capital–backed firms in creating self-sustaining industrial transformations. These causes suggest that venture capital is an ill-suited investment vehicle — let alone policy framework — for fostering a clean-technology revolution. Yet, venture capital investing remains active within cleantech.

The promise and success of venture capital in fueling Schumpeterian creative destruction is undeniable in the information and biomedical technologies. However, generalization from these cases without understanding the structural and market conditions in which venture capital investing has traditionally helped open new economic spaces and brought about industrial transformations can be misleading. Because industries differ in terms of their market conditions, maturity, and technological trajectories, not every industry provides the same conditions for, or responses to, venture capital investing.

Some have recently argued that the venture capital model can be adjusted to account for the conditions we have identified as constituting a fundamental blockage (Marcus, Malen, and Ellis 2012). These authors suggest that the venture capitalists are making larger investments with longer time horizons with presumably lower risks and also smaller investments at earlier stages. Finally, they suggest that the venture capitalists are investing more at the intersection between clean energy and the information technologies. Whether this will overcome the obstacles we have identified is, of course, unknown at this time. It is also possible that venture capitalists will find cleantech niches within which to invest. However, we do not believe that during the next decade venture capital will find cleantech to be a field that provides enormous capital gains. Also, the firms supported by venture capital investment are unlikely to make a significant contribution to addressing the global climate change trajectory.

Given the political economic changes expected to result from global warming and the possibility that peak oil has been reached, there are ample

76   opportunities for innovation and entrepreneurship in clean technology. Many cleantech businesses can and should grow using self-financing and investments from friends and family, and the Danish wind turbine industry is a classic case of such growth (Garud and Karnøe 2003). In Denmark, there was no need for venture capital. The technology was developed in use, as both performance and reliability advanced together. There is every reason to believe that the desire to decrease carbon emissions will offer many such opportunities. Large existing multinationals such as General Electric, Siemens, Alstom, Hitachi, and Toshiba in energy and Toyota, Daimler, Nissan, General Motors, and others in transportation are leveraging their competences to produce clean-technology solutions. In addition, existing small- and medium-sized firms, which have strong technical abilities in various machinery industries and in components and subcomponents of larger energy solutions, will respond to these business opportunities.

5

THE GREEN SPIRAL

Nina Kelsey and John Zysman

Part I of this book made three strong arguments: green growth may prove necessary to sustaining the political support for long-term emissions reduction; present proposals for green growth do not create the scale of economic gains necessary to build political support; and therefore creating sufficient green growth will require experimentation to discover how a low-emissions energy systems transformation may become a foundation for large-scale, durable economic growth. These arguments present a paradox: if climate policy requires supportive coalitions that only green growth can bring together, but green growth itself requires policy experimentation, then where does the support for experimentation come from, and how can states make progress?

Part II addresses this paradox through cases that study how and under what conditions different countries have escaped, or failed to escape, the political paradox of green growth. To explain how states have successfully initiated green policy experimentation despite the near-term uncertainty surrounding green growth, we introduce the idea of a "green spiral"—a process of policy feedback in which initial, incremental steps to jointly address economic and environmental issues might over time build up industrial coalitions with material interests in favor of sustaining and expanding efforts at climate change mitigation. This process is not straightforward or necessarily intentional. In our successful cases, these efforts have rarely involved climate change as the primary motivator for action. Rather, they often begin with policies created in response to other concerns, such as local pollution or energy crises. How, then, does this process ultimately create viable coalitions with political will to support aggressive emissions reduction policy?

At its core, the notion of a green spiral reflects a process of mutually rein-forcing feedback between climate policy and industrial interests. Initial policy moves—perhaps minor, and possibly peripheral to environmental concerns—create economic constituencies with vested interests in "green" models of value creation. In turn, these interests develop material reasons to stabilize existing policy and advocate for further policy action. Taken as a whole, our cases illustrate a long-term, path-dependent feedback process by which the conditions for increasingly aggressive "green growth" policy are created: a policy spiral. Put simply:

First, early policy moves—in energy security, pollution, or other related fields—create or grow relevant green industry or commercial constituencies.

Second, these new constituencies create political viability for additional policy moves.

Third, additional policy making in turn strengthens and creates additional green constituencies.[1]

Repetition of this cycle of self-reinforcing policy can, over time, push in-dustries and markets to restructure around "green" paradigms. It is critical to note that in this process, success involves recruiting industry, commercial, and other allies that directly benefit from *and are often created by* the policies being enacted. Ideally, this process ultimately shifts the structure and expecta-tions of the market in which industries—green and otherwise—operate.

But if our success cases benefit from the supportive political dynamics of a green spiral, from where did the initial impetus for the policies that started it come? Explaining the origins and development of green spirals requires that we consider "green" policy broadly. In Part II, we are interested in patterns of early moves and experiments that could end up leading to durable industrial support for a low-emissions energy systems transformation. Consequently, this means we are interested in a diversity of approaches. We see the notion of "green growth" entangled with the specifics of local political and economic stories: efforts to expand access to energy, to transform the energy system, to address pollution problems, to secure national energy supplies, and to estab-lish competitive industries in new green technologies. Thus, we include in our scope not only policies specifically and explicitly designed to produce "green growth" but also a wide variety of policies that have, intentionally or not, become building blocks in the drive toward green growth. In many cases, these individual efforts were motivated by goals far removed from climate change mitigation—but still contributed to coalitions that would eventually come to support climate action. Therefore, we do not assume that different states taking the first steps toward a low-emissions energy systems transformation either arrived at that point intentionally or followed the same templates to getting there. But across the diverse economic and political characteristics of our cases, and their varied commitments to green policy, we observe one thing in common: a green spiral of self-reinforcing policies and industrial interests accompanies real movement toward low-emissions energy systems.

By implication, our cases suggest that the presence of green parties, or green agendas in major political parties, is certainly significant but definitely not sufficient for a green spiral. Instead, the cases generally echo the theme that environmentalism does not typically win on its own. Where green growth policy is a reality, it has typically found support from a coalition of industrial as well as environmental or social interests. Conversely, where green has not won, it is because a coalition capable of supporting green has not (or has not yet) emerged.

We consider two sets of cases that face two different kinds of problems. The *developed countries* face principally a challenge of replacement — moving mature economies with largely sufficient energy sources from a high-carbon/low-efficiency system to a low-carbon/high-efficiency system. This requires going far beyond simply attaching green energy production to today's existing power grid. The system will, to vastly oversimplify, need to be fundamentally reorganized: from centralized production and decentralized consumption over dumb networks to decentralized production over intelligent networks that enable responsive consumers and more efficient demand management. In contrast, *developing countries* face fewer barriers from their legacy energy systems but greater challenges in reconciling emissions reduction with rapidly growing economies and energy demand. Developing countries lack the sunk costs of an existing brown energy system, which can in some ways be thought of as an advantage. But given their rapidly growing demands for energy to power economic development, it is not clear that green energy alone will suffice. Using green to leapfrog brown will not be simple, if it is possible at all.

The key question, then, is how such coalitions come to be. First and foremost, they rarely represent the triumph of "good" policy over "bad." Nor do these "green" coalitions necessarily result in policies that might resemble an ideal economically efficient outcome, however defined. Rather, we consistently see that politically viable and sustainable policy has been more important than policy that narrowly targets economic efficiency.

GREEN SPIRALS IN THE ADVANCED COUNTRIES

To get a sense of how a green spiral might take hold in practice, consider the Danish and Californian experiences we present in Chapters 6 and 8. Both

82   have seen green coalitions serendipitously emerge from feedback between environmental policies and economic interests. In the California case, policy making occurred in several phases. First, in the 1950s and 1960s, the Los Angeles smog pollution crisis led to a set of policies addressing particulate air pollution by restricting auto pollution and energy efficiency to avoid extension of nuclear power. Then, in the 1970s, the oil crisis provided impetus for the adoption of statewide energy efficiency standards. Finally, in the past decade, concern over carbon emissions has led to a program of relevant regulations ranging from more stringent auto emissions regulations to renewable electricity mandates. The interest group dynamics that emerged alongside this policy-making process illustrate how each round of policy making helped to create the political potential for the next phase by supporting the creation of interest groups that were structured around environmental regulation: relevant research capacities were created; technology industries and the venture capital community gained green industry experience and skills; and the business community as a whole adapted to these forms of regulation. In the latest round of renewable energy policy making, the clean-energy business community that grew out of these early rounds of regulation has become a major source of political support for increasingly aggressive policy. Currently, the California narrative is in a critical transition period as venture capital shifts toward other outlets, due to the venture capital energy industry mismatch discussed by Kenney and Hargadon in Chapter 4. The question is whether green industry will, in the meantime, become a strong enough force to sustain the trend toward green.

Denmark displays a similar pattern of self-reinforcing policy phases. In the 1970s, the oil crisis initiated policy making aimed at curbing Denmark's dependence on imported energy. By the 1990s, this policy had built up wind power into a significant component of Denmark's energy supply and policy strategy. Finally, recent policy making has explicitly been aimed at significantly reducing carbon emissions through a variety of regulatory strategies. Just as in the California case, each phase of policy making created the conditions that make the next round viable by creating interest groups that will benefit from further policy action. The early push for energy security led to a focus on alternative energy technologies, the development of wind technology expertise, and widespread, grassroots ownership of wind turbines. Out of this pattern of industrial development and adoption, a new alliance of landowners and manufacturers emerged in support of renewable energy policy. The more aggressive policy moves made possible by this shift in interests are in turn feeding back into the Danish economy, with major companies like Vestas and DONG Energy now building commercial strategies around the expectation of

future zero- or very low-carbon policy environments: a structural reorientation of the market as a whole. Policies initially oriented simply toward developing wind power are now culminating in a national commitment to a fossil fuel–free energy system, with backing from significant industrial interests.

THE TWIN CHALLENGES FOR DEVELOPING COUNTRIES

Where the developed countries face one challenge — transforming their domestic energy systems without undermining economic growth — the developing countries face twin energy challenges, which are always potentially in tension with each other: expanding energy supplies to rapidly growing economies while simultaneously "going green." The advanced wealthy countries must move their mature economies away from high-emissions energy systems without undermining economic growth. Certainly the emerging economies must *also* shift their existing energy systems to a low-carbon structure. But at the same time, the ambition, and reality, of rapid economic growth means rapidly expanding demand for energy. Even if these countries succeed at reducing their energy intensity — the amount of energy required to generate a given unit of GDP — their economic growth rates will overwhelm these efficiency gains and continue to drive both energy demand and emissions.

Our cases suggest that developing countries have managed this tension in two quite different ways, based on two different situations developing countries may find themselves in. The *first* is the story of developing countries like China (see Chapter 11) that face a significant tension between parallel green and brown growth objectives, often because they have significant domestic fossil fuel resources. Here, meeting energy demands with cheap, secure domestic fossil fuel will be overwhelmingly tempting. For China in particular, this dynamic has emerged alongside the development of significant economic interests in green technology. China's emerging dominance in some green industrial sectors will generate a form of green spiral on the manufacturing side: China is already clearly set to derive significant growth from green industry and policy that supports it. But that spiral will develop in parallel with brown, fossil fuel–driven domestic energy growth. Whether the green manufacturing spiral will spill over to the dynamics of the entire economy remains to be seen.

The green manufacturing spiral poses a second tension: between China's green growth at home and its trading relationships abroad. China's green success has come, as in many other areas of its economy, through heavily subsidized export industries. Those industries have recently generated significant pushback — particularly in solar energy technologies — from countries accusing China of unfair competition. As countries around the world seek export-led growth abroad to justify green investments at home, this dynamic illustrates the risk of "green mercantilism" discussed in Chapter 1: increasing tensions in international trade amidst a global struggle for position in green export markets.

The tension between green and brown growth stories expresses itself differently in the case of Brazil (Chapter 12). Brazil has shown leadership in developing biofuels, while at the same time undermining climate stability directly through its ongoing destruction of the rainforests and indirectly via its oil exports. What is noteworthy in both cases is that development proceeds through parallel green and brown pathways dictated by the basic developmental needs of the state. In each case, *both* green and brown developmental pathways appear to be dictated by the structural realities — in terms of economics and resources — that these states face. They cannot therefore be simply separated; neither China nor Brazil can easily give up its brown development just because it is also pursuing green growth.

The *second* situation is that of countries, such as India, that have more limited or nonexistent domestic fossil fuel reserves but still need to build out their energy systems to meet both current and future demands. Cases of this type raise the question of whether, in the long run, green options such as renewable energy and distributed solar power, along with efforts to press energy efficiency, can provide partial or comprehensive solutions to the basic developmental needs of such countries. In other words, are there cases of developing countries for which green strategies may be *more effective* solutions than brown, rather than just (expensive) alternatives? In India, for instance, energy efficiency and renewable energy technologies might offer solutions to the problem of development in the context of limited domestic fossil fuel sources and high import costs. Meanwhile, distributed renewable energy generation might offer a solution to India's need to electrify a broad subset of its population currently living without access to the grid.

In countries that see a need to expand access to power similar to China's but have limited domestic fossil fuel reserves, we can thus imagine something close to the core concept of green growth religion, in which green solutions open up developmental and economic growth possibilities that would not be available or would be more expensive in a fossil fuel–based system. Of course, such a developmental path depends on the ability to establish the institutional and bureaucratic capacities to implement policies at all. In India, at least, it is not clear that the institutional and bureaucratic capacity necessary to cash in on the growth potential of green solutions exists.

Our cases largely focus on what we might term *serendipitous* green spiral politics, where states came to find themselves with green constituencies they did not necessarily set out to create. Can an analysis of these unplanned processes tell us something about future *planned* policy? Thus far, we have suggested that these processes are largely unintentional and path-dependent. In both the developing or developed economies, however, we find that states making progress toward green growth rely on political processes that go well beyond a simple ideological victory of environmentalists or climate crusaders over the nonbelievers or the selfish. Thus, the presence of green parties, or green agendas in major political parties, although significant, is definitely not sufficient, and in some cases is not even necessary, for a green spiral. Instead, the cases generally echo the theme that environmentalism does not typically win on its own. Where green growth policy is a reality, it has typically found support from a coalition of industrial as well as environmental or social interests. The green spirals leading to these broad coalitions often grew out of chance events or emerged from policies originally designed to solve simpler problems. Conversely, where green has not won, it is because a coalition capable of supporting green has not (or has not yet) emerged.

But this analysis begs the question of whether the green spiral can be intentionally kick-started on a faster timescale. Our cases shed some light on this question: both Colorado and South Korea represent cases in which policy makers appear to have deliberately pushed to restructure their energy economies around new interest configurations. Colorado's 2004 renewable energy initiatives created a surprisingly fast shift toward wind interests in a state not traditionally green in many areas, as conservative landowners in the eastern plains — otherwise skeptical of climate policy — realized that new renewable energy adoption mandates potentially turned their land into valuable wind turbine sites. Interviews suggest that at least some players in the legislative game at the time hoped for and attempted to accelerate this process. South Korea's government, meanwhile, in the Lee administration explicitly attempted to restructure its economy and business interests around a green growth model that would provide its domestic industries with a new green business paradigm. Whether that policy will be sustained by the new government is not yet clear. These cases provide interesting tests for exploring whether such green policy feedback effects can be created intentionally under a variety of circumstances. We should be wary of the possibility for overanalysis or cheerleading in these cases, given that their stories have not fully played out and that they face some significant challenges. However, they provide some tentative evidence that policy makers are actively considering these types of legislative dynamics and may be able to deliberately, and perhaps successfully, manipulate them.

INDUSTRY ALLIANCES, INTERESTS, AND CAPTURE

Environmentalist/industry alliances, our cases show clearly, are essential to the move to green energy and sustainable green growth. Our analysis suggests that initiating a transition from green growth religion to green growth reality requires a concerted attempt to create or identify benefits, benefits that are perhaps themselves ancillary to green policy, which help industrial interests perceive gain from green policy. Those interests then help make the search for viable long-term green growth strategies self-sustaining.

Of course, the "side payments" and accommodation of diverse interests that come with viable policies raise the issue of industry capture of policy. Such "green capture" of the policy process may be an inevitable — and in some cases desirable — precursor to longer-term policy stability. But it raises risks of its own. In some sense the move may have to be from "capture" of policy by brown interests to capture by green. So we begin by considering whether there is a typical policy process that can lead to green growth experimentation and the long-term formation of green policy coalitions.

Despite the importance of allying industrial interests to climate policy, our cases suggest the difficulties and pitfalls of doing so. The beneficiaries of an existing energy system are typically the strongest constituents for status quo policies, and their influence often allows them to capture the policy process. We see this in Japan, where nuclear interests joined forces with fossil fuel advocates to limit attempts to reconsider Japan's reliance on heavy industry and nuclear energy or to reconfigure its energy system. While the country's reliance on renewable energy will likely increase in the wake of the Fukushima crisis, it remains to be seen whether this will represent a critical juncture that sets the stage for the emergence of a Japanese green spiral. Examples from other countries suggest that this will require finding firms and industry groups poised to benefit from the new transition. For instance, the green spiral phenomenon in Denmark led both heavy industry like the Danish wind turbine firm Vestas and major energy sector firms like the utility DONG Energy to become constituents for Denmark's emergent fossil fuel–free energy policy. Both benefitted from credible expectations of direct, material benefits from green policy action, without which building industry alliances becomes much harder.

The necessity of building strong political foundations for green growth raises clear policy implications. Hands-off, economically ideal policies like carbon taxes may not create the kinds of coalitions we observe in the successful cases described in Part II. These types of polices may indeed minimize the overall costs of transition, and where it is politically viable, putting a price on carbon may be a useful part of policy packages. But high emissions prices create significant practical political problems. These policy approaches typically have broad negative consequences in the form of higher energy costs, while providing diffuse future benefits. As Chapter 2 discusses at length, these are precisely the types of conditions that theorists have suggested are theoretically unlikely to lead to successful passage (Oye and Maxwell 1994) or survival (Patashnik 2003, 2008) of regulations. Without the ability to deliver acute, near-term benefits, carbon pricing lacks the ability to build supportive coalitions of long-lasting, organized interest groups. As our cases show, the prospects for real "green growth" policies depend on such coalitions and the interlinked bargains among at times antagonistic interest groups and firms. The European policy portfolio, discussed by Huberty in Chapter 7, is just such a case, with quite divergent national interests reconciled across a set of separate policies.

Our findings are consonant with some existing lines of analysis that have investigated the possibility of an interplay between politics and political desirability/viability of regulatory standards. However, this literature has tended to focus on the potential for regulation to generate support by manipulating the incentives of existing industry, typically by offering opportunities for rent extraction by established entrants to the market. Thus, for instance, Oye and Maxwell (1994) suggest that the regulation imposed by the Montreal Protocol, governing ozone-depleting chlorofluorocarbons (CFCs), was politically viable because it offered key companies in the United States and Britain the ability to capture rents based on their comparative advantage in CFC substitutes. Examining this interplay from the policy side, Urpelainen (2012) suggests that the ability of more stringent regulation to motivate scattered or weak renewable energy industry interests—by providing greater rewards for organization and lobbying—might actually motivate politicians to pass more stringent regulation than they otherwise would. In a broad sense, our findings are in keeping with this line of literature. We find that the ability of regulation to offer particularist benefits, supportive of a broad policy coalition, does in fact appear to be a common thread in green growth "success stories."

As we have described, however, the specific logic we find in our cases is that different regulation can create new interests as actors discover themselves

88   either benefited or harmed by the new rules. In a long-term, multiround process, early regulation that often is not even intentionally aimed at stringent carbon emissions reduction in fact *creates* new interests. These emergent interests in turn lobby for and support the imposition of stronger regulation in later rounds of policy making.

Our results match well with other recent analyses of the feedback processes that sit behind green interests. Particularly important is Eric Biber's (2013) excellent examination of the defeat of Proposition 23 (a California ballot measure that would have suspended AB32, California's major global warming policy legislation). Biber's analysis comes to essentially the same conclusion as our own analysis regarding this dynamic: he argues that Prop. 23 was defeated because prior rounds of policy (AB32 and earlier) had altered California's interest configuration, weakening opposition from sectors like utilities and petroleum, and creating pro-policy interests in high-tech industry, venture capital, and green labor. In other words, changes to interest configurations resulting from earlier rounds of policy supported the passage of AB32 and later acted to stabilize it in the face of challenges. Laird and Stefes's 2009 analysis of the development path of renewable energy in Germany also bears some resemblance to our argument. Although they present it as a smaller part of a broader story that relies more heavily on public opinion, key electoral victories, and policy makers' early cognitive consensus, Laird and Stefes's account of this story suggests some similarities: early shocks to the system opened a public opinion window for renewable energy policy, and the interests created in response to that policy ultimately served to reinforce and support these policies in the long term.

CONCLUSION: READING THE CASES

Our cases provide a window onto the variety of responses countries have made and are making to the problem represented by climate change and the potential opportunity represented by green growth. As we have noted, the cases vary both by levels of development and by the nationally idiosyncratic roles played by economic and energy system legacies. Hence we suggest the following questions as touchstones for the reader: What background (in terms of resources, industry, and prior policy) does each state bring to the green policy table? What is the political story that has brought each state to its policy position today? What particular mix of contemporary interests has this history created, and how? How have these background conditions supported or undermined the formation of green coalitions, and why? These are the questions that our cases attempt to answer.

6

DENMARK

A Classic Case of a Green Spiral

Jakob Riiskjaer Nygård

Denmark is a good example of a classic "green spiral." Today, Denmark aims to eliminate fossil fuels from its heat and electricity supplies by 2035 and from its energy mix completely by 2050. Forty years ago, the economy depended on oil for 90 percent of its energy needs. In 2010, oil remains the dominant fuel, but the energy mix has become more diversified, including a significant share of renewable energy (20 percent). The past 40 years have seen a relatively constant overall level of energy consumption, while GDP nearly doubled in the same period, which corresponds to an average annual growth rate of 1.78 percent per year.[1]

Beginning with the oil crisis in the 1970s, a strong coalition has emerged that is determined to drive the long-term transformation of the Danish energy sector. In a first phase, beginning roughly at the start of the oil crisis until the early 1990s, policies pursued initially to ensure energy security had the derivative effect of decoupling emissions and economic growth.[2] The current phase, aimed at a fossil fuel–free energy system by 2050, has the objective of driving growth as well.

We develop the story in four phases, arguing that the policies of the first two periods fostered the industry, infrastructure, and energy mix that, combined with domestic political pressure and international developments, facilitated the present multiparty commitment to a zero-carbon economy. We conclude by situating the Danish story in a Nordic context.

GREEN GROWTH PART I: ENERGY SECURITY (1973–1993)

The first explicit formulation of Danish energy policy was a response to the oil crises of the 1970s. The first Danish energy plan of 1976 emerged in the context of an economy highly dependent on oil, a civil society highly supportive of wind energy and critical of nuclear energy, and the limitations and opportunities inherent in Danish geography and existing infrastructure.

The primary political objective in this first period was to achieve energy security. The intent was to insulate the economy from future energy price shocks and sustain economic growth. The three energy plans enacted during this period (1976, 1981, and 1990) employed a range of policies to achieve energy security, which can be categorized under four headings: substitution and exploration; support for alternative sources of energy; energy efficiency; and infrastructure investment (Hadjilambrinos 2000; Mendonca, Lacey, and Hvelplund 2009).

Substitution and Exploration.   The electricity industry responded independently to the oil crisis by beginning a transition from oil to coal as the primary fuel in electricity production. Oil and electricity taxes were enacted to support the shift, and within a few years, the electricity industry had almost completely substituted coal for oil, a condition that would persist until the mid-1990s. This substitution does not eliminate the issue of energy security because coal was imported as well. However, there is no OPEC in world coal markets, which makes dependence on coal imports significantly more desirable than dependence on imports of oil. In the 1990s, the share of natural gas in electricity production and heat generation gradually increased (Grohnheit 2001; Hansen 2003; De Lovinfosse 2008).

At the same time, exploration of natural gas and oil in the North Sea was accelerated, although many believe the division of oil rights unduly favored the Norwegians, and Danish conflicts over control and exploitation of the fields may have restrained the pace of expansion (Rüdiger 2011). In 1972, Danish Natural Gas (renamed DONG for Danish Oil and Natural Gas in 1973) was established as a state-owned company with the exclusive right to extract oil and natural gas from the North Sea (Ibsen and Poulsen 2007). By 1995, Denmark had become a net exporter of oil and natural gas, and the move largely assuaged fears of another oil crisis. According to the Danish Energy Authority, Denmark is expected to remain a net exporter of natural gas until 2020 and of oil until 2018 (DEA 2010a, 2011a). Substitution and exploration went a long way toward reducing dependency on oil by 1980. In 1971, oil contributed 78 percent of electricity generation. By 1980, oil contributed 18 percent of electricity generation.

Support for Alternative Sources of Energy.   The first energy plan also explored alternative sources of energy. The rationale at the time, of course, was to exploit every potential avenue of energy security. Initially, nuclear energy was the favored option of policy makers and the electricity industry, but a strong and broad coalition of civil society movements opposed nuclear power, and in 1985, the Danish Folketing (Parliament) passed a moratorium on nuclear energy. The coalition strongly favored wind rather than nuclear energy, and with a geography that enabled wind—a flat country with lots of wind potential—and a history of experimenting with windmills dating back to the 1890s, the result was a gradual increase of wind as a share of electricity production. Today, wind energy accounts for roughly 20 percent of annual electricity production, and in some months, more than a 40 percent average wind supply is handled in the grid (Sovacool, Lindboe, and Odgaard 2008).

Early policies supporting local cooperative ownership helped strengthen public support for wind power production and ease barriers to implementation of projects. By the early 1990s, 120,000 people, out of a total population of roughly 5 million, were registered as owners of wind turbines—either individually or through cooperatives (Mendonca, Lacey, and Hvelplund 2009). While the trend of local ownership has been reversed since the late 1990s, it was a crucial part of the initial success of wind power deployment and helped to build a foundation and broaden grassroots support for the strong wind power industry that exists in Denmark today, which was spearheaded by wind turbine manufacturer Vestas and DONG energy. Political support for renewables consisted of electricity taxing schemes, investment subsidies, a feed-in tariff, a mandatory capacity target, and R&D support for renewable energy. The total share of renewables gradually increased to roughly 27 percent of electricity production and 20 percent of final energy consumption in 2009 (Hvelplund 1997; Toke 2002; Hansen 2003; McLaren Loring 2007; Karnøe and Buchhorn 2008; Sovacool, Lindboe, and Odgaard 2008; Toke, Breukers, and Wolsink 2008; DEA 2010b).

Collectively, Danish wind policy aided the emergence of an industrial ecosystem of wind energy firms and technologies. During the 1970s, a number of experiments with wind turbine technology were carried out independently of one another. Most were regionally located within a radius of 100 km—*not* coincidentally in the same region that houses the Danish wind cluster today. In 1976, a 22-kW windmill was connected to the grid. This achievement generated massive media attention and interest in wind-power generation, which had the dual effect of opening a market for distributed wind power production and broadening the coalition described above. The incident led to the creation of the Danish Windmill Owners' Association, two years later (Karnøe and Garud 2012).

In 1978, a $1 million grant was given to support a test center at Risø for small-scale wind power generation. In 1979, a subsidy scheme for small-scale wind generation was enacted, transforming the economics of wind power generation, and by 1980, "about ten firms were actively selling wind turbines in Denmark" (Karnøe and Garud 2012, 745). Interestingly, the justification for the scheme was to create "production opportunities for the Danish industry in such a way that series production could be achieved" (Van Erst in Karnøe and Garud 2012, 744). In other words, a form of systems-transforming green growth argument was evident here, although it could hardly be said to define the broader contours of energy policy at this point. Due to a set of regulatory co-incidences, the Risø center became the locus of cooperation among industry, research, civil society, and business, and a Danish wind cluster had emerged.

Energy Efficiency. Energy efficiency measures were an important comple-ment to the other policy tools employed during this first phase of the story. By mandating energy efficiency in buildings, taxing delivered energy, and subsi-dizing energy efficiency measures, Denmark reduced specific heat demand by nearly 40 percent between 1981 and 1997. Overall CO_2 intensity was reduced by 50 percent from 1980 to 2006 (Grohnheit 2001; DEA 2009). Crucially, as pointed out above, the share of natural gas in electricity production and heat generation increased as energy efficiency policies rewarded combined heat and power (CHP) plants using natural gas and biomass. This brings us to the final category of energy policies during the first part of the story: infrastructure investment (Grohnheit 2001).

Infrastructure Investment. The development of district heating grids began in the 1950s but was accelerated as energy policy became explicit during this first part of the Danish energy story. It enabled the introduction of natural gas and conversion of conventional power plants to CHP plants in electricity pro-duction, since only transmission capacity to the central CHP plant was needed; the distribution grid was already in place in the shape of district heating and electricity grids to which gas-fired CHP plants could be connected (Grohnheit 2001). Utilizing waste heat from electricity generation in CHP plants increases the primary energy efficiency of a plant by turning waste heat into a useful resource in district heating grids. Further, it massively decreased the capital costs of a natural gas grid, thus rendering it a desirable policy option. Next we discuss how the widespread existence of district heating grids in Denmark was to become a key enabler of the further integration of biomass in the energy mix.

Results of the First Phase of Policy

As the fears of another oil crisis subsided — in part because of the success-ful substitution of fuel sources and in part because of the passing of time —

new policy priorities emerged. Energy security to sustain economic growth remained the primary priority of Danish energy policy, and although becoming a net exporter of oil by 1995 meant that the Danish economy would now also benefit from future increases in the price of oil, because oil is traded in a world market, it also meant that oil-consuming parts of the economy would still be exposed to any future "oil shocks." In that sense, becoming a net exporter of oil acted as a sort of hedge for the overall economy, but further diversification of the energy mix to ensure stable growth in the rest of the economy remained a central driver of energy policy.

GREEN GROWTH PART II: THE RISE OF ENVIRONMENTALISM IN THE AUKEN YEARS (1993–2001)

After the 1993 elections, a new social democratic-led government came into power, and with it came a significant addition to energy policy under the direction of Minister of Energy and the Environment Svend Auken (1993–2001). Auken's original portfolio — environment — was merged with the ministry of energy in 1994, symbolic of the further integration of the two policy areas (Hansen 2003; De Lovinfosse 2008; DEA 2011b). The policies of previous years were largely carried on, but there was an increased focus on the environmental benefits of renewable energy. Following the World Commission on Environment and Development's publication of *Our Common Future* (WCED 1987) — better known as the *Brundtland Report* for its chair, former prime minister of Norway Gro Brundtland — environmental concerns became an increasingly important issue in public debate. The 1996 energy plan put emphasis on the environment, containing more than 100 initiatives aimed at CO_2 reduction (Karnøe and Buchhorn 2008).

Under Svend Auken's tenure, focus on the environmental benefits of renewable energy increased. "The energy plan of 1996, 'Energy 21,' contained more than 100 initiatives designed to reduce CO_2 emissions" (Karnøe and Buchhorn 2008, 76). Among these were an annual target of 1 percent additional renewable energy in the energy supply, electricity taxes to finance energy efficiency programs, continued support for investments in district heating grids, and continued support for the development of oil and gas resources in the North Sea (Danish Government 1996). As such, the policies in the new plan represented a continuation of previous policies as described above, with an increased focus on the GHG emissions associated with energy consumption.

Moreover, the 1990s marked the golden age of wind power deployment in Denmark, with rapidly increasing shares of wind power in electricity generation. From 1993 to 2003, 2.7 GW of wind generation capacity was added.

94   At this point the integration of electricity grids in Europe deserves mention. The integration of Nordic and European electricity grids with increased interconnection capacity is crucial to the expansion of wind power in Denmark by allowing imports of electricity to offset imbalances between supply and demand in the context of intermittent wind production (Grohnheit 2001). As explained in Chapter 2, electricity grids depend on constant balancing of supply and demand. In the case of Denmark, Energinet.dk—the state-owned transmission systems operator—is responsible for ensuring this balance and for maintaining and expanding the grid. As the expansion of wind power continues, transmission bottlenecks impose an upper limit on the ability of grid interconnections to offset the fluctuations of Danish wind energy production. As we will see, this, in part, leads to the idea of transforming the electricity grid by creating a Smart Grid.

The Birth of the Green Growth Argument

The idea of supporting the cleantech sector to create export-led growth via "green exports" can also be traced back to this period. The energy plan of 1996, Energi 21, points to a Danish interest in positioning itself in international energy markets by investing in cleantech: "It is the Government's intention to support a continuation of this [the massive growth of Danish energy technology exports in recent years] positive trend through the initiatives in Energi 21" (Danish Government 1996, 13).

The environmentalist policies deployed during this period did not represent a break in the pursuit of long-term energy independence; this objective remained as a fundamental driver. It would be more accurate to describe the new environmentalist drivers as creating a second, complementary layer of policy objectives on top of energy security objectives. The ability of Auken to increase the focus on environmental policies in overall energy policy is a result of the increasing public awareness of the adverse impacts of environmental pollution and the developments during the first part of the story. The public awareness provides the political justification, and the bottom-up support for renewable energy in the first part of the story helped form broad public support for and acceptance of renewables, as well as an industry with which a strong coalition could be built to support further policies for renewable energy.

Two things are important to note in the development of public opinion. First, the environment was never seen as the most important problem among the Danish electorate. While many Danes were interested in energy and environmental politics, historically, only a relatively small minority has subscribed to the notion that "the environment" is the *most* important problem facing politicians (Andersen 2002, 2008; Arbo-bähr 2010). Most Danes thus considered themselves interested in energy and environmental politics, but few considered it the most important problem facing the nation. It is not insignificant at all however, whether 3 percent of the population consider it the most important problem, as was the case in 2001, or over 10 percent do, as was the case during most of the 1990s and again in 2009. That is the difference between a statistically insignificant group of voters and a very significant group of voters and thus, for policy makers, the difference between a "good" and a "bad" political sell.

Second, the most important issues, aside from the recent advent of the immigration issue, had generally been those of economic politics. The environment did, however, become a more important issue in the 1987 election following the publication of the *Brundtland Report* (WCED 1987) and, after an initial dip in the 2000s, again during the 2007 election. The report was published in May 1987, and it propelled the issue of the environment and sustainability onto the political agenda of the September elections later that same year. The issue remained relatively important until the 2001 election, with around 10 percent of the electorate declaring it the most important problem that politicians needed to address. Subsequently, other priorities rose to the forefront of public attention, as discussed next.

GREEN GROWTH PART III: LIBERALIZATION (2001–2006)

Liberalization: A Political Intermezzo

Following the Auken years of 1993–2001, a new right-wing government came into power in 2001, led by Anders Fogh Rasmussen. To avoid confusing him with the prime minister who followed him, Lars Løkke Rasmussen, we refer to him hereafter as Fogh. Energy policies were reversed; funding for environmental and renewable energy programs was cut in favor of deregulating energy markets and privatizing state functions. Annually installed wind capacity rates dropped accordingly. This rather sudden shift from a political environment that was quite supportive of green policy to one where green policy initiatives were slashed had diverse sources. Ideologically, subsidies and other support mechanisms for renewable energy were seen as directly in conflict with the objective of liberalization. The Environmental Assessment Institute under Bjørn Lomborg, established after the election, challenged the environmental part of the rationale for supporting renewable energy: that climate change was "worth" fighting by questioning the science of climate change and suggesting that, for instance, supporting sustainable development in Third World countries was a more cost-effective way of pursuing environmental priorities. Andersen (2008) suggests that a "Lomborg effect" explains the dip in the importance of the environment on the political agenda in the early 2000s (Meyer 2004a, 2004b; Andersen 2008; Karnøe and Buchhorn 2008).

But it is also very likely that environmental issues were simply drowned out by other issues coming to the fore at the time. It is important to note that energy and environmental politics played a very minor role in the 2001 elections, in which the core themes were the future of the welfare state and immigration. Jørgen Goul Andersen shows that the two major issues for voters in the 2001 elections were "welfare" and "immigration" (Bille 2002; Andersen 2008; Larsen and Andersen 2009). The issue of energy and environmental politics was not important to voters, and it was not a central issue in the election. Fogh's campaign was, among other things, based on a deregulation and privatization agenda to improve efficiency of the welfare state. Because of the unpopularity of the "broken promises" of the incumbent social democrats, his campaign was also based on the idea of "keeping promises," as expressed by his coining of the concept of "contract politics." This concept became a central theme of his successful 2005 and 2007 reelection campaigns (Andersen 2008, 19).

Part of grasping the sudden shift in policy is also understanding the very coalitional nature of the Danish multiparty system of politics. In a parliament where governments have historically depended on center parties for parliamentary backing, the 2001 election marked the first time since 1929 that parties right of the middle held a majority in the Folketing on their own (Bille 2002). In other words, the government did not depend on a center party for parliamentary majority, which likely would have limited the subsequent deregulation and liberalization drive. Finally, some political commentators also assert that part of the reversal was simply a narrowly motivated, short-term political effort to rein in some of the previous government's policies. The subsequent resumption of green policy later in Fogh's term, after the prior government had faded into the past, gives credence to this view.

The following five years thus marked a period of Danish energy policy in which the political objective of liberalization was the main driver of policy. The change came about as a result of EU pressure that began the process of deregulating energy markets in the late 1990s, but with the election of 2001, the process received strong backing from the Danish Folketing and government as well. The primary goal of energy policy was still to ensure stable economic growth, but in the eyes of the new government, liberalization of energy markets was the appropriate mean toward that end (Nørgaard and Tornbjerg

2002; Karnøe and Buchhorn 2008; Mendonca, Lacey, and Hvelplund 2009; Jakobsen 2010).

Despite the significant change in policies away from alternative energy support and environmental priorities during this period, the foundation for another critical change in policy had been laid. The changes to the energy mix and the investment in industry and infrastructure had created a context in which the goal of the fossil fuel–free economy could emerge.

GREEN GROWTH PART IV: THE COMMITMENT TO A FOSSIL FUEL–FREE ECONOMY (2006–2050)

A multiparty consensus committing to green growth has emerged over the past few years. As we turn to that story, we should note that green growth was never an explicit primary goal of Danish energy policy during these first three parts of the story, but the combination of policy tools used to achieve the primary objectives of supply security and economic growth had the derivative effect of decoupling emissions and economic growth (Danish Government 1996; Grohnheit 2001). Thus, although emissions reductions did not attract substantial focus as a political objective until the 1990s, the decoupling of growth and emissions began in the 1970s. In the clarity of hindsight, we can thus describe these first three phases as a form of green growth *compatible* with emissions reductions.

Around 2006, a combination of international developments, domestic political circumstances, and the policies pursued during the first phases of green growth had created the industry, infrastructure, energy mix, and global market conditions that enabled Denmark to commit to pursuing the goal of a fossil fuel–free economy. This commitment occurred in spite of the fact that Denmark was still governed by the liberal-conservative administration that had initially slashed green policy support. With the fall 2011 election bringing a center-left coalition government into power, reinforcing the drive toward the fossil fuel–free economy has been reinforced. But how did the initial reorientation occur?

The Political Circumstances

One part of the reorientation story is purely political. First, the Danish public service does not change with elections. That is, aside from natural turnover and ministerial portfolio reshuffling, ministerial employees largely remained the same as during the Auken years, except for the staff that was downsized as a result of funding cuts after the 2001 election. This implies that the policy ideas created during Auken's tenure remained nascent in the ministries. Importantly as well, the increasing scientific consensus on the adverse impacts of climate change, and the communication thereof, clearly also had an impact on the change in policy—though whether it was directly by changing attitudes of policy makers, by empowering the views of environmental activists who had remained in government, or through increasing public awareness and pressure is unclear. But by the late 2000s, the environment was again becoming an increasingly important issue on the Danish political agenda. Moreover, according to public opinion polls, "already in May 2002, the environmental cuts were the most unpopular of the government's new measures (50 percent against, 35 percent for)" (Andersen 2008, 17).

The stage was set for a shift in direction. During the government's attempt to liberalize energy markets, it sought to adhere to environmental obligations via the EU emissions trading scheme and joint implementation projects under the Kyoto Protocol. Meilstrup (2010), based on interviews with ministers and high-level civil servants, argues that Fogh decided he needed to "green" the government in response to public pressure. He did this by appointing Connie Hedegaard as Minister for the Environment from 2004 to 2007 and as Minister for Climate and Energy from 2007 to 2009. In the heat of the Jyllands-Posten Muhammad cartoons controversy of 2006, she suggested to Fogh that pursuing the presidency of COP15, which was expected to deliver the next global climate change treaty, was a unique opportunity for Denmark to shift international focus away from the cartoon crisis (Meilstrup 2010). The change in policy, then, is seen in part as a way for the government to position itself in the race for the presidency of COP15 and later to bolster diplomatic efforts to achieve an ambitious treaty.

The shift led from the center right by Rasmussen was then reinforced by a significant center left victory in September 2011. The election resulted in a new center-left coalition government led by Helle Thorning-Schmidt. The coalition consists of the Socialist People's Party, the Social Democrats, and the Social-Liberal Party dependent on support from the small red-green alliance for parliamentary majority.

Details aside, the election entrenched a cross-party commitment to a fossil fuel–free economy. Two key developments occurred as a result of the election and the shift in government that reinforced the path of green growth embarked upon by the previous center-right government. Martin Lidegaard was appointed Minister for Climate, Energy and Building. The very order in the naming of his portfolio and the addition of the building sector to it imply the priority of climate change in relation to energy politics. Preceding his appointment, Lidegaard cofounded and was chairman of the environmental think tank Concito, which, since its inception in 2008, had been vocal in arguing for a greener climate and energy policy. The naming and expansion of his portfolio, together with his background, point to the increased emphasis on green energy policy by the newly elected government. Second, Lidegaard immediately announced that he would seek to negotiate a broad compromise on the long-term direction of Danish energy policy by the end of 2011. Though he did not make the deadline, he succeeded in terms of securing a framework for the long-term development of the energy sector. The energy plan, established on March 22, 2012, is supported by all but one (minor) party in the Folketing, and it provides the general framework for the development of the energy sector from 2012 to 2020.

Structural Reorientation of the Energy Market

Simultaneously with the political reorientations, a sea change was occurring more broadly in the general economy. Structural changes were playing out in industry at international, domestic, and local levels. This is best exemplified by DONG Energy's decision to pursue a green strategy in 2008.[3] The main tenets of the strategy are to stop new investment in coal-fired power plants and increase the amount of wind- and natural gas–fired power plants in its portfolio. The goal is to increase the ratio of renewables to fossil fuels in the portfolio to 85/15, to cut CO_2 emissions per energy unit in half over ten years, and to reduce it to 15 percent of current levels by 2040 (Bøss 2011).

In addition to this, DONG has also pulled back from coal-power activities generally, making the decision not to pursue any more coal-fired power plants in the future. Indeed, as of 2009, it has pulled out of all new coal-fired projects — including projects to build coal power plants in Scotland and Germany — in spite of the fact that it has expertise in this area, had won these contracts, could potentially make money from them, and had already sunk some investment into them. This seems to indicate a *uniquely* strong commitment to pulling back from carbon-heavy power sources like coal. Why would DONG cancel projects it had already signed, secured, and invested in?

The best way to understand this shift is to see it as representing a structural shift in the expectations created by regulation and the market for energy companies. DONG's current strategy reflects a belief that coal is no longer a good investment — in any form. Pulling back from coal-fired plant projects that have already been won is a reflection of DONG's growing expectation that conditions in the market — ranging from increasingly stringent projected carbon regulation to public opinion trends — will make it increasingly difficult to bring coal projects to completion as countries shift away from coal as a desirable power source and that (even if completed) such projects will have increasingly uncertain returns on investment. In part, this is because of the surrounding regulatory environment, which places a growing cost on CO_2; free CO_2 quotas will disappear as of 2013, meaning that full CO_2 costs will be incurred from that point on. Pursuing a coal project—even one that is already in process—no longer makes good business sense to DONG because it could lead to an expensive waste of effort and uncertain profitability over the long lifetime of these projects. Given that funds for investment are limited and that the alternative investment—renewable energy—is desired and stimulated from a societal perspective, DONG sees this situation as prompting a strategic reorientation toward low-carbon investment (Bøss 2011). Once expectations within the market have changed to this extent, green growth policy becomes in a sense self-sustaining, since perceived incentives lead to the growth of constituencies with a vested interest in green energy and shrinkage of constituencies with a vested interest in fossil fuels. DONG itself has adapted to the transformed market structure and now supports CO_2 taxes and increasing emissions reductions goals, as these regulations incentivize the continuing transition to the renewable energy world DONG is restructuring itself for (Bøss 2011). Indeed, DONG belongs to a group of Danish companies that would like to see tighter regulation of CO_2 emissions—for example, for EU measures to increase the CO_2 price under its Emissions Trading Scheme.

On top of this, DONG Energy is a market leader in offshore wind energy, and with expertise built up through its offshore exploration activities, it is well positioned to pursue booming offshore wind energy markets (Kragh 2012).

THE GREEN SPIRAL: FROM ENERGY SECURITY TO A ZERO-CARBON OBJECTIVE

The policy suite used today to pursue Denmark's fossil fuel–free goals represents an integration of trends during the first phases of Danish green growth in a holistic approach to transforming the entire Danish energy system. To eliminate fossil fuels from the energy system, the new energy plan focuses on increasing the use of renewables in electricity generation, electrifying heating and transport, and leveraging both as distributed battery capacity in future "smart" energy grids.

The linkage of growth, security, and environmental priorities represents a reimagining of policy priorities. As renewable energy and cleantech industry investments become drivers of economic growth and energy security, the political rationale for investing became significantly more robust. Crucially, the policy change occurred under a right-wing government that has historically been more skeptical of environmental priorities and alternative energy sources. The question is no longer whether Denmark should invest in renewables or transform its energy system, but how fast it can, and how it should, eliminate fossil fuels from the energy mix (Vestergaard 2006). Political resistance to green growth policies has virtually disappeared.

Goals for a Systems Transformation

The energy plan, totaling investments of DKK17.7 billion, picks up the historic support for renewable energy. The overall goals of the plan, which covers the period 2012–2020, is to increase the share of renewables to 35 percent overall, to cover 50 percent of electricity consumption with renewables, and to reduce gross energy consumption by 12 percent compared to 2006 — all by 2020. Specifically the plan calls for tenders on two new offshore wind farms (400 + 600 MW), seeks to install 500 MW of near coastal windmills, and envisions a net increase of onshore capacity of 500 MW, thus totaling an expansion of wind capacity of 2 GW. In other words, the plan seeks to increase installed wind capacity by more than 50 percent by 2020 and to stimulate the integration of renewables in combined heat-and-power plants by supporting the production of and infrastructure for biogas and biomass. For areas where there is no business case for district heating, the plan seeks to stimulate the exchange of oil- and gas-fired furnaces with small-scale heat pumps and solar heating (Regeringen et al. 2012).

To improve the economics of wind power, the plan seeks to leverage the district heating system by using large heat pumps to run at times of excess wind power production. In other words, the plan seeks to use large-scale heat pumps as battery capacity for times of low electricity demand and high wind power output. To ensure system stability at times when transmission bottlenecks limit the ability of grid interconnections to compensate for wind power output volatility, the plan seeks to promote the implementation of a "smart grid." Aside from the rollout of smart meters, the plan is rather vague in terms of concrete initiatives and definitions as to what this implies (Regeringen et al. 2012).

The Danish state-owned transmission systems operator Energinet.dk and the Danish Energy Association published a report that envisions the Smart Grid in the Danish context as a transformation of the electricity grid, which enables an effective interplay among wind power production, heat pumps, and electric vehicles (Danish Energy Association and Energinet.dk 2010). The combination of real-time dynamic pricing of electricity through smart meters and distributed battery capacity in the grid — in the form of electric vehicles and electric heat pumps — to offset the volatility of wind electricity production is thus envisioned to enable Denmark to massively increase the share of wind production in electricity generation.

The plan thus aims to reap a double dividend of the electrification of the transport sector by leveraging it as battery capacity for the entire energy system, while decarbonizing it as electricity generation goes green. Electrification is not seen as a suitable alternative for heavy-duty traffic, however, and as such, biomass is seen as the solution for decarbonizing this part of the transport sector (Regeringen et al. 2012). Finally, energy efficiency is promoted throughout the energy system as a complimentary layer on top of other goals to increase competitiveness and decrease consumption, thus reducing the size of the challenge of fossil fuel independency (Regeringen et al. 2012).

Tools for a Systems Transformation

Realizing these goals entails massive investments and a continuation and reinforcement of the concerted efforts of industry, academia, and politicians described in the first phases of this chapter. The emergence of cluster support policy and efforts to leverage the efforts of those three actors will be covered below. First, we briefly discuss the Danish government's tools of change. Expansion of wind capacity is supported from both the supply and the demand sides: calls for tenders on new offshore wind farms, subsidies, and funding for R&D. This applies also to other types of renewable technologies, such as wave, solar, geothermal, biomass, and biogas. Specifically with regards to biomass and biogas, the parties behind the plan have agreed to renegotiate the law on heat supply to ensure that incentives are in place for the transition from fossil fuels to biomass and biogas in heat production. Further, the parties have agreed to increase subsidies for biogas and to ensure that natural gas infrastructure enables its increasing use. Remaining oil furnaces will be mandatorily phased out gradually from 2013 and replaced by forms of heat generation based on renewable energy, as described above. Energy efficiency measures include obligation schemes for energy companies, a strategy for building renovation leveraging energy service companies, R&D support, support for use of combined heat-and-power generation, and capture of waste heat in industrial processes. Smart grid promotion includes the rollout of smart meters, increased international interconnection capacity, and the development of a strategy for the implementation of a smart grid, including an overhaul of relevant regulations to ensure incentives for "the green transition, cost-efficiency, competitiveness, and consumer protection" (Regeringen et al. 2012). Finally, a strategy will be developed to promote "energy efficient vehicles" in the transport sector, including hybrid plug-in electric vehicles. Charging infrastructures, subsidies, and tax incentives for electric vehicles are intended to promote their uptake.

Because the rationale for the policies described above is now economic growth as well as environmental protection and energy security, it should be understood against the backdrop of the developed cleantech cluster that emerged as a result of the first phases of green growth. Two government studies from 2006 and 2009 investigating the green business potential in Denmark identified a cluster of highly competitive cleantech businesses in Denmark producing and exporting "clean" solutions to environmental problems. As of 2006, the sector consisted of 720 companies that employed roughly 120,000 people, with total added value in the sector amounting to DKK86 billion — roughly 5 percent of GDP (Andersen, Bertelsen, and Rosted 2006; FORA 2009). Export and revenue in the sector have exhibited strong growth rates from 2000 to 2008 compared to the rest of the economy as well as the EU (Danish Government 2010). In other words, Denmark currently enjoys a strong position in parts of the global cleantech market. This position in turn becomes interesting politically because the demand for green energy globally is high and is projected to increase massively in the future. There is a huge global market potential for cleantech, and global investments in the sector are projected to increase rapidly over the next 20 years (Meilstrup et al. 2010).

This position and the knowledge base built by the FORA studies of 2006 and 2009, as well as similar studies commissioned and published by the Nordic Council of Ministers, have led to attempts at building policies of cluster support to further nurture and develop the Danish cleantech cluster, with the explicit aim of maintaining and increasing global market positions in emerging cleantech markets. Specifically this involves public-private partnerships building on the historically high level of trust and cooperation between stakeholders. These partnerships are intended to foster and nuture start-ups, identify and correct regulatory barriers, and bridge knowledge from academia to the private sector. According to former permanent undersecretary at the Ministry of Economics and Business Jørgen Rosted, efforts lacked sincere political backing during the Fogh and Løkke governments, but the 2011 election can be expected to speed up political backing to these initiatives, which is crucial for adapting regulation to provide the necessary incentives (Rosted 2012).

Challenges Going Forward

A broad coalition in Danish politics has, then, agreed to an energy strategy with very ambitious targets for promoting green growth and emissions reduction. The relative coherence of policies across the past four decades gives reason to believe it can be sustained, but for Denmark to achieve its goals, stakeholders must invest heavily and sustain collaboration.

DENMARK IN A NORDIC CONTEXT

Before we conclude, let us set the Danish case in a Nordic context. Danish achievements are clearer in contrast to its small, wealthy Nordic neighbors. The varying impacts of the oil crisis of the 1970s on the Nordic energy systems serve to highlight the uniqueness of the Danish case as well as some common traits of the Nordic story. While the oil crisis effectuated swift and radical transformation of the Danish energy system, the impact it had on the other Nordic energy systems was very different.

Sweden responded to the oil crisis by initiating construction of 12 nuclear plants. Historically, Swedish electricity generation had depended almost exclusively on hydropower. However, due to political and geographic constraints on further expansions of hydropower and a lack of domestic fossil fuel resources, Sweden opted for nuclear power in response to increasing demand for electricity in the context of the oil crisis. Just as heating was highly dependent on oil, the oil crisis had effects similar to those in Denmark in terms of promoting biomass-fired CHP for district heating and energy efficiency measures to reduce overall consumption (TemaNord 2007; Chen and Johnson 2008).

The oil crisis had primarily positive, if any, impacts on the Norwegian economy. Because electricity generation historically depended (and still does today) almost exclusively on hydropower and heating mostly was covered by electricity, the oil crisis's primary impact was to speed up exploration of oil following the first discovery of oil and natural gas in the North Sea in 1969. By 2006, Norway was the third-largest exporter of crude oil in the world. Due to its abundant hydropower resources, the oil crisis had little effects on Norway's incentives to alter its energy mix or promote energy efficiency (Gan et al. 2005; TemaNord 2007; Knudsen and Larsen 2008).

With fairly abundant hydropower resources—although more limited than those of Norway and Sweden—Finland turned to nuclear power and energy efficiency measures, including CHP and district heating, as a response to the oil crisis. Already in the 1950s and 1960s, Finland had begun turning to coal-fired power generation in response to increased demand for electricity. Though biomass production of energy became a political priority early on, it did not, as in the case of Denmark, translate into significant impacts on the energy-generation profile until the 1990s (TemaNord 2007; Kivimaa 2008).

Two observations can be drawn from this very cursory description of the impacts of the oil crisis on the Nordic energy systems. First and crucially, and perhaps also obviously, energy choices are highly constrained by the legacy energy system in which they occur and by available natural resources. Second, Denmark's policies — particularly the support for wind and the character of that support — are unique in the Nordic context, while the energy efficiency, CHP, infrastructure, and exploration policies were mirrored by Sweden, Finland, and Norway to varying degrees.

Today, as they did in response to the oil crisis, Nordic energy policies vary significantly. While all of the Nordic economies explicitly aim to foster green growth, the challenge facing Denmark is greater than that of its neighboring countries in that they are all endowed with large amounts of low-carbon energy supplies. The goal of eliminating fossil fuels rather than focusing on emissions reductions further sets the Danish strategy apart from those of its Nordic neighbors (Spongenberg 2011).

CONCLUSION: ACHIEVING GROWTH WITH COMPATIBLE EMISSIONS REDUCTIONS

The Danish strategy of energy independence, described in Parts I and II, successfully achieved growth compatible with emissions reduction. It further created the industry, infrastructure, and energy mix that, combined with international developments, have enabled Denmark's current attempt to achieve a fossil fuel–free economy (as described in Part IV). The idea is to create growth that is not only compatible with emissions reductions but also driven by them, thus fulfilling the triple underlying policy objectives of energy security, climate change mitigation, and green growth.

The ability to move from phase to phase of this progression has been an evolutionary process, with early phases creating the conditions that make later phases possible. Over time, evidence suggests that this has led to a very real transformation of the structure not only of the Danish energy system but of its industry and markets as well. The current behavior of Denmark's energy industry suggests that expectations have been fundamentally reconfigured. Denmark's policy objectives have thus proven to be self-reinforcing in two ways: across objectives in the sense that they are intertwined, each contributing to the fulfillment of the others, and over time in the sense that policy actions taken at one point in time help to create the context that enables and supports policies within the next phase.

To be sure, the extent to which the lessons of the Danish experience can be applied internationally has its limits. Denmark is a small open economy, and its energy system benefits from a high degree of domestic integration as well as interconnection capacity with its neighbors with abundant baseload power to compensate for intermittent renewables. Put more boldly, Denmark depends on Norwegian hydropower and the continental grid to ensure the stability of its own energy system amidst Denmark's commitment to intermittent renewable energy sources.

However, some aspects of the story provide valuable insights to policy makers who are seeking to promote green growth: Denmark is a global champion in terms of its ability to handle high amounts of intermittent renewables in the grid. And though part of the reason is geographical and thus hard to replicate, another part of it has to do with its unique political climate and close cooperation across stakeholder groups and the coherence of policies pursued over time. While the specific policies pursued by Denmark since 1973 may serve as inspiration for countries seeking to reduce their carbon footprint, the key is to understand that any such effort has to be undertaken in the context of stable coalition to sustain it in the long term. It is this type of long-term progression that is likely necessary to create a transformation in societal and industry behavior and expectations.

7

THE EUROPEAN UNION

*Green Growth without Borders: Transnational
Energy Systems and the Politics of
Transformation*

Mark Huberty

INTRODUCTION

In the last decade, energy systems transformation has become the new and
unheralded frontier of European deepening. Starting in 1996, the European
Union mandated the liberalization and integration of national energy systems,
put a price on greenhouse gas emissions from electricity generation, established binding targets for renewable energy adoption, mandated the breakup
of state energy monopolies, and sponsored the creation of EU-level regulatory and standards-setting bodies for energy infrastructure and markets. Most
recently, the Europe 2020 program has established enforceable goals for the
integration, liberalization, and decarbonization of the European electricity
supply system and ambitious but aspirational targets in energy efficiency.

Most analysis of this European policy history has emphasized the role of
environmental politics in driving progress on emissions reduction. Appeals to
environmental politics in this context appear to explain the apparent willingness of the European economies to trade off the economic costs of climate
change mitigation for the perceived ecological and social benefits it might
bring. Consistent with this understanding of the politics of European energy
policy, green parties and social movements have been given significant ex-
planatory weight.

This chapter argues that the environmental politics approach falls well
short of a satisfying explanation for both the evolution of European policy
and the characteristics of the policy suite. The attention to environmentalism,
rather than to the details of European energy policy and the constraints of the
current European energy system, overemphasizes the role of environmental

108 concerns. It also leads to the conclusion that the European policy suite may be fundamentally unstable — prone to reversal when the costs of environmental action exceed the altruism of European publics. This poses particular problems when faced with the fact that progress on emissions and renewable energy continued even after European enlargement added 12 member states with significantly less enthusiasm for climate change mitigation and significantly greater reliance on fossil fuels.

Instead, European policy must be understood as an attempt to transform the energy system amidst, on the one hand, the need to maintain a stable political coalition of EU member states supportive of the transformation and, on the other, the technological and economic complexity of the energy system. This trifecta of constraints — political, technological, and economic — complicates the process of policy design. But it also improves the prospects for sustaining policy through cross-subsidization across policy domains. These constraints and opportunities arise from the common role played by energy in emissions, security, and technological change. That role is closely intertwined with the possibilities for technological change in the energy system. Thus, only by understanding both the technological challenge of energy systems transformation and the political conflicts implicit in that transformation can we understand the resulting policy suite.

GREEN PARTIES FOR GREEN ENERGY? COMPETING EXPLANATIONS FOR EU POLICY LEADERSHIP

While the energy sector itself accounts for only 2 to 4 percent of European GDP, the central role of energy in modern industrial society gives changes to the energy system an importance that is far in excess of their immediate economic valuation. Today, Europe's energy system provides abundant, reliable, relatively inexpensive energy. Disruption of any of these characteristics would pose major challenges to the rest of the economy. Thus, it is not surprising that both the EU and its member states have approached climate and energy policy as an attempt to restructure the inputs to the energy system while leaving the outputs untouched. Technologically, that has meant switching away from imported fossil fuels toward domestic renewable energy. Economically, this has meant marketization of the energy system; dismantling of vertically integrated state-owned energy firms; and differential regulation of energy production, distribution, and use. These initiatives all seek to accomplish the decarbonization of European energy supplies and the integration of European energy markets, while leaving the industrial superstructure of the EU unperturbed.

On their own, these technical and regulatory changes pose significant challenges. Ongoing changes in the political landscape of the EU have only compounded these challenges. Europeanization of energy policy has taken place amidst an enlargement program that has made Europe's climate and energy interests more, not less, diverse. The industries of eastern Europe and the Baltic states in particular were more dependent on greater quantities of less expensive carbon energy than their Western counterparts. The publics in those countries were less enthusiastic about climate change mitigation and more likely to support exploitation of domestic fossil fuel resources — many of which, like Polish lignite coal, were particularly dirty energy sources. Yet, despite the increased diversity of interests, the EU continued to make progress after enlargement on the decarbonization of the energy supply and the deployment of more expensive renewable energy.

Explaining this ongoing progress poses two challenges for policy analysts. First, most contemporary accounts of European progress in energy systems transformation or climate change mitigation have relied on either domestic party structures — the role of green parties in particular — or foreign policy entrepreneurship — chiefly leadership in the United Nations COP process — to explain ongoing progress.[1] Yet, energy reform has continued despite the enlargement of the EU to include countries without strong green movements and amidst the return of center-right parties to government in countries like Denmark, Germany, and the United Kingdom.[2] Furthermore, the failure of EU policy leadership to secure binding emissions targets at the 2009 COP-15 negotiations has made no appreciable difference to the goals of EU climate policy.

Second, these political accounts of Europe's energy systems transformation have little to say about the particular contours of European policy. The choice of a policy suite that includes a carbon emissions trading system, a renewable energy mandate, and energy market liberalization is in many cases at odds with European green parties' preferences. Indeed, if the green parties were as important to policy outcomes as is claimed, we would expect to see much more radical policy than we do: more aggressive targets, less dependent on market-based instruments like carbon pricing, founded on a stronger critique of the ecological and equity costs of capitalism.[3] Moreover, progress on both energy market reform and emissions reduction has continued despite, as in Denmark and Germany, the return of center-right parties to government.[4]

Beyond these theoretical arguments, an improved understanding of the policy rationale at work in Europe is critical for two purposes. First, it provides a response to the self-styled "price fundamentalism" of economic analysis (Nordhaus 2010). Such fundamentalism usually leads to the conclusion that

110   the EU policy mix represents an inefficient departure from a ideal price-based emissions control mechanism. But this conclusion arises from an emphasis on emissions reduction to the exclusion of other policy prerogatives, and in doing so, it obscures the potential reality that, absent this policy suite, the political economy of energy and climate policy would not have tolerated a carbon price at all. The choice, in other words, was not between the first and second best but between the second best and nothing.

Furthermore, a better understanding of the policy rationale will improve our ability to predict the success and longevity of the policy itself. To a great degree, the stability of the European energy policy suite relies on spillover benefits in energy security and competitiveness to justify ongoing emissions reduction. This "green growth" strategy promises to turn on its head the core problem of climate change mitigation — the tradeoff of present consumption for future benefits — by reconciling emissions reduction to economic growth in the present. If successful, this would mark a radical shift in the potential for serious emissions reduction. If not, it marks a critical weak point in European ambitions and an implicit limit to the tolerance for the costs of emissions reduction.

THE EUROPEAN ENERGY POLICY SUITE

As of 2010, the EU has deployed a range of policy mechanisms to reduce emissions, secure energy supplies, and incentivize energy sector innovation. This suite of policies should be seen as an attempt to simultaneously address three energy-centered externalities: global climate change, energy security and price instability, and competitiveness and technological innovation. The existence of multiple energy-related externalities complicates the problem of policy formation. But it also provides a means to build sustained policy coalitions through linkage of objectives in one domain to action in others. That linkage generates policy stability in two ways: first, the beneficiaries develop acute interests in ongoing progress that allow emissions reduction policies to move beyond mere cost minimization, and second, linkage provides for cross-subsidization of transition costs among political and economic actors both within the member states and between them. Indeed, whether intentional or not, the policy suite that has developed in Europe over the last decade shows all the signs of fulfilling these political economy functions.

Progress in European Energy Policy, 2000–2010

As of 2010, the European energy policy suite consists of four major initiatives:

1. The Emissions Trading Scheme, which sets a price on energy-derived carbon emissions for approximately 40 percent of the European economy via annual limits on emissions and a secondary market for emissions permits within that limit.
2. The Renewable Energy Directive, which puts binding targets on member states to consume, as an EU average, 20 percent of their electricity from renewable sources by 2020.[5]
3. The Energy Market liberalization program, which mandates the breakup of vertically integrated national energy markets into separate domains of production, distribution, and retail, and that sets new terms for market competition in wholesale and retail energy provision (Jamasb and Pollitt 2005).
4. The SET-Plan and Framework Programmes, which provide significant European and Member state funding for research, development, and deployment of new energy technologies (European Commission 2007b, 2009a, 2009b).

Figure 7.1 shows that this policy suite did not arrive at once but rather evolved over time. As it did so, the political justification for each policy evolved as well. The liberalization of the energy market began in 1996 as a fairly standard extension of the Common Market, in parallel with other EU attempts at services and goods market integration.[6] In its initial form, the European Commission justified the program on the basis of more competition in energy markets, lower prices for retail and industrial customers, and improved investment in energy infrastructure (European Commission 2001). By 2003, the Parliament and the Council had adopted the second gas and electricity directive to begin the process of integrating national markets via network connection and market reform. Those reforms were extended and deepened via the third market directive, issued as part of the 2008 Climate and Energy Package.

In contrast to these market reforms, which have a long history in European widening and deepening, the Emissions Trading Scheme was a direct response to external events. At the Kyoto talks in 1997, EU member states had committed to emissions reductions of 8 percent below the 1990 baseline by 2012.[7] The EU believed it could achieve these reductions more efficiently acting as a body than if each member state did so on its own. Economic costs figured heavily in this decision. Since the majority of EU trade takes place among the member states themselves, a pan-EU emissions regulation mechanism would minimize potential distortions to the Common Market that state-level policy regimes could have introduced. It also had the potential to lower compliance costs by allowing member states to invest in emissions reductions (via the indirect mechanism of emissions permit purchases) where the marginal cost of reduction was lowest. The Emissions Trading Scheme thus began largely as a carbon market, intended to price carbon and thus incentivize emissions reduction via efficiency, investment, and innovation.

1996

2020

- **December 1996** Adoption of the Directive on rules for a common internal market in electricity
  - **March 2001** Commission proposes completion of the internal energy market via the 2nd Energy Market Directive
    - **September 2001** Adoption of the Directive on the Promotion of Electricity from Renewable Sources
      - **June 2003** Revised rules for the common internal market in electricity adopted; market dis-aggregation mandated and defined.
        - **August 2003** Second Gas and Electricity Directive endorsed by the Parliament
          - **October 2003** Emissions Trading Scheme (ETS) adopted
            - **January 2005** First trading period of the ETS begins
              - **October 2005** Climate and energy prioritized at Hampton Court Palace summit under British Presidency
                - **January 2007** Commission White Paper on EU Energy Strategy
                  - **March 2007** European Council adopts 20/20/20 targets
                    - **January 2008** Second trading period of the ETS begins; Commission proposes legislation for 20/20/20 targets
                      - **June 2008** ENTSO-E establishes operations
                        - **December 2008** Climate and Energy Package, synthesizing rules for electricity market integration, renewable energy, and emissions trading, endorsed by the Parliament and Council

FIGURE 7.1   Timeline of EU energy and climate policy

In 2007, two years into the operation of the ETS, the Commission proposed strengthening the ETS and implementing aggressive targets for renewable energy deployment. In what became the so-called 20/20/20 goals, the 2007 Commission white paper (European Commission 2007a) proposed that, by 2020, Europe obtain 20 percent of its energy from renewable sources, use energy 20 percent more efficiently, and reduce emissions by 20 percent relative to 2005 levels. To do so, it proposed moving beyond the emissions trading scheme to use direct subsidies to renewable energy — so-called feed-in tariffs or other support schemes — to incentivize renewable energy adoption and decarbonization of energy production.[8] This proposal was eventually adopted in December 2008 as a set of legislation known as the 3rd Climate and Energy Package.[9] In addition to the renewable energy and emissions targets, the Package also provided for EU-level coordination of national energy market regulations, established an EU-level energy regulator, and reinforced the mandate for the breakup of vertically integrated national electricity monopolies into separate markets for production, transmission, distribution, and retail.

Finally, the EU has moved to implement significant support for energy R&D relative to its budget. The Strategic Energy Technology Plan (European Commission 2009b) laid out a series of innovation and pilot program investments seeded with EU funding but completed by a consortia of private corporations and member states. Those investments complemented existing investments in energy R&D in the 7th Framework Programme, which invested €2.3 billion in energy-related research over the period 2007–2013.

Policy Redundancy in the European Union Emissions Reduction Suite

This energy policy suite marks a major accomplishment for the EU. It has significantly expanded EU authority over a major sector of the European economy. It has created new EU institutions that usurp some member state authority over energy market regulation. It has led to the formal or legal dismantling of state-owned energy monopolies, foot-dragging by Germany and France notwithstanding. All these developments have given the EU new influence over the evolution of the rest of the economy, via regulation of how energy is produced, distributed, and used.

But, theoretically, much of this policy should not be necessary for the EU's climate policy goals. Emissions reductions, in particular, should not require parallel programs to incentivize renewable energy, energy efficiency, or research and development. Rather, the consistent message from economic analysis has emphasized carbon pricing in isolation.[10] Given the right emissions price, market actors should of their own accord determine the most efficient way to optimize their investment in greenhouse gas emissions reduction. By this argument, separate policies to promote renewables and push energy efficiency may constitute market-distorting industrial policy.[11] Indeed, it now appears that most of the 2020 emissions goals in the EU will be satisfied through widespread deployment of renewable energy, even though many cost estimates (such as Enkvist, Nauclér, and Rosander [2007]) show that energy efficiency improvements are often much cheaper.

This problem only compounds other issues of the design of the ETS itself: rights to emit are granted via the member states, rather than auctioned by the EU, leading to all kinds of chicanery among the member states;[12] allocation is based on prior-period emissions, providing perverse incentives to overemit and thus keep the baseline high; and the price of emissions permits on the secondary market has proven somewhat volatile and unpredictable. All of these institutional designs raise the price of emissions and reduce the effectiveness of the ETS.[13]

This gap between theory and policy implementation is puzzling in light of the political economy of climate change action. As Chapter 2 discusses, and the other country studies have shown, the costs and benefits of major emissions reduction have led other major emitters — notably the United States in the developed world, and China and India in the developing — to reject aggressive or explicit climate action. In the case of the EU, they are powerful arguments for choosing the least-cost means of action. Indeed, interviews with the European Commission in late 2010 suggested that the EU abandoned earlier ideas for a command-and-control approach to emissions regulation largely because of fears about cost. Despite those concerns, however, they have subsequently added to the carbon price framework a range of policies regarded as more costly, and less efficient, than a carbon price alone.

This is all the more surprising given that the Renewable Energy standard was adopted *after* the accession of the new member states. As Figure 7.2 shows, these new member states were considerably more reliant on energy and fossil energy than the EU-15. Given that the EU-15 were already concerned about potentially detrimental effects of carbon pricing on competitiveness, the addition of 12 new members with even greater concerns should have made progress even more fraught. Under any theory of policy formation that gives primacy to efficiency and cost minimization, we would expect that this would make the EU more likely to pursue carbon pricing as the low-cost option. But this did not occur.

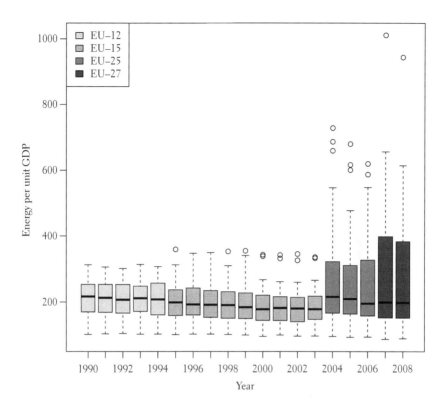

FIGURE 7.2   Emissions intensity of economic activity in the EU across enlargements

SOURCE: Emissions data are taken from the Carbon Dioxide Information Analysis Center at the U.S. Department of Energy Oak Ridge National Laboratory and are expressed in MMT carbon.

NOTE: Emissions data are expressed as millions of metric tons (MMT) carbon per constant 2005 €.

Complementarity, Not Redundancy: Climate Policy as Energy Policy

This portrayal of the puzzle of policy redundancy relies on viewing policy goals as *either* climate *or* energy focused. This is incorrect. EU actions on climate and energy cannot be separated. Analytically, such a separation fails to account for the vital role played by the energy system in any serious attempt at emissions reduction. Politically, this separation ignores the immediate conflation of climate and energy goals and interests — and the political battles this brings — that occurs as soon as an emissions price is introduced. Substantively, it fails to recognize the underlying technological characteristics of the European energy system, the profound barriers to change those characteristics pose, and the actions required to overcome these barriers.

Climate between Energy and Security

Resolving these analytic shortcomings must begin with the recognition that EU policy is optimizing across three separate externalities: emissions, energy security, and economic compeitiveness.[14] But those externalities are closely connected to one another via mutual dependence on the energy system. Implicitly, solutions to any one of them suggest some form of energy systems transformation.

This has two important consequences. First, because of the variation in national energy markets, summarized in Figure 7.3, the importance of each externality varies by member state. Spain and Portugal are energy islands due to

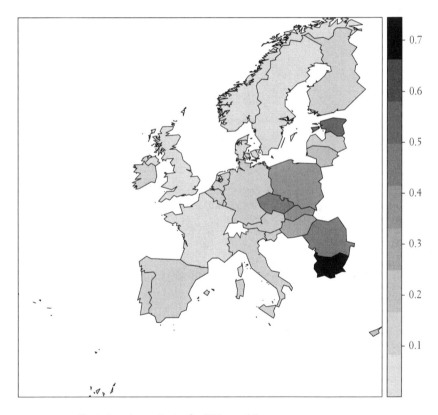

FIGURE 7.3   Emissions intensity in the EU-27 + Norway, 2005

SOURCE: Energy intensity data from Eurostat. Emissions intensity data based on author's own calculations using GDP data from Eurostat and emissions data from the Carbon Dioxide Information Analysis Center at the U.S. Department of Energy Oak Ridge National Laboratory.
NOTE: Greece omitted due to lack of data.

the isolation of the Iberian peninsula; most of eastern Europe remains dependent on fossil fuels, either domestic coal or gas imported from Russia; Denmark is, at least for the near term, a net energy exporter that has decoupled GDP growth from energy consumption; and France has already decarbonized 80 percent of its electricity supply through reliance on nuclear energy. These national differences in the structure of energy production, distribution, and use alter the importance that each member state attaches to the goals of competitiveness, energy security, and emissions reduction.

Second, isolated solutions to one externality may well exacerbate the others. Thus, pursuing individual solutions to each of these externalities could well fracture the coalition required to maintain policy at all. The climate policy mix, therefore, should be viewed not as an attempt to resolve the emissions externality alone but to optimize policy within the constraints imposed by these three energy-related externalities.

Those constraints come in two parts. Politically, each externality has its own constituency inside the EU. Energy security is most salient for the new member states, whose exposure to Russian influence through their dependence on energy was made clear by the 2005–2006, 2007–2008, and 2009 Ukraine gas crises. The western European states, who depend less on Russian energy, are correspondingly less concerned (though balance-of-payments concerns over imported fossil fuels remain salient). Emissions reduction is most important to some states with strong green parties and to those who view international European climate leadership as vital. But states with relatively high-carbon energy shares view emissions reduction as a potential drag on economic competitiveness. Competitiveness, of course, is a universal concern, but states with strong renewable energy technology industries (like Denmark or Germany) stand to benefit substantially from EU-wide emissions reduction programs, while other states may become net importers of these technologies. Thus, each policy domain has separate, though sometimes overlapping, member state constituencies.

Optimizing at any one externality would risk fracturing the coalition along these lines. Pursuing emissions reduction through a high emissions price would have two immediate effects: first, it would substitute Russian gas for domestic coal in electricity generation, at an immediate 40 percent reduction in carbon per unit energy. Second, it would raise retail electricity prices substantially and disproportionately in high-carbon-share economies. These developments might lead to defection by member states concerned about energy security and reduced economic competitiveness.

Likewise, pursuit of energy security alone would lead to significantly greater use of domestic EU coal. Much of the remaining coal in Europe, such as that

118   around Silesia in Poland, is of the soft brown lignite (World Energy Council 2010) variety, which in addition to its carbon emissions carries a much higher share of other pollutants compared to the hard coal of earlier generations. This would alienate member states more committed to emissions and pollution reduction and would frustrate EU attempts to achieve its commitments under the Kyoto protocols.

Furthermore, a renewables target alone would generate significant benefits for member states with strong wind and solar power industries. Those countries would stand to benefit from increased exports of capital goods, such as wind turbines and solar cells, to other member states lacking domestic production capacity.[15] But that would come at large costs to technology-importing countries, both in absolute terms and in the secondary effects on trade balances.

Finally, linkage of security, competitiveness, and climate change goals was made easier by energy market reform. Adoption of significant volumes (greater than 20 percent) of nonhydroelectric renewable energy — a cornerstone of energy security, emissions reduction, and competitiveness policy — poses significant challenges to the power grid. Technologically, the intermittency of most renewable energy sources can destabilize the power grid and lead to supply disruption. Those problems can be offset through grid reinforcements and investments in new technologies. Making those investments, however, would not have been in the interest of older, vertically integrated state power monopolies. Their control of both production and transmission of electricity gave them large incentives to favor their own energy production assets in making new grid investments and allocating grid capacity. As a corollary, it also gave them few incentives to invest in new transmissions connections for renewable energy resources or to harden the power grid to effectively manage intermittent generation. In this context, the breakup of the power monopolies and the creation of independent markets for production, transmission, distribution, and use was a critical step in pushing for the adoption of low-carbon energy sources.[16]

Thus, each policy problem carries with it unique interests for and against that would frustrate attempts to pursue them in isolation. Instead, the EU energy and climate policy suite has evolved to yoke progress along any one policy dimension to progress along the others. The mix of costs and benefits to any one interest group varies by the policy instrument, implicitly cross-subsidizing policy compliance. Finally, the ability to pursue all of these policies was highly contingent on the market reforms that enabled their implementation.

This analytic framework suggests that the arguments of the price fundamentalists cannot see the forest for the trees. As emissions policy alone, the ETS may be inefficient and cumbersome compared to a pure carbon price. As energy policy, the renewable energy mandates crowd out other, cheaper emissions-reducing fuels and efficiency investments. As market policy, energy market liberalization makes only partial sense in a world of massive, highly centralized fossil fuel–generation plants.

But in practice, the policies manage the tradeoffs among the three externalities. The renewables mandate accomplishes four ends: it provides emissions reduction largely through renewable electricity adoption; it expands domestic renewable energy markets, generating profits for firms in renewable energy leaders like Denmark and Germany; it provides indigenous energy substitutes not subject to Russian influence; and it shifts the cost incidence of emissions reduction from retail electricity prices to subsidies paid, at least partially, from general taxation.

Absent some means of subsidization, the renewables mandate might generate opposition among either those less concerned with emissions or those net renewable energy technology importers. But the Emissions Trading Scheme, together with reallocated EU Structural Adjustment Funds, provides a political framework for implicit cross-subsidization. As Zachmann (2011) has shown, the new member states—for whom energy security via renewables is more expensive than via domestic coal—receive relatively more permits than they should compared with historic baselines. Conversely, countries like Germany and Denmark—who stand to benefit from the expansion of the renewable energy market—receive relatively fewer.[17] Since those permits have value on secondary markets, this represents an implicit subsidy to the same member states who are most exposed to the costs of renewables-led emissions reduction. Thus, the renewables mandate solves the security problems of new energy sources and generates significant income for some member states. But some of that income is recycled via the ETS permit process, cross-subsidizing energy security via renewables rather than domestic coal.

Finally, the pursuit of emissions reduction raises concerns about European competitiveness in the face of high energy prices. To offset these concerns, both the renewable energy mandate and the ETS provide compensating incentives. First, renewable energy has become a significant area of European comparative advantage. Maintenance of that advantage will require ongoing innovation. As a range of studies have shown, many aspects of energy innovation respond better to learning by doing than by laboratory or "big science"

120 research alone (Heymann 1998; Kamp, Smits, and Andriesse 2004; Meyer 2007; Acemoglu et al. 2009). The renewables mandates, by expanding the market for installation of new technology, provide the means for that kind of innovative activity. Meanwhile, the emphasis on energy technology support in the SET-Plan and the Framework Programmes underpins basic research. Economically, these programs intend, at least, to generate signficant innovation and job growth via investment in new high-technology sectors. Politically, they create new constituencies of firms and workers supportive of emissions reduction, offsetting the acute costs of emissions mitigation with the acute benefits of industrial competitiveness.

GREEN GROWTH AND THE EUROPEAN UNION

This study has so far demonstrated that EU climate policy cannot be understood in reference to emissions reductions alone. Were that the case, a range of simpler, and potentially even cheaper, alternatives for climate change mitigation might have emerged as preferred policy options. Instead, the EU has, whether by design or not, embarked on a policy suite that couples progress on emissions reduction to action on energy security and economic competitiveness. Doing so has allowed the cross-subsidization of different policy goals between the member states, keeping together political coalitions for action where action on only one goal might have generated defection.

In doing so, the EU has embarked on a strategy that knits together many of the green growth proposals discussed in Chapter 3. Improved competitiveness from reduced reliance on imported fossil fuels, export-led growth in renewable energy industries via market promotion at home, and revenue recycling from emissions pricing to research and development all represent prominent green growth strategies. That the EU understands this is clear from statements by the commissioners themselves. Commissioner for Energy Günther Oettinger argued for increased European spending on low-emissions energy technologies by stating that "in global competition we need to avoid that we start lagging behind China and the USA."[18] EU Commissioner for Climate Action Connie Hedegaard has also endorsed the growth potential of climate change mitigation (Hedegaard 2010).

Many of these strategies have worked well for individual member states. As Chapter 6 shows, Denmark has profited from both export-led growth in the wind turbine industry and increased global competitiveness through insulation from fluctuating fossil fuel costs. Germany has done well through promotion of renewable energy firms like Siemens at home (though as Frondel et al. [2009] show, that has come at a very high cost, particularly for solar energy technologies). Portugal and Spain both sought to use domestic market expansion to drive export competitiveness abroad and industrial redevelopment at home (Rosenthal 2010). Finally, a range of countries, from the United Kingdom to Poland, view offshore wind energy as a new source of demand for skilled labor displaced from declining sectors such as offshore gas and oil exploration (in Scotland) and shipbuilding (in Poland).

As Chapter 3 notes, however, each of these strategies remains limited in scope and potential duration. In the case of the EU, four threats in particular stand out.[19] First, the process of market integration, critical to cost containment, has run into various regulatory problems on the ground. This is principally true in the case of power grid integration. Integration of renewable energy in the European power grid will be cheaper and less complex if accompanied by integration of the current regional energy markets. By averaging intermittency and resources over a wider geographic range, market integration can improve the stability of the power grid and lower the price of renewable electricity. A European grid capable of drawing wind energy from northern Europe and solar energy from southern Europe would allow averaging of renewable power production across the entire European continent.

But actually building the power grid interconnectors required to make this a reality has encountered two significant problems. First, local resistance to new power lines has delayed new interconnector construction. Discussions with several European energy firms in late 2010 suggested that the time from project announcement to the start of operations could be as long as a decade. Second, potential solutions to local resistance — chiefly burying cables to minimize their aesthetic impacts — face significant technical hurdles[20] and raise construction costs dramatically.[21] Thus, despite ambitious goals for EU-level adoption of renewable energy and reform of power markets, the disconnect between EU-level goals and local regulatory and political reality may slow progress and increase costs.

The second problem is closely related to the first. The 2008–2009 policy reforms left untouched the essentially national nature of renewable energy support schemes. While the implicit fiscal transfers embedded in the ETS and the renewable energy mandates flow across borders, policies implementing renewable energy subsidies remain essentially national. This is, in many ways, suboptimal, particularly when many European economies face significant financial difficulties. Given Germany's weather, building even more solar energy capacity there would be less optimal than expanding solar capacity in sun-drenched countries like Spain, Italy, or Greece. Funding EU-level subsidies for building renewable energy capacity in the most optimal areas remains, however, off the table. Whether the Europeans decide to harmonize support for renewable energy across countries so renewable energy investment is pushed where returns are highest remains to be seen. This would involve a move from implicit to explicit fiscal transfers, at a scale that the member states have been reluctant to embrace.

The third problem stems from the political economy of the Common Market itself. As Figures 7.4 and 7.5 show, significant disparities in competitiveness in renewable energy technology presently exist among different EU member states. Given the lack of tariff barriers inside the EU, mandates to adopt renewable energy technology may exacerbate rather than even out these disparities. This harkens back to earlier debates about the impact of the euro and a common monetary policy on member state heterogeneity. Then, the debate over optimum currency areas turned on whether a common monetary policy would generate convergence of business cycles among the member

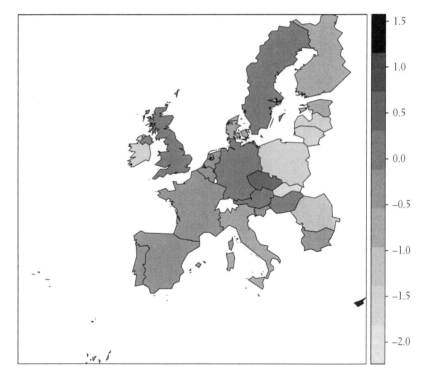

FIGURE 7.4 Geographic disparities in regional comparative advantage for photovoltaic technology, 2008

SOURCE: Revealed comparative advantage calculations based on the six-digit United Nations COMTRADE data and are shown as base-10 logs.

FIGURE 7.5 Geographic disparities in regional comparative advantage for wind turbines, 2008

SOURCE: Revealed comparative advantage calculations based on the six-digit United Nations COMTRADE data and are shown as base-10 logs.

states or, alternatively, reduce transaction costs and so increase the specialization and heterogeneity of the EU economies. Now the question is whether renewable energy standards will provide new industrial opportunities to all member states or instead generate substantial windfall profits for already competitive firms in specific member states.

Finally, the fourth problem reflects the risk of relying too heavily on policy schemes alone to generate green growth markets. The 2008–2009 financial crisis left many European renewable energy firms and support schemes on shaky ground. In Germany, prominent solar firms QCells and First Solar both encountered financial troubles in 2012 as a consequence of both intensified competition from China and flagging demand. The Spanish and Portuguese

124   wind industries have seen home markets collapse as their respective governments have pursued fiscal retrenchment amidst high unemployment and deep
recession. These developments reflect the concern, raised in Chapter 1, that
green growth dependent on climate policy did not necessarily help stabilize
the long-term politics of climate change mitigation. The cycle of industrial
development, retrenchment, and renewal has played out in every industry.
But to the extent that Europe has relied on the causal connection between
emissions reduction and growth to stabilize its climate policy ambitions, it
now risks reversal as its renewable energy industry goes through that same
cycle.

CONCLUSION: RISKS AND OPPORTUNITIES FOR GREEN GROWTH IN THE EUROPEAN UNION

The EU, intent on climate change mitigation, has yoked emissions reductions to the cause of energy security on the one hand and the promise of
innovation-driven jobs and growth creation on the other. In doing so, it has
created significant incentives for otherwise reluctant actors to maintain their
commitments to emissions reduction in the face of the costs. Eastern European member states concerned about the price of renewable energy nevertheless benefit from reduced dependence on uncertain foreign suppliers and
receive subsidies to offset the costs. Northwestern European countries offset
the costs of those subsidies with the expanded markets for the products of
their high-technology industries. Emissions prices provide near-term signals
for energy market evolution and efficiency, but not at levels that would generate significant political backlash. In contrast to recommendations for "price
fundamentalism," this analysis would suggest that, given the interaction of the
EU climate and energy policy suite with the political interests at stake, the
superficial inefficiency of EU climate policy is a feature, not a bug.
    Whether that translates into green growth is, of course, a different matter.
As we have seen, EU policy faces obstacles to policy implementation and
economic solidarity stemming from the dynamics of renewable energy adoption. Hopefully, the gains from green growth will remain large enough to
help offset the costs implicit in these obstacles. If so, then the strategy of cross-
subsidization of interests can remain viable and help sustain emissions reduction in the future. If not, however, EU policy will face significant challenges
in sustaining the transition to a low-emissions economy.[22]

8

THE UNITED STATES

Local Green Spirals, National Ambiguity

Nina Kelsey and Alice Madden with Juliana
Mandell and Sean Randolph

American climate and energy policy must be thought of as 50 semi-independent policy experiments, nested in a permissive but otherwise generally neutral national policy environment. Despite largely ambiguous national outcomes, state-level experiments have generated successful instances of what Chapter 5 termed a "green spiral." Whether either this ambiguous national position or increasingly active state-level experimentation will coalesce into a national green growth experiment remains largely unclear. This chapter studies the state-level successes in California and Colorado in the context of federal policy. We find that Colorado provides evidence of intent to bring into being a latent interest coalition—and in doing so, potentially initiate a process of positive policy feedback loops. In contrast, California's ambitious climate and energy policy regime—including long-run targets for ambitious emissions control—emerged out of past successes in solving environmental or energy policy problems only loosely related to carbon emissions. Hence, despite national policy stasis, empirical evidence points to the flexibility of U.S. states in building a politics of green growth and using that politics to launch a variety of experiments in starting and sustaining a low-emissions energy systems transformation. But as we discuss in the conclusion, it remains largely unclear whether these state-level green spirals presage national momentum for green growth.

THE NATIONAL CONTEXT

Events over the last 15 years have made it clear that the United States cannot be considered a success story at the national level. Despite the ambitions of the Obama administration as it entered office, the United States has not established a sustainable federal green strategy. Nor have the elements of a green coalition emerged at the national level. The United States has abundant fossil fuel reserves — coal, oil, and shale — and associated interests defending them; also, for now, fossil fuels are less expensive than green alternatives. Consequently, a shift to green energy, all else equal, means higher costs for industry and consumers. It is therefore not surprising that no national green coalition has emerged. Now the emergence of shale as a low-cost, lower-emissions alternative to coal is further complicating the national context.

Nationally, the weight of policy continues to support fossil fuels. Although the federal government has provided incentives for the development of green energy, this must be viewed in the context of broader funding structures: the federal government also provides many forms of generous incentives for development and use of fossil fuels, and indeed, the balance of subsidy overall has been in favor of fossil fuels. Between 2001 and 2011, fossil fuels captured 25 percent of Department of Energy (DoE) research and development spending, while renewables received 12 percent (Pfund and Healey 2011). Outside of the DoE, the legislative context to date provides little sustained impetus for a real energy systems transition. Even the relatively moderate domestic cap-and-trade deal that was recently proposed ultimately proved impossible to pass. The United States did not ratify the Kyoto Protocol, and it has made little progress toward any global initiatives since.

However, the federal government does provide some support for green business and policy experimentation. The federal government has provided financial incentives — in the form of guaranteed loans, tax incentives, and similar measures — for the development of green industry and renewable energy. This has been particularly true in recent years, as stimulus funding under the American Recovery and Reinvestment Act (ARRA) following the 2008 financial crisis provided a wave of incentives, much of it targeted at green industry. ARRA included significant funding of various forms for renewable energy and efficiency measures.

This green support has done two things overall. First, it has generated pools of available *innovation* and *technology*, serving as an accelerant for the creation of green industry where it has occurred. Research takes place in a variety of units in the federal government and in institutions funded by the federal government, often through the DoE, including the national labs, research universities, and the struggling ARPA-E unit. In addition, the Department of Defense can be an important player in technological innovation because it is not just an R&D funder; it often also provides an initial purchaser for expensive prototype or early-stage products, helping to provide a bridge to commercialization for many U.S. technological advancements. Second, in both of the case studies below, we find that this type of funding has helped supercharge green policy moves at the state level, providing greater political motivation for state-level policy. This effect is discussed in greater detail in the cases.

However, the effectiveness of federal incentives is complicated by the politics of green subsidies. Pfund and Healey (2011) suggest that tax credits have supported the development of renewable energy sources such as wind, biomass, solar, and others. But the tendency of renewable energy tax incentives to be temporary and subject to recurrent extensions means funding is uncertain and development is subject to boom and bust cycles — "tight and frenzied windows of development" (Pfund and Healey 2011, 27). The temporary nature of the ARRA funding creates similar problems. This has had detrimental effects on the growth of renewable energy overall. Although we find that federal incentives have in some cases assisted the development of green policy and green interests in our cases below, it is equally the case that sudden drop-offs in federal funding may put these developments at risk if they lead to green industry "busts" and abandonment by investors.

In addition to these issues, creating coherent policy at the federal level is simply difficult. Policy-making authority and responsibility is fragmented: there is an array of federal-level policy administered by several groups within the executive branch, including the DoE; the Federal Energy Regulatory Commission (FERC), which has authority over the national energy grid; the Environmental Protection Agency (EPA); and various R&D units, such as the newly created Advanced Research Projects Agency — Energy (ARPA-E), as well as existing units in the national labs, EPA, and Department of Defense.

The EPA policies declaring carbon to be a pollutant do set the framework for a potential longer-term approach to a green energy policy. Under the Clean Air Act, the EPA has regulations coming on line covering vehicles and point sources such as factories and power plants; these powers, though limited in places, may have significant effects in the future (Burtraw and Woerman 2012).[1] However, such regulations have not been a part of the national picture until very recently, and they are facing a series of legal challenges (thus far unsuccessful) as well as likely legislative attempts to curtail the EPA's power.

In keeping with this fragmentation, there is a general failure to coordinate what is being done at the national level. National/regional policy making is not strategically coordinated well either across departments or with state-level policy making. National-level groups often do not have practical control over local responses. For instance, FERC's actual authority over the grid is largely limited to purely national-level issues, such as the regulation of the transmission,

128 reliability, and wholesale sales of electricity between states. More local distribution systems and pricing are administered at the local level, with FERC
holding advisory powers at best; even multistate, regional planning is handled
by state consortia (Fox-Penner 2010; FERC 2011; NERC 2011).

Overall, then, federal-level policy to date can be characterized largely as su-
percharging state-level policy by providing permissive conditions and energy
in the form of funding. We emphasize that the U.S. federal structure delegates
a great deal of regulatory power to state governments to begin with. In the
absence of clearly articulated national policy, state-level energy regulation remains preeminent. Given the lack of an overarching and coherent emissions
policy at the federal level, state-level powers are relatively strong in the area
of carbon emissions and green industry. State autonomy is compounded by
exemptions from federal rules that have been granted to states, like California,
that are interested in experimenting with stricter environmental standards than
those created at the federal level. Indeed, lack of coordination can increase
freedom to experiment, but the lack of coordination also makes attempts to
transform state-level systems that are linked to national systems problematic.
This serves as an obstacle to success in some policy areas. This effect is seen,
for instance, in the California deregulation story, where California state policy
clashed with regional energy market policy, creating problems for successful
deregulation (Sweeney 2002).

As a result, all 50 states have the potential to diverge along separate green
growth trajectories, each implementing different policy mixes in response
to different situations and goals.[2] An interesting question that remains un-
answered is whether the states' policy progress could lead to a national-level
deal, just as individual national-level stories have led to an EU-level deal in
Europe. For now, though, policy experimentation remains largely at the state
level, and we turn now to our state-level cases.

CALIFORNIA

Key Lessons

The California story has two important features.[3] First, California is often an
early mover in environmental policy. This in combination with its large size
means its policy decisions can be leaders for policy throughout the United
States. Second, it has significant commercial interests in green technology.
These two points are related and build on the state's prior history.

The California case suggests three key lessons. First, California provides
a key example of the green spiral process. Green policy in California was an

iterative process in which each round of green or environmental policy helps to broaden the set of constituencies that are tolerant or supportive of further green policy steps. Thus, initial rounds of pollution and energy efficiency policy are credited with building familiarity and support among consumers and industry that created a permissive environment for green policy like Assembly Bill 32 (AB32—California's landmark 2006 emissions reduction legislation). AB32 is, in turn, continuing to grow an industry group with a direct stake in seeing green policy survive and expand. Industry coalitions work to create sustainable policy across partisan shifts. This lesson echoes the lessons learned in Denmark and Europe, and we see the possible beginning of a similar process in the Colorado case (below). Much of the analysis that follows lays out how the California spiral developed and how each round feeds back into subsequent rounds.

Second, the California case took place over decades and with mistakes made along the way. Energy systems are large and slow to change; the industry sometimes requires time and incentive to experiment until it finds successful investment and business models. This in turn requires some level of policy stability. Because energy systems and the economy are large, complex, slow-moving systems, designing well-matched policies for these systems is an inherently difficult problem. This suggests green policy will work best when it is relatively simple and open-ended, providing support for industry growth but allowing for experimentation.

Third, green growth policies and initiatives must take into account and coordinate with the characteristics of existing systems and context, both at the public and private levels. In the case of deregulation, California's deregulatory moves failed partly because they were mismatched with conditions in the regional electricity system California participated in. In that case, mismatch led to failure. California's cleantech venture capital community now stands at a critical juncture. The current venture capital investment model appears mismatched to the characteristics of cleantech development. However, it appears that the business community may be adapting. How well these investment models are able to adapt to cleantech characteristics may determine their success.

Overview

In 2006, California passed AB32—one of the most important climate policy moves in the United States to that point, given California's size and the scope of the measure. AB32 called for emissions reduction through a variety of measures targeting multiple sectors, including energy generation, transportation,

130 efficiency, and others; its overarching goal is a reduction of emissions to 1990 levels by 2020. By the last quarter of 2010, the state had captured 50 percent of global venture capital funding for cleantech. These developments were made possible by a historical trajectory of policy and business community development dating back to the 1940s. Early pollution policy laid the foundation (though not intentionally) for future emissions policy. Building on this foundation, California's already established venture capital community, supported by the state's top-tier research universities and policy makers, made a wave of investment in cleantech. By the late 2000s, venture capital, green business, and state climate policy enjoyed a synergistic relationship, supporting increasingly aggressive green policy. The heyday of the venture capital–focused interest group structure has likely passed, as we discuss toward the end of our analysis, due to declining federal incentives and increasing recognition that the venture capital model may not be well tailored to the energy sector. What remains to be seen is how much will be consolidated and what will emerge in its wake.

California's green growth history began in the mid-twentieth century as a period of green growth *compatible with* emissions reductions. The primary focus of policy was reducing air pollution, and emissions reductions were only a derivative effect. There were two policy debates during this period. There was a drive for air pollution and energy efficiency programs — programs that were successful. The deregulation of the electricity industry proved to be a failure. We comment on lessons from that deregulation later. Importantly, energy efficiency programs, in combination with structural factors, were able to keep California's per-capita electricity use relatively flat, while permitting significant economic growth (discussed below). On the other hand, deregulation of the California electricity industry was troubled by unintended consequences and was largely unsuccessful.

Recently, a third strand of green growth development in California began taking hold. This movement represents a more emissions-aware energy movement, based around the idea that growth could be *driven by* emissions reduction and that the cleantech industry could represent the next new major source of economic growth for California. Next, we explore this evolution.

*Phases 1 and 2: Pollution and Clean Air Standards, and Oil
and the Rise of Efficiency Policy (1940s–1970s)*

By the late 1970s onward, electricity use per capita in California flattened (electricity use per capita increased by 50 percent nationally), while the state experienced long-term economic growth — successfully decoupling growth and

TIMELINE: THE PHASES OF CALIFORNIA'S GREEN SPIRAL

Phase 1: 1940s–1960s — Air Pollution Crisis and Clean Air Standards
In response to increasingly severe air pollution, California creates county-level Air Pollution Control Districts and begins setting motor vehicle air quality standards. California wins the legal right to deviate from national policy and impose more stringent air pollution regulation (1967). Creation of this regulatory structure paves the way for later policy rounds.

Phase 2: 1970s — Oil Crisis and the Rise of Efficiency Policy
OPEC oil embargo creates incentive for energy efficiency. California Energy Commission is created, and California adopts widespread efficiency standards for appliances and buildings. These measures continue to build constituencies tolerant of or in favor of additional policy measures.

Interlude: 1990s–2000 — Energy Deregulation: A Policy Detour
California implements aggressive electricity deregulation, eventually leading to fiscal and energy crises.

Phase 3: Mid-2000s — Politically Viable Emissions Policy
Interest configurations created by rounds of policy making above, which left industry familiar with, and in some cases supportive of, environmental legislation, allow passage of climate-related legislation, including AB1493 (GHG emissions reductions in California motor vehicles); SB1078 (a 20 percent renewable electricity mandate); and, in 2006, AB32: the California Global Warming Solutions Act.

Phase 4: 2010 — Growth of Interests Helps Green Policy Survive a Challenge
2010's Proposition 23 threatened to suspend AB32 indefinitely, but it was defeated. Lack of in-state backing for Prop. 23 combined with a wide variety of in-state interests that benefited from and supported AB32 led to Prop. 23's failure.

electricity consumption (Roland-Holst 2008). In the later part of the 1970s, the state put into effect an aggressive energy efficiency policy package comprised of building and appliance standards and utility programs. In addition, the state introduced policies to decouple utility profits from total electricity generation. These policies provided a compensatory revenue stream and performance incentives for utilities that met or exceeded efficiency savings. Regulators used a new investment metric — "cost of conserved energy" — to calculate savings

132   from avoided use and thus justify the program costs (Rosenfeld and McAuliffe 2008; Rosenfeld and Poskanzer 2009). Approximately 25 percent of the reduction in per-capita electricity consumption growth patterns can be attributed to efficiency policy measures (the remainder was driven by a combination of, on the one hand, demographic and structural effects and, on the other hand, changes to industrial profile — largely a shift away from heavy industry toward light industry, services, and IT) (Sudarshan and Sweeney 2008; Mitchell 2009).

The viability of these policies stemmed from a combination of effects of previous policy moves with political circumstance. California's history of severe air pollution problems in previous decades (Phase 1) meant it had regulatory infrastructure — such as the California Air and Resource Board — in place and existing regulatory latitude from the federal government, in the form of legal rights to pass more stringent air pollution regulations than the national level. These circumstances played a central role in the later implemented energy efficiency measures (Haneman 2007) and lowered costs and barriers to further policy making. Early investments in public research fed back into the policy environment: policy makers were also able to take advantage of the established research universities in the area. A symbiotic relationship between regulators and researchers emerged in which regulators funded research and modeling that in turn greatly benefited policy implementation, confirming the practicality of efficiency policy and increasing political will for it, in something of a virtuous circle (Hanemann 2007; Rosenfeld and Poskanzer 2009), again lowering perceived barriers and costs. A lack of state coal reserves also helped limit resistance (Sweeney 2002). Finally, against this background, the OPEC embargo and rising fuel prices helped to create a political will for regulation that ultimately overcame Republican Party and industry objection.

Interlude: Energy Deregulation — A Policy Detour (1990s–2000s)

At this point, California engaged in a round of industry deregulation. This period stands apart from the broader green spiral policy story, but it offers important lessons of its own. We therefore cover it here as an "interlude" in the California policy story.

Rising electricity prices, declining capacity relative to per-capita use, and federal policy trends all made deregulation attractive to California in 1996.[4] Proponents argued it would lower prices by introducing competition, efficiency, and flexibility into the market. In 1996, the state passed deregulation policies that separated generation and distribution within utilities; required all electricity produced from fossil fuel–fired plants to be sold on the power exchange; and promoted more open access to transmission.

California's deregulation further tightened already tight electricity supplies in the West. Amid this tight market, prices began to rise. While other states in its regional grid could respond by ensuring electricity supply through generation facilities or medium- to long-term contracts, California's utilities were mandated to use spot markets and thus bore the brunt of price spikes. In essence, deregulation policies combined with market manipulation and political incapacity greatly exacerbated California's electricity concerns and plunged the state into crisis. In combination with continued regulation of retail rates (retail rates were in fact initially deregulated as well, but this was reversed due to consumer reaction), this crisis led to bankruptcy for some utilities.

Two implications can be drawn from this story. First, restructuring energy markets is a difficult process fraught with potential for unintended consequences. Second, trying to transform just one part of a system can create problems; California faced a troublesome conflict between local and regional practices. Local deregulation must interface with conditions at the regional and/or national level.

Phase 3: Politically Viable Emissions Policy (Mid-2000s)

California arrives at the modern period of policy making with two relevant legacies from Rounds 1 and 2 of policy making: air pollution and energy efficiency. The first is the result of the narrative that has occupied the previous two sections: California's history of successful leadership, within the context of the United States, in pollution and energy efficiency policy, and resulting regulatory infrastructure. This experience has made California more willing and able — in terms of politics, industry, and policy infrastructure — to enact green policy that could lower emissions and build green markets.

The second derives from California's general economic history of successful innovation and new business creation. This background and its commercial infrastructure legacy prepared California to undertake a new wave of business creation in a highly technical field such as clean technology. California has in place the financial expertise, related services, and intellectual infrastructure to support a thriving high-tech venture capital community, and has constituencies in place who stand to profit from venture capital activities (Lecar 2011; Randolph 2011). This venture capital community has a strong backing in technical know-how local to the state, with an emphasis on innovation and high-tech light manufacturing (Sudarshan and Sweeney 2008).

134   In addition, California's strong network of research and innovation centers
supports basic research and nurtures a community of scientists and engineers.

As the wave of industry growth from the information technology industry
boom drew to a close, all this venture capital "machinery" was in a sense left
idling. Venture capital participants began searching for the next major investment wave (Lecar 2011). This search led business interests to focus on green
technology as a rapidly growing, policy-driven market.

AB32: Green Business and Venture Capital Interests
Help Create a Cleantech Market

These conditions set the stage in 2006 for the passage of AB32, California's
climate legislation. AB32, the most expansive of a range of green policies
California has recently passed, established binding emission reduction targets
and increased policy requirements for renewable energy portfolio standards;
required vehicle efficiency; and introduced a statewide carbon cap-and-trade
program. AB32 orders the reduction of California GHG emissions to 1990
levels by 2020, a 30 percent reduction from projected business-as-usual levels.
The bill further requires an 80 percent reduction in GHG emissions by 2050.
A suite of new and existing state laws and policies intended to meet these goals
(CARB 2008) includes the following:

- Development of a *cap-and-trade program* intended to link with regional
  market systems. This will cover power plants, electricity importers,
  and high-emitting industrial combustion and processes — an estimated
  37 percent of economy-wide emissions. By 2015, coverage will extend to
  transport fuel and fuel distributors and is estimated to cover 85 percent
  of aggregate emissions.
- Increase in the preexisting *renewable portfolio standard* to 33 percent.
- California *Energy Efficiency Strategic Plan*.
- Implementation of *light-duty vehicle GHG standards*.
- Implementation of *low-carbon fuel standards*: requires major distributors
  of transportation fuels to reduce the carbon intensity of their fuels by
  10 percent in 2020.

California has also implemented other related measures, such as SB375,
which calls for regional sustainable community strategies to better integrate
housing and land use planning, to reduce transportation emissions.

In addition to their impact on emissions, it is hoped that these policies will
create long-term growth in the California economy. AB32 sent a clear signal to
cleantech business and venture capital of policy stability and support for low-
carbon technologies. The Berkeley Energy and Resources (BEAR) economic
model finds that the state's Draft Scoping Plan for AB32 will increase the gross

state product by about $76 billion, create up to 403,000 new jobs, and increase real household incomes by about $48 billion (Roland-Holst 2008).

California's general receptiveness to green energy policy was amplified by venture capital community interest. AB32 found ample support in California's business and venture capital communities (Hanemann 2007; Prabhakar 2011), in contrast to attitudes toward climate legislation seen in the business communities of many heavy manufacturing and coal-producing U.S. states. A recent analysis (Knox-Hayes 2012) of the passage of AB32 as a path-dependent outcome of "crystallization" of supportive policy coalitions based on the history of green-compatible policy (as described above) found that policy actors gave strong credit to industry within policy coalitions: venture capital support "pouring into the Bay Area" (11), "strong business communities of support," and "an active clean technology industry" (12). California's venture capital community advocated climate policy as a means to establish a market for cleantech and to ensure continuity and stability of expectations (Walsh 2010; Prabhakar 2011).

The policies have not been free of opposition. For instance, vehicle GHG standards have been challenged by national automakers in federal courts, while Proposition 23 in 2010 attempted to suspend AB32. But these challenges have thus far not found success. As we discuss below, the result of the ongoing evolution of business interests in California is that overall business opposition subsequent to AB32's passage has in fact been quite low and is continuing to decrease over time.

Post-AB32 Cleantech Investment Growth in California

While cleantech venture capital had started to grow in California prior to AB32 with a more global market focus, investment numbers in California following the initiative grew considerably (Randolph 2011). By the late 2000s, California had established a leading role in cleantech venture capital both nationally and internationally. In 2008, California captured 57 percent of U.S. cleantech venture investments, totaling $3.3 billion (BACEI 2010). Cleantech investment dipped worldwide in 2009, but it rebounded in the first half of 2010. In the second quarter of 2010, California captured 70 percent of all U.S. cleantech venture investment and 50 percent of global venture investment, with total investments of more than $1 billion (BACEI 2010). The Bay Area accounts for a particularly large and steady share of this activity. The state leads the United States in cleantech patents, with 458 registered cleantech patents between 2007 and 2009. Cleantech and green business have had positive gains on California employment as well;

136   between 1995 and 2008, it is estimated that employment in green business in the state grew 36 percent. During the 2007–2008 recession in California, when total state employment fell by 5 percent, green jobs grew 5 percent (BACEI 2010).

California's Capture of Federal Funding Supercharges Post-AB32 Cleantech Growth

California's cleantech industry growth has simultaneously benefited from an external driver: federal funding, especially from the federal stimulus package following the 2008 economic crisis. Federal funding for cleantech has come in boom and bust cycles over the last 30 years. Following an initial fervor of investment in the 1970s after the OPEC oil embargo, federal funding fell significantly (Nemet and Kammen 2007), decreasing by over 75 percent since 1978 (CBO 2010). In the last ten years, however, DoE funding has rapidly increased, supercharged by the American Recovery and Reinvestment Act following the 2008 financial crisis.

California has managed to capture a disproportionate amount of federal funding in the cleantech sector. The number of top-tier research universities exploring the issue, and their established connection to a network of early developers and venture capital, has given the state a competitive edge (Randolph 2011). California received the lion's share of U.S. stimulus funding in a number of green initiatives. Figure 8.1 shows California's dominance as a recipient of DoE funds. Out of the $34.19 billion of stimulus funds available through the national DoE, California received more funding than any other state in the categories of renewable energy, modernizing the electricity grid, and science and innovation (RATB 2011). California received almost one-quarter of total DoE stimulus funding on science and innovation, although a significant section of this funding is earmarked for security and maintenance of state nuclear arsenals. It also received large sums of funding for energy efficiency work.

Between 2008 and 2010, the Lawrence Berkeley National Laboratory and Lawrence Livermore National Laboratory received between 49 and 76 percent of the total DoE funding to California (OMB 2011). The DoE also funds more developed stages of cleantech via loan guarantees, tax credits, energy bonds in the forms of grants in place of tax credits, and direct grants (DoE 2011a). A number of cleantech venture capitalists have profited indirectly from recent DoE loan guarantees of considerable size, such as those to Solar Trust, Sunpower, Bright Source Energy, and Nordic Wind Power (DoE 2011b).

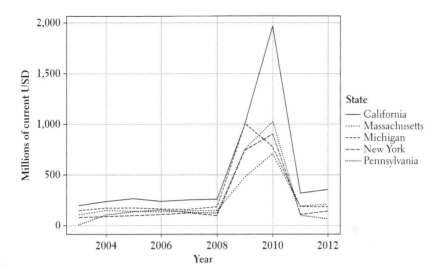

FIGURE 8.1   U.S. Department of Energy spending, contracts excluded
SOURCE: OMB 2011.
NOTE: The five states shown above are the recipients of the largest percentages of grant money from the DoE.

Phase 4: Growth of Interests Helps Green Policy Survive a Challenge (2010 and Beyond)

As the cleantech industry has grown in California, a community of advocates for climate policy has grown in the business sector. This community has both defended existing gains in green policy and pushed for more. Eric Biber's (2013) excellent and detailed analysis of the political fight surrounding Proposition 23 illustrates this dynamic. Proposition 23 was a 2010 effort to suspend AB32 until and unless the state achieved very ambitious employment levels. Biber found that the defeat of Prop. 23 relied on two shifts. First, state industry interests that might have benefited from less stringent green policy shrank, in many cases because previous policies had already forced them to commit to green improvements. Thus, for instance, the large utility Pacific Gas and Electric opposed Prop. 23. Biber suggests that that is due to PG&E's previous investment in renewable energy — made due to prior energy legislation — and the fact that previously imposed policies had rewarded utilities for focusing on consumer energy conservation. Meanwhile, Chevron stayed neutral, perhaps because of efficiency investments it had already made. Second, state industry interests that had a stake in seeing green policy continue helped to defend against Prop. 23. The state's cleantech venture capital community contributed

138   financially to the campaign to defeat Prop. 23 (although Biber notes that these interests donated more toward the end of the campaign and represented a minority of donations), while Biber suggests that growing green employment in California may have contributed to a sense among voters that Prop. 23 represented a threat to total employment rather than an economic boost.

The effects of AB32 and other prior rounds of policy thus fed back into increasing support for green policy, creating a local, predictable, growing market and source of employment, and thus strengthening its own business constituency. In essence, California's green industries are creating a symbiotic relationship with California's green policy; each supports the other and helps it grow.[5]

The Future of California's Green Spiral: Developing Challenges

Will the green spiral continue? Could it collapse? California has thus far benefited from largely unintentional feedback effects. The defense of green policy by green industry against Prop. 23 suggests that the spiral has become meaningfully self-reinforcing at this point, but its continuation is by no means written in stone. In particular, the ebbing of federal funding and the likely shift or exit of venture capital interests could lead us to anticipate changes in policy support. Below, we review the challenges that could affect — and potentially derail — the spiral.

Policy Stability

The stability of existing policy, especially federal funding and incentives, is unclear. Cleantech, to a far greater degree than its IT predecessor, relies on policy and regulation for market creation and thus finds itself at the whim of political climate. Changes in the policy environment can lead to collapse of investment, as seen with the first failure of renewable energy policy in the 1980s (Kenney 2011b). The ongoing success of California's current phase of green growth depends on its ability to maintain political will and positive feedback over time, and how the current policy experiments will play out is difficult to predict. The growing size of green industry makes for positive momentum, and AB32 provides some long-term policy stability going forward. But the tendency of federal funding, still important to maintaining momentum, to come in boom and bust cycles may be one threat to policy stability in practice.

The venture capital sector has been quite important in supporting green policy throughout the most recent rounds of policy making. However, the fundamentals of the energy market mean it is likely not a long-term match for venture capital, and venture capital's potential exit from the energy market could be an important challenge to the continuity of future policy making. The limits of venture capital investment in the energy sector and the sources of its possible exit from the sector are dealt with in depth in Chapter 4, but a few comments are called for here.

Briefly, venture capital generally works best when it enters markets that are large and rapidly growing, with technology that is scalable, non-capital-intensive, and profitable. Although the energy market is large, it tends to be slow growing, slow and expensive to scale, and capital-intensive, with long-term investment horizons and conservative buyers (see Chapters 2 and 4; also Lecar 2011). This is particularly the case in energy generation, where new plants are not built often and are expected to last decades. The volume of activity seen in cleantech venture capital in the 2000s is surprisingly large given these realities. One possible explanation is that the availability of federal funding and loan guarantees has had a distortive effect, encouraging venture capitalists to pursue not only solid investments but also some that might otherwise not make sense. As a result, the ebbing of federal funding could exacerbate the problem of venture capital exit, though it could also be beneficial to the extent that it removes incentives for unproductive investment.

The standard venture capital model is likely incompatible with cleantech development in the long term if it continues to pursue technological pathways not well suited to its strengths. Indeed, 2008 saw a reduction in cleantech investments compared with the 2003–2008 period (Moore 2011). However, it appears that something of a shift may be underway. As results come in from early rounds of investment, venture capital is in a "period of reassessment"; many are shifting their focus to more scalable, less capital-intensive, more rapidly profitable technologies like efficiency technologies (Prabhakar 2011). The year 2008 saw an increase in activity from cleantech-specialized venture capital investments (Moore 2011). Rather than following projects to completion in the more traditional venture capital model, these firms are instead focused on capturing a part of the cleantech supply chain, such as early- or later-stage development (Redman 2011). The cleantech venture capital industry has also witnessed the entrance of a number of large corporate players, which may prove better suited to handle the capital

140   intensity and long investment horizons of cleantech. Some of these take a traditional corporate investment form, while others are invested in third-party venture funds focused on cleantech (Reuters 2010), some significantly (Kanellos 2010; Danko 2011).

COLORADO

Key Lessons

In Colorado, constituents with an existing desire for lowering GHG emissions passed emissions-reduction legislation whose feedback effects then helped create the interest configuration needed to sustain it, crystallizing a latent coalition of interests they perceived.[6] In essence, they consciously initiated a green spiral. This is a contrast with the California case, in which an unintended feedback loop of green policy ultimately created the will for political action. Colorado's movement toward green growth policy has developed recently through the relatively rapid creation of a supportive coalition behind it. Thus, unlike California, Colorado's green growth policy did not emerge as a long history of iterative, path-dependent rounds of policy making that predated conscious concern over climate and emissions, building supportive interests and neutralizing potential obstacles only incidentally. Rather, policy in Colorado was crafted with conscious intent to both address carbon emissions and overcome the typical obstacles to green policy—such as business community skepticism and political opposition. It generated bipartisan support such as that of Republican Speaker Lola Spradley. So here we analyze the Colorado case by laying out the question of how and why a green policy has come together, and come together quite rapidly, in Colorado.

Colorado's experience suggests two lessons. First, Colorado was able to make a relatively rapid shift toward a green industry path because policy leaders identified a *latent* potential partnership between multiple, very different constituencies who all had interests that could be served by similar green growth policies. This provided an opportunity for an eventual policy realignment based on an informal partnership among these groups. Once the tangible benefits of policy manifested, this latent coalition solidified.

Second, Colorado's story demonstrates the importance of policy moves that have immediate, tangible, ongoing benefits for constituencies that otherwise might be skeptical of green policy. Such policy moves can fundamentally alter the political landscape, creating new supporters for green policy and thus broadening the potential coalition for green policy. In a conceptual sense, this is the heart of "green growth" policy: environmentalists have always supported renewables, but the "green growth" argument focuses on showing other groups that they have real, direct economic interests in green policy as well. In Colorado, a latent coalition existed, but the tangible benefits of early policy moves for potential members of that coalition helped bring that coalition together and solidify it.

141

Overview

Despite its vast reserves of fossil fuel,[7] the state of Colorado has recently embarked on a surprising green growth path. In 2004, a grassroots advocacy movement in support of renewable energy put a renewable portfolio standard (RPS) on the ballot: Amendment 37 called for renewable energy standards and several related measures. Despite opposition from major stakeholders like the utility company Xcel, the measure passed by slightly more than 50 percent (Broehl 2004). Colorado met its initial RPS goals ahead of schedule and

---

COLORADO TIMELINE—PURPOSIVE CREATION OF GREEN SPIRAL

Phase 1: 2004—Initial Policy Movement: The Renewable Portfolio Standard (RPS) and Related Policies
Amendment 37, a citizen ballot measure with bipartisan support calling for renewable energy standards and several related measures, passes in the general election. Democrats gain a majority in the state legislature. Previously, Colorado's Republican-controlled General Assembly defeats multiple attempts to pass clean energy and RPS legislation.

Phase 2: 2006—The Green Coalition Comes into Its Own
Following a period of blockage where support built and additional green bills were passed by the legislature but vetoed by Republican Governor Bill Owens, Governor Bill Ritter, a Democrat, is elected after making green energy a primary issue in his campaign.

Phase 3: 2007–2010—Turning Opponents into Allies: Results of Policy Moves Feedback
Colorado passes over 50 pieces of legislation intended to advance the "New Energy Economy" (Clean Air Clean Jobs Act 2010, among others). In March 2007, the legislature ups the RPS to 20 percent by 2020; in 2010, it is again raised to 30 percent.

Phase 4: 2011–Present—Challenges
Shrinking federal funding and cuts to state funding begin to create future challenges for green policy.

142   has since raised the standard twice, making its current goals second only to California's among U.S. states (Minard 2010). Colorado's green industries have been booming in the past few years; the state has attracted global green technology leaders like the wind turbine maker Vestas, which will hire 2,500 local workers (Ritter 2010).

Phase 1: Initial Policy Movement — The Renewable Portfolio Standard (2004)

The critical questions in the Colorado story are first, what allowed Colorado to pass a citizen-supported RPS measure like Amendment 37 (a particularly startling achievement given that similar legislation had repeatedly died in the state's General Assembly), and second, once Amendment 37 passed, what drove Colorado on the relatively fast track of green policy that it has seen — from a 10 percent RPS, to 20 percent, to 30 percent — with accompanying growth in installed energy base and local green business? Below, we argue that the answer lies in a combination of (1) a public advocacy effort that attempted to show very different constituencies in Colorado how clean energy could meet their different needs, thus building a proto-coalition among several communities; (2) a fertile environment provided by local centers of research and business innovation in cleantech; (3) coincidental funding assistance from the federal government; and (4) immediate reinforcement generated by early successes.

The Latent Coalition: Sources of Public Support

Colorado's population can be divided into three major geographic groups, each of which has its own economic and ideological makeup regarding renewable energy. The *front range area* in central Colorado includes Colorado's major urban centers and tends to be more progressive and Democratic-leaning than the rest of the state. Colorado's urban, Democratic administrators are more likely to implement renewable energy projects (Davis and Hoffer 2010). Eight out of Colorado's 13 coal-fired power plants are also near front-range cities, and there have been recent protests in Coloradan cities against coal-fired plants (Finley 2009; Espinoza 2010).

The *rural plains counties* in eastern Colorado tend to be more conservative and Republican. Republican support for renewable energy is generally lower. However, agricultural communities have a history of utilizing wind as an important power source (Davis and Hoffer 2010). With an RPS, they can increase their income by selling homegrown renewable energy back to utilities or by leasing land to wind farms. The support of Republican former

Speaker Lola Spradley, who represented a rural constituency in eastern Colorado from 2003 to 2004, was indispensable to the eventual creation and passage of Amendment 37 and provided significant rhetorical support for the effort (Plant 2011).

Finally, the *western mountain counties* are rural and relatively independent politically. These areas tend to have less in the way of exploitable wind energy. But tourism is a major industry, meaning that protecting the natural landscape is important.

In other words, advocates of Amendment 37 had arguments to offer voters in each area. In addition, rate payers in all areas had opportunities to gain from the RPS if they installed solar. The legislation offered consumers rebates, potential buybacks of homegrown renewable energy, and guaranteed low impact on rates.

Precisely how critical the arguments made to each constituency were to the success of Amendment 37 is difficult to determine definitively. It is clear that support from urban front-range and western mountain counties formed a core part of the vote for 37. Voting returns show that *all* of the Colorado counties in which Amendment 37 received more than 50 percent of the vote were front-range or western mountain counties. In the rural eastern plains counties, the amendment faced not only general ideological opposition but direct, specific opposition from rural power generation co-ops that felt threatened by the measure (Baker 2011). A poll roughly a month before the election did show that a plurality of Republicans in the state supported the measure (45 percent favoring and 33 percent opposed [Frates and Cox 2004]), and Spradley made a concerted effort to reach these voters with an economic message about potential monetary benefits of local wind installations (Olinger 2004; Paulson 2004; Purdy 2004).

Ultimately, the measure failed to win any of the eastern plains counties outright. However, without efforts to court these voters, 37 might have done even worse in these areas, potentially resulting in a statewide loss. These efforts may also have paved the way for a subsequent quick turnaround to acceptance of the benefits of the RPS in following years (discussed below).

Phase 2: The Green Coalition Comes into Its Own —
Additional Sources of Policy Support (2006)

Research, Development, and Green Industries

Colorado has a longer history in green innovation and industry than in green policy per se. Colorado houses three national laboratories, all of which

144   contribute to research and development in climate change mitigation technologies. The state of Colorado has created a "collaboratory" of higher-education centers and research institutions that works closely with the private sector to ensure the rapid transfer and commercialization of new technologies. A fourth national laboratory, the National Institute for Standards and Technology, is playing a leading role in establishment of smart grid standards. Colorado also has successful renewable energy and energy efficiency firms that predate the key legislations of the mid-2000s.

Since Governor Ritter's "New Energy Economy" program began to take off, green industries have been expanding rapidly, with help from the research community and federal support in Colorado. (ASES [2008] provides a detailed overview of Colorado green industry.) By 2007, the renewable energy and energy efficiency industries had generated $10.2 billion in revenue and hired 91,285 workers (Bezdek 2009, 47). During the same year, the total revenue for the oil and gas industry was $17.2 billion, and the industry employed 70,779 workers (MacDonald et al. 2007, 55). Though green industries generated less revenue than the oil and gas industry, it hired more workers.

In addition, Colorado also has a generally attractive business environment, featuring low corporate and income tax rates and a highly educated workforce. Forbes rated it the fourth best place to do business in the United States (Baden-hausen 2010). In combination with the low-carbon/green growth policies of 2004 and later, these conditions proved attractive to global cleantech leaders that have located in Colorado, like Vestas and its suppliers.

Policy Viability Funding Gives the Green Spiral a Boost

Colorado also benefited, at least in the short term, from a coincidental conjunction with federal funding trends. Green policy took off in 2007 and 2008 with incoming Governor Ritter. Shortly thereafter, the global economic downturn led to the passage of the U.S. stimulus bill, the American Recovery and Reinvestment Act (ARRA). Since a meaningful percentage of ARRA funds were focused on renewable energy and efficiency in both new and existing programs, the sudden influx of funding from the federal government in areas like efficiency, weatherization, and renewable energy provided both a safety net for existing programs (that might otherwise have been cut in the face of state budget difficulties) and a kickstart for programs that would otherwise have been slower or impossible to start, providing levels of funding larger and faster than those that states had envisioned for themselves (Plant 2011).

Phase 3: Turning Opponents into Allies—Results of Policy   145
Moves Feed Back (2007–2010)

In addition to the growth of its green industry sector, Colorado's green policy support was ultimately strengthened by the eventual tolerance or active support of several critical allies in the conventional energy industry, spurred by the configuration of policy proposed. In several cases, the immediate outcomes of Amendment 37—which turned out to be easier to achieve than utilities expected and provided tangible benefits to rural plains voters— significantly raised support for renewables and green policy, particularly in the eastern plains counties.

Energy Industry

Given Colorado's extraction industries, it is not surprising that energy industry stakeholders at first strongly resisted low-carbon legislations. Colorado's Republican-controlled senate rejected the RPS in 2003 and 2004, before Amendment 37 passed as a ballot initiative. However, subsequent to Amendment 37, several important players in Colorado's energy industry have found reasons to support green policy, at least in the short to medium term. Xcel Energy, the most influential utility company in Colorado, opposed the 10 percent RPS in the beginning but quickly had a change of heart and ultimately supported the increase of the RPS, first to 20 percent and then to 30 percent. Xcel realized it would not be difficult to meet the 20 percent target, as federal tax credits after 2008 made wind energy affordable (Minard 2010). With Colorado's significant wind potential, improving technologies, and volatile, increasing fossil fuel prices, wind energy may become competitive faster than envisioned. This could be stalled if the price of natural gas remains low and the production tax credit, upon which companies like Vestas heavily rely, is not renewed by Congress.

A large sector of Colorado's oil and gas industry has also jumped on the green-growth wagon, at least temporarily, offering full support for Colorado's latest Clean Air Clean Jobs Act. Under implementation of this act, Xcel will retire two old coal-fired power plants and retrofit one of them to burn natural gas. Given that coal provided for 65.2 percent of Colorado's electricity in 2008, while natural gas only provided 25.2 percent (EIA 2010a), natural gas producers stand to gain a much bigger market share at the expense of the coal industry. Indeed, there has been a publicity battle between the coal and the oil and gas industries over the Clean Air Clean Jobs Act.

While natural gas burns cleaner than coal, it is a nonrenewable energy source that produces greenhouse gas emission and can only serve as a bridging fuel rather than a long-term solution. Support from the oil and gas industry may become shakier if Colorado moves further along the green growth path, although self-reinforcing effects of green policy–created constituencies, like those seen in the California case, may compensate for this if such interests are sufficiently developed.

Consumers

Meanwhile, experience with renewables, and particularly wind, has increased support for green policy among rural consumers. By 2006, some of these constituencies had begun to receive tangible benefits from local eastern plains wind installations. Observers familiar with Colorado politics suggest support has risen throughout the state, but especially among Republicans and in the eastern plains counties.

A demonstration of this effect is found among electoral returns for races that touched on this issue. Governor Bill Ritter made renewable energy a critical part of his campaign platform in 2006, making 2006 something of a referendum on the program's success thus far. Ritter did well in the 2006 election, and notably, he did significantly better among eastern plains voters than Amendment 37 had done two years before. Although Ritter generally did not receive an overall majority in these politically conservative areas, he was competitive; in eastern plains counties that had major wind installations in place or under construction by 2006 (Bent, Logan, Prowers, and Weld), he received between 47 and 57 percent of the vote. In the eight eastern plains counties that had given Amendment 37 less than one-third of their vote, Ritter typically received around 13 percent more of the vote than Amendment 37 had.

Phase 4: Challenges (2011–Present)

Green growth policy nonetheless faces clear obstacles in both the present and the near future. As discussed in the previous section, natural gas is only a bridging fuel. Colorado's policy makers likely cannot count on long-term support from the oil and gas industry, especially when the price of natural gas is low. Also, Colorado lacks the transmission capacity to best exploit renewable energy. Xcel Energy tried to kickstart solar projects in southwestern Colorado, but an influential local landowner successfully fought running a transmission line across his ranch (Minard 2010). Public resistance is especially pronounced against transmission lines crossing residential areas or private lands (Davis and Hoffer 2010). The promotion of distributed generation at customers' facilities also requires the grid to be able to accommodate distributed, intermittent power sources. As it is everywhere, upgrading to a renewable-friendly transmission grid will be a major challenge for Colorado.

Colorado, like most other states, also faces some political and structural challenges to green policy. These include uncertainty over future federal funding (Plant 2011). As noted above, Colorado's green policy has benefited from federal funding. The corollary to this, however, is the potential challenge facing Colorado and other states as ARRA winds down. Funding for many of these programs, such as weatherization, is expiring or being cut. The need to replace these programs at the state level as the influx from the federal level ebbs will be a huge challenge in the near future, and it is uncertain how effectively states will respond. An inability to find replacements could slow down industry growth significantly (Plant 2011). This could have a significant potential to derail Colorado's shift toward green policy in the same sense that the trailing off of federal subsidies and exhaustion of the cleantech venture capital wave could derail California's story.

In addition, other possible obstacles include potential exhaustion of the renewable energy "low-hanging fruit," leading to higher future costs; a return to partisanship after a honeymoon period of general support; and some internal fracturing of the green energy community (Baker 2011). Colorado Governor John Hickenlooper, elected in 2010, has not made renewable energy a top priority. The critical question for Colorado going forward is similar to that in California. To what extent have the strong successes of existing policy created a stable, embedded constituency for green industry — from new manufacturing installations to rural landowners that have made wind leasing a part of their income base to houses that have invested in solar panels — that will carry it forward through funding uncertainties and the challenges of increasing scale?

CONCLUSION: STATE-LEVEL GREEN SPIRALS

Federal funding and research support have created broadly permissive conditions that have accelerated policy movements in particular states. But states' individual decisions about whether to pursue particular green growth policy options differ significantly. They differ partly because the particular characteristics of states differ — in terms of resource profile, industrial profile, infrastructure, geography, and political and policy history. Similarly, states have a wide variety of locally specific policy veto points, key players, and gatekeepers. These can range from physical blocks like unsuitable infrastructure to political blocks like resistant citizens. Again, these emerge from the particular political and economic structures of states and are separate from the veto points found at the federal level. Ultimately, successful green growth stories happen

148   when (a) a high enough proportion of relevant key players support specific green growth policies and (b) veto points are avoided or overcome.

In a sense, of course, this is a truism, but it is important to clearly state the point, because it suggests precisely what we see in our case studies: that green policy will be most successful over the long term when it increases the number of supporting interests or decreases the number of interests with incentives to block further policy. Our cases suggest that individual moves toward green growth policy (such as energy efficiency and renewables policies) can be self-reinforcing. This occurs if green policy moves create observable benefits and learning effects, encourage investment, and increase comfort levels in ways that increase the proportion of key players that are willing to support or tolerate green growth policy. The evolution of green growth policy is path-dependent, with prior history shaping the tools accessible to policy makers. Particular choices regarding infrastructure or policy at one point in a state's history serve to enable or choke off access to subsequent choices in the next phase of policy making: in effect, the concept of the "green policy spiral" suggested in the introduction to Part II.

This effect emerges in different ways in the two cases examined in depth. California's story is one not of intent but favorable and self-reinforcing accident: early crises triggered early energy policy moves, which created the grounds for later, stronger policy. By contrast, Colorado's story is a more intentional one: policy makers were able to identify a latent coalition that could be formed among different groups with the potential to profit from green policy. This coalition was then able to harness the reinforcing effects of the immediate, tangible benefits provided by that policy, which strengthened the argument pulling coalition members together and now shows signs of becoming self-reinforcing in the way the California story has.

This should not be taken to suggest that an ongoing march toward ever more stringent regulation of carbon emissions is inevitable in any of the U.S. states. The growth of constituencies around existing green policy makes the creation of additional green policy in the future easier and more likely. But it is certainly the case that countervailing forces or shocks to the system could derail these "spirals." In our analysis of California and Colorado, we see that the policy spirals of both are being challenged by recent events such as the subsidence of federal funding and the venture capital mismatch. An important question for both cases, therefore, is whether sufficient green interests will remain to support the symbiotic business/policy relationship as the venture funding and federal subsidy waves recede and whether alternate and more appropriate funding models can be found to fill the space left by this change.

What does this mean for green policy at the national level? Chapter 7 presents the European case as one in which individual stories eventually coalesced into a federal story. Partly as a result of the particular policy narratives of European countries, Europe ended up with an aggregate configuration of interests that had a large enough proportion of green interests and a small enough proportion of brown/fossil fuel interests that a green deal was politically viable and served multiple players. The United States as a whole has, at best, not traveled far enough down that road to see similar federal-level results. Although there has been some unilateral movement by the executive branch, the United States is not at a point where Congress will move on green legislation. Green interests are growing in particular areas, such as California and Colorado. But they are not yet large enough at the national level to create a coalition capable of outweighing fossil fuel interests like coal, oil, and energy-intensive manufacturing. The green spiral remains local, location-specific, and tentative. Whether the balance will shift in the future remains to be seen.

9

JAPAN

*Paragon of Energy Efficiency, Green Growth
Laggard*

Brian Woodall

INTRODUCTION

A rich country with strength in innovation, Japan has compelling reasons to
move its large, mature economy onto a sustainable, low-carbon trajectory. Yet,
despite heavy dependence on imported fossil fuels, Japan has yet to create a
policy environment that enables achievement of the country's full potential
in reducing emissions, expanding cleantech capabilities and use, and exploiting untapped endowments of renewable energy resources.[1] Faced with rising
fossil fuel costs and supply risks, Japan's core strategy was to increase reliance
on nuclear power, which, tragically, produced the 2011 Fukushima crisis. Putting aside concerns about energy security, diversification of supply, and calls
for policies to mitigate climate change, it is logical to assume that Japan's
R&D prowess would translate into a dominant position in the development
of renewable energy technologies (Kitazuma 2008).[2] Yet, even a government
report conceded that Japan's "excellent technological strength at the highest
global standards, including registered patents in the environmental field, . . .
has not necessarily led to the full penetration of the global market or development of new products" (MOE 2010, 161). In fact, Japan ranked 20th on the
2012 Global Cleantech Innovation Index, whose authors concluded that the
country has not translated innovation into entrepreneurial cleantech start-ups
(Knowles et al. 2012, 15, 23; also Pew Environment Group 2012, 44). These lackluster results stand in puzzling contrast to Japan's leading role in introducing
and commercializing green technologies in the automotive sector.

Japan's "surprisingly unambitious" commitment to a green growth strategy is
even more puzzling considering earlier success in reducing pollution, enhanc-

ing efficiency, and still maintaining economic growth.[3] By the late 1960s, an environmental movement emerged to protest the consequences of a business-first strategy that allowed companies to reap profits without heed to the social costs of the pollutants emitted from their factories. In response, pro-business policy makers deftly reversed course, passing legislation that brought pollution levels on par with those of other industrialized countries. Then the oil shocks of the 1970s exposed the fallacy of a national strategy premised upon a continuous supply of cheap imported oil to fuel an export-oriented economy driven by heavy industry. Government responded by passing an energy conservation law in which industry took the lead in making Japan into an exemplar of energy efficiency. Japan bounced back faster than any of the major industrialized countries from the downturn that followed the 1973 oil shock and went on to realize two decades of sustained economic prosperity. How was it that the Japanese were able to do all this, but have not committed to a national strategy that alleviates concerns about energy supply and security, better exploits renewable resources, and incentivizes Japanese companies to take a leading position in the $5 trillion global energy market with increasing demand for cleantech?

Japan's failure to fully buy into a green growth strategy is the result of regulatory capture by an alliance of policy makers and strategic parts of industry with a commitment to carbon-intensive and nuclear energy. This Brown + Nuclear Coalition (hereafter referred to as the Coalition) formed in the mid-1950s and evolved into a formidable subgovernment. The Coalition's key actors include government bureaucrats, officials of the ten regulated regional electrical utility monopolies, and elected politicians. The main bureaucratic actors are officials at the Ministry of Economy, Trade, and Industry (METI), which, until recently, was responsible for promoting *and* regulating the energy sector. As with all Japanese government officials, many METI bureaucrats retire early and "descend from heaven" (*amakudari*) into "second careers" in the private sector. Between the early 1960s and the 2010s, 68 METI "old boys" descended into positions at the regional utility companies.[4] In exchange for these postretirement sinecures, it is rumored that METI officials provide lenient regulatory oversight and ignore safety violations. Bureaucrats also supply policy information that is akin to staff support to their allies in the Diet (Japan's parliament), and they reportedly direct the utility companies to fund supportive candidates for elective office.[5] In return, the favored lawmakers ensure a robust energy budget and enact policies that serve the interests of the utility companies (Onishi and Fackler 2011). In addition, official deliberation councils (*shingikai*), labor unions, academic researchers, construction contractors, and localities hosting those plants (especially the nuclear facilities) play supportive roles in the Coalition.

The Coalition pressed policies that fortified Japan's commitment to fossil fuels and nuclear energy, which ensured that a Green Coalition never achieved critical mass. Japan's piecemeal green growth policies were forged in four phases. Phase I (1955 to 1969) was characterized by a national strategy that assumed an uninterrupted supply of cheap energy, while companies in the favored industries paid little heed to the social costs of high-speed growth. Phase II (1970 to 1989) was ushered in amidst the environmental movement of the late 1960s and the angst spawned by the oil shocks of the 1970s. It was during this period that Japan curbed pollution and achieved energy efficiency without sacrificing economic growth. Phase III (1990 to 2000)—which followed the bursting of the "bubble economy"—was characterized by economic stagnation and policy immobility, while Phase IV (2001 to 2010) was marked by efforts to deregulate and privatize energy markets. It remains to be seen whether the natural disasters and nuclear crisis unleashed on March 11, 2011, will create a supportive policy environment that actively encourages new infrastructure and energy approaches that produce a Japanese green spiral.

PHASE I: CHEAP ENERGY AND HIGH-SPEED GROWTH, 1955–1969

By the mid-1950s, Japan was on the cusp of a decade of double-digit annual economic growth rates. In 1961, the government launched a plan to double GNP by the end of the decade, but the goal was achieved in just six years. Much of this growth was generated by export-oriented "strategic industries"— particularly heavy materials industries such as steel, shipbuilding, machine tools, and automobiles—that were nurtured by policies crafted at the Ministry of International Trade and Industry (MITI—the predecessor of today's METI). These favored industries were assured ready access to inexpensive electricity supplied by coal- and oil-powered thermal as well as nuclear power plants operated by ten regional electric utilities (Murota and Yano 1993, 91–97).[6] And these strategically important industries—which later came to include semiconductors and consumer electronics—were allowed to mature in a relatively stable, predictable, and *insulated* domestic market that gave advantages in production and international competition to Japanese firms (Borrus, Millstein, and Zysman 1984, 147). With the founding of the Liberal Democratic Party (LDP) in November 1955, the captains of these smokestack industries and their MITI allies found powerful patrons among lawmakers of a political party that would rule the country for the next five and a half decades. And so it was that the Coalition was formed, initiating more than five decades of uninterrupted regulatory capture.

The Coalition's vitality and staying power derived, in part, from the fact that one political party dominated Japan's parliamentary realm from 1955 until 2009. Over the course of the more than half a century of almost unrivalled dominance, mutually beneficial ties binding the LDP to METI and the utility companies became institutionalized. As one of the "three noble houses" (*go-sanke*)—along with steelmakers and financial institutions—that supplied political funding to the LDP, the utility companies could count on the perpetually ruling party to sponsor beneficial policies. Even after Japan's campaign finance law was tightened in 1974 to limit corporate donations, the utility companies continued to funnel political money to preferred candidates by ordering top officials to make *individual* donations to the People's Political Association (*Kokuminseijikyōkai*), the LDP's political fund agent. For example, between 1995 and 2009, some 448 officials of Tokyo Electric Power Company (TEPCO)—the largest of the utility companies—donated a total of nearly $750,000 (¥59,570,000) to the fund agent.[7] Reportedly, TEPCO was pressed to fund the campaign of its former vice-president, who was running with the LDP's endorsement in the 1998 Upper House elections (*Asahi Shinbun*, October 8, 2011). Would-be challengers confronted the specter of a perpetually ruling party with ironclad ties to an elite ministry of the government bureaucracy and deep-pocketed corporate backers. And the labor union supporters of the Democratic Party of Japan, which, in 2009, unseated the LDP, have steered the new ruling party to embrace pro-Coalition policies (*Akahata*, August 17, 2011).

Sustained economic growth became the driver of a "business first" strategy premised upon an unimpeded supply of low-cost energy. The rationale behind Japan's strategy was articulated by economist Hiromi Arisawa, who argued that "providing cheap energy engenders immense economic benefit for the nation . . . [and] interruption of supply is a rare danger. We cannot, because of such a small possibility of danger, demote this cardinal principle of cheap energy to a secondary position" (quoted in Murota and Yano 1993, 103). In the unlikely event that shipments of imported oil were to be disrupted, low-cost nuclear power would ensure an adequate energy supply. The nuclear option was made possible by the Diet's passage, in December 1955, of the Atomic Energy Basic Law, whose stated aims included the enhancement of energy security, industrial promotion, and people's living standards. Japan's first nuclear reactor was a research plant that began operations in 1963, while the first commercial reactor started up in 1966. Meanwhile, companies in the favored smokestack industries powered by this supposedly unrestricted supply of cheap energy reaped windfall profits without concern for the social costs of

154   the pollutants emitted from their factories. Consequently, as the 1960s drew to a close, Japan's badly polluted air and waterways became emblemized in the "four great pollution diseases," including Minamata disease, Niigata Minamata disease, Itaiitai disease, and Yokkaichi asthma.

The Coalition met little resistance in pressing its cheap energy, growth-at-any-cost strategy. Policy makers ignored a mounting body of scientific evidence linking human deaths and disease to decades of unrestrained environmental pollution.[8] And government turned a blind eye when pollution-emitting companies hired thugs to intimidate victims and physicians who pressed lawsuits against those companies (George 2001). In the meantime, energy consumption increased dramatically as the economy grew at a breathtaking pace and more citizens came to enjoy the fruits of economic prosperity. Between 1965 and 1969, Japan's overall energy consumption expanded by 60 percent, while reliance on petroleum more than doubled (METI 2010).[9] But as long as the economy kept growing and giant oil tankers continued to offload their cargoes at Japanese refineries, the Coalition's business-first policies enjoyed nationwide support.

PHASE II: CURBING ENERGY CONSUMPTION IN A BUBBLE ECONOMY, 1970–1989

Policy Drivers

By the end of the 1960s, Japanese policy makers could no longer ignore a dangerously polluted environment. An environmental protection movement emerged in the mid-1960s and coalesced around victims of pollution-related diseases and denizens of heavily industrialized urban areas (Reich 1984, 390).[10] Buoyed by court rulings in favor of victims of the pollution-related diseases, thousands of citizens' groups sprouted up (McKean 1981, 17, 20; Mason 1999, 189). Opposition parties championed environmental protection, which became the dominant issue on the political agenda.[11] The threatened embargo by the Organization of Petroleum Exporting Countries (OPEC) in October 1973 led to a quadrupling in the price of oil that necessitated a rethinking of energy strategy (ANRE 2010, 4). By this point, however, Japan had become more reliant on oil than any other developed country (Stewart and Wilczewski 2009). While Japanese manufacturers pondered how to deal with radically higher fuel costs and an uncertain energy supply, panic-stricken homemakers stocked up on toilet paper and other commodities. And everyone in this nation of "workaholics" dreaded the approaching winter months with the possibility of no heating oil to warm the "rabbit hutches" in which they lived.[12] A second oil shock—set loose by the ouster of the shah of Iran in January

1979—sent the price of oil spiraling to $34 per barrel and further exacerbated
Japan's sense of energy insecurity.

Policy Tools

Policy makers responded by enacting laws to reduce pollution, promote energy efficiency, and develop new and renewable sources. The Basic Law for Environmental Pollution Control, enacted in August 1967, was the first clear sign that the pro-business, LDP-led government was willing to do something about the effects of decades of environmental degradation. While the law was carefully crafted to ensure that environmental protection would not impede economic development, it set the stage for the passage of 14 pollution-related laws by the "Pollution Diet" of 1970. A cabinet-level Environment Agency was established the following year, and MITI's *Vision for the 1970s* made the case for "technology driven clean energy in an ecological context" (Watanabe 1995). Although the government dragged its feet in responding to environmental concerns, progress in cleaning up the air and waterways came swiftly, and Japanese companies soon became world leaders in the production of pollution-control devices (Pempel 1982, 232).

The government enacted measures to encourage "energy conservation" (*shōenerugii*) through tax incentives, subsidies, and preferential loans, most of which were directed at the industrial sector. In November 1973, the Diet passed an Emergency Petroleum Countermeasures Policy to encourage energy conservation, and five years later, public funds from MITI's budget were combined with private-sector monies to establish the Japan Energy Conservation Center, which was tasked with administering examinations to certify enterprise-level "energy managers" and collect efficiency data (ECCJ 2010a). The 1979 Energy Conservation Act—known officially as the Law Concerning the Rational Use of Energy—established criteria to constrain energy use within the industrial, commercial and residential building, machinery/equipment, and transport sectors. It featured measures to encourage efficiency, including low-interest loans, tax breaks, grants, and the mandatory appointment of an energy manager within individual factories and workplaces (Shiel, Jeffers, and Dyar 2011, 7–23).

A crucial moment arrived in 1973, when the decision was made to dramatically expand Japan's reliance on nuclear power. In July, just prior to the OPEC oil embargo, the Agency for Natural Resources and Energy (ANRE) was established within MITI, consolidating administration of petroleum, coal, electric utilities (including nuclear power generation), and energy conservation under "one powerful unit" (Johnson 1982, 296–297). ANRE's mission was to ensure

156   a stable, efficient supply of energy and mineral resources and to promote their appropriate and safe usage. In the aftermath of the first oil shock, government enacted laws providing generous subsidies to municipalities hosting nuclear power plants. These plants brought jobs, and the subsidies funded recreation centers, roadways, and parks for towns and villages suffering from the loss of tax revenues caused by depopulation. In addition, construction contractors, suppliers of nuclear technology, and large manufacturers, which viewed nuclear power as a reliable, low-cost option, rejoiced. Despite local protests and safety concerns, the government steadfastly pressed the case for greater reliance on nuclear energy, which grew from 1 percent of total energy supply in 1973 to 5 percent in 1980 to 10 percent in 1986 (ANRE 2010). Not even the Three Mile Island or Chernobyl nuclear crises prompted a rethinking of policies in support of atomic power and the partial self-sufficiency it promised (of course, Japan must import the uranium needed to power the nuclear plants) (Fackler and Onishi 2011).

Japan's first tentative steps to promote cleantech development were taken in the aftermath of the 1970s oil shocks. The "Sunshine Program," which began in 1974, provided R&D funding for renewable energy technologies (Daily Yomiuri Online, August 16, 2011). But the sun did not shine brightly on the project's budget, which, between 1974 and 1978, accounted for only 3 percent of MITI's energy-related special accounts budgets.[13] By 1978, Sunshine Program funding had produced a handful of small-scale solar, geothermal, and coal liquefaction generating plants, most of which were research facilities (Murota and Yano 1993, 115). That same year, MITI launched the "Moonlight Program" to administer large-scale R&D projects for improving energy efficiency (Daily Yomiuri Online, August 16, 2011). But it, too, was hamstrung by a minuscule budget amounting to less than 1 percent of energy-related allocations (Murota and Yano 1993, 116). And in October 1980, the Law Concerning the Promotion of the Development and Introduction of Alternative Energy established the New Energy and Development Organization, which distributed R&D subsidies and conducted studies to develop solar and geothermal power, coal gasification and liquefaction, and other new energy sources (NEDO 2000, 19).[14]

Obstacles

The Coalition was forced to pay heed to environmental concerns and pursue an energy strategy that no longer assumed an unlimited supply of cheap oil. A rising chorus of demands to clean up the polluted air and waterways was largely silenced following the enactment of antipollution laws that produced palpable results without derailing the export-driven industrial juggernaut. By the outset of the 1980s, Japan's most egregious environmental problems had been solved, and the country boasted standards of air and water purity that rivaled those of most any major industrialized country. Meanwhile, the Coalition promoted LP gas and nuclear power, while refusing to commit to more fully developing renewable energy. As a result, the contribution of renewables to Japan's total primary power supply did not exceed 1 percent until 1990. With considerable sunk investment in fossil fuel and nuclear energy systems, and disdainful of the concentrated costs and diffuse, distant benefits likely to derive from greater reliance on renewables, the Coalition easily brushed aside resistance to its policy agenda.

Results

Japan responded to the oil shocks by diversifying its energy supply, promoting energy efficiency, and curbing pollution. Between 1973 and 1989, petroleum's share of the primary energy supply dropped from 75 percent to 56 percent. Meanwhile, the shares of LP gas (2 percent to 11 percent) and nuclear power (1 percent to 10 percent) increased, while those of coal (which ranged between 17 and 20 percent), hydroelectric (4 to 5 percent), and renewables (1 percent) remained essentially unchanged (ANRE 2010). In the aftermath of the 1979 oil shock, the industrial sector led an aggressive efficiency campaign. Although energy consumed by the transportation, commercial, and residential sectors continued to expand, the industrial sector's consumption of energy was reduced and held in check thereafter. And enormous strides were made in cleaning up the country's air and waterways. According to government data, the annual average of sulfur dioxide in the air was cut from 0.034 parts per million to 0.006 ppm between 1970 and 1985, while significant reductions were also seen in the nitrogen oxides, carbon monoxide, and suspended particulate matter. These achievements were aided by the efforts of municipalities, such as Kawasaki City, which transformed itself from a polluted wretch of a place into a vibrant, "environmentally friendly city" (Environmental Measures in Kawasaki City).[15] And Japan was able to do all this while continuing to grow the economy, which expanded by threefold between 1974 and 1989.

PHASE III: "LOST DECADE," LOST GREEN OPPORTUNITY, 1990–2000

After the "bubble economy" abruptly burst in late 1989, Japan's banks found themselves buried under a mountain of nonperforming loans, much of which

158   was collateralized in real estate now worth a fraction of its hyperinflated values. Throughout the "lost decade" (*ushinawaretajūnen*) of the 1990s, the economy remained mired in stagnation, while a succession of governments proved unable to make the difficult choices needed to pull the economy out of a prolonged malaise. The captains of industry could no longer take refuge in a large, stable, and insulated domestic market that had nurtured the country's world-class steel, automobile, and semiconductor manufacturers. Because many de facto protectionist barriers had been grudgingly dismantled, Japanese firms faced withering competition from foreign competitors with lower-priced labor. Moreover, while Toyota and Honda were able to take advantage of energy efficiency branding to produce and market green automobiles, other Japanese cleantech products did not have the same branding appeal and suffered from lack of access to venture capital, which had never been Japan's strong suit (e.g., Pew Environment Group 2012). The "lost decade" would become a decade of lost green opportunity.

The decade's only significant green policy initiative was the *New* Sunshine Program, essentially an amalgamation of the *old* Sunshine Program and the Moonlight Program. Launched in 1993, the New Sunshine Program was a comprehensive national project whose aim was to promote technological development in new energy fields, with particular emphasis on solar energy (Daily Yomiuri Online, August 16, 2011; DeWit and Iida 2011). Its most palpable accomplishment was the "Rooftop Program," the world's first large-scale development of photovoltaic technology, which demonstrated its feasibility as an energy source.[16] In contrast to previous initiatives that focused on energy security, the New Sunshine Program explicitly aimed to combat global warming.[17] This dovetailed with the position taken at the 1992 "Earth Summit," when the Japanese government pledged to use foreign aid and technology transfers to promote the utilization of green technologies and to help solve environmental problems in the developing world (Meakin 1992).[18] And Japan assumed the spotlight by hosting the 1997 United Nations Framework Convention on Climate Change, which produced the Kyoto Protocol. For a time, it seemed that the Japanese were on the verge of putting forth a comprehensive program to reduce greenhouse gas emissions. And yet, nine years later when California's Assembly Bill 32—the Global Warming Solutions Act of 2006—became law, Japan's climate change mitigation strategy remained adrift.

Meanwhile, only marginal progress was made in reducing Japan's reliance on fossil fuels. In fact, petroleum, coal, and LP gas continued to account for more than 80 percent of the total primary energy supply.[19] At the same time, hydroelectric energy declined both in absolute terms and as a percentage share of primary energy supply, while the contribution of other renewable sources remained stuck at 3 percent. The contribution of nuclear energy grew from 10 percent to 13 percent (ANRE 2010).

PHASE IV: RETRENCHMENT AND DEREGULATION, 2001–2010

In April 2001, under the LDP-led government of Prime Minister Junichiro Koizumi, support for renewable energy programs was cut in favor of deregulating energy markets and privatizing state functions. While energy security remained the central objective, liberalization and deregulation of energy markets came to be viewed as a crucial means to its achievement. The Democratic Party of Japan (DPJ), which supplanted the LDP as ruling party in August 2009, campaigned on a platform calling for greater emphasis on renewable energy and stricter controls on greenhouse gas emissions. And yet, even in the immediate aftermath of the Fukushima crisis, campaign rhetoric and prime ministerial pledges did not translate into fundamental change in the nation's energy policy.

Drivers

The September 11th terrorist attacks and skyrocketing oil prices that followed refocused attention on Japan's energy *in*security, with its heavy reliance on petroleum imports from the Middle East. This gave added urgency to the quest to geographically diversify energy supply, leading to negotiations with Russia over the trans-Siberian oil pipeline and the expansion of LNG facilities on Sakhalin Island. It also upped the ante in the territorial dispute with China over control of the Senkaku (Diaoyu) Islands and their potentially rich energy reserves.

The Fundamental Law on Energy Policy Measures, popularly known as the Basic Act on Energy Policy, was passed by the Diet in 2002. This law enshrined the 3Es goals of energy policy: energy security, environmental sustainability, and the utilization of market mechanisms to generate economic development (Duffield and Woodall 2011, 3742). METI was tasked with formulating and drafting basic energy plans (BEPs), three of which were issued between 2003 and 2010.[20] In the 2010 BEP, four additional goals were tacked onto the familiar 3Es: ensuring the safety of the energy supply; ensuring efficiency in energy markets; restructuring the energy industry; and gaining public understanding of a vastly expanded role for nuclear energy (3743). The Plan set a number of targets, including a doubling of Japan's "energy self-sufficiency" and "zero-emission power supply" ratios by the year 2030. In addition, targets were set to halve CO_2 emissions of the residential sector, maintain energy efficiency of the industrial sector, and obtain "top-class" shares for energy-related products and systems (Duffield and Woodall 2011).

The DPJ's victory in the August 2009 lower house elections seemed to herald a turning point in Japan's energy policy. Indeed, the party's election manifesto called for "measures to prevent global warming," introduction of a "fixed-price purchase system for renewable energy with mandatory purchase of all power generated," promotion of "environmentally friendly, high-quality housing," achievement of world leadership in "environmental and related technologies," and the establishment of "secure energy supplies" (DPJ 2009, 23–26). Shortly after taking office, Prime Minister Yukio Hatoyama boldly pledged that by 2020, Japan would reduce greenhouse gas emissions to 75 percent of 1990 levels, and in March of the following year, the DPJ submitted a "Global Warming Countermeasures" bill to the Diet (Duffield and Woodall 2011, 3742). The DPJ-led government also oversaw the formulation of the 2010 BEP, which called for a dramatic reduction in carbon emissions.

Tools

The government took a variety of actions on the green energy front. In January 2001, the Environment *Agency* was transformed into the *Ministry* of the Environment (MOE) as part of an overall reorganization of government organs. Then, in June of the following year, a Renewable Portfolio Standard was created, requiring utility companies to purchase a portion of their supply from renewable energy sources. But critics argued that the METI-set utilization targets were too low and offered little incentive to induce potential suppliers to enter the market (Dollery 2010, 8–9). In June 2009, Japan became party to the OECD's Green Growth Declaration that called upon countries to "pursue green growth strategies . . . , acknowledging that 'green' and 'growth' can go hand-in-hand" (MOE 2010, 160). In August, the Diet passed a new law creating a feed-in tariff (FIT) under which the national government would set rates to be paid by utility companies to households, private firms, and public facilities that generate photovoltaic solar power. Significantly, the FIT did not apply to wind, biomass, and other renewables (DeWit and Iida 2011).

In the summer of 2005, Environment Minister Yuriko Koike announced a "Cool Biz" campaign requiring that central government ministries set air conditioner temperatures at 82.7°F (28°C) to reduce energy usage, and workers were encouraged to dress in casual attire during the hot summer months. Then, in May 2007, Prime Minister Shinzo Abe announced his "Cool Earth 50" that aimed to reduce greenhouse gas emissions by 50 percent by 2050. The following year, the cabinet of Prime Minister Yasuo Fukuda, Abe's successor, adopted a detailed "Action Plan for Achieving Low-Carbon Society" (Duffield and Woodall 2011, 3742).

Japan's energy policies were spelled out in the Basic Energy Plans, which unfailingly argued that nuclear power is a clean, low-cost source of a "self-sufficient" (even though Japan has no domestic uranium reserves) energy supply. The 2010 BEP called for expanding nuclear power's share in the primary energy supply from 10 percent to 25 percent by constructing 14 new nuclear power plants in the upcoming two decades (Duffield and Woodall 2011, 3743). Meanwhile, the BEPs highlighted the intermittency problems and high costs associated with renewables. The Plan called for measures to promote nuclear power generation, advance utilization of "clean coal" and other fossil fuels, and expand the use of renewable energy through an expanded FIT, targeted tax breaks, subsidies and R&D support, and efforts to create a "smart grid." It also called for the substitution of natural gas for petroleum and coal, the introduction of measures to promote the use of hybrids and other advanced low-emission vehicles, and the construction of net-zero-energy houses and buildings (3744–3745).

The government also offered incentives to produce and purchase environment-friendly products. Introduced in 1999, the "Top Runner" Program employs government-set fuel efficiency and energy efficiency standards based upon the most energy efficient products on the market for specific types of vehicles and appliances. The idea is to encourage energy efficiency in the transportation and residential sectors by promoting competition among manufacturers, provision of pertinent information by retailers, and the purchase of energy efficient products by consumers (ECCJ 2010b). An "Eco-point" system was created in July 2009 as part of Prime Minister Taro Aso's economic stimulus strategy. This enabled consumers who purchase government-designated air conditioners, refrigerators, and television sets that receive terrestrial digital broadcasting to apply for points that can be used to buy gift certificates, prepaid cards, and other "green products" (*Japan Times*, June 20, 2009).The program was subsequently expanded to include construction or renovation of eco-friendly houses and a subsidy for the purchase of hybrid cars (METI 2009).

Obstacles

The Coalition was wary of the emphasis on renewable energy and countermeasures to combat global warming trumpeted by the new DPJ-led government. Prime Minister Hatoyama's pledge to reduce Japan's greenhouse gas emissions to 75 percent of 1990 levels by 2020 stirred controversy in September 2009. While foreign leaders such as Connie Hedegaard, Denmark's minister for climate and energy, praised the action pledge as a "bold step"

162 that should "inspire other countries to follow suit," it received an icy response from Japanese government bureaucrats and business leaders (McCurry 2009). In interviews conducted in Tokyo during June 2010, officials of three different government ministries expressed dismay that Hatoyama had made the pledge without first consulting with domestic stakeholders. One interviewee opined that a 17 percent cut might be feasible but that 25 percent was out of the question. Meanwhile, a succession of business leaders — including officials of the Federation of Electric Power Companies, Japan Business Federation, and the Japan Automobile Manufacturers' Association — described Hatoyama's initiative as "unrealistic" and a "burden on the people" (Ryall 2009).

Buoyed by support from the DPJ's labor union supporters, the Coalition set about diluting and creating loopholes in the new green energy policies (DeWit and Iida 2011). Having effectively trivialized green energy policies in Japan's overall energy strategy, the Coalition quietly worked to undermine what were perceived as excessively eco-friendly pillars of the 2010 Basic Energy Plan. These efforts bore fruit at the December 2010 Cancun Climate Summit, where the Japanese representative declared that Japan "will not inscribe its target under the Kyoto Protocol on any conditions or under any circumstances" unless India and China were also legally bound to make similar cuts (Vidal 2010).

Results

The contribution of renewables in the total primary energy supply changed very little during the lost decade. In fact, from 2001 through 2009, the contribution of renewables and hydroelectric power hovered around 6 percent, while fossil fuels and nuclear power accounted for 94 percent of the country's energy supply (ANRE 2010). The fact that the FIT applied only to solar photovoltaic–generated electricity offered no incentive to develop and deploy wind, geothermal, and other renewables. And the Renewable Portfolio Standard required that utility companies purchase only that portion of the solar electricity in excess of the producing household's actual consumption (DeWit and Iida 2011). When subsidies for photovoltaic installation were terminated in 2005, solar cells had been installed on 320,000 rooftops nationwide. As soon as the subsidies expired, domestic shipments of photovoltaic modules plummeted, and Japan fell behind China and Germany in the production of photovoltaic cells (Roney 2010). Although subsidies were restarted in 2007, Japan did not regain world leadership in photovoltaic production.[21]

Meanwhile, deregulation produced disappointing results. An instructive example is seen in the Koizumi government's attempt to liberalize the electricity market. In 2005, the government moved to allow power producers and suppliers (PPS) to act as brokers in buying electricity (mostly from manufacturers that generate their own) and selling it to commercial customers. The Japan Electric Power Exchange was established to act as a wholesale trading market, which was to open 60 percent of the country's electricity market to competition, thereby breaking the utility companies' virtual monopoly and reducing costs for consumers. But six years later, results had fallen far short of expectations. In fact, despite offering rates as much as one-third cheaper than those charged by the utility companies, the PPS companies had managed to capture only a 2 percent market share. This was largely a result of having to depend on the utilities' transmission lines (Onishi and Fackler 2011). This problem became apparent in the aftermath of the 3/11 disasters, when Tokyo Electric Power announced plans to raise electricity charges to large-lot users by an average of 17 percent. When the large-lot users began looking to save money by turning to PPS companies, it was discovered that only 26 of the 50 PPS firms registered with ANRE were actually operating (*Yomiuri Shinbun*, February 24, 2012).

And yet Japan *did* make some efforts on the renewable energy front. The Top Runner and Eco-points programs offered incentives to produce, sell, and purchase eco-friendly products, while FIT led to a near doubling in the number of residential rooftop solar photovoltaic panels between 2005 and 2010.[22] Meanwhile, Toyota launched the world's first commercial hybrid car in 1997, and Japanese manufacturers dominated the green car market (Dashboard 2012). Nevertheless, Japan's considerable latent renewable energy resources were left largely untapped, and the green growth cause failed to attract a champion with the determination or political stature of South Korean President Lee Myung-bak. And even without the barriers erected by the Coalition and its allies, it would have been challenging to formulate and implement a coherent green growth strategy that capitalized upon the country's considerable strength in R&D and cleantech-related patents. The period's most forceful leader, Junichiro Koizumi, pressed an agenda of deregulation and liberalization that was not conducive to incentivizing green energy innovation and usage. And the succession of ephemeral governments that ruled the country after Koizumi's departure in 2006 did their best to provide the least possible long-term strategic direction to national policy.

PHASE V: BEYOND FUKUSHIMA—TOWARD A GREEN GROWTH STRATEGY?

Drivers

The Fukushima crisis prompted a fundamental rethinking of the role of renewables in Japan's energy strategy.[23] It cast doubt upon Japan's reliance on

164   nuclear power, which, according to the 2010 Basic Energy Plan, was projected
to provide nearly one-quarter of the country's total primary energy supply —
and half of electricity generated — by 2030. The Fukushima crisis exposed
the "mythology" of nuclear safety and made pipedreams of the government's
plans to build 14 new nuclear power plants in the next two decades (Duffield
and Woodall 2011, 3743; Kushida 2012, 40).[24] In the wake of the crisis, Prime
Minister Naoto Kan ordered the shutdown of three reactors at the Hamaoka
Nuclear Power Plant, which was constructed on a tectonic fault line. Then
the government decided that nuclear reactors that had been shut down
for scheduled regular inspections would not be restarted until their safety
could be assured. Consequently, nearly two years after the Fukushima crisis,
only 2 of Japan's 50 reactors — a pair of units at the Oi Nuclear Power Plant,
which were restarted on the orders of Prime Minister Yoshihiko Noda, Kan's
successor — were operating.

Policy Tools

A host of policy measures were proposed in the aftermath of the March 11th disasters. The loss of power supplied by the crippled Fukushima Daiichi nuclear
reactors led to orchestrated power outages and rolling blackouts over a broad
area that included the Tokyo metropolitan area. Aiming to achieve a 15 percent reduction from 2010's peak-period summertime levels, the government
imposed a mandatory cut in electricity usage for all large-lot users in the areas
served by the Tokyo Electric Power and Tohoku Electric Power companies
(Asako 2011). In addition, private citizens and companies were asked to vol-
untarily cut energy usage by the same amount. Many companies shifted work
hours to weekends and extended summer vacations, and some moved production facilities to unaffected areas. Workers were encouraged to "Light Down"
by turning off home computers after 8:00 p.m. The Environment Ministry
also expanded the scope of the original Cool Biz campaign from government
workers to all workers with the launch of the *Super* Cool Biz campaign, which
likewise encouraged setting office thermostats to 82.7°F (28°C) and adopting
a casual dress code during the summer (Song 2011, 28).

    On June 15, 2011, Kan agreed to step down as prime minister once the Diet
passed three bills, including a new basic law on renewable energy.[25] Amidst
widespread criticism for his government's handling of the 3/11 disasters, particularly its response to the nuclear crisis, Kan told critics in the Diet that they had
better swiftly pass the bills if they wanted to get rid of him and vowed to display
the renewable energy bill in the Prime Minister's Office until it was enacted.
A DPJ ally observed that Kan had long supported an expanded role for renewables in Japan's energy policy and that passage of the bill would allow him to

exit the premiership on a high note (Azuma and Sugita 2011). On August 26, Diet's upper house approved the renewable energy bill (it received lower house approval three days earlier), and Kan and his cabinet resigned six days later.

The new renewable energy law laid the foundation for future legislation and generated a variety of policy proposals. It created a feed-in tariff mandating that the utility companies purchase energy generated by solar, wind, geothermal, and other renewable sources at above-market rates (Leone 2011). In the first month after the FIT went into effect, nearly 34,000 projects valued at $2 billion emerged (DeWit 2012). One proposal called for the exemption of *mega*–solar power plants from acreage restrictions in the Factory Location Law, while another proposed relaxing the River Law to increase the number of small hydro-electric plants. Other proposals suggested utilizing empty farmland for solar or wind power generation and rebuilding areas devastated by the 3/11 disasters into "smart cities" utilizing renewable energy sources and intelligent grids (*Yomiuri Shinbun*, February 4 and January 24, 2012, and September 13, 2011).[26] In March 2012, the Environment Ministry relaxed the ban on the drilling of diagonal wells into national parklands, which contain as much as 80 percent of Japan's geothermal resources (*Yomiuri Shinbun*, March 13, 2012).

And the Noda government attempted to recast national energy strategy. On September 19, 2012, the Nuclear Regulation Authority (NRA) replaced the much maligned Nuclear and Industrial Safety Agency as Japan's atomic watchdog. The NRA was placed under the Ministry of the Environment to separate nuclear safety *regulation* from industrial *promotion*, which remained METI's charge. In addition, the government tasked the Energy and Environment Council with taking account of public sentiment in forging a new energy strategy. On September 14, 2012, the Council submitted its "Innovative Strategy for Energy and Environment," which aimed to realize a society not dependent on nuclear power, a green energy revolution, a stable energy supply, reform of the electric power system, and global warming countermeasures. The plan recommends a 40-year life span for nuclear reactors (which require the NRA's safety assurance to be restarted), no new plant construction, and mobilization of "all possible policy resources to such a level as to even enable zero operation of nuclear power plants in the 2030s" (Energy and Environment Council 2012b). While the details remained fuzzy, the new strategy seemed to commit the government to make nuclear-free, green energy a fundamental component of Japan's energy future.

Obstacles

Anticipating a showdown in the wake of the Fukushima crisis, the Coalition's spokespeople spotlighted the higher relative costs of renewables. Previous

METI estimates showed that the unit price of electricity generated from photovoltaic solar is five times greater than that of nuclear power and double that of petroleum (ANRE 2010, 25).[27] Critics maintained that a shift to renewables will strap Japanese manufacturers with higher energy costs that will disadvantage them in competitive markets and force them to move operations overseas. Japan's largest business federation estimated that a zero-nuclear policy would result in an unemployment rate of 7.2 to 7.3 percent in 2030, as opposed to 6.0 to 6.1 percent with continued reliance on nuclear power (Harlan 2012). And a panel commissioned by the Science Council of Japan estimated that closing down all of Japan's nuclear reactors by summer 2012 would result in a ¥2,121 ($26.50) increase in the average household's electricity bill by 2030 (Daily Yomiuri Online, July 4, 2011). Meanwhile, the utility companies countered antinuclear protesters by instructing their employees to send emails expressing their support for atomic power and to fill seats at hearings to discuss restarting nuclear power plants. Additionally, two utility companies were accused of falsifying data to allay safety concerns about construction of a proposed pluthermal plant (Daily Yomiuri Online, July 31, 2011).

Statements issued by the Kan and Noda governments sparked confusion and controversy. In May 2011, the Kan government's chief spokesperson asserted that nuclear power will remain a major part of Japan's energy policy, but at a July press conference, Kan stated that "Japan should make itself not dependent on nuclear power" and that efforts should be made to "achieve a society that can function without nuclear power in the future" (Associated Press, May 8, 2011; Daily Yomiuri Online, July 15, 2011). The very next day, Kan said the statement reflected his own *personal* opinion — not the official position of his government — prompting cabinet ministers to complain about Kan's habit of making policy proclamations without consulting with the stakeholders (Daily Yomiuri Online, July 16, 2011). Two weeks later, Kan asserted that the government's "de-nuclearization" efforts would be carried out "systematically and in stages" (Daily Yomiuri Online, July 31, 2011). In September, the economy and trade minister in the newly appointed Noda government was forced to resign after describing the evacuated area around Fukushima Daiichi as "death towns" (*Yomiuri Shinbun*, September 13, 2011). One year later, the Noda government further contradicted itself by announcing that construction could resume on partially completed reactors, which meant that they would still be operating for decades beyond the nuclear phaseout set for the 2030s.

Under pressure from big business, localities that host nuclear plants, and foreign allies, the Noda government's "Innovative Strategy" came to be riddled with ambiguities, contradictions, and escape clauses. Leaders of Japan's most powerful business federations described the zero-nuclear strategy as "unrealistic and unreachable" and "totally unacceptable" (Hesse 2012; *Japan Times*, September 18, 2012). Fearing the loss of jobs and subsidies — and not wishing to become the permanent storage sites for unused nuclear fuel and radioactive waste — representatives of local areas voiced their concerns. Meanwhile, representatives of the U.S. government, which, apparently, was led to believe that Japan was merely *considering* the zero option when the original pronouncements implied otherwise, pondered the impact on energy prices if the world's third largest economy were to begin snapping up fossil fuels (DeWit 2012; *Japan Times*, September 14, 2012). And the governments of Britain and France, where spent Japanese nuclear fuel is converted into mixed-oxide fuel, made it clear that their countries did not wish to become permanent storage sites for reprocessed materials that a nonnuclear Japan might refuse to repatriate (*Asahi Shinbun*, September 13, 2012).

Results

It remains to be seen whether the Fukushima crisis will become a green tipping point. The "Innovative Strategy for Energy and the Environment" proposes cuts in electricity usage, measures to promote greater energy conservation, and a near tripling in the contribution of renewables. But the increased emphasis on renewables will come at the cost of a steep reduction — if not its outright elimination — in the role envisioned for nuclear power, which was supposed to supply half of the country's electricity needs in 2030. As observed earlier, big business and the regional electrical monopolies, localities dependent on nuclear power plants, and even some of Japan's allies and other foreign governments all looked on the nonnuclear option with disdain and distrust. Meanwhile, the muddled responses to the Fukushima crisis on the part of both the Kan and Noda governments ushered new actors to the bargaining table, including citizens' groups championing antinuclear and green causes, bureaucrats in ministries other than METI, and local governments (DeWit 2012). Consequently, it is likely that the debate over the Japanese energy future will not be settled anytime soon.

Three additional lessons have thus far emerged. First, the mandatory energy cuts and the voluntary conservation efforts of the general public and companies demonstrated that even the world's "efficiency superpower" could tighten its belt even further.[28] Second, an expanding coalition favors breaking up the ten regional utility companies (Kushida 2012, 51). For example, Softbank CEO Masayoshi Son pledged to invest ¥1 billion ($12.5 million) in a new natural energy foundation and announced plans to build ten solar plants

168   on the condition that the utility companies are deregulated (*Christian Science Monitor*, May 3, 2011; Song 2011, 31). And third, some of the most innovative ideas for solving Japan's energy problems and combating climate change are coming from the local level. For example, the Tokyo Metropolitan Government issued its own policy vision that promotes "the generation of locally produced, locally consumed energy and the advancement of independent, distributed power production" (TMG 2011, 28). So perhaps going forward, innovative cities, *not* the national government, will come to set Japan's energy policy agenda.

CONCLUSION: SLOW TO GO GREEN

Despite compelling reasons to do so, Japanese policy makers have failed to forge a coherent policy strategy to reduce emissions and grow cleantech capabilities. Indeed, with a domestic resource endowment almost totally devoid of fossil fuels, it seems strange that Japan's energy strategy would rely on imported supplies of petroleum, natural gas, and coal. Moreover, in light of Japan's seismic conundrum, nuclear energy is a very risky source of green energy, although closing the nuclear fuel cycle by bringing the Rokkasho reprocessing plant to full operational capacity would lend credence to the government's claim that nuclear atomic energy should be seen as a "quasi-domestically produced power source" (*junkokusandengen*) (Energy and Environment Council 2012a, 3). It is puzzling that Japanese policy makers have not made a more concerted effort to more fully exploit the country's rich endowments of solar, wind, and geothermal energy resources. And considering the strong position of Japanese companies in the environmental technology and renewable energy fields, one is left to ponder why it is that the national energy strategy does not seek to capitalize on this area of comparative advantage in establishing a strong position in international markets.[29]

There are many reasons behind Japan's puzzling failure to fully buy into a green growth strategy. From the mid-1950s until the 1970s oil shocks, a business-first strategy propelled Japan into the ranks of the world's richest countries, albeit at the cost of a dangerously polluted environment. Massive sunk investments went into installing the infrastructure for an energy system designed to deliver fossil fuel–derived and nuclear energy to the entire country. Many of today's most successful companies were nurtured under that strategy, while many of the institutions and organizations that continue to shape energy policy were established during the period. Moving to a green energy system would mean retiring energy assets that remain useful and profitable, and doing so on the proposition of weak, diffuse benefits that may not materialize for decades, if ever. Despite considerable strength in R&D and success in the green car market, Japanese companies have, as a rule, underpunched their weight in most other cleantech markets. These self-reinforcing mechanisms have produced inertia and "lock-in" that complicate any attempts to shift policy in a green direction (North 1990).

Japan's energy policy domain was long dominated by a Brown + Nuclear Coalition. In contrast to Denmark and South Korea, where pro–green growth alliances came together and effected a political realignment, such has not been the case in Japan. Indeed, strategic parts of Japanese industry and allies in the government bureaucracy and political realm remain opposed to green growth based upon a commitment to renewables, despite its potential for enhancing Japan's energy independence, leveraging its comparative advantage in key high-technology markets, and combating climate change. There are interesting similarities between the Japanese and California cases in the challenges faced (reducing both pollution and energy intensity) and in the outcomes realized (enhanced energy efficiency). In some ways, the Japanese and California stories are similar. California is an exemplar of energy efficiency among U.S. states, while Japan is the exemplar among rich countries. But California has pushed harder on emissions control, and Japan has yet to enact an equivalent to Assembly Bill 32. Japan has produced some innovative green policies, but, to date, the policy environment has failed to generate a green spiral. It remains to be seen whether the Fukushima crisis will lead to the emergence of a Green Coalition with the will to see cleantech policy survive and expand.

10

KOREA

From Authoritarian to Authoritative:
The Path from Heavy Industry
to Green Growth

Irene Choi

The Korean government has attempted to initiate a "green spiral." The Lee Myung-bak administration proposed plans to immediately address the emissions problem and to promote a restructuring of the Korean economy that would support growth and competitiveness. The recent push for green growth is reminiscent of the 1960s and the Heavy and Chemical Industry (HCI) drive under the authoritarian leadership of President Park Chung-hee. In the 1960s, an authoritarian government forced the development of heavy and chemical industries, imposing its purposes and directions on society and the economy. In this democratic era, the government has shown that it can exert authoritative leadership in beginning a transition to a greener society. What accounts for this commitment to green and the effort to build an alliance with industry to accomplish it? One explanation is that the executive branch traditionally — and sometimes unilaterally — made major economic decisions, while President Lee's background as a former Hyundai Construction chairman provided close ties with the country's major industrial players. However, now the government must build a coalition — initially one with the industrial community. Ultimately, the Korean green growth strategy intends to create a partnership with the advocates of "green" and the advocates of "growth" to promote more balanced and sustainable future growth. It will, though, be for the new government to extend the coalition to include the environmentalists, should it so wish. International commitments, including the Korean creation of a Global Green Growth Institute, were intended in part to anchor the coalition against a change of direction after a new president was elected. That fight has now begun, and it will be some time before it is evident whether Korea pulls back from its commitments to "green growth" or shifts its focus — and the political labels—while broadening the political base. Hence, the path to green from heavy industry is also marked by what we call a shift from authoritarian to authoritative governance.

THE OVERALL VISION

The Lee Myung-bak administration set impressive goals. According to its plans, Korea would reduce carbon emissions and thus increase energy security, reap economic benefits, and improve the quality of people's lives with green innovations. In essence, green growth was proposed as the single answer to many of the country's needs: first, the need for a more stabilized energy supply for a country that imports 96.7 percent of its energy from overseas and has the fastest-growing emissions among OECD countries; second, the need for a new engine for economic growth; and third, the possibility of establishing itself as a leader among those countries. Ultimately, Korea's green growth plan intended to induce an economic and social paradigm shift that would revolutionize Korea's energy systems, industry, and urban management systems, including buildings and transportation. The Korean government was determined to realize this vision. By 2009, Korea had recorded the highest green stimulus per capita, as well as the highest green fund percentage of total GDP among the G20 countries (UNEP 2009).

Understandably, there were limits to the extent to which the government could meet these goals during a single presidential term of five years. Yet, what may be unique and noteworthy in the Korean case is that President Lee's growth strategy, though explicitly framed around green growth, was more successful at creating a coalition of interests in the industrial sector than it was at capturing support from environmentalist groups. One of the major issues that concerned environmentalists was that the government's agendas were too growth oriented in that they would hardly improve the environmental attractiveness of outcomes. For example, the Four Major Rivers Restoration Project, which involves building 16 dams and extensive dredging, and renewable energy development policies have sparked heated debates on whether the government's real intention lies in truly greener growth. The critique deals with the government's need, at least in the short run, to concentrate on the economic benefits of green growth in order to engage the industrial sector. However, to bring about an economic and social *paradigm shift* that will revolutionize the daily lives of Koreans, the support and participation of civil society are mandatory.

As a long-term vision, we emphasize that the Korean ambition goes well beyond the definition of green growth proposed in the first part of this book:

172   growth *compatible with* emissions reductions or growth *driven by* emissions reductions. The Korean green growth strategy intends a multilevel transformation that, if realized, will be more than a simple growth strategy and will affect many more aspects of Korean life than just the economy.[1] The political challenge is correspondingly greater as well. Shifting from an authoritarian regime to an authoritative one, the government has been faced with the challenge of building a coalition of interests with the industrial sector. Yet, the challenge does not stop there. As a critical step toward realizing the multilevel transformation, the government intends to create broader support for green growth. This is because the prospect of a full social paradigm shift empowers the drive for economic growth through emissions reductions. However, while President Lee's administration made meaningful progress in the former, accomplishments to the latter task were relatively limited.

KOREAN GREEN GROWTH OBJECTIVES

In 2008, Korea faced two problems. First, concerned voices had been raised about whether Korea, as a nonannex country to the Kyoto Protocol, was ready to start bearing global emissions reduction requirements under post-Kyoto systems (Kim, Kim, and Park 2009, 2). Meanwhile, after the global financial crisis in 2008, Korea was also searching for stimulus policies that would get the Korean economy back on track. The Green New Deal that was announced in January 2009 was the Korean government's effort to solve both problems. It was followed by the creation of the Presidential Committee on Green Growth; the Green Growth Development Strategy, a longer-term effort extending through 2050; and the Five Year Plan for Green Growth.

The Presidential Committee on Green Growth released a progress report between 2008 and 2009 that described the Green New Deal as a plan to invest ₩50 trillion ($45.4 billion) from 2009 to 2012 in nine key green projects that included the restoration of four major rivers, green transportation, green cars and clean energy, waste resource catchment, and reuse projects (PCGG 2010a, 9). The Green New Deal predated, but did not include, the establishment of the Presidential Committee on Green Growth, preparation and publication of the Green Growth Development Strategy (for the period up to 2050), and the Five Year Plan for Green Growth (2009–2013). The government also promised an investment of 2 percent of GDP to initiate developments in the green sector as part of the Five Year Plan for Green Growth (PCGG 2010b, 22). By 2013, the Lee Myung-bak administration had made it clear that the government was serious about its commitment to its vision of green growth and that an overarching plan for action in the near future and beyond was firmly in place.

The Korean goals for green growth, as outlined in the national strategy, are (1) reducing greenhouse gas (GHG) emissions and improving energy security, (2) creating new engines for economic growth, and (3) greening the country and Korean lifestyles, with the objective of becoming a model green growth country internationally. Together, these three objectives constitute (and require) a transformation of Korean society and the economy. The objectives are closely intertwined, with business opportunity and improvement in quality of life springing from the need to reduce emissions and increase energy security. As noted above, the Korean green vision goes beyond the focus and scope of this project, particularly in the realm of the third objective (greening the country and Korean lifestyles, which includes greening land space and transportation). Our discussion below therefore focuses on the first two Korean objectives, which are most closely related to our central focus on green economic growth, defined for this project as growth that is compatible with and driven by emissions reductions.

First Objective: Reduce Greenhouse Gas Emissions and Improve Energy Security

The first objective set by the Korean government involves two major goals that are intertwined, in the sense that achievements in one tend to imply (but do not guarantee) achievements in the other: reducing carbon emissions and enhancing the nation's energy security. Three strategic approaches contribute, to varying extents, to accomplishing these two goals.

The first strategic approach is *increasing energy efficiency*, thereby reducing fossil fuel consumption. According to the Ministry of Knowledge Economy (MKE), the Korea Electric Power Corporation (KEPCO) plans to invest ₩4.7 trillion ($4.2 billion) on smart transmission and distribution to decrease energy loss (MKEEID 2010, 4), while the introduction of the smart grid and demand-side management will bring further improvements in energy efficiency. The strengthening of energy efficiency standards, the introduction of energy management systems, the use of smart grid techniques, the deployment of high-efficiency appliances, and the rationalization of the energy pricing system are all expected to boost energy efficiency. With better energy efficiency leading to lowered consumption of fossil fuels, both GHG emissions and import dependency are expected to be reduced.

The second method is *deployment of clean energy*: generating more energy from greener sources. The law on renewable energy development, usage, and dissemination has been amended in 2010 as part of the effort. As described in a report issued by the Korean Institute for Industrial Economics and Trade

(KIET), the government has been using feed-in tariffs (FIT) to subsidize small- and medium-sized renewable energy producers in the past. It is now shifting from FIT to a Renewable Portfolio Standard (RPS) system beginning in 2012 (Choi 2009, 35). RPS targets are 2 percent by 2012 and 8 percent by 2020, with quotas concentrated on solar energy during the initial five years from 2012 to 2016 (MKE 2010a). The current goal is to increase renewable energy usage to 11 percent of total energy consumption by 2030 (PCGG 2010a, 8) (see Figure 10.1).

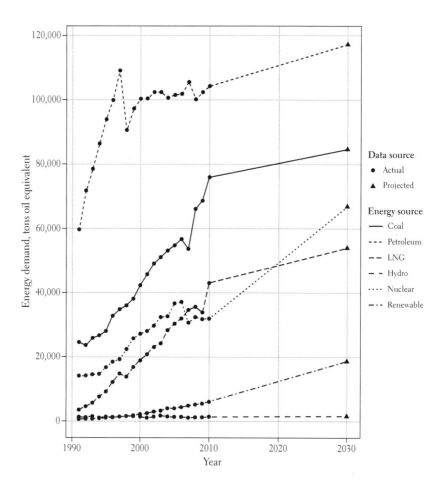

FIGURE 10.1   Planned shift in Korean energy mix, 2008–2030
SOURCE: PCGG 2010a, 8.

In absolute terms, Korea's renewables goal appears modest compared to those of renewables powerhouses like Denmark. This apparent modesty reflects in part the low installed base from which Korea must start (Korea's goal of 10.7 percent is a fourfold increase from 2009's 2.7 percent). It is also a reflection of the relative dearth of strong renewable resources (Korea's renewable plans are constrained by the fact that Korea's wind and solar potential is limited compared to many nations). Korea believes that, given these limitations, it has set quite challenging goals.

The third method is to *produce more energy from nuclear power plants*, a carbon-free but nonrenewable source. Korea is already the fifth largest nuclear energy producer (151 TWh), generating 5.5 percent of the world's total nuclear energy (IEA 2010a, 17). By 2030, Korea aims to produce 59 percent of its domestic electricity from nuclear energy. According to the *Korea Herald* (Cho 2010), the Basic Energy Plan of 2008 further shows that nuclear energy will take up to 27.8 percent in the country's overall energy mix. In addition to the potential to reduce carbon emissions, Korea hopes to emerge as a major exporter of nuclear power technologies and plants in the global market.

Whether nuclear power constitutes green energy has been as controversial an issue in Korea as it has been elsewhere. The Presidential Committee had attempted to include provisions for development of nuclear power in the Framework Act on Low Carbon Green Growth enacted at the end of 2009, but it had to abandon this because of objections regarding the safety and cleanliness of nuclear power. Still, nuclear power is included in Korea's blueprint for future energies as a major alternative energy to fossil fuels.[2]

Second Objective: Provide an Engine for Economic Growth

The second major objective of Korea's National Green Growth Strategy and Five Year Plan for Green Growth is to create new growth engines from green technologies, promoting green industries. Korea has the market clout and technical skills to capitalize on green markets like those that objective #1 (with its goals of increasing national efficiency, renewables, and nuclear power) would create domestically. The Korean government's choice of the next generation's growth-driving green industries, such as solar panels, fuel cells, LED, and green cars industries, reflects well on the strengths of its current industrial sector. The country is home to some of the top global corporations in many high-tech industries such as the electronics, semiconductor, IT, automobile, and shipbuilding industries. Korea also owns some of the most advanced technologies in related areas, and since 2005, the government has been spending ₩253.2 billion ($230 million) on research and development in heavy electric equipment and semiconductors (MKE 2010d, 14). Technological capabilities, experience, and knowledge on market trends and consumer taste in those industries could help the Korean firms make a fast start in some of the new green industries.

Korean companies are in fact making major moves in target industries. Hyundai Heavy Industries is building a 175-MW generator (at a cost of $7 trillion) in what is to become America's largest solar energy–generation project (a total of 900 MW) in California and Arizona (Park and Lee 2010). Samsung will invest ₩23 trillion ($20.9 billion) on solar panels, fuel cells, LED, and medical devices by 2020. It will also start building a green industrial complex by 2021 with ₩7 trillion ($6.3 billion) in initial investments (Ryu 2011). Hyundai-Kia Automobile has developed the Sonata Hybrid and K5 Hybrid using its own independent technologies, acquiring 1,000 new patents. Hyundai also produced prototypes for a new plug-in hybrid electric vehicle (PHEV) model in 2012 and a fuel cell car model in 2013, strengthening its environmentally friendly automobiles lineup (Cho 2010).

The electricity and smart grid businesses also represent major opportunities for Korea. According to the International Energy Agency (IEA), $13.6 trillion is expected to be spent worldwide on the electricity industry by the year 2020. In addition to leveraging a significant domestic market, Korea can also hope to export to developed countries, as well as to China and Asia, where the markets for smart grids are expected to grow exponentially in the near future (quoted in MKE 2010b, 96). In the best-case scenario, Korea would see an annual increase of 50,000 jobs, a ₩74 trillion ($67 billion) increase in domestic demand, and ₩49 trillion ($44.5 billion) increase in exports of smart grid–related products by the year 2030 (MKE 2010c, 33).

The Korean government is attempting to create possibilities and opportunities for the industry to achieve major transformations in energy systems, industrial structure, and lifestyle changes. The intention is to have an industrial sector that is prepared and eager to take advantage of the market opportunities inherent in capturing this new industry.

Playing the Global Standards Game

Korea will face increasing necessity to meet, or in many cases set, global standards — that is, the technical standards that govern interoperability, and thus the usability, of products. Standards are critical in some of the emerging industries Korea wants to play in, particularly smart grid and related products. With a relatively small domestic market, Korea's ability to satisfy scale economies without exports has limits. This means it will do best if it can sway international decisions on use of standards, ultimately acting as a leader in the international development of newly emerging standards and therefore ensuring a broad market for its own producers. If Korea can lead the international development of newly emerging standards, this will place it at the center of global innovation and position it to reap a strong share of the benefits from a global green transformation.

Korea intends to expand its influence on global standards by actively participating in international discussions and consortia. For example, the selection of Korea and Italy as leading countries for the smart grid project during the expanded G8 summit in 2009 presented one early opportunity. Korea plans to lead international discussions of global standards for smart grid by holding the World Smart Grid Forum and other conferences. Furthermore, through close cooperation with Japan, the government seeks to improve product compatibility in the energy storage, electric vehicle, and smart home fields. Efforts in other fronts such as renewable energy and green shipbuilding are also visible. For example, the Korea-China consortium for renewable energy development is being organized to promote cooperation in entering third-party markets. Finally, in all aspects of green technology development, the government supports small- and medium-sized enterprises participating in global consortia through the Korea Trade Investment Promotion Agency's (KOTRA) Global Green Cooperation Support Center.

Already, there have been successful results in this regard. Xeline's Broadband Power Line, developed together with the United States and Spain, was selected as the global standard by the International Standard Organization (ISO) in 2009. In terms of exports, Korean firms such as LS Industrial Systems, Nuri Telecom, and RadioPulse have secured major sales of solar energy generation and advanced metering infrastructure hardware to countries such as Japan, Australia, Mexico, Norway, Italy, and Sweden (MKE 2010b, 127–128).

The Role of Emerging Firms

Interestingly, much progress is being made by smaller firms like Xeline and Nuri Telecom, which are not the traditional conglomerate industrial leaders in Korea. This suggests that Korea's green growth is not entirely led by the familiar *chaebol* organizations but offers new opportunities to smaller businesses as well. To further improve these small- and medium-sized firms' brand recognition and to facilitate international cooperation, the government has introduced various measures such as *Green Certification* and *Green Financing*.

Green Certification, for example, reduces uncertainty for investors by presenting government-selected green technologies and businesses. Investors who choose to invest in these green-certified businesses can enjoy tax benefits, and selected businesses also receive credit benefits, get additional points when applying for foreign conventions, export incubator projects and R&D investment projects, and enjoy priority treatment in patenting (Chung 2011).

However, the success of efforts to encourage the growth of small- and medium-sized firms (SMEs) in Korea has been controversial. Some argue that support measures for SMEs are not efficient or effective in the long run because they preserve vulnerable and unsustainable businesses that are not helpful in creating a competitive economy. For instance, the various support schemes during and after the financial crisis to failing SMEs have allowed them to survive without the necessary restructuring (Pascha 2010). The current system — which is directed at supporting as many SMEs as possible — could be streamlined to give more comprehensive assistance to a few select firms.

THE GOVERNMENT AND THE GREEN SPIRAL

Historically, economic development in Korea has been particularly dependent on government policies that are intertwined with the interests of major businesses — such as Samsung, LG, and Hyundai — in the manufacturing sector. Today, the government is concentrated on maintaining such relationships amid the growing influences and sometimes diverging interests of conglomerate firms. Challenges to changing the pricing structures of the electricity market or introducing carbon pricing systems come in part from a need to earn the cooperation of the industrial sector, which has a critical part in the government plans for green growth.

This points to a more fundamental dynamic in the Korean economic story, which is being expressed within and through the green development strategy: the shift from what might be termed an *authoritarian* to an authoritative economic policy framework. Korea has a long history of planned industrial transitions. In the past, however, Korea's economic course has been charted under firm, authoritarian government control expressed through top-down control of the industrial sector, largely represented by chaebols. Today, while the Korean strategy is still orchestrated, this planning is applied in a softer manner, requiring directed leadership of a wider variety of firms; we call this approach *authoritative*. But this raises uncertainties. How well will the new approach work? Will it require a broader coalition of business to support than the old authoritarian approach? Will it suffer if there is a lack of social buy-in — for example, if Korea's green growth strategy fails to convince environmentalists?

Despite such challenges, President Lee made a compelling case for big businesses that there was something in it for them as well. As a president who endorsed an "economy first" slogan throughout his campaign and was associated with corporate-friendliness during his administration, he always made sure that *growth* was an integral part of the plan. The fact that the president was a former chairman of Hyundai Construction further helped with the process of convincing industrial players, and his Grand National Party's victory of 153 out of the 299 seats in the 2008 parliamentary elections allowed him to more comfortably exert his influence on the Korean economy. However, the president's closer ties to the industrial sector made it harder for the government to develop a broader coalition with green society.

In fact, environmental groups opposed many of the government's green growth agendas, such as the Four Major Rivers Restoration Project and renewable energy development projects. Opponents to the Korean green growth strategies argued that green growth was deployed as a mere instrument to sugarcoat business interests into something more desirable. While the government was quick to lay out the vision and framework for greener economic growth, would a lack of debate with such opposing groups in civil society turn out to be the downfall of Korea's green growth strategy? Korea seems to be laying the groundwork for the economic gains to specific interests needed to motivate the industry portion of a green policy coalition. But it remains to be seen whether this groundwork will translate into strong enough support to kick off a green spiral, as well as whether the industry side of such a coalition is sufficient for (good) policy if environmentalists do not join in.

Critique and Debate

Critiques of the Lee administration's green growth programs could be summed up with one main question: How green is its green growth vision? Debates on major issues such as restructuring the energy and electricity markets, the Four Major Rivers Restoration Project, and energy development plans all revolve around this issue. Thus, the key to entrenching a green spiral in Korea will be getting the environmentalists on board with the government's green growth programs. The government, which continues to play a critical role in leading the coalition—both with industries and with the broader civil society—will have to respond to the issues discussed in this section in order to realize the larger vision of green growth.

Restructuring the Market

To realize its vision of a green economic engine, one of Korea's biggest challenges is providing the right set of incentives in the domestic market and energy system. One such challenge is introducing a carbon pricing system such as an Emissions Trading Scheme (ETS) and carbon taxes. In 2009, the government announced its plans to implement cap-and-trade policies starting in 2013. The Federation of Korean Industries (FKI), representing Korea's top conglomerate firms, strongly advised the government against the cap-and-trade policies, thus causing delays both in debate and implementation. The bill finally passed Congress in May 2012 and will be put into effect in 2015. However, the government has yet to form a concrete plan for implementing a carbon tax due to opposition from the business sector.

Delays in implementing a carbon trading policy had to do with concerns about the policy's potential economic effects. According to the FKI, the proposed carbon trading schemes will raise production costs for Korean firms and erode their price competitiveness in global markets, especially because Korea's major trading partners like America, China, and Japan are also delaying the implementation of similar carbon pricing systems. Also, the FKI argued that Korean firms, except for a few conglomerate ones, are lacking the appropriate tools to measure their own greenhouse gas emissions and that the government should first construct a national carbon measurement, report, and management system. It acknowledged that introducing the *greenhouse gas target management system* that allowed the collection of data on carbon emissions was the right step toward national carbon emissions management—and a sufficient one. On the other hand, the ETS bill passed in 2012 envisions the parallel running of the systems, with graduation clauses for the emitters in the target management system with emissions over a certain amount required to move into ETS (it would be optional for those with less than this amount).

Yet another change that the government must supervise is the restructuring of the electricity market. While the restructuring of electricity markets is a complex and often controversial challenge in most settings, some rearrangement of the market dynamics may be necessary for two reasons. First, better price incentives could drive domestic efficiency, reducing consumption and emissions. Second, it would make Korea a more suitable nursery for refining and commercializing effective new products in these areas by providing the appropriate structure and market incentives for the development and use of energy efficiency and smart grid products. Responsiveness within the energy system is likely necessary to support the kind of green transformation of the economy and society that Korea seeks.

In 1999, the government recognized the need for a more open and competitive market for electricity. Consequently, KEPCO's generation has been divided into five separate power-generation firms (excluding nuclear). However, while the government guarantees certain amounts of profits to independent power-generation firms with Power Purchase Agreements (PPA), generation capacity of the private sector has not been increasing since 2001 (Kim and Kim 2010, 13). Also, further restructuring of the market has stopped since 2004, and significant improvements in efficiency have not been made. According to Kyung Hoon Kim and Hye Soon Kim (2010), the Korean electricity market is currently structured so that KEPCO monopolizes transmission and distribution of electricity, while 93.3 percent of generation is also produced by KEPCO and its six subsidiary firms. Transactions of electricity over 20 MW are required to go through the Korea Power Exchange (KPX), where wholesale price is determined by the actual variable costs of the generators and not by a market mechanism (Kim and Kim 2010, 13).

Current subsidies for electricity create distorted incentives for electricity usage and efficiency. In Korea, electricity usage is classified into six types — residential, general, educational, agricultural, industrial, and streetlight — and each type pays different rates. Electricity rates for consumers are determined by the government, based on consideration of KEPCO proposals and inflationary pressure. For residential and general usages, the government imposes six levels of progressive utility rates to induce energy conservation. However, the industrial sector, which consumes more than 50 percent of the total electricity generated in Korea (quoted in MKE 2010c, 50) uses electricity at a price that is only 86.59 percent of the production cost (MKE 2010c, 11). This cost recovery rate varies over time and year, and is said to have been between 89.4 and 90 percent in 2010.[3] While cheap utility prices have helped Korean industries to be price-competitive in the global market, distortions in the pricing structure of the electricity market fail to induce industries to reduce electricity usage.

Furthermore, low electricity prices have been pointed out as one element that caused the rapid increase of demand for electricity in Korea. According to the government's past prognostication, demand should have grown by 2.4 percent during the years 2006 and 2011; this fell short of the actual 4 percent increase. Indeed, for the last ten years, Korea has been experiencing a particularly rapid growth in electricity demand. With electricity demand increasing 1.5 times faster than the country's economic growth, this ratio is larger than most advanced countries and even China (Lee and Chun 2011). The fact that the government has shown little success in containing the large increase in demand for electricity is a factor in the tension between the broader ambition of a greener society and the specific objectives of green growth policies.

With the current constraints on increasing the supply of electricity, at least in the short term, the fear of total blackouts in Korea has been rising, especially after the occurrence on September 2011, when power reserves fell to 240,000 kWh and 37 percent of households across the country lost power

(Ho and Chun 2011). Despite efforts to fix the problem, the supply and demand imbalance remains an issue.

However, yet another problem with current subsidies is that it may limit the introduction of real-time pricing of electricity that is critical to the effective utilization of the smart grid and generally weaken natural incentives to develop and use energy efficient and smart grid products in the domestic market. A combination of these factors makes creating a pricing system that effectively conveys market incentives — a key feature of the smart grid — very difficult.

Currently, the Presidential Committee on Green Growth is trying to reform the retail electricity market by introducing a variable pricing system for electricity. The Ministry of Knowledge Economy submitted its Electricity Price Revision Plan to Congress in February 2013, suggesting a simplified pricing system for residential electricity. Specifics include reducing the progressive utility rates to at least three or four from the previous six levels and also reducing the discrepancies between the highest and lowest rates. As prior attempts at deregulation and privatization have shown — both in Korea and in other cases — the task of introducing responsiveness into the market is complex, and the solutions that will ultimately work to support the type of transformation Korea seeks may need to be the product of experimentation.

Four Major Rivers Restoration Project

The current administration's corporate friendliness is indeed a double-sided coin. Though industry support is a critical factor if the green spiral is to be initiated and maintained in Korea, it also raises concerns that economic growth, rather than climate change mitigation or adaptation goals, may be the overwhelming content of Korea's green growth policies. Adversaries pointed out that President Lee's policies and programs were "green washed," meaning that simple construction projects were conveniently relabeled as green projects, despite their possible adverse effects on the environment. In essence, these arguments hint at the possibility that climate mitigation goals have come only as an afterthought to promoting a new model of economic growth and improving energy security.

On this matter, the Four Major Rivers Restoration Project, along with the Grand Canal project, is at the center of the debate. Together, these projects in the water and waste sector take up a significant portion (45 percent) of Green Stimulus Spending (UNEP 2009). While aiming to prepare for climate change, mitigate damages from annual floods, satiate water needs, and promote rural development, these projects have consistently met severe resistance from academia, environmentalists, and the general public. The nation was, and still is, sharply divided on this issue. Experts from both sides make valid arguments on the pros and cons of the river restoration project, but there are other concerns besides the environmental side effects. Critics point out that the actual economic benefits of the restoration projects fall short of those suggested by the government. On top of that, the immense annual maintenance costs have recently been brought to public attention, further undermining the case for proponents of the river restoration projects. By 2010, public opinion surveys showed that almost as many were opposed to the government plan as were showing support.

Yet, despite vigorous opposition, President Lee pushed through with the project. The Ministry of Land, Transport, and Maritime Affairs (MLTMA) announced in January 2013 that 99.4 percent of the construction had been completed. The debate, however, seems far from being resolved. While the government reported a stunning reduction in flood damages in 2012 (one-tenth compared to the previous year), despite a twofold increase in rainfall in 2011, opponents still argue that the government's claims are groundless and contend that the government used faulty measurement tools. Furthermore, they believe that because annual sedimentation would require massive maintenance costs, the river restoration project would perpetuate unnecessary government spending.

Energy Development Plans

As mentioned above, Korea's goal is to get 59 percent of its total energy from nuclear power plants by 2030. Although many reluctantly acknowledge nuclear power to be the only feasible alternative to fossil fuels, the government's aggressive goal toward nuclear energy development has been controversial, not only because of its environmental effects but also due to safety concerns and its ambiguous effect on future energy security.

Nuclear energy's safety concerns have increased substantially after the fears of nuclear explosion and radiation exposure in Fukushima, Japan. When Korea won the bid in 2010 to construct nuclear power plants in the United Arab Emirates, with expected profits of $4 million, the country was excited about becoming the next major nuclear power exporter. Yet, despite such major accomplishments, safety issues regarding nuclear energy generation, including proper disposal methods of the nuclear wastes, continue to be debated. In response to the recent concerns regarding the safety of nuclear power plants, the Korean government has announced the Domestic Nuclear Energy Security Check Plan. The government expects to continue discussion about this issue.

It is also worth noting that the effect of nuclear power on energy security is unclear. Despite KEPCO's recent discovery of uranium in Waterbury Lake,

Canada, Korea would have to continue importing a major portion of its uranium from Russia, Kazakhstan, and/or Australia. While Korea is potentially simply trading one dependency for another, expanding nuclear power in the country's energy portfolio will reduce its high dependency on oil coming from the Middle East. At the moment, Korea is more concentrated on tackling the potential safety issues of nuclear power plants; potential dependency issues related to uranium are not considered a major concern.

The government's relative lack of enthusiasm about developing renewable energy, on the other hand, has caused concern. Because only 6 percent of the Green Stimulus Package is devoted to this area, along with the seemingly modest goal of producing 11 percent of total energy production from renewable energy sources by 2030, many believe the government's green rhetoric is insincere. Although a simple numeric comparison with the targets of China (15 percent by 2030) and Europe (20 percent by 2020) may be unrealistic and insignificant, the government's plan to focus on nuclear energy generation has estranged environmentalist groups and the opposing Democratic Party.

Between 2002 and 2011, Korea experienced the largest growth (19,584 percent) in electricity generation from wind, solar, geothermal, tidal, and hydro among the G20 countries. In absolute terms, however, Korea still produces only 4.13 billion kWh — 0.9 percent of total electricity generation — from those renewable energy sources (quoted in Schmidt and Haifly 2012, 3). The government has been allocating an annual amount of ₩1 billion for the last five years on FITs, renewable energy R&D, and infrastructure building (approximately $850 million in 2011), but many claim that it has not been sufficient to induce substantial growth. The recent euro-zone crisis has been especially detrimental to the solar energy industry. OCI Corporation, the world's second largest polysilicon producer operating in Korea, made a tentative decision to cancel the construction of two major plants. Other firms in the industry, such as LG Chemical and SK Chemical, have similarly put off investment plans, while eight out of nine domestic solar battery producers have been shut down. Critics explain that the allocated budgets are being used ineffectively without sufficient preparation or evaluation tools (Han and Lee 2012).

However, environmental activist groups are responsible at least partially for the slow progress in renewable energy development. Several renewable energy projects have been delayed or even repealed due to objections from local environmentalists. A wind farm in Moojoo and a tidal power plant in Incheon are just some of the examples. According to those opposing organizations, tidal power plants destroy mudflats, wind farms create noise pollution, and solar power plants desolate forests. The absence of a unified effort to promote renewable energy development exacerbates the problem.

While various individual environmentalist groups condemn the government's plan on nuclear energy development, each one has been unsuccessful in providing a feasible alternative.

Can the Spiral toward Green Continue?

The government, as discussed, is no longer in a position to completely dictate economic development and must work with conglomerate firms that are major players not only in the domestic but also in the global market. These firms, which were once very much dependent on government guidance, now have the resources to conduct market research, invest in R&D, read global market trends, examine customer taste, and, most importantly, follow their own agendas. While such eye-opening progress made by major firms is appreciated and applauded, it also implies that the government may have to compromise, at least in the short run, to get the industrial sector participants on board with its green agendas.

On this note, the government's role is nonetheless critical in nurturing firms and allowing them to make preparations to cope with Europe's green protectionism. The introduction of a national GHG inventory report system is a meaningful step in the right direction. The system requires that target firms (with more than 25,000 tons of GHG emission) set individual GHG emissions- and energy consumption–reduction goals and report back to the government with results. If successful, the system would not only contribute to realizing the country's emission-reduction targets but also allow for proper measurement, reporting, and verification in the country. Yet, this plan is again criticized for its leniency toward the industrial sector. According to the current agenda, the industrial sector would be responsible for 18.2 percent of the total GHG emissions-reduction target, and the transportation sector would be responsible for 34.3 percent (MKE 2011). Critics suspect that the government may have laid the entire burden on the transportation sector, which is not represented by a significant interest group.

With the news that Korea will be hosting the UN Green Climate Fund's headquarters in Songdo, the country felt a growing optimism about becoming a leader on future developmental and climate issues. Though it seems that politicians share common interests in pursuing "green" growth, political delicacy is involved in defining exactly what they mean by it. President Park Geun-hye has shown some caution in following her predecessor's exact footsteps since her inauguration in February 2013. To the public eye, "green growth" was President Lee's most publicized agenda and achievement, and it is understandable that the current administration wishes to put some distance

186   between itself and some of the more controversial projects like the Four Major
Rivers Restoration Project. Pundits are already worried about President Park's
apparent lack of enthusiasm about the issue. The PCGG has been demoted
to an office under the prime minister, and other responsible bureaus and divi-
sions have been downsized or renamed to exclude the word "green." Nevertheless, President Park has promised to continue pursuing the country's major
goals of reducing GHG emissions and promoting low-carbon growth even if
it is under a different label of sustainable development and creative economy.

What gives hope to proponents of green growth is that public support for
green growth policies has gained momentum in Korea. The public sees green
growth as something helpful and advanced: according to Korea's Presidential
Committee on Green Growth, 96.7 percent of the population believe that
green growth policies should continue to be implemented by the Park administration. The government's R&D investment has increased from ₩2 trillion
($1.7 billion) in 2009 to ₩2.7 trillion ($2.3 billion) in 2011, and during the
same period, the country's technological levels have risen from 50.9 percent
of those of leading countries to 77.7 percent. The 30 largest corporations in
Korea have been projected to invest ₩22.4 trillion ($19 billion) between 2011
and 2013, compared to the ₩15.1 trillion ($13 billion) invested between 2008
and 2010. Within three years, the renewable energy sector experienced a 3.7
times growth in employment, a 6.5 times rise in sales, and a 7.3 times surge
in exports (PCGG 2012). Importantly, as part of an effort to entrench its green
growth initiatives, the Lee administration has with fanfare and international
attention established the Global Green Growth Institute (GGGI) to explore
ways of creating and implementing green strategies that drive growth. Specific
agendas may have to be changed or forgone, but the country and its government would hardly miss a chance to become a leader in the green world.

CONCLUSION: CAN A GREEN SPIRAL BE SUSTAINED?

Two distinctive features of the Korean case should be emphasized. First,
the Korean government has sought to consciously initiate a domestic green
growth spiral and to entrench that domestic effort with international commitments to promote green strategies for growth. Second, Korean policy has
pursued multiple ambitious objectives — energy security, economic growth,
and emissions reduction — that intertwine to create a common purpose. As its
goals are currently formulated, there is little conflict among these three objectives. According to the plan, green growth will reduce emissions, improve
energy security, create significant employment, and drive economic growth,
all in a greener way. This unity of purpose could translate to an unusually uni-

fied coalition of interests supporting these goals, assuming the different actors involved (government, business, consumers) can reach comparable unity on the tools to use to get to the desired outcomes.

However, there has been an unresolved conflict on the concept of green between the government and the environmentalists. As a result, relatively little has been accomplished in building a coalition that involves the broader civil society and enables the multilevel transformation that culminates in a social paradigm shift. On the other hand, there have been considerable developments to the coalition of business interests. The Lee administration formed a uniting economic incentive pushing for green growth, and such a strong perception of a purely economic motive strengthened the overall rationale for Korea's package of energy objectives and should continue to help build a coalition of industries. As the government moves forward with initiating the green spiral, it will have to concoct strategies to engage opposing parties and embed its vision beyond party politics.

Hence, Korea does face meaningful challenges in achieving many of its goals. Yet, considering that green growth is still at a very early stage of development, the government has definitely taken significant steps, such as laying out the institutional framework necessary for green growth. It is prepared to take active roles in delivering many of its promises to emerge as a role model for later-developing countries in realizing the green growth paradigm for sustainable and balanced growth.

Korea may also be somewhat unique in the scope and timeline of its ambitions. In this discussion we have, directly or implicitly, discussed a variety of transformations that are being undertaken or must be undertaken as part of Korea's desired paradigm shift: a shift in power sources and use; a restructuring of the energy market and its pricing structure; a possible shift in industrial structure toward more incorporation of small- and medium-sized firms that are natural fits for emerging niches in new industries; and a shift in the international role toward a more assertive leadership in standard-making. And these are just a subset of the range of changes Korea wants to make; shifts beyond our scope of discussion here range from changes in ecological approaches to mass transit to building and urban planning to citizen lifestyle.

Individually, these shifts are important. But taken together, the whole may be greater than the sum of its parts if Korea succeeds in restructuring the expectations, logic, and behavior of Korean society and the economy into a new, self-sustaining green whole with a momentum of its own—what President Lee Myung-bak termed "a new national development paradigm" (Lee 2008). We have argued that we have seen such self-reinforcing transformations occur, to greatly varying degrees, in the companion cases of Denmark and California.

188   However, if Korea succeeds in a similar paradigm shift, its transformation will be somewhat unique in being the result less of the kind of path-dependent, evolutionary process seen in those cases and more of a conscious effort undertaken at a historic moment. It remains to be seen how fully Korea will succeed with its goals — individually and as a coherent whole — but the process commands attention from scholars of green growth policy.

11

CHINA

Green Industry Growth in a Brown Economy

Crystal Chang and Huan Gao

INTRODUCTION

China presents a puzzling case of green industry growth in an otherwise brown economy. The country is at once the world's largest exporter of solar panels and its largest greenhouse gas emitter. This seeming contradiction can be explained if the Chinese government's recent promotion of green technologies is viewed not as a domestic antidote to fossil fuels but rather as another facet of the country's manufacturing-based and export-led industrialization strategy. We argue that the Chinese government's continued promotion of energy-intensive manufacturing is a political choice. The Chinese Communist Party (CCP) has made an implicit bargain with the Chinese public to provide sustained rates of economic growth and rising incomes in exchange for social stability and the continued right to rule. The economic potential of green industries alone is not enough to sustain the Party's side of the bargain.

To be sure, the politics of green growth in China are more complicated than the tension between the country's energy-intensive economy and emissions reduction. China lacks the type of broad coalition between policy makers, environmentalists, and industrialists necessary to drive and sustain green growth policies. Such a coalition is unlikely to emerge for a number of reasons. State agencies, especially the State-Owned Assets Supervision and Administration Commission, control many of China's energy-intensive and highly polluting industrial assets, making the regulation of those assets by other state agencies difficult, and there are conflicts among them. And while public protest over China's environmental degradation has been growing, the focus has been on both water and air contamination that pose immediate dangers to public health. Furthermore, organization around environmental issues is severely limited due to the government's paranoia over collective opposition.

On the ground, there has been little, if any, buy-in from local governments as to the necessity of curbing carbon emissions, especially if doing so could negatively affect the local economy. Scientific voices in the government have expressed deep concerns about the impact of climate change on average air temperatures, precipitation, and extreme weather events across China. But the fact that their 2007 National Climate Change Programme (NDRC 2007) has seen little action suggests scientists have yet to find powerful political allies.

Because of the country's size, China's energy policies and green industry growth have stirred global controversy. A binding international agreement to curb carbon emissions would be useless without the commitment of the world's largest emitter. Yet, the Chinese government has repeatedly contended that because China is a "developing country" with hundreds of millions of its citizens living in poverty, the country should not be bound by the same emissions standards as advanced industrialized nations. Meanwhile, sophisticated Chinese firms are flooding global markets with state-subsidized green technology products, in some cases pricing foreign competitors like Solyndra out of the market. Is this unfair trade? If foreign governments enact tariffs to curb the importation of Chinese green products, a trade war could ensue that could hamper global economic recovery.

In the remainder of this chapter, we endeavor to clarify the reality of green growth in China. First, by shedding light on the politics of economic and energy policy making, we explain why the Chinese government has aggressively promoted green industries but has yet to adopt a more comprehensive green growth strategy. Second, we evaluate five key areas of China's energy strategy to show how the current policy framework is set up to stretch the limits of its existing energy system but not to fundamentally transform it. Third, we touch on some of the international implications of the government's promotion of domestic green industries. We conclude with a few unconventional ideas about how the international community might nudge China toward a greener economic growth trajectory.

THE POLITICAL ECONOMY OF ENERGY IN CHINA

Like many developing countries, China faces the twin challenges of reducing emissions and keeping up with rapid growth in energy demand. The 12th Five Year Plan (FYP) encourages local officials to cut emissions, but it gives them considerable leeway to make adjustments as the Chinese economy continues to expand. The plan's target is to reduce energy *intensity*[1] — not total energy consumption — by 16 percent. Not only is this a step backward from the 20 percent reduction target set in the 11th FYP, but it also means that as China's economy continues to grow, energy consumption and related emissions will also continue to grow, albeit at a slower pace. This modest emissions reduction goal reflects the government's ambivalent attitude toward — and lack of commitment to — an economic growth strategy that is compatible with emissions reduction. In this section, we argue that China's ambivalence toward green growth can be attributed to the absence of a broad-based coalition necessary to promote and sustain a green growth strategy.

During the reign of Mao Zedong, the CCP derived its legitimacy through the banner of communism. With the winding down of communist ideology in China's reform period (1978–present), the ability to create tens of millions of jobs annually and raise living standards for China's vast population became the new source of legitimacy for the CCP's continued rule.[2] It is no accident that the first goal listed in Section 3 — "Main Objectives" — of the 12th FYP remains an economic growth target of 7 percent. China's emergence as a global manufacturing powerhouse has sustained CCP rule by generating impressive employment growth and keeping a lid on social instability.

During the communist period, state-owned factories were responsible for all industrial output. Economic reforms have permitted some growth of the private sector, especially in light industries such as textiles and consumer products. State-owned enterprises (SOEs), however, remain dominant in many capital- and energy-intensive upstream industries such as iron, coal, and steel, as well as downstream industries like heavy machinery, automobiles, and construction. Such firms benefit from a number of preferential policies, including state-subsidized loans, lucrative government procurement contracts, lax enforcement of environmental regulations, and access to subsidized energy inputs.

The industrial sector — which continues to be dominated by state-owned firms — is estimated to comprise 46.8 percent of China's economy in 2010 (CIA 2011b), much higher than those in other prominent industrializing and developing economies, such as 28.6 percent in India or 26.4 percent in Brazil (CIA 2011a, 2011c). The dominance of steel, cement, electronics, and other energy-intensive industries, coupled with double-digit GDP growth, has led to soaring energy demand in China and made it the world's largest energy consumer.[3] In its *World Energy Outlook 2010*, the International Energy Agency predicts that between 2010 and 2035, China's energy demand will increase by 75 percent (IEA 2010c, 5). Equally alarming is the U.S. Energy Information Administration's prediction that China's electricity generation alone will triple between 2009 and 2035, producing 10,555 billion kWh of electricity in 2035 (EIA 2010b, 16). Though China has had a good track record when it comes to improving energy efficiency, the 12th FYP's stated goal of reducing the energy intensity of GDP by 16 percent over the next five years is simply not enough to level off energy consumption and related emissions.

As Figure 11.1 shows, China's energy production relies heavily on coal. According to official data from its National Bureau of Statistics, China's total

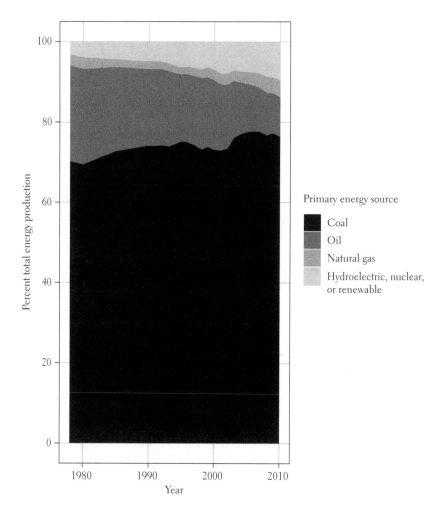

FIGURE 11.1   Chinese energy production by primary energy source, 1978–2010
SOURCE: NBS 2011.

primary energy production measured 3.25 billion tons of standard coal equivalent in 2010, of which 68 percent came from coal.[4] While the production of hydroelectric, nuclear, and renewable energy in the past decades has steadily increased to 9.4 percent, such sources have tended to displace the use of natural gas and gasoline, but not that of coal. On the contrary, the share of coal in China's energy production profile has steadily increased since the 1980s.

China's electricity production, more specifically, is overwhelmingly reliant on coal. In 2010, 80.8 percent of China's electricity was generated by thermal power plants, the majority of which are coal-fired, with some fueled by natural gas. Hydroelectric power generated 16.2 percent of electricity; nuclear power, 1.8 percent; wind, 1.2 percent; and all others, such as garbage incineration plants, solar energy, and geothermal power, were less than 0.1 percent (State Electricity Regulatory Commission of China 2011, 10).

China's recent development of domestic shale gas has been touted as a cleaner alternative to coal, but these sources are unlikely to significantly displace coal in the near future. According to the EIA's assessment, China has 1,275 trillion cubic feet of shale gas, the largest reserve in the world (EIA 2011, 4). However, shale gas exploration and development are still in the infant stage in China. Thus far, Chinese companies remain focused on surveying, drilling test wells, and acquiring technology through collaboration with foreign firms on overseas projects. According to the NDRC's "Shale Gas Development Plan 2011–2015," as of the end of 2011, there are only 15 domestic test wells, with 9 producing gas. The NDRC's goal is to raise the annual production level to 6.5 billion cubic meters, or 229.5 billion cubic feet, by 2015 (NDRC 2012, 7). Though this figure sounds ambitious, it amounts to less than 10 percent of China's gas consumption in 2009 (EIA 2011, 4). The government's ambitious development of shale gas is further evidence that China's leadership has little intention of moving toward an emission-free economy.

The state's continued ownership of productive industrial assets including shale gas production complicates its role as regulator of emissions. The output of state-owned entities, though much lower than during the communist period, remains significant. While accurate data do not exist, various estimates put the share of gross domestic product of state-owned and partially state-owned entities at somewhere between 30 and 40 percent (OECD 2009; Szamosszegi and Kyle 2011).[5] The Ministry of Environmental Protection is limited in its ability to enforce Chinese environmental laws and regulations, especially when the polluting assets are highly lucrative and protected by other powerful state agencies.

The problem of conflict of interest is particularly salient at the local level. As one prominent China scholar has noted, China's environmental strategy resembles their economic strategy (Economy 2010, 95). China's leaders provide administrative and legal guidance but devolve far greater authority to provincial and local officials. As it embraced the market as a force for change, the central government allowed local officials to become the agents of economic reform by giving them full control over local resources and industrial assets.

This decentralized model of development has been wildly successful in spurring economic growth, but it has proved insufficient to protect an already fragile environment. Typically, when a new law is issued by the central government, local governments issue their own version of the national law (Stalley 2010, 25). Not only is the implementation of environmental directives often a matter of interpretation, but many local governments lack the capacity to enforce national targets. Take, for example, the unintended consequences of energy efficiency programs. Struggling to meet the energy intensity–reduction targets, some local officials scheduled brownouts, which caused the temporary shutdown of factories, schools, and hospitals. When the lights were turned off, manufacturers fired up diesel generators to compensate for the loss of electricity from the grid. These actions had the perverse effect of driving up diesel prices and ultimately food prices (Xinhua 2010), not to mention promoting an uncontrolled source of energy use and emissions in the form of off-grid diesel generation.

The low capacity of local governments is exacerbated by endemic corruption. In 2007, the Chinese Academy for Environmental Planning estimated that only half of the national budget for environmental protection was spent on legitimate projects (Economy 2007). The loss of public funds due to graft is particularly egregious in a country that already suffers from a poorly funded environmental protection regime. Local officials knowingly shield local enterprises from national regulations, sometimes turning a blind eye to their pollution of local water and land resources. When faced with the choice between upholding environmental protection laws and supporting an energy-intensive factory employing thousands of residents, local officials often choose the latter.

In 2006, Zhou Shengxian, the director of the State Environmental Protection Administration, said, "It is clear the conflict between economic growth and environmental protection is coming to a head. Fraud in project approval was prominent with many projects passing their environmental assessment without fulfilling the necessary criteria" (Lague 2006). Zhou admitted that a government investigation into pollution control approvals for construction projects worth more than $12.5 million found violations in almost 40 percent of cases. Without an autonomous central agency to serve as the lead monitor and enforcer of environmental laws and regulations, local economic interests often prevail. And although there have been thousands of localized public protests over poor natural resource management in recent years, public outcry has not led to significant policy change.

Chinese leaders remain highly sensitive to collective efforts with the potential to criticize the CCP leadership. As a result, the government has instituted registration restrictions that require nongovernmental organizations to find a government sponsor, which, in addition to various other legal measures, severely constrain the number, size, and reach of environmentally concerned citizens. Furthermore, the self-censorship of the state-run media has limited its bite as a corporate watchdog. And although social networking sites are increasingly becoming platforms to spread news of local scandals, they have yet to produce an Arab Spring–like social movement pushing for significant political reform. These are some of the reasons why a grassroots green growth coalition has yet to emerge in China.

The other problem with carbon emissions is that unlike deforestation and water pollution, they are not visible to the naked eye. Even though many scientists find that China's endemic problems of water shortage or desertification are in large part due to climate change, their claims are hard to "prove" to ordinary citizens. As a result, there has been little public pressure on the government to act on the climate issue; most of that pressure has come from the international community. To be sure, the lack of public consensus over climate change is not a uniquely Chinese problem, evidenced by widespread climate change skepticism in the United States.

To sum up, the legitimacy of China's single-party government largely rests on its ability to secure the energy required to sustain the country's manufacturing-driven economy, not on its ability to solve the emissions problem. And while environmental protection is an increasingly salient social issue, the public's attention is primarily focused on issues such as water pollution that visibly impact public health. The problem of carbon emissions has not yet reached the radar of the average citizen, and thus little public pressure has been put on the government to reduce emissions. Public action is further limited because of a censored media and strict regulations over social organization. The national laws and initiatives that do exist are often lackadaisically implemented by local officials who often prioritize economic growth and personal enrichment over environmental protection.

OPPORTUNITIES AND CONSTRAINTS IN CHINA'S ENERGY POLICY FRAMEWORK

In this section, we evaluate five key components of China's energy policy framework: energy efficiency, expansion of renewables, electricity transmission, economic restructuring, and electricity pricing reform. China is making strides in the first three areas, but overcoming hurdles in the last two — economic restructuring and electricity pricing reform — will be difficult. Despite its progress in these areas, China's current policy framework is not designed to reduce the country's *total* carbon emissions, let alone achieve a full decoupling of emissions from economic growth within the next two decades.[6] Rather, China's ad hoc basket of energy and environmental policies are designed to extend the boundaries of the existing energy system, not to fundamentally transform it. We now turn to examine in greater detail each of these five areas of China's energy policy.

Energy Efficiency: Grabbing the Low-Hanging Fruit

In 2006, China consumed 48 percent more energy per unit of GDP compared to the United States and nearly twice as much compared to Japan or France (EIA 2008). The high energy intensity of the Chinese GDP is the result of a combination of factors, including, but not limited to, inefficient technology, a manufacturing-driven export-led economy, and price controls that distort energy usage by industrial and residential consumers. In many ways, creating policy incentives to improve energy efficiency reflects an effort to grab the low-hanging fruit in the existing economic and energy system.

From the late 1970s to the late 1990s, China had a strong track record of reducing the energy intensity of its economic growth. But after China's accession to the World Trade Organization, manufactured exports began to soar, and with it the energy intensity per unit of GDP. To curb this unwelcome trend, the Chinese government began to adopt a number of policies to promote energy efficiency in 2004. Those policy measures included fiscal incentives such as tax breaks for purchasing energy-conserving equipment, stricter standards for new buildings and appliances, mandated closures of inefficient coal-fired power plants and manufacturing plants, and information-driven programs like appliance labeling and media advertising (Zhou, Levine, and Price 2010). Despite the blip in the early 2000s, the Chinese government has been fairly successful with its energy efficiency programs.

The government has been particularly aggressive in closing small and inefficient power plants and producers of energy-intensive products. Between 2006 and 2010, China shut down 72.1 GW of small coal-fired generators (Wen 2011). Many inefficient producers of coal, steel, concrete, and coke were also closed down. Perhaps most importantly, the central government has signaled that it will begin to evaluate the performance of local officials based on their ability to meet not only economic growth targets but also national energy intensity– reduction targets. The 12th FYP states that the government will strengthen the

evaluation of energy conservation goals and improve the reward and punish-
ment system to ensure that local governments have the proper incentives to
carry out energy efficiency policies (NDRC 2011).

Between 2006 and 2010, the implementation of energy efficiency policies
has helped China to reduce energy intensity by 19.1 percent from 2005 levels, just shy of the 11th FYP's stated target of 20 percent. The use of ad hoc
measures — brownouts, shutdowns, off-grid generation, and so forth — suggests
that China was already pushing close to its practical limit of energy intensity
reduction within the current policy framework and energy system during the
last FYP. This is probably why the government lowered the energy intensity–
reduction target in the 12th FYP from 20 to 16 percent. A 16 percent reduction
in energy intensity appears achievable under the current policy framework,
but it hardly amounts to a dramatic transformation of the current system.

*Renewable Energy: Promoting the Growth of Green
Industries*

Renewable energy has witnessed explosive growth in China. As of 2010, the
country had a total of 25.8 GW of installed wind capacity, second only to the
United States in absolute terms. More than half of that capacity, 13.8 GW,
was added in 2009 alone (Li, Shi, and Gao 2010, 4). China has become a
large market for renewable technology deployments, which has enticed the
world's leading energy companies as well as the participation of new domestic
entrants. With the help of the Chinese government, homegrown green firms
have become major global players. Yet, despite the impressive export performance of China's green industries, renewable sources will not significantly
displace fossil fuels in China's overall energy mix.

To be fair, the central government has made some efforts to increase the
share of renewable sources at home. The two national grid companies are
required by law to purchase energy from wind and solar farms at higher rates,
which ensures that renewable power plants can cover their cost and maintain
a profit margin. China's major power producers, especially the state-run "Big
Five," have been in negotiations with local governments to secure rights on
land and at sea to develop new renewable resources. Oceanfront investment
agreements from the Big Five exceed RMB 100 billion (about $15 billion) in
committed funds (C. Zhang 2010). Similarly, there has been a wave of land
deals in western China's vast deserts with high solar potential (Dong 2009).
Numerous hydroelectric projects are also on the drawing board. China's grid
companies are also investing in a new transmission system that will help overcome transmission bottlenecks and facilitate the integration of renewable
sources into the grid.

Zero emissions are a benefit of renewable energy installations, but they are not the primary reason for the Chinese government's massive investments. Rather, such investments allow China to both diversify its energy portfolio and expand its domestic energy supply. A bird's-eye view of China's energy strategy suggests that the government is not only investing in the expansion of renewables but also in the expansion of fossil fuel sources and other nonfossil fuel sources like nuclear power. The government's target of 15 percent non-fossil fuels in the primary energy consumption by 2020 is significant (Zhou 2010), but, once again, it does not amount to a fundamental transformation of China's existing fossil fuel–based energy system.

Though the impact on the domestic energy landscape is limited, China's green industries are booming abroad. China's green firms enjoy many advantages: cheap labor, an extensive electronics supply chain, price supports, state-subsidized loans, and cooperation from the central and local governments. As a result, China's solar cell producers, such as Suntech Power and JA Solar, are some of the most competitive in the world. China's solar industry has enjoyed an annual growth rate of more than 100 percent for the past five years and has produced more than half of the world's photovoltaic cells in 2010 (SEMI, PV Group, and CPIA 2011, 6). According to the *New York Times*, up to 95 percent of China's solar panel output in recent years was exported (Bradsher and Wald 2012). China was also the world's largest producer of wind turbines in 2009 (Bradsher 2010a), led by the state-owned Sinovel, the second largest wind turbine manufacturer in the world in 2011 (Xinhua 2011a). Industry experts find that Chinese solar firms are contributing to the falling prices of photovoltaic cells worldwide (SEMI, PV Group, and CPIA 2011), thus reducing the costs of renewable energy deployments around the world.

We see the government's promotion of domestic green industries as a logical extension of its export-oriented, manufacturing-driven economic strategy rather than as a tool for a fundamental energy system transformation. Given the Chinese government's commitment to investing and deploying renewables, it should be able to reach its rather modest 15 percent nonfossil fuel target by 2020. Ironically, Chinese greentech products will likely help turn the "religion" of green growth into a "reality" in other countries long before they are able to do so at home.

Ultra-High-Voltage Transmission Grid: Integrating More
Than Just Renewables

Grid connectivity and long-distance transmission have been two of the greatest obstacles to expanding renewable energy in China. To overcome these obstacles, China is building an ultra-high-voltage (UHV) transmission grid. The problem is that the majority of China's hydroelectric, wind, and solar energy resources are located in western and northern regions, far away from the eastern and southern regions where energy demand is the greatest (State Grid Corporation of China 2010). To make matters worse, the regions where renewable opportunities are the greatest are also those in which grid networks are the weakest (Li, Shi, and Gao 2010).[7] Lack of transmission capacity in part explains why a shocking 30 percent of China's wind-generation capacity is not connected to a power grid of any kind (Xinhua 2011b). The new UHV grid is intended to integrate existing and new renewable sources to the national grid, but as we explain below, it is also intended to integrate new fossil fuel sources, including coal and natural gas.

To overcome the transmission bottleneck, State Grid Corporation of China, China's largest transmission and distribution company, is building a new UHV transmission grid that is scheduled to be completed by 2020. By 2015, there will be seven long-distance, alternate-current UHV transmission lines, as well as eleven 800-kV direct-current UHV transmission lines. Together, these lines are capable of transmitting electricity across a distance of more than 2,000 kilometers, linking renewable energy resources in northern and western China to load centers in the east (State Grid Corporation of China 2010, 28; Y. Zhang 2010). State Grid Corporation of China predicts that in 2015, the grid will be able to accommodate three times more clean energy sources compared to 2005 (2010, 53).

This same UHV transmission grid will also expand the transmission capacity and reach of coal-fired electricity plants. The use of coal has been somewhat constrained by the transportation capacity between coal-producing regions and those regions where energy demand is greatest. Currently, coal is transported from mines in northwestern China to coal-fired power plants in the eastern seaboard via railroads, or first via rail to a northern seaport and then via boats to southern cities. In 2008, 49 percent of the freight cargo by weight traveling on national railroads and 21 percent of China's total port throughput were coal, most of which was destined for power plants (NBS 2010, 15–20; State Grid Corporation of China 2010).[8] The transportation of coal is one of the greatest bottlenecks to meeting China's energy demand. The new UHV grid will allow more coal-fired power plants to be built where the coal is mined. Instead of transporting coal across the country, which is costly, dirty, and inefficient, electricity will be produced where coal—including low-grade lignite—is abundant and then transmitted to load centers via a new long-distance transmission network (State Grid Corporation of China 2010, 34).

The extension of the UHV grid to reach new coal deposits reflects the Chinese government's continued commitment to coal as the primary energy input. According to many estimates, China has 114.5 billion tons of proven coal reserves, or 14 percent of the world's total coal reserves (EIA 2008; Morse and He 2010).[9] Coal's abundance and relatively low costs make it the most attractive option to satisfy China's rapidly expanding energy demand. There is little incentive for the government to reduce the use of coal, despite its contribution to atmospheric greenhouse gases. In countries that lack large domestic sources of fossil fuels, such as Denmark and Korea, the desire to curb fuel imports and enhance energy security naturally coincides with the need to develop nonfossil fuel energy sources. However, in countries where fossil fuels like coal are abundant, such as the United States and China, enhancing energy security means exploiting available domestic sources first, even if they are highly polluting.

To be fair, the central government is seeking ways to mine and burn coal more efficiently, safely, and cleanly. These measures address economic efficiency as well as energy efficiency and local pollution. As mentioned earlier, China is overhauling its fragmented coal mining industry via the closure of small mines as well as merger and acquisition.[10] The 12th FYP emphasizes consolidation of the coal mining industry to create larger and more efficient mining conglomerates (NDRC 2011). The Chinese government is also actively closing down small coal-fired power plants and installing larger power plants that produce less pollution, including CO_2 emissions, per unit of energy produced (Yang, Guo, and Wang 2010). Finally, the government is exploring carbon capture and sequestration (CCS). In 2009, China's first near-zero-emission coal plant won state approval. Other similar pilots are in the works, including one in Inner Mongolia that could become the largest sequestration project in the world (Friedman 2009). Because it is still unclear how much CCS projects will cost to build and operate, not to mention what the environmental consequences might be of putting tons of CO_2 into the ground, it is too early to project the impact that CCS could have on China's emissions.

Economic Restructuring: Shifting China's Economic Growth Machine

In the 12th FYP and elsewhere, the Chinese government is emphasizing the need for economic restructuring to both achieve more balanced and sustainable economic development and mitigate the depletion of China's limited natural resources. Increasing the efficiency of China's manufacturing-based

economy is important, but alone it is not enough to significantly curb energy demand or carbon emissions. A transition to a more services-based and
consumption-oriented economy will be key. The question is how much of a
shift is enough to make a difference?

The 12th FYP calls for a modest 4 percent increase in the share of services
in the economy (NDRC 2011), which stood at 43.6 percent in 2010 (CIA 2011b).
It is not clear, however, how the government practically intends to speed up
that transition. Instead of a detailed plan, there are only ad hoc measures. For
example, the government claims to be offering firms in the service sector the
same rates for water, electricity, and natural gas enjoyed by firms in the industrial sector (NDRC 2011), which it hopes will boost the business of service
sector firms.

How quickly the Chinese economy can shift away from export-oriented
manufacturing and large infrastructure investments and toward increased
services and domestic consumption is open for debate. In our view, an accelerated transition away from energy- and carbon-intensive industries to more
service-centered industries will require more innovative policies than simply
lowering energy rates. Economic restructuring is hampered by the fact that
SOEs tend to be concentrated in manufacturing-based industries, banking
and telecommunications notwithstanding. Is the Chinese leadership prepared
to curb subsidies to SOEs in traditional sectors and increase policy support
to private firms and entrepreneurs? There has been no precedent for such a
shift. Government officials have yet to realize that economic restructuring will
require a paradigmatic shift in the state's role in the economy.

*Electricity Pricing Reform: Squeezing China's
Power Producers*

The Chinese energy sector remains under tight state control. While prices
for petroleum and natural gas have been allowed to move more or less with
global prices, the government continues to tightly control electricity prices for
residential and some industrial users. Electricity subsidies distort the market
and may prove to be the single greatest obstacle to reducing energy use and
overall energy intensity in China.

China's National Development and Reform Commission (NDRC), the
main agency in charge of national economic policy, sets the prices of energy
inputs and retail energy. The NDRC has been reluctant to raise utility rates
for fear of public backlash, despite the fact that market-based coal prices have
climbed precipitously due to China's exploding energy demand. The average
price of coal at Qinhuangdao port, a major coal terminal in China, increased

from roughly $60 per metric ton in early 2005 to $160 per metric ton at the height of energy prices in 2008 (Morse and He 2010, 7). During that period, there were only one or two modest electricity rate hikes per year of less than 5 percent. Chinese power producers and grid companies have been squeezed between rising coal prices and state-controlled retail electricity prices, often suffering huge operating losses. Rather than allowing electricity prices to rise, the NDRC and other government agencies have instead opted to support state-owned utilities and grid companies by helping them negotiate for lower coal prices or, in some cases, by offering government handouts to compensate for losses.

Another problem with subsidized electricity prices is that they encourage residential and industrial users to consume more energy than they otherwise would under market prices, thus making lowering emissions or per capita more difficult. Price supports may also make China a less effective test market for new energy efficiency products that Chinese firms could eventually export to the rest of the world. If such price distortions cannot be removed, then efforts to reduce energy intensity will be severely constrained. The NDRC has expressed its intent to adjust electricity prices. For example, the NDRC is planning to introduce tiered rates for residential users in order to promote conservation (Liu and Huang 2010). On the other hand, as a new round of inflationary fears grips China, increasing retail energy prices may continue to be socially and politically unpalatable.

BROADER IMPLICATIONS OF CHINA'S INVESTMENT IN GREEN INDUSTRY GROWTH

Given the rapid pace with which Chinese greentech firms have flooded renewable energy markets with inexpensive products, it is not surprising that many foreign executives and policy makers view Chinese firms and the government that supports them with increasing suspicion and hostility. In March 2012, the U.S. Commerce Department announced that it would impose tariffs on solar panels imported from China after concluding that the Chinese government provided illegal export subsidies to domestic manufacturers (Bradsher and Wald 2012). In this section, we argue that the international implications of China's green industry growth are more nuanced than the view that Chinese competition is unfair and therefore bad for world markets.

Let us begin with the effects of China's green energy investments on global markets. On the one hand, the government's subsidization of Chinese greentech exports is squeezing the profits of many global players and potentially reducing the incentive for such firms to invest in long-term research and development of next-generation technologies. Danish Vestas and German Siemens have in fact seen their sales and profits drop precipitously in recent years due to stiff Chinese, as well as Indian, competition. The fall of erstwhile industry darling Solyndra is perhaps the most high-profile case; it filed for Chapter 11 bankruptcy in 2011, despite having received $535 million in federal loan guarantees. Solar panels from China now control about half of the American market, while panels from the United States control less than a third (Bradsher and Wald 2012).

On the other hand, Chinese competition is making some foreign firms stronger and more efficient. General Electric, for one, is investing hundreds of millions in the development of thin-film technology to make larger and lighter panels, which it reckons will cut installation costs by about half (*The Economist* 2012a). It is currently completing America's biggest solar panel factory in Colorado. Furthermore, General Electric and other foreign technology firms are winning contracts to provide equipment and services in China. In 2010, General Electric signed contracts to supply 88 wind turbines to HECIC New Energy Co., Ltd, one of China's leading wind energy developers, for three new projects in Hebei and Shanxi Provinces (General Electric 2010). In 2009, American firm First Solar signed a memorandum of understanding with the Chinese government to build a sprawling, 2-GW solar power field in Inner Mongolia (Daily 2009). These are just a few examples of the many foreign firms participating in the Chinese domestic market for clean energy. Experience, learning, and scale gained from playing in the large Chinese market will help these firms scale and bring their overall costs down. Intense competition drives down the costs of renewable energy deployments in many parts of the world that otherwise would not have been able to afford it.

Then there is the issue of how China's strength in greentech markets will affect its negotiating position on climate issues. Many wonder whether China can simultaneously dominate in these markets and demand technology transfer or compensation in exchange for emissions reduction at home. The answer is, probably not. But is this the right question? Trying to get the country's leaders to sign onto a binding emissions-reduction agreement is unlikely to be successful because the international community will not promise enough technology transfer and compensation to satisfy them. In other words, China may be using the issue of technology transfer and compensation as a way to buy itself more time, guessing that other countries will not agree. We argue that the advanced industrialized countries should be less focused on how to get China to commit to a significant reduction in emissions and more concerned about how to help China restructure its economy such that its energy consumption and emissions will naturally fall.

In China, green growth is neither a "religion" nor a "reality." The problem of greenhouse gas emissions continues to take a backseat to more pressing concerns over economic growth and social stability. Since the initiation of economic reforms in 1978, there has been an implicit bargain between the CCP and the Chinese people such that, as long as the party can generate jobs and raise living standards, it will be allowed to maintain a monopoly over political power. In this light, the government's financial support of green industries can be viewed primarily as another effort to boost China's exports rather than fundamentally transform the country's domestic energy system. The composition of the new 18th Politburo Standing Committee, China's most powerful decision-making body, suggests that the party is likely to stay focused, first and foremost, on the economy. Most of the new members, including General Secretary Xi Jinping, are viewed as politically conservative and committed to preserving the vested interests of the party elite. If growth stalls and public unrest deepens, the new leadership may even roll back the already modest energy targets laid out in the 12th FYP.

It is difficult to envision a scenario in which emissions reduction emerges as a stand-alone goal or driver of economic growth in China. As this chapter shows, state-owned firms are entrenched in energy-intensive industries and are therefore unlikely allies of emissions reduction. If anything, they are likely to oppose more stringent environmental regulations. Meanwhile, because the livelihood of China's green industrialists depends more on markets abroad than at home, they are often more concerned about trade policy than environmental policy. The emergence of a grassroots coalition to combat climate change is further hindered by the public's understandable preoccupation with more tangible pollutants, as well as by the government's tight restrictions on social organization.

In our view, emissions reduction will be the result — not the driver — of a fundamental shift in the structure of the Chinese economy. Efforts to force China into a binding international agreement to cap emissions will be futile. Why do we say that? China lacks the broad coalition of political, industrial, and social interests required to transform China's manufacturing-based economy and fossil fuel–based energy system. Simply put, the political will is not there. Until the state can disentangle itself from the economy, or until the implicit bargain between the CCP and the Chinese people is recast on new terms, it is unclear where the political desire for greener growth will come from.

So what, if anything, can concerned members of the international community do? First, we must continue to collaborate with those in Chinese society who are concerned about climate change — especially scientists, environmental activists, and even some sympathetic members of the government. Together, we can leverage the Internet and social media to educate the Chinese public about the ways in which climate change is already affecting their lives and practical ways in which they can combat it. We can also facilitate capacity building at the local level and find ways to incentivize local officials to be better enforcers of environmental regulations. The Natural Resource Defense Council, for one, is already involved in such efforts.

Second, we may have to learn to live with cheap Chinese solar panels and wind turbines. Placing tariffs on Chinese goods in order to protect manufacturers in the advanced countries is unlikely to produce the desired results. It is our view that Chinese competition will push foreign manufacturers to focus on new materials and methods of production and move further up the value chain.

Third, we should invest in cleaner coal solutions. In 2009, the European Union pledged up to €50 million ($70 million) to help China build a near-zero-emission coal plant. Mongstad — a billion-dollar development owned jointly by the Norwegian government and three oil companies — could be on the verge of a technological breakthrough that could make carbon capture and sequestration more economically viable (*The Economist* 2012b). The goal is not to "give away" this technology to China but rather to deploy it as widely as possible to reduce the costs for all countries that rely on coal. Telling China — or the United States — to quit coal is a nonstarter.

There is no silver bullet to solve the global climate problem. In China, as in other countries, the problem will have to be tackled on multiple fronts. Attempts to force or shame China into significantly reducing emissions will not be effective. A transformation of the country's enormous and complex economic and energy systems will require greater international cooperation and the emergence of a domestic coalition pushing the country's leaders to make tough political choices.

12

BRAZIL

Disentangling Green Industry from Brown Consequences

Benjamin S. Allen

INTRODUCTION

In Brazil, there is political tension between the goal of achieving energy independence and green growth through the country's renewable energy sectors
and the need to preserve the country's Amazon, Cerrado, and Atlantic forests.
In contrast to most industrialized countries, whose greenhouse gas (GHG)
emissions are largely caused by energy production and consumption, in Brazil, almost 80 percent of GHG emissions stem from large-scale burning of
forests, and ranching and agricultural production on cleared forestlands. Indeed, energy production and consumption accounted for just over 19 percent
of Brazil's GHG emissions profile in 2005 (MCT 2010).

However, Brazil's principal renewable energies — ethanol, biodiesel, and
hydropower — require land to be cleared for cultivation or construction, and
as domestic energy supply expands over the next decade to meet growing
demand, each renewable source risks directly and/or indirectly worsening
deforestation rates. The tradeoff between energy independence through renewables and GHG reductions from conservation pits a concentrated coalition of developmentalists and agribusiness elites against a looser coalition of
environmental nongovernmental organizations (NGOs), bureaucrats in environmental agencies, environmentalist politicians, and public prosecutors. In
consequence, renewable energy often conflicts with efforts to reduce GHGs
through forest conservation in Brazil.

This chapter analyzes the relationships among agribusiness, energy, and
deforestation-related GHG emissions to highlight the challenges Brazil faces
in crafting coalitions capable of setting its economy on a path toward green

growth. The contributions of deforestation, agriculture, and energy to Brazil's overall GHG emissions profile are surveyed. The chapter then discusses the political trajectory of environmentalism in Brazil since 1981, arguing that the last few years constitute a period of environmental retreat. It examines GHG emissions in different economic sectors, including how ranching and agriculture contribute to Amazon deforestation, the leading cause of GHG emissions in Brazil. It also discusses the potential for Brazil's nascent modern forestry sector to aid in fostering green growth in the region. The chapter argues that, despite renewable energy's potential to reduce energy-related GHG emissions in the long run, ethanol, biodiesel, and hydropower threaten to increase medium-run GHG emissions from deforestation if conservation laws are not strengthened and enforced.

ENERGY, DEFORESTATION, AND GHG EMISSIONS IN BRAZIL

Overview of Energy and Deforestation in Brazil

Brazil is a federal democracy of 190.7 million people, has a diversified economy (Baer 2008, 1–3, 405),[1] and is by some estimates the fourth largest greenhouse gas emitter in the world—responsible for 5 percent of world emissions, or 2.2 gigatons of carbon dioxide equivalent, in 2008, according to the World Resources Institute (stated in McKinsey & Company 2009, 2). Eighty percent of these emissions are driven by deforestation, cattle ranching, and agriculture, while only 20 percent are driven by energy and nonagricultural industry (IPEA 2010b, 133). However, because Brazil's renewable energy sector is principally based on agriculture and on the clearing of forests to build dams, it has ties to deforestation and may not be as green as it first appears.

Brazil, therefore, faces political and economic challenges to green growth, defined here as growth consistent with an overall reduction in GHG emissions. First, the cattle and soybean industries—which produced 25 percent of gross domestic product (GDP) in 2008[2]—fear that their growth potential will be reduced by the enforcement of legal restrictions on forest clearing contained in Brazil's landmark 1965 Forest Code. These sectors, along with the mining industry, are members of the Congressional Business and Ruralist Blocs (DIAP 2010, 39–41).[3] Second, several of the powerful political and economic players who invest in renewable energy have little sectoral interest in preserving forests and reducing total GHG emissions. Petrobras, Brazil's national oil company, owns and operates six biofuel distilleries but also exploits the country's oil reserves.[4] In January 2012, Brazil's National Development Bank (BNDES) established an ambitious loan program to increase sugarcane production for ethanol (Leahy and Pearson 2012)—a move that may place pressure on the Atlantic forest in the southeast and northeast regions of Brazil if cash infusions stimulate horizontal expansion of cultivated land.[5] The beef and soy industries invest in bovine fat- and soy-based biodiesel to take advantage of recent national legislation enacted to broaden the biodiesel market. Finally, the Brazilian federal government and the construction industry clear patches of the Amazon to dam rivers to meet the growing domestic electricity demand—a project envisioned in the federal government's 2007 Growth Acceleration Plan (PAC).

Third, Brazil produces petroleum—and plans to increase production by 2020 (MME/EPE 2011). The financial incentives are hard to resist: sales to Brazil's top-ten export destinations—including the United States and China—netted US\$18.2 billion in revenues in 2010–2011 (Greenpeace 2012). Since Petrobras discovered an offshore presalt layer of oil in 2007, the federal government and Petrobras have sought to turn Brazil into an oil exporting power and plan to invest R\$686 billion from 2011 to 2020 to increase oil and gas production (Greenpeace 2012). However, investments in oil extraction and consumption will likely increase Brazil's total GHG emissions in the long run (Greenpeace 2012). Meanwhile, because oil exploration promises to increase Brazil's wealth and international profile and to reduce the country's poverty rate, public debate in Brazil generally avoids the oil-related GHG issue, focusing instead on the distribution of oil receipts among states and municipalities.

Sources of Brazil's GHG Emissions

McKinsey & Company (2009, 7) estimates that 55 percent of Brazil's GHG emissions result from deforestation, much of which is carbon dioxide (CO_2).[6] A further 25 percent of Brazil's GHG emissions stem from the agriculture and cattle ranching industries, which emit methane (CH_4) and nitrous oxide (N_2O) (McKinsey & Company 2009).[7] Figure 12.1 shows the share of CO_2 emissions by economic sector.

In contrast to most OECD countries, where energy and industry drive emissions, in Brazil, GHG emissions are currently largely a rural problem. Nevertheless, energy-related emissions are likely to rise in the coming decades. First, Greenpeace (2012) estimates that increasing oil production and consumption will cause Brazil's CO_2 emissions to skyrocket by 197 percent—canceling out gains made from reducing deforestation.[8] Second, the recent decline in deforestation rates may not last. Ruralist efforts to weaken environmental institutions may cause forests to be cleared to expand soy and sugarcane production (in part, for biodiesel and ethanol) and to build new hydroelectric dams.

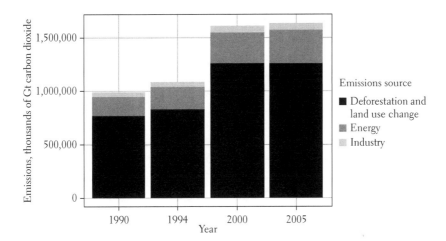

FIGURE 12.1   Brazilian CO_2 emissions by source, 1990–2005

SOURCE: MCT 2010, 12.

NOTE: To measure GHG emissions from deforestation, the Brazilian Ministry of Science and Technology (MCT), in its 2010 Second National Communication on GHGs to the United Nations Framework Convention on Climate Change, used satellite images taken from 1994 to 2002 of selected forested areas to estimate GHG emissions in those years. The MCT then extrapolated deforestation's contribution to GHG emissions for 1990 and 2005, and compared these estimates to emissions data from other sources.

Environmentalism in Brazil from 1981 to the present is examined later in the chapter in relationship to the country's current green growth challenges.

OVERVIEW OF BRAZILIAN ENVIRONMENTAL POLITICS, 1981–2012

Environmental activism in Brazil began in earnest in the early 1980s and professionalized in the wake of the 1992 United Nations Earth Summit in Rio de Janeiro. After 1992, Brazil restructured and strengthened its environmental bureaucracy, leading to reduced deforestation rates in the Atlantic and Amazon forests (Hochstetler and Keck 2007; McAllister 2008a). These laws and agencies, however, have been weakened since 2008 — a process that threatens Brazil's potential to foster green growth in the long run.

This section examines two key, overlapping periods in Brazilian environmental politics. The first, which lasted from about 1981 to 2008, was characterized by expanding environmental activism, legislation, and enforcement. The second, since about 2000, is characterized by stronger agribusiness political organization and, more recently, the weakening of environmental institutions and legislation to increase agricultural profitability. The Workers' Party (PT), which has held the presidency since 2003, has presided over the last phase of expansion (2003–2008) and the current phase of retreat (2008–present).

*Expansion of Environmental Laws and
Institutions, 1981–2008*

Brazil's military dictatorship, which ruled from 1964 to 1985, enacted the country's first major green growth initiative in 1975. The ethanol program, Pro-Álcool, was implemented in the wake of the 1973 Middle East oil shock to promote energy independence, and ethanol has since evolved into Brazil's premier renewable energy industry (Hira and de Oliveira 2009; Levi et al. 2010, 76–79).

The North American and Western European environmental movements of the 1960s and 1970s influenced scientists, university students, and activists in Brazil in the 1980s. In 1981, the military regime enacted the National Environmental Policy, establishing Brazil's first federal environmental institutions. During this period, the regime's political liberalization, and local environmental crises — such as in the petrochemical city of Cubatão, São Paulo — induced environmentalists in Brazil to organize politically around issues of air and water pollution (Hochstetler and Keck 2007, 192).[9] Meanwhile, activists in the wealthy industrial states of Rio de Janeiro, Minas Gerais, and São Paulo also expressed concern about the future of the Atlantic Forest. The conservation agenda gained momentum when, in 1985, the rubber tappers' union leader, Chico Mendes, in the far-flung Amazonian state of Acre, adopted an environmental discourse to attract national and international attention to his workers' rights movement (164–165). Domestic and international NGOs began to bring world attention to the struggle to save the Amazon, linking conservation to human rights and issues of poverty and inequality in a new socioenvironmentalist agenda.

The fact that environmental activism emerged during democratization is no coincidence. The military regime was guiding a transition to democracy in the 1980s, which created the opportunity for political movements of all stripes to emerge. The first civilian president, José Sarney, was elected by Congress in 1985, and the Constitutional Assembly took place in 1988. Social movements from throughout the country, including environmentalists, elected delegates to attend the Assembly. The resulting Constitution contains an article (225) that promises protection of the environment.[10]

That same year, President Sarney launched Brazil's candidacy to host the first UN Earth Summit in 1992 in Rio de Janeiro (Hochstetler and Keck 2007, 113). In preparation, environmental activists both within and outside of Brazil began organizing in earnest to present their proposals to the UN delegates at the summit. Civil society organizing continued during the summit and long afterward. It was at this time that the environmental movement began professionalizing, accepting money from international donors, and lobbying effectively for environmental reform (Hochstetler and Keck 2007, 99). The movement's influence on national policy waxed through the 1990s and 2000s, and it has waned only since 2008. In addition to the impetus provided by the Earth Summit, environmental organizing was aided by the murder of Chico Mendes in 1988 by hit men hired by Acrean landowners. Mendes's death turned him into a martyr to the Amazon cause and attracted worldwide condemnation.

In addition to professionalizing environmental activism, the 1992 Earth Summit affected Brazilian government institutions. In 1989, to increase the effectiveness of environmental management and law enforcement—and to demonstrate progress to the outside world—the federal government conjoined four environmental agencies into the new Brazilian Institute for the Environment and Renewable Resources (IBAMA). In 1992, Brazil created the Ministry of the Environment (MMA) and placed IBAMA under its auspices.

The years 1992 to 2009 saw the enactment of several major environmental laws. First, the 1998 Environmental Crimes Law (9,605) facilitated prosecutions of environmental crimes (McAllister 2008a). In 1992, environmentalists proposed legislation to streamline conservation area creation and governance, resulting in 2000 in the National System of Conservation Units (SNUC, Law 9,985).[11] Agribusiness was largely absent from the legislative debate over the SNUC in the 1990s,[12] and the resulting law facilitated the rapid creation of conservation areas in the Amazon rainforest during the 2002–2008 period.

In 2003, with the inauguration of Luiz Inácio "Lula" da Silva of the left-wing PT, Acrean environmental activist and PT politician Marina Silva was appointed Minister of the Environment. She brought NGO allies into federal environmental agencies and pushed an aggressive agenda in the Amazon, creating new conservation areas in high-deforestation zones in southern Pará and imposing fines and other punishments for illegal deforestation throughout the region as part of the 2004 Action Plan to Prevent and Control Deforestation in the Amazon (PPCDAm; see Assunção, Gandour, and Rocha 2012, 7–9). Silva was aided in part by the 2005 murder of an American nun—and socioenvironmental activist—Sister Dorothy Stang in Pará. Much as Chico Mendes's murder had done in 1988, Sister Stang's death outraged the world community and opened political space for the creation of new conservation areas and stricter law enforcement in the Amazon (Hochstetler and Keck 2007, 181).[13] In 2007, the Lula administration issued Presidential Decree No. 6,321/2007 to subject rural property owners who practice illegal deforestation to strict command and control regulation—including embargoes on their products—and to forbid federal credit agencies from approving "credit of any kind not only to agricultural or forest activities performed within [illegally deforested and embargoed] areas, but also to any service and commercial or industrial activity that involved the acquisition, intermediation, transport, or commercialization of goods produced in embargoed establishments" (Assunção, Gandour, and Rocha 2012, 10).[14] In August 2008, President Lula signed Decree 6,527 to create the Amazon Fund within BNDES to receive international donations for the reduction of GHG emissions from deforestation and forest degradation. This was followed in 2010 by congressional legislation allowing private landowners to market carbon credits for any deforestation that was avoided (May, Millikan, and Gebara 2011, 38).[15] Finally, in 2009, Brazil enacted the National Climate Change Policy to stem GHG emissions from various sources (especially from deforestation).

How were these environmental laws and decrees able to pass in a developing country primarily concerned with economic growth? The answer is that the empirical context in which the agribusiness industry operated was less threatening to its interests in the 1990s than in the 2000s. In the 1990s, there were few large conservation areas, so agribusiness did not concern itself with the SNUC law. Moreover, though agribusiness and mining had never liked the 1965 Forest Code, before the 2000s, enforcement of the code had been weak, so there had been little incentive to overturn it. Until the 1998 Environmental Crimes Law was enacted, illegal deforestation in the Amazon and elsewhere had been enormously difficult to prosecute, and the *Ministério Público*, or MP (which had been granted autonomy in the 1988 Constitution, and to this day is the most effective enforcer of environmental law in Brazil), could do little to suppress illegal deforestation. As a result, although the agribusiness lobby proposed revisions to the Forest Code in Congress in 2000, it did not assemble enough support to overcome environmentalist resistance and get its proposals passed until 2012.

International concern and money, and weak political organization on the agribusiness side, produced a political environment conducive to adopting environmental legislation and, in the 2000s, to strengthening environmental restrictions on credit for farmers and ranchers. However, these legislative and enforcement changes induced agribusiness to improve its political organization in the 2000s to fight to protect its interests.

The Political Rise of Agribusiness and the Weakening of Environmental Institutions, 2000–Present

In the 1990s and 2000s, the area of land cleared for ranching and brought into soy production expanded significantly, pushing farming and ranching further into the Amazon and aggravating deforestation in the region. Most soy farms violated (and still violate) a Forest Code provision requiring that a certain percentage of farmed land be set aside for conservation.[16] When the federal government began enforcing the Forest Code aggressively and creating new conservation areas in the Amazon, agribusiness began to organize around the goal of overturning the legislation that now threatened its interests.

In 2002, soy kingpin Blairo Maggi was elected governor of Mato Grosso, a state that straddles the Cerrado and the Amazon rainforest and is on the deforestation frontier. As governor, and later as federal senator, he and Kátia Abreu, the senator from Tocantins who heads the congressional Ruralist Bloc (*Bancada Ruralista*), lobbied the federal government to weaken environmental regulations and helped focus the Bloc on this task. This effort has been aided by sympathetic *developmentalists* in most political parties — including the PT — who support rapid economic development at any cost. Mining and construction industries are core developmentalist constituencies and are represented in government by the Ministry of Mines and Energy (MME) and in Congress by the *Bancada Empresarial* (Business Bloc), which is the largest congressional bloc, and represents over 45 percent of the National Congress as of 2010. Representatives of agribusiness and developmentalist interests are also members of parties in congressional coalition with the PT, including the PT's largest partner, the Brazilian Democratic Movement Party (PMDB) (DIAP 2010, 39).[17]

The environmentalists, whose strongest political ally is the PT, found themselves trapped after 2003. Many of them joined the government or allied with the government when Silva became the Minister of the Environment. The progress she made in environmental policy during her tenure incited the Ruralist backlash, and having lost Lula's support, she resigned in 2008, removing the environment's strongest advocate from the government. Before, during, and after that time, Lula and the PT began making decisions that were harmful to the environment in the interest of promoting economic growth. The 2007 Accelerated Growth Plan (PAC) promotes the building and paving of highways in the Amazon, as well as the construction of new hydroelectric dams there — several near or inside the current boundaries of protected areas. Meanwhile, there is no other party of national importance through which environmentalists can advocate for their interests.[18]

In 2000, Ruralists in Congress proposed revisions to the Forest Code, loosening conservation requirements on private lands. The acrimonious debate lasted a decade and ended with agribusiness's victory in 2012 when the new Forest Code passed Congress and was signed into law by President Rousseff. Environmental activists and politicians were able to postpone votes on the new Forest Code, but the bill worked its way slowly through Congress due to the persistent efforts of the Ruralist Bloc and its agribusiness constituents.

214   Bending to the environmentalist pressure that remained, but not wishing to alienate agribusiness—which could paralyze her agenda in Congress by blocking her legislative proposals or defecting from the government's congressional coalition—President Rousseff line-item vetoed several provisions, and wrangling continues over a provisional measure to fill the gaps created by the vetoes. Rousseff further showed her independence from environmental interests in 2012 by altering the boundaries of several conservation units in the Amazon to begin hydroelectric dam construction. She did this by provisional measure, which has since been ratified by Congress.

Finally, on December 8, 2011, while the country's attention was focused on the Forest Code revision, the Rousseff administration sanctioned Complementary Law No. 140, which strips IBAMA of much of its environmental licensing and enforcement power. The law decentralizes licensing for activities such as deforestation to states and municipalities. In addition, the law prevents IBAMA, which is federal, from monitoring and enforcing the rules of licenses issued by state and municipal governments.[19] This institutional change leaves the fate of the forest in the hands of state and municipal environmental agencies that are often underfunded, understaffed, and subject to political pressures to issue licenses irrespective of ecological consequences.[20]

In sum, Brazilian environmentalism has taken two steps forward and one step back: activists and their representatives have enacted key environmental laws and constructed a competent environmental bureaucracy. However, since 2002, these successes have engendered a countermovement in which antienvironmental interests have become better organized and have begun to curtail conservation laws and the power of enforcement agencies. This current period does not portend a complete retreat from environmental governance. Most conservation laws have not been overturned, and some state-level agencies are building their capacity to issue environmental licenses and enforce laws responsibly. Nevertheless, agribusiness and developmentalist interests continue to pose a threat to conservation and to efforts to reduce Brazil's deforestation-related GHG emissions.

RANCHING, AGRICULTURE, AND AMAZON DEFORESTATION

Brazil's commodities, including beef and soy, are increasing their shares in Brazil's export profile (De Negri and Alvarenga 2011)—and thus their importance to Brazil's national politics and its emergence as a regional economic power. Both industries have a history of encroaching on the Amazon rainforest and provoking deforestation there, and after oil, they present the strongest challenge to green growth in Brazil.

Amazonian deforestation was not considered a serious problem before the 1980s, when satellite images of massive cleared areas and photographs of the forest burning began to be published in national and international media outlets. Brazil began to monitor annual deforestation rates by satellite in 1988 through the National Institute for Spatial Research (INPE). INPE's images show that deforestation rates spiked in 1995 when about 29,000 km2 were deforested and in 2004 when the forest lost 27,400 km2 of forest cover (IPEA 2010b, 82; INPE 2011). Since 2005, however, due in part to the appreciation of Brazil's currency against the U.S. dollar and to conservation policies in the region (Banco Mundial 2010, 40), the deforestation rate has steadily declined, reaching 7,000 km2 in 2010 and 6,418 km2 in 2011.

Despite this decline, forest loss in the Amazon and elsewhere has been severe. The Amazon lost 18 percent of its forest cover from 1970 to 2007, the Cerrado lost 20 percent, and the coastal Atlantic forest—of which only 11 percent of its historical expanse remains today—lost 8 percent (Banco Mundial 2010, 39–40; S.O.S. Mata Atlântica 2011). Cattle ranching and soybean cultivation contributed to forest loss in the Amazon and Cerrado, while sugarcane farming, coffee plantations, logging, urbanization, and other population pressures have decimated the Atlantic Forest over centuries (McAllister 2008b; S.O.S. Mata Atlântica 2011).

Why Ranching and Agriculture Have Expanded in the Amazon

Estimates show that today about 80 percent of deforested lands in the Amazon have been converted to pasture (Walker et al. 2009, 732). Since 1990, the Amazonian cattle herd has grown from just under 26 million heads to over 74 million in 2005 (738), and IMAZON, a Belém, Pará-based research institute, estimated total Amazon beef production at about 2.8 million metric tons that year—much of it sold in domestic consumer markets (Barreto et al. 2008, 13). The share of Amazon beef in total Brazilian beef exports rose from 5.35 percent (10,000 metric tons) in 2000 to 21.53 percent (263,787 metric tons) in 2006 (Walker et al. 2009, 740). Meanwhile, soy cultivation in the Center-West Cerrado and along the Amazon deforestation frontier increased from just under 3 million hectares in 1990 to 10 million hectares in 2011 (CONAB 2011), pushing ranching further into the Amazon. The rise of ranching has been facilitated by three sets of policies.

First, territorial integration and production policies enacted since the 1960s have induced massive population migration to the Amazon from other regions

216   of Brazil. In the 1960s and 1970s, the military dictatorship encouraged settlement to secure territorial sovereignty in the region to prevent the emergence of opposition insurgent groups and to reduce land conflicts elsewhere in Brazil. With the military's retreat in the 1980s, the interior of Amazônia was left ungoverned, leading to violent land speculation and rampant deforestation (Hochstetler and Keck 2007, 144–146). Investments in roads and highways have aggravated speculation, land conflicts, and deforestation by opening faster land routes from ranches in the Amazon to consumer and export markets in São Paulo and Rio de Janeiro and promoting the growth of towns along Amazonian highways.[21]

Second, the federal government began a campaign in 1992 to eliminate foot-and-mouth disease, which was endemic to Amazonian cattle herds at the time (Barreto et al. 2008, 25). By 2005, the southern Amazon—Rondônia, Mato Grosso, Acre, Tocantins, and the southern half of Pará—had been declared free of the disease and therefore eligible to export beef. Cattle herds have grown rapidly in these regions since 1990 (Walker et al. 2009, 738); not coincidentally, Pará, Mato Grosso, and Rondônia also present the highest deforestation rates in the Amazon.

Finally, until 2008, subsidized credits the Brazilian federal government granted to Amazonian farmers and ranchers aggravated deforestation by creating financial incentives to invest in increasing land holdings rather than productivity.[22] Despite lenders being prohibited from loaning funds to ranchers to deforest, subsidized credit indirectly worsens deforestation. A rancher logs an area adjacent to her land to increase herd size and production, sells the wood, and claims title to the land (often falsely).[23] She then takes out a subsidized loan to buy cattle to graze that land. From 2003 to 2007, IMAZON found that ranchers in the Amazon received R$1.89 billion in subsidized loans (Barreto et al. 2008, 22).[24] An upshot of these loans is that ranchers may earn higher profits by expanding land holdings through deforestation and illegal appropriation of public lands than they would by investing in productivity enhancements.[25] Lula cracked down on these loan practices in Decree No. 6,321/2007, but residents of the Amazon need alternatives to ranching if they are to survive while keeping the forest standing.

Creating a Legal, Sustainable Timber Industry

An effort currently underway to cultivate economic growth without aggravating deforestation in the Amazon and elsewhere is the creation of a legal, modern forestry industry that employs sustainable logging practices and creates jobs and income for local families.[26] Since 2000, federal and state governments in the Amazon have aggressively created new national and state forests and worked with environmental NGOs and local communities to design concession plans.[27]

The federal government is leading this effort, creating 7.7 million hectares of new national forests in the Amazon since 2000.[28] By 2010, the Amazon contained over 28 million hectares of land in 43 national and state forests, with the (still unrealized) potential to produce R$1.2 to R$2.2 billion in timber per year (Medeiros et al. 2011, 15). Meanwhile, the SFB's (2011, 5) auctioning of 1 million hectares in forestry concessions in 2010 is expected to create about 7,500 new formal jobs in ten poor municipalities in Rondônia and Pará. If this potential is realized in these and future concessions, then the modern forestry sector may indeed begin to place the Amazon on a path toward green growth: employment and income generation *via* the sustainable harvesting of timber rather than extensive forest clearing to open pasture for cattle.

Institutions to support forestry concessions are in their infancy but are making headway. In 2006, the federal government enacted the Public Forest Management Law, which created the SFB, an *autarquia* of the Ministry of the Environment, to issue and manage forestry concessions in national forests, and a National Fund for Forest Development (FNDF) to promote the creation of new state and national forests and to fund research into natural resources (Banerjee and Alavalapati 2009, 245). Combined with the *Amazônia Legal* program to legalize landholdings in the Amazon, implemented by the federal government in 2009, these moves are beginning to bring logging into the realm of legal commerce and to create jobs.[29]

Coordination challenges, however, remain within the state. As conservation areas, national forests are managed by ICMBio, which must approve their management plans — including zoning and concession plans. The SFB, meanwhile, issues and monitors forestry concessions and may develop criteria for concessions that undercut sustainable zoning and practices prescribed in ICMBio's management plans.[30] Both ICMBio and the SFB are young agencies and are still developing their norms and procedures. Thus, priorities sometimes conflict, delaying implementation of concessions. One upshot is that to date, the SFB has only signed two 40-year concession contracts with logging companies for 144,800 hectares in Amazonian national forests (SFB 2012).[31] In addition, it is still unclear how well the SFB's monitoring of concessionaires' compliance with contractual items — including sustainable practices — works.[32]

This section shows how cattle and agribusiness in the Amazon and Cerrado regions drive deforestation and how through deforestation and their own emissions, these industries contribute to about 80 percent of Brazil's total GHG

218   emissions. It suggests that the creation of a sustainable, modern forestry sector is essential to providing Amazonian residents with economic incentives to leave trees standing. Brazil has already taken some steps in this direction, but this effort must be fortified in the coming years if the country is to foster forest-based green growth. Brazil's energy sector, discussed next, presents a more mature vision for green growth in the country, but there are environmental risks in hydropower, ethanol and biodiesel, as well — though renewable, these energy sources require extensive land and, often, forest clearing.

BRAZIL'S ENERGY GENERATION: A RENEWABLE POWERHOUSE WITH A POSSIBLE DARK SIDE

Brazil's energy matrix is remarkably green, with 45.9 percent of its domestic energy supply provided by renewables in 2008 —well above the world average of 12.9 percent (IPEA 2010b, 133). Though petroleum and derivatives still account for the largest source of energy in the country, the renewable energy sources of sugarcane products and hydroelectricity come second and third, respectively (EPE 2010, 31). This impressive performance results from policies enacted since the 1970s that have aimed to secure Brazil's energy independence, and growth is expected to continue due to recent technological breakthroughs (such as flex-fuel cars), global demand for ethanol, the political organization of the sugarcane industry, and government investments in agroenergy and hydroelectric dams.

Nevertheless, there is a possible dark side to renewable energy in Brazil. To meet domestic and world demand, Brazil must increase both sugarcane crop productivity and the amount of land cultivated. The latter may displace food crops and force farmers to move into the Center-West Cerrado by pricing them out of their lands in coastal regions, exacerbating deforestation in both the Cerrado and the Amazon (IPEA 2010b, 417). Opening new land in the southeast and northeast regions of Brazil for sugarcane cultivation, meanwhile, is expected directly to worsen deforestation in the Atlantic Forest (IPEA 2010b, 431–432), especially if the revised Forest Code is enacted as written.[33] In addition, because the current major ingredients in Brazilian biodiesel are soy and bovine fat, Brazil's current investments in biodiesel production may increase Amazon and Cerrado deforestation in the medium run. Finally, large hydroelectric dams, such as the proposed Belo Monte dam in Pará, require logging of surrounding lands and displacement of local residents and may have deleterious downstream effects from diverting river flows.

In this section we examine tradeoffs between greenness and growth in Brazil's renewable energy sector. We first profile the share of renewable energy sources in Brazil's domestic energy matrix. Then we analyze environmental risks in the ethanol and biodiesel sectors. Finally, we discuss the consequences hydroelectricity may have for the Amazon rainforest.

Profile of Brazil's Energy Matrix

Brazil has succeeded in providing a large share of its domestic energy supply from renewable sources such as ethanol, biomass, and hydropower—and in the coming years, increasingly from biodiesel. Figure 12.2 shows the changes in the composition of Brazil's energy supply from 1940 to 2009 by source. Overall domestic energy supply rose from about 23 million t.o.e. (tons of oil equivalent) in 1940 to 243 million t.o.e. in 2009. Concomitant with growth in the total domestic supply of energy, production grew among all sources.[34] However, the share of petroleum and other fossil fuels in total domestic supply peaked in 2000 at 50.9 percent and was down to 46.6 percent in 2009. Meanwhile, the share of hydropower has risen substantially, from 1.5 percent in 1940 to 25.2 percent in 2009. Much of this is consumed as electricity. Sugarcane products (ethanol and biomass from sugarcane bagasse) have also increased their share, from 2.4 percent in 1940 to 8 percent in 1980 and 18.2 percent in 2009. This changing balance between renewable and nonrenewable sources of energy over time makes Brazil an impressive case of energy systems transition.

Ethanol

Ethanol is Brazil's signature biofuel, and its production and consumption both within Brazil and abroad are growing due to the advent in 2003 of flex-fuel cars (which can run on any combination of petroleum-based gasoline and ethanol; 90 percent of new cars sold in Brazil are flex-fuel) and to national law, which requires 20 to 25 percent ethanol blends in petroleum gasoline (Chambers 2010). Ethanol currently constitutes 40 percent of fuel used by cars (Levi et al. 2010, 7) and is taxed at a lower rate than petroleum gasoline (15). In addition, laws passed in the United States, the European Union, and elsewhere establish minimum biofuel content standards in gasoline, providing international markets for Brazilian ethanol.[35] State support from 1975 through the 1980s provided by the Pro-Álcool Program enabled the sugarcane-based ethanol industry to grow and thrive. Despite market liberalization in the 1980s and 1990s (Levi et al. 2010, 77), there are currently 434 ethanol distilleries in operation in Brazil (IPEA 2010a, 14) that are sustained by high domestic and global demand. In 2007, Brazil exported 185 million gallons of ethanol to the United States and consumed just under 6 billion gallons domestically (Hofstrand 2008).

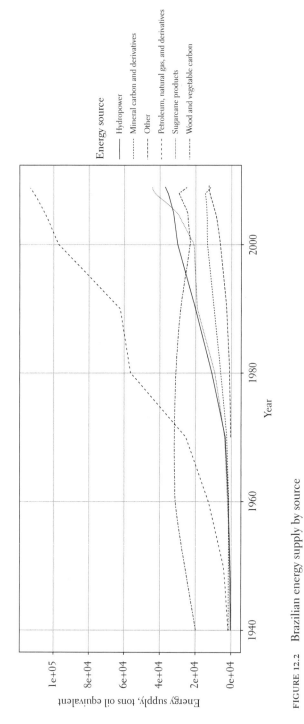

FIGURE 12.2   Brazilian energy supply by source
SOURCE: Adapted from EPE 2010, 31–32.

Brazilian sugarcane-based ethanol is widely considered to be a net carbon-efficient fuel when compared to petroleum because it is extracted from crops, the next generation of which reabsorbs some of the carbon emitted from the burning of the previous generation. When the widespread use of sugarcane bagasse — rather than fossil fuels — to power distilleries in Brazil is taken into account, sugarcane-based ethanol can reduce GHG emissions by up to 92 percent per liter when compared to one liter of petroleum-based gasoline. (The United States' corn-based ethanol, in contrast, only reduces carbon emissions by 19 to 47 percent compared to petroleum (see La Rovere, Pereira, and Simões 2011, 1031).[36] In addition, at about US$23/liter in 2005, Brazilian ethanol is more cost-efficient to produce than sugarcane-based ethanol produced in other leading countries, such as Thailand and Australia, where prices per liter are higher (Nassar 2009, 70). Part of these advantages lies in favorable climatic conditions, and part is due to bagasse burning to power distilleries, which reduces distilleries' energy costs (Hofstrand 2008; Nassar 2009, 71).

However, though Brazil's sugarcane-based variety of ethanol may reduce net GHG emissions from fuel, sugarcane requires land on which to grow, and extension of farm land devoted to sugarcane may directly worsen deforestation rates in Brazil's Atlantic forest, as well as indirectly increase Amazon deforestation by displacing other crops and cattle ranching in coastal regions toward the Cerrado and the Amazon (McAllister 2008b, 10,876). Furthermore, given the amount of land that IPEA researchers predict may be cultivated by 2035 — 22 to 23 million hectares — if existing conservation laws in the Atlantic Forest are not effectively enforced, ethanol production may directly increase deforestation in the region in the coming decades (IPEA 2010b, 431).

Land area devoted to sugarcane cultivation grew from 1.9 million hectares in 1975 to 5.62 million hectares in 2005 and 9.67 hectares in 2009, due to the Pro-Álcool Program and expanding world market for ethanol. To understand ethanol's contribution to this trajectory, in the 1975/1976 harvest, only 14 percent of sugarcane harvested was used to produce ethanol; the other 86 percent was converted to sugar. In contrast, in the 2009/2010 harvest, 57 percent of the sugarcane harvested was used to produce ethanol, while only 43 percent was converted to sugar (MAPA 2010). Continuing growth in world demand for ethanol, as BNDES and CGEE (2008, 192) estimates show, may lead cultivated land in Brazil to reach 25 to 40 million hectares by 2025.

Though the prediction for 2025 may suggest that deforestation is inevitable, the BNDES study argues that, in fact, Brazil has about 136 million hectares with good potential for sugarcane cultivation, mostly in the Cerrado, without additional direct deforestation (BNDES and CGEE 2008, 192).[37] To reduce potential deforestation, Brazil passed a sugarcane zoning law in 2009

222 to prohibit sugarcane cultivation in the Pantanal and Amazon biomes (IPEA 2010b, 144). In addition, the state of São Paulo — where much sugarcane cultivation is concentrated — signed a voluntary Agroenvironmental Protocol in 2007 with the state's sugarcane producers to eliminate harvest burning by 2017, to recover 400,000 hectares of riparian forests and water springs on sugarcane farms, and to encourage respect for environmental zoning regulations (Lucon and Goldemberg 2010, 343–344). However, state capacity to enforce laws and accords is greater in São Paulo than elsewhere (McAllister 2008a), and political deals in São Paulo may be easier to implement because the Brazilian Sugarcane Industry Association (UNICA) is headquartered in the state.[38] In contrast, large investments in state capacity building will be necessary in the other states in which sugarcane is cultivated — Espírito Santo, Mato Grosso do Sul, Minas Gerais, Goiás, Paraná, and all nine northeastern states — if the expansion of land for sugarcane is to occur in a way that avoids GHG emissions from deforestation in the Atlantic Forest.[39]

Finally, sugarcane yields have improved considerably since 1975. Tons of sugarcane produced per hectare rose from 65 in the 1977/1978 harvest to an average of 85 from 1989 to 2004 (IPEA 2010a, 13). Productivity is expected to continue to rise, from 6,900 liters of ethanol per hectare now to about 7,160 liters by 2020 (IPEA 2010a), and if such progress is combined with the maintenance of strict conservation policies and effective environmental law enforcement, ethanol's future contribution to deforestation may be lower than current estimates.

Biodiesel

Brazil's federal government began investing in biodiesel production in 2005, and the country's 2008–2017 Decennial Energy Plan aims to produce enough biodiesel not only to power vehicles but also to integrate the fuel into the electricity grid (IPEA 2010a, 21). Though the industry is currently small, growth in the coming decades may worsen deforestation rates because of biodiesel's links to soybean farming and cattle ranching: Despite government efforts to diversify the agricultural ingredients in biodiesel, soy and bovine fat currently account, on average, for 75.04 percent and 17.79 percent of raw materials used in biodiesel, respectively. Large-scale soybean and meatpacking companies in the Cerrado and Amazon — the principal drivers of deforestation in both regions — are investing in biodiesel production to diversify and take advantage of state support for the sector.[40]

Although in 2008 biodiesel accounted for less than 1 percent of Brazil's domestic energy supply, it is being gradually integrated into the energy matrix. National standards required that all diesel gasoline sold in Brazil contain 3 percent biodiesel by 2008 — and most diesel sold now contains 5 percent biodiesel (IPEA 2010a, 20–22).[41] A 2005 law established state support for biodiesel research and provides financing from BNDES and other public institutions.[42] These investments have increased production of biodiesel in Brazil, from 69 million liters in 2006 to 1.167 billion liters in 2008, placing Brazil fourth in world production — behind Germany (3.193 billion liters), the United States (2.644 billion liters), and France (2.063 billion liters) (27).

Growth in biodiesel is good news for Brazil's energy-related GHG emissions profile, but its effects on land use and its consequent potential to contribute to GHG emissions from deforestation mean that enthusiasm over biodiesel's overall greenness must be tempered. Indeed, if biodiesel production grows considerably in the long run, the risk of a rise in deforestation is alarming. Walker (2011, 933) estimates that without adequately enforced conservation policies, biofuel growth from expanding soy production may cause 61,332 km2 of Amazon deforestation by 2020.[43] The risk is already present: area devoted to the planting of soybeans has increased from 6.9 million hectares in 1976 to an estimated 24.2 million hectares in 2010 (CONAB 2011), of which 6.4 million hectares are in Mato Grosso — one of the two leading Amazon and Cerrado deforesters, where soy and other large-scale agricultural interests have held power in state government since 2002.

As the domestic and global markets for ethanol and biodiesel grow, agroenergy is likely to contribute both more directly and indirectly to deforestation than it currently does. This, in turn, will (at least partially) offset ethanol's and biodiesel's potential contributions to reducing overall GHG emissions and fostering green growth in Brazil.

Hydropower

Finally, hydroelectric dams present another paradox in Brazil's potential to foster growth. Hydropower has the third largest share in Brazil's domestic energy supply (see Figure 12.2), and it is essential if electricity generation is to meet growing demand over the coming decades (OECD/IEA 2006, 9–10). Currently, the Brazilian federal government plans to invest R$96 billion to generate 42,000 MW of hydroelectricity by 2020 and plans to build 24 new hydroelectric dams in the water-rich Amazon (MME/EPE 2011). However, large hydropower projects require that surrounding lands be deforested (to build the dam, store materiel, and house workers) — with the corresponding release of GHGs — and dams may damage ecosystems by altering river flows, causing downstream forest die-offs.

Brazil's 852 hydroelectric plants (of all sizes) nationwide produce 72.5 percent (79,182.3 MW) of Brazil's domestic electricity supply, and 311 new plants are under construction (potentially adding another 15,336.7 MW) (IPEA 2010b, 137). Given the abundance of rivers in Brazil, hydropower is key to the federal government's economic growth strategy, but up-front environmental costs generate opposition from domestic and international environmental groups. This is the case of two recent controversial decisions by the federal government. The first reduces the size of seven conservation areas in the Amazon to facilitate the issuing of environmental licenses to build four new hydroelectric dams in the Tapajós River Basin (in Pará and Amazonas). The second is to push ahead with the construction of the Belo Monte Dam—a point of contention between the federal government and environmentalists.

First, 13 of the government's planned hydroelectric dams in the Amazon are to be located near or within ecologically sensitive conservation areas, and the construction contractors cannot acquire the environmental licenses necessary to build in or on the border of such areas. In January 2012, this fact prompted President Dilma Rousseff to take the unprecedented step of issuing a provisional decree (MP No. 558)[44] to reduce the size of seven federally protected areas in the Tapajós River Basin by 1,500 km2 to facilitate the licensing process (Araújo et al. 2012, 1). The decree has since been ratified by Congress (Bragança 2012). There are both legal and ecological ramifications to this issue. First, MP No. 558 sets a new precedent by which the president may reduce other conservation areas by decree—opening up new areas for deforestation and associated carbon emissions. Second, if the 1,500 km2 of mostly pristine Amazonian rainforest removed from the Tapajós River Basin conservation areas is deforested to build the planned dams, IMAZON estimates that more than 152 million tons of CO_2 will be released into the atmosphere (Araújo et al. 2012, 8).[45]

The deforestation and greenhouse gas risks associated with dam building in the Amazon are encapsulated in the case of the Belo Monte dam, which is currently under construction on the Xingu River in Pará. Belo Monte has become a symbol of progress for developmentalists and of irresponsible environmental destruction for environmentalists. When completed, the dam will be the world's third largest, and the Brazilian government estimates that it will produce 11,200 MW of electricity, though environmental activists believe this figure is exaggerated because of the river's seasonal variation in flow (Inter-American Dialogue 2011). However, building the dam requires altering the course of the Xingu River and displacing local indigenous communities to clear and flood 400 to 500 km2 of currently standing forest—a process that may release "enormous quantities of methane" (Amazon Watch 2011), a powerful greenhouse gas, into the atmosphere. Finally, dam construction and operation will attract an estimated 100,000 migrants to the region, which will urbanize the area and exacerbate deforestation.[46] In sum, like the Tapajós River Basin dams discussed above, Belo Monte's long-term clean energy–generating potential may be canceled out by its up-front environmental impacts.

The question of if—and how—environmental damages are mitigated during and after Belo Monte's construction will likely shape the future of large hydroelectric projects in the region. IBAMA required that the bidding contractors present projections of the scale and distribution of deforestation and that they propose measures to offset the damages (IBAMA Parecer No. 06/2010). The winning consortium, Norte Energia, has committed R$3.9 billion to mitigation and compensation (*The Economist* 2013).[47] Proposed mitigation actions, including the creation of 14,000 km2 of conservation areas, the strengthening of environmental licensing procedures, and stronger law enforcement, may be capable of neutralizing effects from deforestation caused by Belo Monte. However, as mentioned previously, IBAMA has been weakened in recent years, and (already high) impunity rates for environmental crimes in the Amazon may rise. President Rousseff's MP No. 558 threatens the legal and ecological security of existing and future conservation areas, so promised investments in mitigation do not guarantee that damage to the forest caused by the dam's construction will, in fact, be offset.

Renewable energy and green growth are new global creeds, and Brazil is playing to its strengths. It is a leading producer of bioethanol, is developing a biodiesel industry, and contains sufficient water resources to satisfy much of its domestic demand for electricity through hydropower. However, each of these renewables contributes, or has the potential to contribute, to deforestation-related GHG emissions. To increase the production of renewables without threatening the country's forests, the Brazilian federal, state, and municipal governments must invest in building the capacity of environmental agencies to enforce environmental laws throughout the national territory. Such capacity building involves increasing agency budgets, hiring competent personnel with career stability, and purchasing planes and all-terrain vehicles and arms that can enable environmental enforcers to reach remote areas where illegal deforestation occurs. To do this, Brazil must reverse its current trend of weakening environmental institutions. Finally, federal, state, and municipal environmental agencies, and the *Ministério Público*, must ensure that the contractors hired to build Belo Monte and other dams follow through on their commitments to offset deforestation resulting from dam construction.

226   CONCLUSION: A DIFFICULT, UNCERTAIN PATH TOWARD
       GREEN GROWTH

This chapter argues that despite the progress Brazil has made in enacting environmental laws and building institutions, and in fostering an energy matrix with a high proportion of renewables in it, the issue of forest conservation prevents the emergence of a coalition of environmentalists, renewable energy businesses, and political elites capable of promoting economic growth, while reducing overall GHG emissions. Due to the connections between renewable energy — ethanol, biodiesel, and hydropower — and deforestation, a political coalition capable of placing Brazil solidly on a path toward green growth has yet to emerge. And current moves to increase oil production and consumption by exploring the presalt layer offshore oil fields will likely undermine any advances the country makes in reducing overall GHG emissions in other sectors.

Why, despite the centrality of environmental issues to Brazil's development and the existence of an environmental movement that has had so much success since the 1980s, has no green coalition among business, government, and civil society that is capable of moving Brazil toward an economic growth path involving an *overall reduction* in GHG emissions emerged? The answer lies in two places. First, a conflict exists between conserving forests and opening more land to cattle ranching, soy farming, and hydroelectric dams. This conflict pits environmentalists in NGOs, the *Ministério Público*, and the Ministry of the Environment against developmentalists, mining companies, agribusiness, and the construction industry — and their allies in Congress and the Ministries of Mines and Energy, and Agriculture and Ranching. This cleavage divides protagonists whose interests, in other contexts, might align to foster green growth.

Second, because Brazil hopes to earn international prestige and windfall revenues from increasing its oil production over the next decade, the political debate over GHG emissions in the petroleum sector is a nonstarter. Indeed, oil emissions may be a politically toxic issue for environmentalists. With respect to oil revenues, government and civil society appear to prioritize fueling economic growth and funding social programs to reduce Brazil's atrocious rates of poverty and inequality over cutting carbon emissions.[48] Petrobras, the state-run oil company, funds several local social and environmental causes, so environmentalists who attack the oil sector for its emissions may alienate allies in NGOs and social movements whose preoccupations with socioeconomic inequality or local pollution trump their concerns for climate change. In consequence, the 2009 National Climate Change Policy avoids setting emissions-reduction targets in the oil sector and instead sets only general energy sector emissions goals to be reached by 2020 (Seroa da Motta 2011, 34).

Nevertheless, Brazil has come a long way since democratization. The *Ministério Público* was granted institutional independence in the 1988 Constitution and since then has prosecuted environmental crimes and pressured environmental agencies to perform to the best of their ability. IBAMA has had its competencies threatened by recent constitutional changes, but it is still capable of carrying out targeted raids and other enforcement actions against perpetrators of environmental crimes. The Ministry of the Environment and ICMBio, established in 1992 and 2007 respectively, work with NGOs and private sector actors nationwide to ensure responsible environmental governance in conservation areas and to implement sustainable development projects. And legislatively, Brazil has made great strides forward since 1992. The Environmental Crimes Law, enacted in 1998, has enhanced the *Ministério Público*'s ability to prosecute environmental crimes; the SNUC has facilitated the designation of new conservation areas; and Lula's Presidential Decree No. 6,321/2007 has increased monitoring and enforcement of environmental laws in the Amazon. In short, although Brazil has not yet embarked on a path of green growth, it has established a foundation on which it may someday do so. First, Brazil must strengthen rather than weaken its environmental laws and enforcement agencies by expanding the legal competencies and operational capacity of IBAMA, which can then increase its efforts to crack down on illegal deforestation. Second, Brazil must accelerate the development of its sustainable timber industry in the Amazon and elsewhere. Third, environmental agencies must ensure that growth in the ethanol, biodiesel, and hydropower sectors is accomplished with minimal impact on forests. Finally, with respect to oil, Petrobras must employ carbon emissions–reducing, or carbon capture and storage, technologies in the extraction and refining processes of the presalt layer petroleum, and the country must begin a wider political debate over oil's GHG emission consequences and how to mitigate them. Clearly, given the shape of political cleavages discussed above, these tasks constitute a "dream list" that is unlikely to be accomplished in its entirety anytime soon. But if Brazil were to complete most of these tasks in the coming years, it would set the stage for long-term economic growth and job creation consistent with reducing overall GHG emissions — that is, green growth.

13

INDIA

*Can Green Be a First-Best Development
Solution for Developing Countries?*

Jayant Sathaye with Juliana Mandell

INTRODUCTION

Developed and developing nations face radically different concerns regarding perceived green growth potential. The green growth story for developed nations centers on the economic opportunities and costs of transitioning a mature energy system to become more efficient and less carbon intensive. For developing nations, however, questions of green growth revolve around a primary need for energy supply. For India this tension takes on a particular importance due to the nation's persistent and growing electricity deficit.

India's significant electricity deficit limits the nation's aspirations for rapid economic growth and sustained development. The deficit is increasingly problematic. Rapid growth in economic output and population is fueling demand for energy. With limited indigenous fossil fuel resources to fall back on, the nation has had to increasingly rely on energy imports at greater cost and at greater detriment to energy security. The nation's current electricity deficit significantly limits productivity, reduces annual GDP, and is a barrier to socioeconomic improvements.

India's electricity deficit is rooted as much in a myriad of operational and institutional problems as in a rapidly expanding energy demand. A comparison of the nation with China highlights these internal problems in producing and distributing electricity. While both nations face pressing energy supply demands as a result of rapid development, China appears likely to meet its energy needs in a "business as usual" scenario. India does not. China plans to address increasing energy demand through aggressive and efficient government action. India, in contrast, has been hampered by fractured and overlapping regulation and inefficient government action. Whereas China contains large reserves of coal, oil, and natural gas, India has limited oil and gas reserves. Moreover, India's population growth rate continues to far surpass that of China, increasing demand for energy. While China appears poised to meet its growing energy demands through heavy infrastructural investment and vast domestic fuel resources, it is clear that a continued energy shares strategy will be inadequate to meet energy demand in India. Barring a significant change in energy policy, India's current electricity deficit and limited green energy infrastructure mean that the country will need to shift more aggressively to energy efficiency and renewable-energy strategies to meet growing demand.

Could India, because of its limited fossil fuel reserves and rapidly expanding economy, actually create a fertile ground for green growth experimentation and returns? Might energy efficiency and renewable energy help resolve the energy deficit in the Indian economy? Energy efficiency offers the potential to reduce demand and thus ameliorate the growing energy deficit; renewable energy provides a means of supplying electricity, including off-grid locations, and reducing fossil fuel imports. Recent studies and on-the-ground projects suggest that energy efficiency programs and renewable energy could potentially provide a means to address the deficit in absolute, disruptive, and geographical terms at a lower cost than business as usual strategies.

India thus faces two related energy challenges. First, it must address its continuing energy deficit, exacerbated by its limited resources and expanding economy and population. Second, to facilitate green growth, India faces the problem experienced by other developing and newly industrialized countries: it must balance an increasing demand for energy with environmental sustainability (Kelsey and Zysman, Chapter 5 in this book). We argue that these goals are not mutually exclusive and that India can solve its energy shortages through investments in green research and development and infrastructure. Such investments have the potential to create a "green spiral," in which newly developed green industrial interests provide support for policies that facilitate additional green growth, creating new green industries (Kelsey and Zysman, Chapter 5).

This chapter focuses on the electricity deficit and potential solutions provided by renewable energy and demand-side management. India's policies to promote a more rapid expansion of the power sector and ways to reduce electricity demand have to be set at both national and state levels. The bulk of the power supply belongs to a state-owned power company that is managed primarily by the state government. Policies set by state governments

230   thus can have a direct and strong impact compared to national draft policies. The number of states that have demonstrated capabilities to set influential policies is very limited. Few states have implemented renewable energy RPOs, and even fewer have set up policies to promote DSM programs to improve appliance, industry, and buildings energy efficiency. Whether these possibilities can be fully realized given the host of operational problems facing the nation remains an open question. This chapter provides information about the rather weak policies that have been implemented to date, but it does not go into the details of what future policies might undertake and ways they could be sustained to ensure their continued use.

THE ELECTRICITY DEFICIT

India's electricity deficit exists in absolute, geographical, and disruptive terms. In *absolute* terms, the state's electrical deficit shifted from 7.7 percent in 1990–1991 to 8.5 percent in 2010–2011 (Sathaye and Gupta 2010).[1] These figures reflect the sum of all utility-level shortages averaged per hour. This definition does not account for the millions in the nation without access to electricity or for the limiting effects of unreliable supply. In *geographical* terms, the electricity deficit speaks to a crisis of access. Presently about 45 percent of the homes in India do not have access to electricity. The majority of these homes exist outside urban areas, often in remote and hard-to-reach locations. Limited geographical access to grid-based electricity, especially in remote and rural areas, remains a persistent barrier to development in the nation. In *disruptive* terms, frequent rolling blackouts and shortages impose economic costs on industry and individuals and require the widespread use of backup generation (Sargsyan et al. 2010).

Moreover, compounding development pressures point to a growing electricity deficit. Rapid economic growth, seen in GDP growth averaging between 7 and 10 percent since 1997 (CIA 2012), has driven a corresponding expansion of energy demand. As noted above, the absolute energy deficit grew almost 3.5 percent over the last two decades. Electricity demand continues to outpace energy production. Demand is expected to grow at an average annual rate of 7.4 percent. Meanwhile, real capacity constructed in both public and private sectors has consistently fallen below even planned capacity over the last few planning cycles (Sathaye and Gupta 2010). In a business as usual (BAU) scenario these pressures will only grow. Energy demand in the nation, commensurate with expected GDP growth, is projected to rise two- to threefold by 2030 (Mathur 2010).

As a result, India faces increasing structural energy insecurity. Compounding this is the fact that, given its limited fossil fuel reserves, the nation has
become increasingly dependent on imports. In 1970, the nation was energy
self-sufficient, albeit at a much lower level of development and with more
limited prospects for growth. In 2010, India was importing 30 percent of total
consumed energy. Furthermore, India's coal reserves are projected to run out
over the next 45 years. In the meantime, the International Energy Agency estimates that nominal prices for coal will triple over the next 20 years (Sargsyan
et al. 2010). India's increasing energy insecurity leaves the nation more vulnerable to fluctuating global energy prices, constricted supply, and price shocks.
Figure 13.1 shows India's increasing energy demands and the distribution of
energy sources used to meet that demand.

India's electricity deficit has immediate negative economic and environmental consequences. Economically, these include shortages, rolling blackouts, and limited energy access, which act as barriers to development and
impose real costs. One estimate found that the numerous electricity shortages of the 2007–2008 fiscal year cost the Indian economy an estimated 6 percent of its GDP (Arora et al. 2010). Furthermore, to compensate for electricity
shortages, many firms and some households rely on expensive and polluting
backup generation. These generators, usually powered by diesel, cost two to
three times more than electricity from the grid and emit harmful local air
pollutants (Sathaye 2011). Lost productivity and additional electricity costs
can make Indian industry less cost-competitive and hamper development
efforts.

The failure to meet electricity demand leaves a significant portion of a state
population reliant on traditional biofuels (wood, charcoal, animal dung, etc.)
or backup diesel generators. Both fuel sources generate significant air pollution and pose a public health threat. Indoor air pollution, caused in large part
by the particulate matter pollutants of traditional fuels, is a major risk factor
and cause of fatalities in India (Smith 2000). Indoor air pollution also has a
significant impact on morbidity and loss of productivity. In their 2001 study,
Bussolo and O'Connor (2001) estimated that the reduced mortality and morbidity caused by reduced particulate concentrations equals to about 334 lives
saved per million tons of carbon abated.

Finally, with the nation's main fuel sources currently coal, biomass, and
oil, continued growth in a BAU scenario will generate a significant increase
in carbon emissions. Under the BAU scenario, with India deriving two-thirds
of its electricity from coal, India is set to become the third largest consumer of
energy by 2030 after only the United States and China (Sathaye 2011). India's

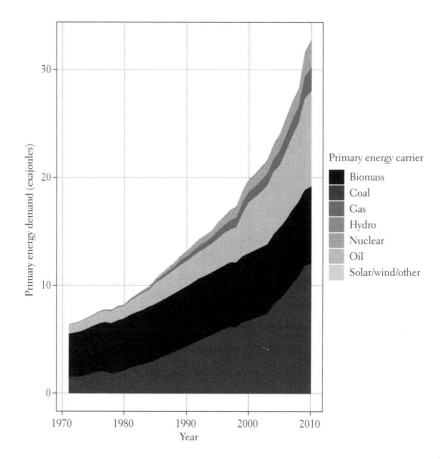

FIGURE 13.1   Indian primary energy demand, 1971–2010

SOURCE: International Energy Agency (IEA) World Energy Statistics and Balances 2012.
NOTE: Excludes traditional biomass.

ratio of CO_2 per capita remains low, but the ratio is currently one and half times 1990 levels and continues to grow (IEA 2009).

In the long run, the effects of climate change will only add to India's developmental stresses. As a developing nation in a tropical region, India has particular reason to view climate change projections with concern. Climate change analysts predict that India will be particularly hard hit, facing moderate to high water stress that will reduce water access and increase droughts and floods. Moreover, as a still developing nation, India relies upon a weaker and less extensive infrastructure to weather such stress. This lack of infrastructure will increase the nation's vulnerability to climate change impact (Sathaye, Shukla, and Ravindranath 2006).

ENERGY EFFICIENCY AND RENEWABLE ENERGY: GREEN GROWTH POTENTIAL

India's inability to address its expanding energy deficit through conventional methods may in fact make it a fertile ground for green growth experimentation. The question arises as to whether energy efficiency and renewable energy can offer India the potential to balance its energy deficit and reap economic gains. How possible this reality will be, however, given the myriad operational problems that plague the Indian bureaucracy and power sector, remains to be seen. In this section, we expand on the arguments for a fit between green development and India's particular needs.

Energy Efficiency

Energy efficiency, with a focus on demand reduction, stands to offer significant potential to the Indian economy, given the state's growing electricity deficit. Despite an overall decline in the energy intensity of the economy over the last ten years, many sectors remain highly inefficient. Since 2000, India has witnessed a 25 percent decline in energy intensity (Sathaye 2011). This decline can be attributed in part to a changing economic and industrial landscape of greater competitiveness and new, less-energy-intensive sectors. In the 1990s, the transformation of the "License Raj" to a more liberalized economy forced industry to become more competitive and focus on bottom-line energy costs. At the same time, the economy began an industry shift away from high-energy-intensive production toward low-energy-intensive services (Mathur 2010). However, as Figure 13.2 shows, the decline in the energy intensity of the Indian economy is less than the decline seen in the United States or China (Sathaye 2011). The discrepancy is due, in part, to ambitious policy implementation by the latter two nations. Moreover, India's rapid economic growth has generated a unique energy-intensity profile, with a significant disparity of energy-intensity levels seen among industries. Rapid growth has enabled old and new firms to compete side by side in the market—the old through scale and depreciation, and the new through efficiency (Mathur 2010). Finally, the nation's built environment stands poised for transformation and growth. All of these factors together illustrate the potential for energy savings and efficiency in the current Indian economy.

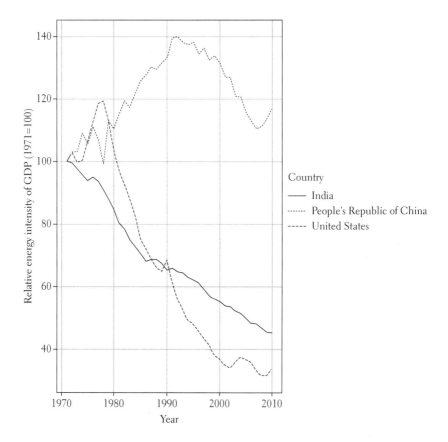

FIGURE 13.2   Comparative energy intensity of economic production, 1971–2010

SOURCE: Author's calculation based on energy consumption and real GDP (constant 2000 dollars) data from International Energy Agency (IEA) World Energy Statistics and Balances, 2012.
NOTE: All data baselined to 1971 = 100.

Recent studies suggest that the effective implementation of energy efficient measures could balance the nation's electricity deficit and increase productivity at a lower cost than building out the supply in a BAU scenario. A recent study from the Lawrence Berkeley National Laboratory projected two scenarios for India's power supply through 2017. The first projection followed BAU patterns, and the second scenario, entitled "supply with energy efficiency" (SEE), met all new demand and all retired appliances with energy efficient technologies. The study found that the SEE scenario enabled the nation to meet peak power demand, eliminate the deficit, and keep supply investment and operating costs below that of BAU. The SEE scenario generated threefold economic benefits: it lowered investment costs for the state and private utilities; it lowered projected fuel and operational costs below that of the BAU scenario; and it increased productivity in commercial and industrial sectors (Sathaye and Gupta 2010).

The use of energy efficiency measures to balance the nation's electricity deficit would generate the largest economic returns, according to the study, through increased productivity in the commercial sector. Balancing the deficit would allow industries, currently hampered by shortages and rolling blackouts, to work at full capacity. According to the SEE scenario, enabling all industries to work at full capacity would generate an additional $609 billion in the commercial sector and $189 billion in various industrial sectors, for a total benefit by 2017 of $798 billion. Moreover, the SEE scenario would improve the fiscal health of individual states. States currently provide heavy electricity subsidies to agricultural and domestic sectors. Not all public utilities are compensated for the costs of providing such subsidies, and they have been a cause of significant debt and even bankruptcy for utilities and states. Energy efficiency would improve the situation twofold: it would reduce the overall energy consumption and thus the need for subsidies, and it would increase the flow of revenue to the state through taxes resulting from increased productivity and GDP growth (Sathaye and Gupta 2010; Sathaye 2011).

Finally, the cumulative impact of not building out supply to the BAU projected extent through the SEE scenario would reduce carbon emissions by an estimated 333 Mt by 2020. Moreover, it would lower projected local air pollutants such as SO_2, NO_x, and fly ash that contribute to direct public health concerns.

Renewable Energy

Renewable energy could provide an answer not only to energy import security concerns but to India's geographic deficit of energy supply. Renewable energy development in India has the potential to provide an accessible and cost-competitive source of off-grid power that would increase productivity and quality of life in rural areas. It has the further potential to generate wealth, spur regional development and employment, and address the nation's increasing energy insecurity.

The current Indian energy electricity supply remains 65 to 70 percent dependent on coal (Arora et al. 2010). With limited fossil fuel reserves and coal reserves projected to run out in the next 45 years, the nation has become increasingly energy dependent and insecure. Spending on oil and gas imports, as a percentage of GDP, has increased and will continue to do so; it

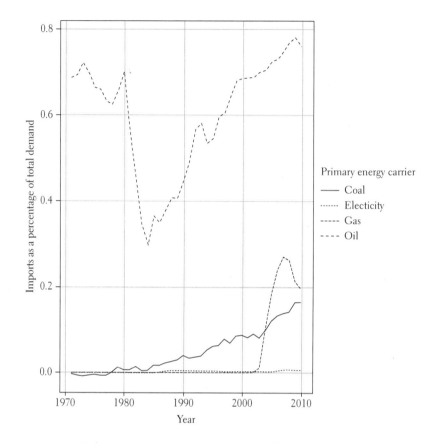

FIGURE 13.3   Indian energy imports as a percentage of primary energy consumption, 1971–2010
SOURCE: International Energy Agency (IEA) World Energy Statistics and Balances 2012.

is projected to rise from 4 percent of GDP in 2010 to 6.9 percent of GDP in 2020 (Sargsyan et al. 2010). Figure 13.3 shows this increase as a percentage of demand.

India's rich renewable resources offer an alternative, indigenous, and abundant energy supply. Large portions of the nation are geographically optimal for solar, wind, biomass, and hydroenergy production. Large expanses of land receive high solar irradiation, the coastline shows regular patterns of high wind velocity, large quantities of biomass are produced annually, and the nation is traversed by a number of rivers and waterways optimal for hydro (Arora et al. 2010).

India has considerable solar and wind power that is largely located from the northwestern to the southern part of the country. The total wind capacity has been estimated to be as high as 2,000 GW, only 10 percent of which would be adequate to supply power in the country over the next 15 years (Phadke, Bharvirkar, and Khangura 2011). Solar power is more expensive but would still be significant to match the demand during strong summer periods (Sathaye 2011).

The current geographical electricity deficit in India acts as a barrier to economic development. About half of the households in India are without access to the grid, the majority in rural and remote areas. Many such villages are situated in locations too remote or difficult to access to achieve grid connectivity at present or in the near future. In these locations, off-grid renewable energy can prove an economically viable source of electricity. Off-grid renewable energy projects provide small-scale, decentralized, and cost-competitive electricity to locations that the grid cannot reach (Arora et al. 2010; Sargsyan et al. 2010). In these locations, renewable energy as compared to the costs and hazards of the other available off-grid lighting sources, such as kerosene, becomes an attractive alternative.

Finding a means to provide electricity to the many rural hamlets and households currently without access to the grid would be a boon to economic development in the region. It would enable increased productivity, permit greater interconnectivity, and facilitate a higher standard of living in these areas.

Current successful off-grid renewable capacity projects installed in India include family biogas plants, solar PV systems, solar streetlights and lanterns, and small hydro plants. For example, in the states of Karnataka and Gujarat, the private company SELCO India found a profitable business model in off-grid solar production. The company enables PV solar generation in off-grid areas through provision of products, services, and access to financing through partnerships with banking institutions. In one example, the company was able to rent solar-powered lanterns to street vendors at a cost less than the operating cost of kerosene lamps (Arora et al. 2010).

At the moment, only 2.4 percent of India's installed renewable capacity consists of off-grid systems. Current projects and trends underway, however, speak to burgeoning development and future capacity. At the moment, government-sponsored programs are paving the way to build out off-grid renewable capacity in rural and remote locations. These programs have resulted in electrification of over 90,000 villages and free electricity connection to over 12 million below the poverty line (Arora et al. 2010; RGGVY.gov).

While independent private sector involvement has been encouraged, as of yet public-private partnerships have been the main business model. In such

238   models, an energy service company, entrepreneur, or outside actor often seeks to provide system maintenance and operations in tandem with government programs. Off-grid renewable energy poses challenges in tandem with opportunities. Due to the remote and rural location of many facilities, it can prove challenging for technical support and backup repair service to reach them. While some off-grid renewable programs have been successful, others have struggled to generate sustainable revenue (Niez 2010).

Renewable energy development offers the potential for off-grid regional economic development in the areas that need it most. Some underdeveloped Indian states are endowed with significant renewable resources. The states of Arunachal Pradesh, Himachal Pradesh, and Uttarkhand are among the poorest in the nation and are endowed with significant small hydro potential. Development of renewable resources could boost economic development, provide an accessible and localized power source, and increase the revenue flow to the state. Furthermore, potential exists from many states to sell excess electricity generated from renewable production to neighboring and distant states, either to satisfy renewable portfolio standards or to address the deficit (Sargsyan et al. 2010).

BARRIERS TO "GREEN GROWTH" AND EXPANDED ENERGY SUPPLY

The market penetration of energy efficient and renewable technologies is often hampered by barriers[2] that are influenced by prices; financing; international trade; market structure; institutions; lack of information; and social, cultural, and behavioral factors. Many papers and reports have documented the pervasiveness of barriers to energy efficiency improvements.[3]

India is moving toward the adoption of policies and regulations that promote competition and more open markets and is thus positively influencing the adoption of energy efficiency technologies. Nonetheless, the adoption of energy efficient technologies faces numerous market impediments and failures that both must work together. Some of the most significant market barriers and steps to address them include the following:

- About 95 percent of the Indian power supply is composed of state-owned companies. A web of complex bureaucracy and regulations plagues its effectiveness.
- Inadequate grid infrastructure and limited data access further contribute to the growing deficit and curtail policy options to address it.
- Consumer discount rates are many times higher than societal discount rates. In industrialized countries, this has meant that incentives have been required to get consumers to adopt new technologies, even when they are clearly already in their own financial interest to do so. Similar

or possibly even stronger incentives will be required in developing
countries like India.

- Financial intermediation by banks and other lending institutions to promote and develop energy efficiency lending is nonexistent. Also, there
are no private sector energy efficiency service delivery mechanisms such
as ESCOs. There is insufficient understanding and assessment of the
risks and benefits that accrue to the parties in an energy efficiency
transaction.

- There are no power sector incentives to build efficient new buildings.
Most new commercial buildings are not occupied by the owner but are
rented. The builder's objective is to construct the building for the lowest initial cost; the renters also have no incentive to invest in efficiency
improvements in a property they do not own.

- The power sector does not treat energy efficiency on the same economic basis as new capacity. This market barrier is being addressed in
industrialized countries by adopting integrated resource planning tech-
niques and by designing and implementing demand-side management
(DSM) programs.

The current state of the nation's electricity grid infrastructure poses further
barriers to addressing the deficit. Inadequate and out-of-date grid infrastructure and interconnections encourage inefficiency and loss. Furthermore, the
current grid and supporting infrastructure, such as approach roads, remain
insufficient to support current rates of electricity use, let alone to expand demand. Finally, the lack of accurate data on energy use per region and by
population undermines the building of sufficient grid infrastructure and fund
allocation (Singh 2006). Further information is needed to understand energy
usage and needs, as well as to map out existing renewable energy resources
(Arora et al. 2010). However, as Kelsey and Zysman note in Chapter 5, the
lack of an adequate "brown" infrastructure provides opportunities to develop
an alternative green infrastructure. While developed nations must overhaul
existing infrastructure in order to substitute green for brown energy, developing and newly industrialized nations such as India have the opportunity to fill
infrastructural gaps with renewable energy.

Administrative problems in the energy sector exacerbate the task of expanding energy supply and modernizing the electric grid, let alone initiating a
spiral of green growth. There are ongoing problems of profit skimming, theft,
and poorly implemented or politically motivated subsidies. Politically motivated electricity subsidies in particular have further widened the electricity
deficit. Since the 1970s, it has become common practice for local and state
politicians to provide large, unregulated electricity subsidies to big farmers
and local leaders in return for delivering voting blocks in rural areas. These
subsidies distort electricity prices and place a financial strain on utilities that

240   often must shoulder their costs (Sathaye and Gupta 2010). These subsidies have often come in the form of unlimited electricity access, the nature of which discourages efficiency and spurs demand, as well as creates a strong constituency with an interest in the political and energy system status quo. These varied forms of corruption negatively impact the financial profile of utilities, accurate data collection, the construction of adequate infrastructure, and the successful implementation of efficiency and renewable policy and programs. Not unexpectedly, all this leads in turn to poor operational and economic performance of utilities; inadequate infrastructure and public access; and difficulty with policy implementation and reform (Lovei and McKechine 2000; Lal 2006).

Reform is difficult because entrenched political interests that stand to benefit from the existing system block reform and new energy plans. Support also suffers among the public, where the widespread perception of utilities as corrupt limits public trust in new programs, including green policies, and even limits public acceptance of subsidy and rate change even when intended to alleviate these problems (Lal 2006). Policy implementation, even once enacted, is often inefficient and weighed down by the resulting additional costs. Indeed, reforming the administration, regulation, and operation of the energy sector is all the more difficult, since they are part of a more general problem in India that acts as a barrier to achieving the country's overall development goals and hampers green growth potential.

POLICY DEVELOPMENTS

What programs are currently underway in India to address these issues? The Indian power sector regulatory setup is quite similar to that in the United States. India has the Central Electricity Regulatory Commission (CERC) and state electricity regulatory commissions (SERC). SERCs, which were established in 1998, promote competition, efficiency, and economy in the power sector; regulate tariffs on power generation, transmission, and distribution; and protect the interests of the consumers and other stakeholders. The SERCs rule on the tariffs proposed by the electricity distribution company, ensuring that the criteria specified in the law are obeyed.

CERC regulates the tariff of generating companies owned or controlled by the Central Government and those that have a composite scheme for generation and sale of electricity in more than one state. CERC regulates and determines the tariffs on interstate transmission of electricity and issues licenses to persons to function as transmission licensee and electricity trader with respect to their interstate operations. CERC specifies the grid standards and enforces them with respect to quality, continuity, and reliability of services by licensees.

CERC does not have direct authority over the decisions of state commissions and utilities unless the issues span more than one state. However, CERC convenes the Forum of Indian Regulators (FOR) — a statutory body consisting of the chairpersons of all the SERCs — that can provide support and guidance on energy efficiency and renewable energy to the SERCs. The objective of FOR is to evolve a common and coordinated approach to various issues faced by the SERCs.

In 2008, the Indian national government announced the National Action Plan on Climate Change (NAPCC), the first of its kind in the country. The plan outlined eight core national missions to be pursued through 2017 to combat climate change. Two of these missions include the National Mission to Enhance Energy Efficiency, with a goal of 10,000 megawatts in savings by 2020, and the National Solar Mission, with a goal of 20,000 in megawatts of solar power by 2020 (Sathaye 2011; Schmid 2011). The mission anticipates achieving grid parity by 2022 and parity with coal-based thermal power by 2030.

The mission's enhanced energy efficiency policy plan draws on a cap-and-trade market-based mechanism scheme and push-pull policies aimed at promoting financing and standards for market transformation. The Perform Achieve and Trade (PAT) program intends to increase energy efficiency within large energy-intensive industries and facilities by setting three-year energy-reduction targets for each plant and then allowing for trading between those that meet targets and those that don't. The Market Transformation for Energy Efficiency (MTEE) aims to accelerate the market shift to energy efficient appliances through promotion of innovative financing models, CDM financing, and a push for uniform standards and labels such as building codes. Finally, the policy plan aims to fund demand-side management programs through finance mechanisms that capture future energy savings. Examples of such mechanisms include tax exemptions for ESCO and CV funds, energy efficient tax reductions, and revolving funds to promote carbon finance. The efficacy of all these programs will depend on the degree to which government bodies enforce real penalties and the actual availability of financing (Sargsyan et al. 2010).

Government-led rural electrification is currently being developed through three federal agencies: the Ministry of Power, the Ministry of New and Renewable Energy, and the Ministry of Rural Development. This development falls into four main avenues. The 2005 Rajiv Gandhi Grameen Vidyutikaran Yojana Act (RGGVY) aims to electrify 125,000 villages and provide free electricity connection to 23.4 million households below the poverty line. This act does not rely exclusively on renewable energy, but it stands as an important part of the portfolio. The second avenue consists of the National Solar Mission that aims to build 2 gigawatts of off-grid solar-installed capacity. Third,

242   the Village Energy Security Program aims to support village energy needs through test projects using locally available biomass. Finally, the Remote Village Electrification Project aims to provide electricity to villages with 300 or more inhabitants not covered under RGGVY and more than 3 kilometers from the nearest point of grid access (Liming 2009; Arora et al. 2010).

Renewable energy development has been further aided by a number of policy developments over the last ten years. The Electricity Act of 2003 aimed to foster competition, private investment, and access to power. It set about delicensing electricity generation. The act specifically recognized renewable projects supplying power to the utility grid. It also established preferential feed-in tariffs and quotas for renewable energy. The reforms enabled captive generation, made provisions for power trading, and phased open access to transmission and distribution. It had substantial impact on attracting private investment to the power sector and increased renewable energy capacity dramatically. It further established demand-side stimulus through RPOs that are set by the state. Current efforts are underway to develop a renewable energy credit trading mechanism across states. The likely next step will be trading as a means for states to meet their RPOs and thus create an integrated market for renewable investment (Sargsyan et al. 2010; Ministry of Power 2011).

Few states have been capable of initiating policies to promote both renewable energy and energy efficiency. But because the sector-dominant, state-owned power company is not federally managed, state government policies have the potential for a strong, direct impact beyond that of national policies. Policy measures to encourage rapid expansion of the power sector while reducing electricity demand must then be enacted at both state and national levels.

CONCLUSION: A GREEN WAY OUT

The nature of India's electricity deficit problems stands in contrast to China's approach to a similar problem of rapidly expanding energy demand. The Chinese case illustrates that India's challenges are not, in themselves, inherent to developing nations. While both nations face problems of increasing energy demand due to high rates of economic and population growth, China alone appears on the road to adequately addressing these challenges of energy supply. The fact that China will likely succeed in meeting its expanding energy needs has a two-part explanation. The first pertains to indigenous fossil fuel reserves and bears limited reflection on government policy. China boasts large coal reserves that ensure a supply of cheap and accessible electricity; India has no such comparable reserves. Second, and arguably more relevant to this study, the Chinese government has made it a national priority to aggressively promote enhanced energy efficiency programs and renewable-energy production. For a party whose political legitimacy depends on a rising national standard of living, securing a sufficient energy supply to meet the expanding demand has become a matter of political survival. The government has executed this directive with aggressive promotion and follow-through aimed at expanding the energy supply through all means possible. National directives seek to simultaneously expand all potential sources of energy from coal to wind turbines, build out the grid, and promote energy efficiency. An aggressive energy efficiency policy currently works to retire inefficient production facilities. The sum total of these measures signals that China will meet the energy needs of its rapid economic growth, but as a heavy greenhouse gas emitter.

In contrast, India, with limited indigenous fossil fuel reserves and an inefficient government bureaucracy, faces an expanding energy deficit. If India continues on a business as usual development track, rapid economic expansion will outpace electricity supply, and the deficit will widen, curtailing productivity, growth potential, and sustainable development. India lacks the fossil fuel reserves China has to fall back on and risks becoming increasingly energy insecure. Moreover, inefficient and uncoordinated policy and regulation offer the potential to exacerbate rather than address deficit concerns. While China too struggles with the issues of policy disruption for personal gain and graft, these issues manifest as inefficiencies in the energy system rather than a lack of sufficient energy supply.

India's insufficient fossil fuel reserves and rapidly expanding economy, however, may offer it a chance and an incentive to explore and derive economic gain from a variety of green growth strategies. Unlike China, India may find it an attractive option to avoid fossil fuel–based development as much as possible, while focusing on economic growth through emissions-reduction strategies such as energy efficiency and renewables. The nation's rapid growth, expanding deficit, and limited fossil fuel resources may in fact create a fertile ground for green growth experimentation and returns. There exists significant potential for the state to utilize energy efficiency measures to address the absolute and disruptive deficit and to utilize renewable energy to address the geographical deficit. Investment in research and development of renewable energy as well as green infrastructure has the potential to create a green spiral in which green industry interests provide support for state-driven green investment and vice versa. However, whether these opportunities will become fully realized remains an open question.

III.   CONCLUSION

14

Can "Green" Sustain Growth?

Mark Huberty, Nina Kelsey, and John Zysman

Green growth emerged as a political justification for pursuing climate policy despite its apparent economic costs. If our efforts to mitigate climate change could generate real economic improvement, then climate policy paralysis might give way to enthusiastic pursuit of the material gains promised by a low-emissions economy. But as we've shown throughout this book, the economic reality of green growth has so far fallen short of its political promise. Today's green growth policy proposals face limited prospects for success outside of a few select countries and as such offer little long-term support for climate policy.

Hence, we conclude as we began: can "green" sustain growth? Answering this question must start with recognizing that serious emissions reduction will require a transformation of modern energy systems. The broad economic growth generated by similar transformations in the past—as in energy, transport, or information technology—suggests the possibility that this transformation may do the same. But growth in those earlier transformations came from the possibilities they created for economic production and job creation throughout the entire economy, not just in transforming the sector itself. Where and how the renewable energy-based economy of the future may generate such possibilities is yet to be identified. But, as Chapter 3 shows, today's most popular paths to green growth are unlikely to create those possibilities. Keynesian green job creation is primarily a short-term tool for depressed economies, not a long-term growth strategy. Export-led growth in so-called green goods can benefit those countries with a well-adapted industrial base in related industries but probably won't generalize to all the countries that need to invest in serious climate change mitigation. Venture capital, as Chapter 4 shows, lacks the enabling conditions that made it a contributor to economic growth and innovation in recent technological revolutions.

With familiar policies unsuited to the task, Part I argues for a period of policy experimentation to discover how best to exploit the full range and potential of a low-emissions energy systems transformation. This prescription for politically driven experimentation raises, of course, a chicken-and-egg problem: if green growth was supposed to generate political support for climate change policy but can't do so until after a period of experimentation that itself requires support, then where does that initial support come from?

Part II of this book addresses this political problem explicitly. As we show, across a range of countries and levels of development, states have pursued a huge range of policy options. But successful states shared a common pattern — what we termed a "green spiral" — in which their early policies, some not even targeted at climate change itself, build broad coalitions of industrial and environmental supporters through actions that delivered near-term, material benefits. Those coalitions later became the foundation for future actions focusing on how countries around the world have begun the political process of building support for long-term policy and policy experimentation.

GREEN GROWTH AND EMISSIONS REDUCTION: THE SHARED PROBLEM OF ENERGY SYSTEMS TRANSFORMATION

The shift to a low-carbon system is a technically and politically daunting task. As Chapter 2 argues, the technical, economic, and regulatory structure of today's energy systems revolve around fossil fuels and their particular physical characteristics. Maintaining the stability of the electricity system and its supply of power to energy-hungry industrial societies depends at its root on fossil fuels' highly dense, portable, and storable fuel sources. As Chapter 2 shows, the move to a renewable energy-based system upends this set of assumptions. Aside from nuclear energy and hydropower, nearly all low-emissions energy resources are intermittent: they vary with the wind, sun, and other sources that supply their power. Absent the ability to easily store electric power, this intermittency can undermine the careful balance of supply and demand that ensures the stability of modern electricity systems. Experience with renewable energy deployment in regions like Denmark or Texas has demonstrated the vulnerability of today's energy systems to such a fundamental change in the characteristics of its energy supplies.

Maintaining stability in spite of these fundamental changes in the energy system will require, we argue, an array of parallel and complementary changes in how we produce, distribute, and use energy. Those changes include the

incorporation of new storage technologies to permit banking of excess power 249
for later use; construction of power grids designed to gather up and redistribute power from geographically dispersed renewable resources; incorporation
of intelligent information systems into the power grid to permit closer and
more responsive monitoring of the system; empowering of consumers to be
more flexible in energy demand and more attentive to the actual cost of power;
and reform of regulatory and market structures to reward more efficient use of
power and to correctly structure investment incentives to ensure a successful
low-emissions development trajectory.

As we and others note in this book, this process of energy systems transformation will require substantial technological innovation. Fostering innovation
in the technologies required for this new energy system poses a complex policy
problem. Experience has provided very good ideas for marginal improvement
of the efficiency and emissions footprint of current energy systems. In contrast,
building out the largely emissions-free energy system of the future poses an array of unknowns. Consequently, we risk taking easier short-term decisions that
optimize today's fossil fuel systems, even if transformative technological innovation offers potentially much larger long-term emissions reduction. Sidestep-
ping the potential for technological myopia will require a concerted effort to
address uncertainty about the long-term technological trajectory of the energy
system. This will require, of course, not merely support for basic research and
development but also consideration of how and when the infrastructure at the
heart of the energy system — the power grid and related technologies — will
evolve and adapt to the new demands placed on it by renewable energy.

The specifics of these tasks aside, the energy systems transformation they
support poses an array of difficult political challenges. For the *developed* world,
effective emissions reduction will require retiring energy assets that today are
useful and profitable, and leaving valuable fossil fuels in the ground, both
now and for the foreseeable future. Replacing these energy sources will require, in absolute terms, very large investments in new energy generation and
transmission infrastructure. The *developing* world, while it lacks some of the
sunk costs that inhibit action in the developed world, faces an equally difficult
problem: making the choice for renewable energy-driven development over
established, reliable, less expensive fossil fuel alternatives. Neither of these
choices — whether to give up fossil fuels or to eschew their adoption — garners
broad political support, even as they generate intense opposition.

In the face of these costs, the environmental benefits from a low-emissions
energy systems transformation offer, at present, little incentive for aggressive emissions reduction. Over the long term, of course, the potential cost
of unchecked climate change makes emissions reduction look like a good

investment. But that benefit—the avoided costs of climate damage—will be widely dispersed, arrive far in the future, and accrue to broad groups regardless of the role they played in emissions reduction today. Diffuse, distant benefits provide little motivation to take action today, and by the time climate damage becomes a real and material threat, the moment for action will have passed.

Nor will the material benefits of a low-emissions systems transformation, as we understand them today, provide much relief. In past eras, of course, the material benefits of energy systems transformation provided more than enough inducement for action. The new capabilities offered by coal, oil, and electricity each ushered in an array of new economic possibilities that were motivation enough for massive investments in new and complex energy systems. But a low-emissions energy systems transformation faces similarly high costs, while offering no comparable functional improvements over fossil fuels. Indeed, the greatest ambition of this transformation is to ensure that industry and consumers notice no difference between the "brown" electricity they use today and the "green" electricity they will use tomorrow.

Immediate costs and distant, diffuse benefits will, inevitably, create powerful political resistance to starting and sustaining a low-emissions energy systems transformation. Neither the presently unfavorable balance of costs and benefits nor the technical obstacles to revamping the energy system, we emphasize, doom the green growth project. As we noted at several points in the book, much of the economic potential of many earlier transformations, most recently information technology, endured periods of discovery before their enormous potential became clear. We should expect the same in this case. But resolving whether and how a low-emissions energy system can open an array of new economic opportunities throughout the economy will require a period of experimentation.

CREATING A POLITICS FOR GREEN GROWTH

Creating support for the experimentation necessary to long-term green growth poses a difficult challenge. Whatever the precise policy approach, a low-emissions energy systems transformation will require long-term, sustained political commitment to investments in new infrastructure, to the development of new technology options, and to the creation of innovative business models across an array of sectors. All these processes are prone to missteps and setbacks that will provide opponents opportunities to stall or reverse the project. Sustaining a long-term policy commitment to emissions reductions and green growth despite inevitable short-term failures will require policies adaptable to changing circumstances.

As the country cases in Part II show, where the political support for adaptability has arisen, it has done so via what we have termed a green spiral. Long-term political support for climate policy did not emerge from thin air. Rather, the green coalitions that underpin such support grew from successes in solving other environmental and economic problems. The political interests that evolved from these successes became supporters for future policy initiatives and provided a counterweight for opposing brown interests. The ensuing policy stability promoted experimentation and insulated the political system from setbacks. As Chapter 5 summarizes, this process of mutually reinforcing feedback between environmental goals and industrial interests helped build a stable politics for green growth experimentation.

The cases of Denmark, California, and Korea suggest the varied possibilities for green spirals. The California and Denmark successes began as narrow responses to specific policy problems. For Denmark, the industrial interests that emerged to solve Danish energy security problems during the oil crises of 1970s evolved into a domestic coalition of industry and labor supportive of emissions reduction and renewable energy adoption. The stable politics of green growth that resulted have shifted Denmark's political debate so far that it now focuses on how fast, rather than whether, to reduce emissions. In California, the roots of a climate policy coalition emerged from a series of responses to acute environmental and energy problems: first the response to the smog problems in Los Angeles in the 1950s and 1960s, then the pursuit of energy efficiency and renewable energy after the oil crises of the 1970s. The green spirals present in both cases illustrate the political merits of strategies that build from concrete material problems toward longer-term green strategies and climate solutions.

By contrast, Korea's green growth strategy explicitly seeks to launch a green spiral. Former president Lee Myung-bak sought to mobilize an industrial constituency for a low-emissions energy systems transformation through the search for new sources of growth for Korea's industrial economy. This strategy has sought to thread a difficult path between Korean industry, which has so far resisted specific commitments to greenhouse gas reduction, and environmental interests, which support the climate goals but fear they amount to mere greenwashing of Lee's industrial objectives. While Lee has successfully launched a green spiral on the basis of industrial transformation, the political task of sustaining it amidst these competing pressures remains. Moving beyond the use of Korea's authoritarian economic tradition, future governments must now bridge these competing interests to build a coalition of industry, environmental groups, and the broader public.

252   These successful cases also illustrate an important related lesson: stable climate politics rarely represent a simple victory of environmental over economic interests. Concerns about climate change are in themselves insufficient for building a stable, long-term green coalition. Rather, they also require the support of a market-driven, profit-oriented constituency for green policy. This support requires building a coalition of industrial interests that jointly and *directly* benefit from green policy. Together, these diverse coalitions of industrial and environmental interests help provide both the economic and political counterweight to offset those economic interests that lost out.

     Finally, as controversies in Korea and several other of our cases illustrate, debates over what counts as green may frustrate attempts at building consensus across environmental and industry groups. Damming rivers for emissions-free hydroelectric power can damage or destroy ecosystems. Nuclear power provides nearly emissions-free electricity once the reactors are built, but it generates highly hazardous wastes and carries the risk of catastrophic accidents like Fukushima. Brazil and China have both adopted strategies with laudable green components, but both must ultimately be judged as brown: Brazil for the destructive forestry practices that accompany its renewable biofuels and China for its rapid expansion of fossil fuel use alongside its enthusiastic embrace of wind and solar technology. These tensions among emissions control, environmental protection, and economic growth are inevitable. Overcoming these tensions to build successful green coalitions requires addressing an array of political as well as technical questions: How should we balance economic and environmental objectives? What balance do we find acceptable? Who gets to decide where that balance lies?

FROM SYSTEMS TRANSFORMATION TO GREEN GROWTH

Policy for green growth must thus simultaneously solve the technical and political obstacles that impede experimentation with the growth opportunities of an energy system transformation. We have noted that fundamental reorganization of the energy system requires the integrated development and deployment of an array of technologies into a new system. It calls for stable and adaptive policy that permits — indeed, encourages — experimentation. But experimentation implies both success and failure, posing a daunting political challenge to those interested in sustaining this transformation in the face of political resistance and opportunism.

     We have argued throughout the book that many conventional climate and green growth policies focus too much on the technical problem of emissions reduction, to the exclusion of this vital political challenge. Chapter 2 considers emissions pricing in particular as an example of the political risks posed by this omission. Technologically, emissions pricing's past successes have come, as in the case of sulfur dioxide and acid rain, where the innovations required for emissions reduction were already in hand. Hence, raising emissions prices could encourage adoption and refinement of existing technologies rather than the creation of wholly new ones. In the case of greenhouse gasses, where many of the technologies required are unknown, emissions pricing risks near-term optimization of our current system in ways that undermine a long-term energy systems transformation. While this may improve conditions in the near term, it risks locking in choices that will prove suboptimal over the long term.

Political as well as technical risks accompany this kind of technology-neutral strategy. Emissions pricing is attractive for its perceived fairness and insulation from political meddling. But it imposes acute, obvious costs on powerful economic interests. Those interests will oppose both the policy itself and the gradual tightening of emissions limits over time. Simultaneously, pricing does little to offset or diffuse these opponents: its technological neutrality deprives emissions pricing of the ability to generate equally enthusiastic and powerful interests in policy continuity. Thus, emissions pricing and related policies risk exacerbating the tensions at the heart of the climate policy dilemma. Even if one disagrees with the potential technological and economic limits of emissions pricing, this political dynamic doesn't bode well for the political viability of emissions pricing or its ability to generate stable long-term incentives for energy systems transformation.

By implication, a viable politics of green growth — a politics that permits an array of experimentation to discover how energy systems transformation might generate broad economic benefits — will require tailoring policy to be conscious of and mobilize the real economic winners from the transition to a new energy system. This can create knotty conundrums. For example, some critics allege that Korean and Danish support for various green technology strategies distorts the pursuit of green growth or environmental sustainability for economic ends. Alternatively, however, these strategies may also generate the foundations of economic and industrial support for green policy continuity. In doing so, they will create winners and losers. However this is done, policy makers need to avoid the perception of corruption, lest — as the discussion of Solyndra, First Solar, and QCells in Chapter 3 suggests — the appearance of unfairness or favoritism undermine progress. Such risks, though real, must be confronted and managed, and they are not reasons for giving up altogether.

To this point, we have focused primarily on national energy systems and national politics. It is here that the problems of green growth appear in greatest relief because it is principally at the national level that the distributional and political questions of energy systems transition play out. Similarly, it is ultimately at the national or subnational level that authority for relevant policy decision making rests. Europe, the obvious exception, succeeds largely because of its uniquely institutionalized transnational political structure.

Nonetheless, climate change is a global challenge, and the world has spent a tremendous amount of time and energy pursuing a *global* emissions mitigation agreement. As of 2012, however, international deal making remains mired in seemingly intractable disputes about who will bear the burden of emissions reduction, who will pay for it, and how much.

This paralysis raises two questions about the implications of this book for international deals. First, does domestic green growth require an international deal? The theoretical and empirical material we present in this volume suggests that, in a green growth–focused world, international agreements need not play a central role in initiating or sustaining the critical green spirals. Our cases suggest that green "success stories" (in a political sense, at least) spiral up from local interests, not down from global deals. International agreements have been a focus of effort because climate policy has traditionally emphasized the high cost of emissions reduction. If climate change mitigation is costly, nations must be concerned that they do not take on unfair shares of those costs, carry free riders, or encourage leakage of industry from cost-bearing countries to those that don't participate. All these concerns have led nations to resist the idea of engaging in green policy without a global deal that somehow ensures collective and fairly distributed effort.

But if, as we have suggested, we could genuinely conceive of green policy in terms of direct benefits for specific local interests, then we need to reconsider the role of international deals.[1] If green growth proves possible, policy will progress not because it fulfills international commitments but because it benefits local stakeholders who influence policy choices. Conversely, if conditions at the domestic level don't support energy system transformation, countries won't sign on to a treaty that forces them to initiate one. Treaties can neither force emissions reduction on nations in a top-down sense nor generate from whole cloth the domestic policies of the fundamental system transition required for green growth. Hence, it is entirely unclear whether international deals, as presently conceived, will play an important or even marginal role in generating a durable politics of the energy system transformation that must underpin green growth.

This analysis raises a second question: Do international deals have *any* role to play in facilitating national policy? As we see in Europe, more ambitious international deals may become possible over time as the politics of green growth at the national level works to expand the boundaries of what countries already find reasonable. As this process develops, green growth may be aided by focusing international cooperation on ancillary policy areas that can support green growth. For example, improved mechanisms for managing innovation, sharing technology, and trading in green goods across countries may provide valuable support for developing green coalitions at home and extending their benefits abroad. Such deals may also help forestall the kind of "green mercantilism" that we warn against in Chapter 3.

NEW DEVELOPMENTS: NUCLEAR, GAS, AND THE FUTURE OF THE ENERGY SYSTEM

Before we conclude, we must note that, for electricity markets in particular, recent developments have made developing the support for green growth more difficult. The rapid development of shale gas in the United States and its impending development in Europe and elsewhere have pushed the price of natural gas down, reduced exposure to international energy price instability, and moderated emissions growth by substituting gas for coal in electricity generation. These developments have made the near-term case for renewable energy more difficult. Cheap natural gas increases the price pressure on renewable energy alternatives. Local natural gas reduces the exposure to international energy insecurity. And lower-emissions natural gas has alleviated — albeit only for the short term — some pressure on emissions.

Pushing against this trend, the post-Fukushima disillusionment with nuclear power has generated new interest in renewable energy and energy efficiency solutions. Japan, Germany, and other countries now look to alternatives to rapidly replace their nuclear power plants. This rapidly changing landscape for nuclear power poses both opportunities and challenges for emissions reduction. In the near term, it threatens higher emissions as fossil fuels come to fill the gap left by retired nuclear capacity. But it also generates strong incentives to find viable low-emissions options to replace nuclear power over the longer term.

For green growth, however, neither shale gas nor nuclear offers much transformative potential. Instead, they only affect the relative price of energy sources we already know of. In doing so, they change the context, but not the ultimate challenge, for green growth. They affect the environment for building a politics of green growth and the economic incentives and opportunities for finding growth opportunities in a low-emissions energy systems transformation. But they don't on their own generate a fundamentally different set of goals or realities for green growth. As we argue, the real potential for green growth lies in how low-emissions energy affects the possibilities for production and productivity in the economy as a whole. These recent developments only intensify the demand for viable green growth strategies to both forestall lock-in to a new natural gas infrastructure and to provide credible alternatives to fossil fuels as some countries look to a nuclear-free future.

CONCLUSION: FROM FAITH TO FACT

Green growth is attractive as a political argument but daunting as a technical and economic task. As we argue throughout the book, the present enthusiasm for green growth is more religion than reality. Translating today's expressions of faith in the possibility of green growth to sustain climate policy into hard economic reality will require moving beyond marginal changes to today's energy systems. Instead, we argue that real success will require thinking much bigger — toward the transformation of the energy system itself and the opportunities that transformation may hold for the economy writ large. Those opportunities could rival the transformative legacy of earlier epochs of large-scale technological change. But finding those opportunities will require substantial experimentation in a supportive policy environment. Sustaining that support through inevitable political, economic, and technical challenges will require a broad coalition. As we show, building such coalitions is a task in its own right. But however the coalitions are assembled, we also show that they must include those seeking abundant and secure energy for growth as well as those who would profit from the development of a new energy system. Closing this book with a prescription for a politics of experimentation, instead of a list of policy proposals, may appear murky and imprecise. But absent the ambition to search for a viable political and technological strategy for green growth, we may foreclose the possibility of stabilizing climate policy through the opportunities created by green growth. Without those opportunities, sustaining emissions reductions now and for the next century will prove very difficult.

NOTES

CHAPTER 1

Earlier versions of this chapter were prepared for the European Council Informal Competitiveness Discussion–Internal Market during the Belgian Presidency of the European Union, Brussels, Belgium, September 30, 2010; and Green Korea 2010: "Strengthening Global Green Growth Strategy: Policy and Cooperation," September 9, Seoul Korea, sponsored by the National Research Council for Economics, Humanities, and Social Sciences (NRCS), the Presidential Committee on Green Growth (PCGG), and United Nations Department of Economic and Social Affairs (UNDESA).

1. While we focus our discussion here on the electrical system, we note that the transportation sector will undergo a similar transformation. Replacing personal transport with more emissions-efficient alternatives may require changes to transportation fuels, their distribution networks, and the vehicles that consume them. The current debate about biofuels, fuel cells, electrically powered vehicles, and other transport options suggests the technological and economic uncertainty surrounding that transformation.

2. The Integration of Variable Generation Task Force (2009) estimates that intermittency becomes problematic at around a 20 percent renewable share of electricity generation. Empirical experience in Denmark and West Texas confirms these estimates.

3. The source of this story and similar stories is unclear and may be apocryphal. Nevertheless, in the early years, few computers were bought or used, and it was by no means obvious that something that would later be called the digital revolution had just begun.

4. Davidow (1986) recounts this story from his time as head of marketing at Intel. There are other versions about how the microprocessor spread. Some contend it spread among hobbyists first, rather than existing businesses. The two stories are, of course, compatible.

5. Rai, Victor, and Thurber (2009) make this point for carbon capture and sequestration (CCS) in particular. The large financial and technological risks that CCS presents, coupled with the huge investment cost and regulatory uncertainty, promise to forestall innovation and investment.

6. There may be some exceptions to this. Renewable energy sources, such as solar and wind, do permit decentralized energy production, reducing energy users' dependence on the grid. Whether this translates into radically new forms of production or the organization of production is still unclear.

7. For the European Union, see European Commission (2007a). For the Danish emphasis on job creation from renewable energy, see Danish Government (2011). For related arguments from prominent figures in the public debate, see Jones (2008) and the European Green Party (2009).

8. Chinese competition in renewable energy industries featured heavily in this debate. In 2010, the United States referred China to the World Trade Organization on the basis of allegations that its subsidies to its domestic wind turbine industry constituted unlawful state aid. China's rapid expansion of capacity in renewable energy also led it to capture 90 percent of the California solar cell market. For the solar market, see Woody (2010). For China's rapidly emerging wind industry and Western responses, see Bradsher (2010b) and Scott (2010).

9. The scale of the energy sector points to the limits of job creation in that sector alone. For instance, Denmark obtains about 10 percent of its overall exports from its wind energy sector, but that sector employs only about 24,000 people, or about 1 percent of the Danish workforce. In most Western economies, the total value of energy consumption runs about 2 to 4 percent of GDP—not insignificant but also not very large compared with the economy as a whole. As such, betting on massive job creation through renewable energy rings hollow.

10. See Engel and Kammen (2009).

11. This argument has reappeared in the European Green Party's Green New Deal, which explicitly calls for a substitution of productivity for employment in pursuit of energy-efficiency improvements and renewable energy installations, among other changes to the economy. While such substitutions may make sense in the guise of lots of labor rendered idle by an employment shock, it does not justify the high wages characteristic of the living standards present in the advanced industrial economies. See Schepelmann et al. (2009).

12. Huberty and Zachmann (2011) provide a tentative test of this proposition for wind turbines and solar cells. The broader point proceeds from both Hidalgo and Hausmann (2009) and the much longer history of trade literature in comparative advantage.

13. See here Bradsher (2010b) and Scott (2010). Chinese entry into the solar photovoltaic market has also put severe pressure on leading solar technology firms in Europe, such as QCells and First Solar.

14. Advocates of nuclear energy or carbon sequestration technologies might object that either or both together provide real alternatives to intermittent renewable energy sources and do not require the kinds of systemic changes we outline. In the case of nuclear energy, this is in fact true. But nuclear energy faces a range of other environmental, economic, and political difficulties that have made it unviable at large scale in most industrial economies. In the case of carbon sequestration, the technology is largely unproven and significantly decreases the delivered power of any power plant (due to the substantial energy required to sequester the carbon in the first place). Thus, while either or both technologies may contribute on the margins to energy decarbonization, neither appears politically, economically, or environmentally viable as of this writing.

15. These three elements of the energy system are configured differently in each country by regulation and ownership structure, creating distinct national dynamics of demand and supply. Hence, there will not be one universal trajectory to a low-carbon future and cannot be a single best regulatory strategy.

16. See Katz and Shapiro (1985, 1986, 1994).

17. For a parallel discussion of this problem, see Noll (2011).

CHAPTER 2

1. Here, as in the rest of the book, we treat green growth as the use of investments required for climate change mitigation to drive broader economic growth. Chapter 3 describes other common definitions and explains in more detail why we adopt this specific definition.

2. We will use "electricity" and "energy" interchangeably for the remainder of the chapter. The liquid fuel energy system that supports transportation shares many of the qualities that complicate the transformation of electricity. However, it differs in one potentially vital respect: given viable biofuels, much of the existing fossil fuel infrastructure could be replaced without wholesale changes to the organization of personal transportation. Whether viable zero-emissions biofuels exist, however, is at present unclear. If, instead, large pieces of the transportation system must move to different fuels, the problems of energy transmission, distribution, and use become more pressing.

3. Biofuels do permit some of these capabilities. Biofuels essentially use photosynthesis to store solar energy in solid or liquid form. At present, however, biofuels face numerous problems for long-term sustainability. Cellulosic biofuels would allow much greater extraction of energy from plant matter but face significant technical challenges.

4. For 2010 market-clearing prices by region and time period, see the electricity balancing data provided by the Electric Reliability Council of Texas. Both west and east Texas showed, for 2010, frequent negative power prices. See http://www.ercot.com/mktinfo/prices/mcpe. Referenced July 10, 2012.

5. Since we have previously said that renewable energy is usually more expensive than fossil fuels, this point merits some explanation. While the average cost of renewable energy is usually higher, the marginal cost can be quite low or zero. Flows of wind or sun cost nothing, while the capital cost of installing wind turbines and solar cells is fixed. Hence, wind and solar farm operators have large incentives to generate whenever the power price is greater than zero. This pushes the market price down until the cost of fossil fuels makes additional fossil fuel–based generation uneconomical.

6. See Cailliau et al. (2011) for a full consideration of the design of capacity markets in the European energy system. They argue that capacity markets can assist in ensuring sufficient backup capacity, but they suggest that such markets should also be accompanied by more transparent retail pricing, better demand response, and more consistent incentive structures for renewable energy generators.

7. Coal also enjoyed support for alleviated fuel wood shortages. Nef (1932) cites anecdotal evidence from seventeenth-century London indicating that well-born women, having earlier disdained the smell and soot of coal, were by midcentury praising its "sweet smell" as firewood shortages threatened.

8. Zysman (1983) argues that this process dominated the successful Gaullist reforms of the French economy after World War II. Rather than defeat agricultural and small business opposition, French President Charles de Gaulle trapped the opposition inside his political coalition by other means and then undermined them from within. Arguably, the Korean case in Part II reflects an attempt to do something similar with green growth. Korea's powerful heavy industries are simultaneously the success stories of Korea's rapid industrialization and the greatest opponents to a more economically and environmentally sustainable future. Whether the Korean state can use green growth to trap and then alter these interests inside a green growth coalition remains to be seen.

9. Note that this does *not* imply that carbon prices lack supporters. But beyond those who desire climate change mitigation for noneconomic reasons or those whose business models derive directly from low-emissions goods, emissions pricing has little obvious constituency. In contrast, high energy prices, and the cost of the investments required for energy systems transformation, affect the entire economy. Hence, it is not the lack of interest groups but rather the imbalance between them that threatens long-term emissions pricing.

10. Victor (2011) makes a similar argument. However, while he grants that the politics of emissions pricing are unpromising, he continues to prefer emissions pricing in the abstract. We, in contrast, argue that pricing would probably prove inadequate even if its political problems could be overcome.

11. Emissions pricing advocates often point out the successful use of pricing to control acid rain emissions in the United States. But as Hanemann (2009) shows, the actual experience of acid rain emissions markets bears little resemblance to the carbon emissions problem. The acid rain challenge required a narrow set of changes by a small group of firms, using readily available technologies. Here, of course, we require a broad set of changes across the entire economy, employing technologies often untested or presently nonexistent. Hence, analogies to the success of acid rain policy have limited relevance for the climate problem.

12. We are not the first to propose this. As noted earlier in the chapter, Nordhaus (2010) has argued for long-term policy credibility, although the origins of credibility are left unaddressed. Helm, Hepburn, and Mash (2004) suggest that credibility could derive from institutions designed with long-term incentives. Victor, House, and Joy (2005) suggested a bottom-up approach in U.S. climate policy, building on state-level experiments tailored to local environs. As our discussion of the United States in Part II suggests, however, local credibility doesn't appear to have triggered federal action as of yet. These discussions of credibility in long-run policy draw on the larger literature on credible commitments as a mechanism of stabilizing long-term economic development. How policy makers should credibly commit, given the political dynamics of climate change mitigation, remains an open question.

CHAPTER 3

1. For definitions of green growth as the pursuit of environmental goals as intrinsic goods rather than for human benefit, see CBO (2009a). For definitions emphasizing

broad mitigation of human impacts on the natural world, see Danish Government and Danish People's Party (2009) and United Green Parties for Europe (2009). For definitions grounded in the assumption of a limited capacity for the earth to support any human activity, see Daly (1990), OECD/IEA (2010), and the World Bank (1992). Finally, Arrow et al. (1995) define *sustainability* as the ability to recover from shocks, not simply the ability to sustain normal patterns of activity.

2. Separate from a debate about which economic strategies qualify as green, there is, of course, another debate that concerns which *technologies* should be considered green. Nuclear power in particular generates substantial controversy in this debate because of its tradeoffs between zero-emissions electricity and the environmental and human health issues implicit in radioactive waste and risk of accident. This debate has become particularly acute in the aftermath of the 2011 earthquake and tsunami in Japan and the nuclear crisis it caused. This chapter reviews economic strategies that could apply to any technology, and it does not take a position on which technologies should qualify as green.

3. Energy investments may also face low opportunity costs. The U.S. National Academy of Sciences makes this point explicitly, arguing that much of the American energy infrastructure requires critical upgrades to remain functional (NAS 2010). The marginal cost of additional changes to support emissions reduction may be quite low.

4. This argument is consistent with a long-standing tradition of treating pollution as a market failure due to negative externalities. In those cases, the correct solution is a Pigouvian tax or an equivalent permit scheme that treats the right to pollute as a property right that can be valued in the market (Baumol 1972; Weitzman 1974).

5. Research priorities remain the subject of intense dispute. Apart from the argument about how to fund technologies, the broader research agenda around behavioral and social actions for adaptation and mitigation continues to evolve. For a comprehensive overview of expert perspectives on research priorities, see Brown et al. (2010).

6. The CBO (2009b), the United States Council of Economic Advisors (Romer and Bernstein 2009), and Romer (2011) all find evidence that the Keynesian multiplier — the ratio of net economic growth caused by stimulus to the cost of that stimulus — is greater than 1, and therefore stimulus is a net boost to the economy. Skeptics of Keynesian stimulus as a jobs creation mechanism find the notion of a positive multiplier implausible. A series of papers on the 2008–2009 stimulus packages in particular found Keynesian multipliers equal to or less than 1 — in other words, government stimulus impeded job creation and economic growth (Cogan et al. 2010; Cwik and Wieland 2009; Mulligan 2010). Krugman (2009) argues that these papers address the wrong problem: the question is not whether private sector investment would have outperformed public spending, but whether private spending would have occurred at all.

7. The bankruptcy of American solar energy firm Solyndra may have long-term effects on American energy policy. Solyndra received federal loans to support development of next-generation solar cells. But Chinese firms drove down solar cell prices to a point where its technologies were not cost-competitive. Solyndra's failure led to calls to cease U.S. support for renewable energy technology firms and investigations into alleged corruption in the loan process itself. See Vlasic and Wald (2012), Glantz (2011), and Lipton and Broder (2011).

We thank William Miller, Donald Patton, Henry Rowen, Rolf Wüstenhagen, and three anonymous reviewers for their valuable comments on earlier versions, with the usual disclaimer that they bear no responsibility for the arguments and conclusions drawn.

CHAPTER 5

1. The political logic of a green spiral shares some traits with the long-standing debate over historical path dependence in political processes. Pierson (2000) argued that many political processes — and in particular processes that centered on institutions like parties, interest groups, or agencies — were prone to inertia borne of the costs and benefits of significant policy change. In a world where founding a new political institution was costly, and where many constituencies benefited from existing institutions already, Pierson argued that new institutions would be rare. Streeck and Thelen (2005) countered that we do see substantial incremental change, even if it's rare to see institutions either radically reformed or thrown out wholesale.

The logic of a green spiral clearly shares some features with Pierson's path-dependency logic. We suggest that the process of policy feedback generates, over time, increasing returns in the form of political support by industrial constituencies who may otherwise have approached climate policy with skepticism. But it's important to note that this support, in our formulation, derives from the material benefits earned from tasks required for systems transformation. This is different from Pierson's formulation, in which increasing returns derive from more efficient institutional operations (learning by doing, in his parlance) or increased opportunity costs from institutional change. Furthermore, our call for experimentation informs against strong attempts to institutionalize climate policy. For if Pierson is right, then very strong policy institutions will inform against experimentation and instead tend to put policy itself on a specific, and potentially suboptimal, trajectory.

Zysman (1994) applies an earlier version of this argument to the problem of economic development. He argues that basic choices at critical junctures in national economic development set enduring trajectories for economic growth and industrial specialization. Energy systems are arguably one instance of this, and national energy systems currently face one instance of such a critical juncture.

CHAPTER 6

1. Source: StatBank Denmark, Nat02. GDP in constant 2005 prices. 1972: DKK785.3 billion; 2010: DKK1,536 billion.

2. Emissions in this case are computed according to the IPCC method, which does not reflect the emissions "hidden" in the outsourcing of heavy industries as a result of globalization. For a discussion of this issue, see Wang and Watson (2008). This caveat, of course, applies to all developed economies.

3. On March 12, 2012, it was announced that long-time CEO of DONG Energy, Anders Eldrup, stepped down. At the time of this writing, the circumstances surround-

ing his departure, as well as the impact it may have on DONG Energy's strategic decision making, are unclear. However, because we argue that DONG Energy's strategic
decision making is largely based on its perception of future market conditions, we
expect the impact of his departure to be minor. Whether the strategy remains in the
wake of his departure will of course be the ultimate test of that argument.

CHAPTER 7

1. See, for instance, Jacobsson and Lauber (2006) on German renewable energy
policy, Christiansen and Wettestad (2003) on the origins and content of the Emissions
Trading System legislation, and Schreurs and Tiberghien (2007) on EU climate and
energy policy.

2. Indeed, amidst extreme austerity measures in the United Kingdom under the
Conservative-Liberal Democratic coalition after 2010, one of the few things that has
not been cut is the United Kingdom's aggressive plan for energy investment and market
restructuring.

3. See, for instance, the European Greens' 2009 election manifesto, which called
for sweeping environmental reforms and an explicit tradeoff of productivity for employment in environmental goods industries (European Greens Party 2009; Schepelmann
et al. 2009).

4. Indeed, in early 2011, the Danish center-right government released a highly ambitious domestic energy and climate policy platform that exceeded the expectations of
nearly every major opposition party. Interviews in Denmark shortly after the platform
was released indicated that this will probably set the terms of the debate for the 2011
election and subsequent energy policy choices. See Danish Ministry of Climate and
Energy (2011).

5. A 20 percent improvement in energy efficiency accompanies this goal, but as of
April 2011, it has no legal force behind it.

6. This is true with one significant exception: unlike most goods industries, electricity does not permit integration via mutual recognition. Rather, integrated electricity
markets require common standards for operation of the electrical grid. Some regions — notably the Nordpool market in Scandinavia — had accomplished electricity
market integration outside of the EU. Now that grid policy has become a European
competence, the ENTSO-E body has been tasked with this process. But the EU has
relatively little experience in standards-based market integration.

7. The Kyoto Protocol's carbon market mechanism was actually something foreign
to the European Union. The EU member states had traditionally preferred top-down
regulatory instruments for environmental policy. They agreed to the permit trading
concept at the insistence of the United States. Despite the latter's withdrawal from
the Kyoto Protocol, the EU continued with the framework and its price and quantity
instruments.

8. The European Court of Justice played a critical role in the evolution of feed-in
tariffs. Many of the member states had adopted feed-in tariffs in the 1990s, but doubts
remained as to whether they constituted illegal state aid under the Common Market
regulations. A 2001 ECJ decision (European Court of Justice 2001) confirmed the legal-
ity of feed-in tariffs and paved the way for their adoption across the EU.

9. Timing here proved critical. The year 2009 saw a rapid worsening of the European economic situation and financial crises in a series of peripheral economies. Interviews with a variety of EU and member state policy makers in late 2010 and early 2011 confirmed that the Climate and Energy package would not have passed under those circumstances. The decision of the French Presidency to push for ratification at the end of its term played a critical role in institutionalizing the Commission's white paper.

10. This echos the discussion of emissions pricing in Chapters 2 and 3. Nordhaus (2010) notes that "under limited conditions, a necessary and sufficient condition for an appropriate innovational environment is a universal, credible, and durable price on carbon emissions." The potentially infinitesimal intersection of the limited economic conditions he refers to, and the limited political conditions that would lead to a "universal, credible, and durable" price, poses major problems.

11. For public criticism of such parallel efforts, see Schmalensee (2012). For attempts to quantify the differential cost of emissions reduction via renewable energy incentives versus emissions pricing, see Palmer and Burtraw (2005).

12. Germany and Poland both had their drafts of the Phase II National Allocation Plan denied by the European Commission on the grounds that they used allocation as a kind of de facto state aid policy that interfered with the functioning of the internal market.

13. The EU has recognized many of these problems. The Third Phase of the trading system, beginning in 2013, will use auctioning rather than free allocation to improve the efficiency of the system and reduce opportunities for collusion. Much of the demand for a shift to auctioning appears to have come from firms that could not rely on smooth adjustments to their allotment quotas under the free allocation system.

14. This mantra has become a common feature of energy policy documents originating in the Commission, starting with the 2007 energy strategy white paper. Interviews with Commission staff in late 2010 suggested that, even within the Commission itself, opinions as to the relative importance or attainability of each goal varied greatly and that the emphasis on any one of the three varied over time.

15. This, of course, is limited to the case in which each member state had binding targets without tradeable certificates. In that case, member states could not satisfy their domestic targets through purchases of excess renewable energy production from abroad. As of 2011, the EU renewable energy goals permit only limited tradeability in renewable energy.

16. Huberty et al. (2011) analogize energy systems transformation to earlier technological transformations like information and communications technology (ICT). Cognizant of the differences between ICT and energy, the breakup of vertically integrated energy systems bears some relationship to the U.S. government's antitrust actions against the AT&T telecom monopoly. In both cases, policy action has attempted to facilitate innovation on the network by separating control of the network from control of the devices and services that operate on it. Whether this will work for energy the way it did for ICT remains to be seen.

17. Note that this will persist even after the move to auctioned permits. Auctioning will only control initial allocation within member states, not between them. Burden-

sharing will still govern member state quotas under the ETS, and the member states retain the rights to use auction revenues however they see fit.

18. Speech of Commissioner Oettinger at ENERI 2010, Belgian Presidency Conference on Infrastructure of Energy research. Brussels, November 29, 2010.

19. As of mid-2012, the uncertain state of European monetary policy poses a third risk. The potential dissolution of the Eurozone consequence of the fallout of the 2008–2009 financial crisis poses an unknown risk to other European commitments. At a minimum, it makes the growth- and security-oriented pillars of the EU climate and energy policy trifecta even more critical. In the limit, however, it could poison European cooperation for a generation. This is akin to what happened in the aftermath of other European policy crises, including the Empty Chair crisis of the 1960s and Margaret Thatcher's rebate and budget moves in the early 1980s. Either of these developments could set back further progress on emissions; whether they would destabilize the prior deal remains unclear.

20. This problem is unique to alternating current transmission. The interface between the cable and the surrounding earth functions as a capacitor. Polarity-switching alternating current thus dumps most of its energy into charging and discharging that capacitor to the point where line losses become very large. Solutions include use of direct current transmission (over very long distances) or shortening of the effective undergound cable length through periodic above-ground stations.

21. See, for instance, the 2008–2009 agreements among the Danish political parties and with the Danish network operator, Energinet.dk, on future construction of interconnectors in western Denmark. The agreement approved the construction of what will be Denmark's last new above-ground transmission line. It also set a framework for moving most of the high-voltage transmission infrastructure underground, albeit at significantly higher cost. See Energinet.dk (2009).

22. This essay was written to cover the politics of EU climate and energy policy up to and immediately after the passage of the Third Climate and Energy Package in 2009. Since then, Europe has endured a sustained recession and a prolonged financial crisis. The Eurozone may yet prove a casualty of these problems if the costs of staying in become too high for member states like Greece, Spain, or Portugal to bear. This would, of course, have profound implications for European climate policy. But those would be dwarfed by the implications for all of EU policy, which would be threatened by the ensuing economic chaos and uncertainty. It would also complicate any assessment of the causes of climate policy changes: was it the political illegitimacy that stained the EU after its inability to solve the fiscal crisis or the subsequent economic chaos that squelched people's appetites for expensive investment?

CHAPTER 8

1. The recently reinforced power of the EPA to regulate greenhouse gas emissions and other executive-level moves could be the beginning of a long-term shift, though it is not yet backed by any clear national consensus on the desirability of climate change policy. A report by Resources for the Future (Burtraw and Woerman 2012) suggests that the United States may be on track to meet President Obama's pledge of 17 percent

reductions in carbon emissions by 2020, due to a combination of subnational measures, consumer and economic trends, and federal regulation under the Clean Air Act. It is difficult to tell at this stage, however, how important the role of the federal government will become.

2. In fact, the story is somewhat more complex than this. Policy can also play out at the regional level, with multiple states banding together on action as in the Western Climate Initiative. For clarity, in this analysis we focus on policy at either the federal or individual state level.

3. An earlier version of this section was originally prepared by Nina Kelsey and Juliana Mandell for the Green Growth Leaders project (see Green Growth Leaders 2011a).

4. James Sweeney's 2002 book *The California Electricity Crisis* provides an excellent analysis of the deregulation story. We base our summary on this work.

5. Though note that our venture capital expert argues that the venture capital story is very much a global story. The local California market is useful but by itself is not enough. Cleantech investors are very much driven by critical global markets as well (Prabhakar 2011).

6. An earlier version of this section was originally prepared by Alice Madden for the Green Growth Leaders project (see Green Growth Leaders 2011b).

7. Colorado has 8 percent of American dry natural gas reserves and roughly one-third of U.S. coal bed methane reserves, as well as oil shale reserves equivalent to the world's proven oil reserves, though it is currently uneconomic to exploit them (Burnell, Carroll, and Young 2008).

CHAPTER 9

This research benefited from a Faculty Foundation Grant from the Ivan Allen College and The Georgia Tech Foundation and from insights gleaned from discussion at the "Take the Lead" Conference held in Copenhagen on October 12–13, 2011. John Zysman, Mark Huberty, Nina Kelsey, and an anonymous reviewer for Stanford University Press offered insightful comments, while Kelsey Hinely provided outstanding research assistance.

1. Japan produces only 18 percent of the energy it consumes, and only 6 percent if nuclear is excluded. Much of the imported petroleum, which accounts for 42 percent of total consumption, originates in politically unstable regions and must pass through precarious chokepoints. In addition, an "Asian premium" adds as much as $6.00 onto the cost of each barrel of Middle Eastern oil, which accounts for 87 percent of Japan's petroleum consumption (ANRE 2010, 31; Stanton 2010). Although Japan's potential geothermal resources are estimated to be the third largest in the world, this energy source accounted for only 0.2 percent of electricity generated in 2010 (*Yomiuri Shinbun*, March 13, 2012).

2. Japan ranked first or second in the world in a country-by-country share of patents registered from 2004 to 2006 in the areas of renewable energy as well as atmospheric, water quality, and waste management (MOE 2010, 134).

3. Ashley Seager, an economics correspondent for the *Guardian*, described the halfhearted commitment of Japan as "surprisingly unambitious" when it comes to the development and use of renewable energy technologies (Kitazuma 2008).

4. "Go-jū-nenkan de 68-nin ga denryoku gaisha ni amakudari—Keisanshō chōsa" (68 METI Officials "Descend from Heaven" to Electrical Utilities Companies in Past 50 Years), *Sankei Shinbun*, May 2, 2011.

5. Japan's national parliament—known as the Diet (*kokkai*—literally, "national assembly")—is composed of a House of Representatives and a House of Councilors. Members of both houses are elected by popular vote. The English-language rendering of the term *Diet* comes from the nineteenth-century Prussian legislative body after which the pre–World War II Diet was modeled.

6. Japan's nuclear power industry was established with the passage of the Atomic Energy Basic Law on December 19, 1955. The Atomic Energy Commission was founded the following year (Murota and Yano 1993, 133). Japan was pushed by the United States, as part of its containment policy, to establish a nuclear power industry. Key actors on the Japanese side included Yasuhiro Nakasone, a future prime minister, and fellow LDP lawmaker Matsutaro Shoriki, who was known by the code name "Podam" in CIA documents (*Mainichi Shinbun*, August 2, 2011).

7. An exchange rate of $1.00 to ¥80.00 is used throughout this chapter.

8. In 1965, for example, scientific evidence linked Yokkaichi asthma to sulfur oxide emitted from the burning of petroleum and crude oil at petrochemical processing facilities and refineries in Yokkaichi City near Nagoya (Murota and Yano 1993, 133).

9. It is worth noting that in 1967, the Japanese government began publishing Long-Term Energy Supply and Demand Outlook (*Chōki enerugii jūkyū mitoshi*) reports.

10. The first, albeit futile, major populist campaign against industrial pollution took place at the end of the 1800s and early 1900s and was directed against the Ashio copper mining company that had, for decades, polluted waterways in Tochigi Prefecture (Mason 1999, 188). In addition, the Ministry of Health and Welfare had attempted to preempt public protest by proposing an environmental protection law in 1950, but industrial interests and their patrons at MITI and in the LDP blocked the bill (Reich 1984, 383).

11. For example, the Clean Government Party won 25 seats in the 1967 lower house election campaigning on an environmental protection platform.

12. The late Sir Roy Denman, director-general for external affairs at the European Economic Community from 1977 to 1982, famously referred to Japan as "a country of workaholics who live in what Westerners regard as little more than rabbit hutches" (*The Times of London*, April 16, 2006).

13. Despite its modest R&D budget, the Sunshine Project can claim some share of the credit for the more than 90 percent reduction realized in the per-watt cost of manufacturing a solar cell, which, between 1974 and 1992, dropped from ¥20,000 to ¥600 (Usami 2004).

14. In 1988, NEDO changed its name to the New Energy and Industrial Technology Development Organization, but the acronym remained.

15. In 1971, Kawasaki began aggressive efforts to clean up the environment, implement pollution-control measures, and provide relief to victims by creating a Pollution Bureau as part of the city government. The following year, Kawasaki became the first city to pass a pollution-prevention ordinance, and in 1976, the "Kawasaki City Ordinance on Environmental Assessment" was approved.

16. Interview with policy experts, Tokyo, June 2010.

17. Interview with policy experts, Tokyo, June 2010.

18. This commitment was reiterated in the "Hatoyama Initiative" announced at the COP15 in Copenhagen in December 2009 (MOE 2010, 154).

19. In 2000, these carbon-intensive energy sources provided 81 percent of the primary energy supply, which was slightly down from the corresponding figure of 83 percent in 1990 (ANRE 2010).

20. The government also issued a New National Energy Strategy in 2006, which, in contrast to the BEPs, focused almost exclusively on concerns about Japan's energy security raised by increasing oil prices, resource nationalism among energy suppliers, and regional conflict over energy resources (Evans 2006).

21. Interview with policy experts, Tokyo, June 2010.

22. The number of households with solar photovoltaic panels installed was 73,000 in 2005. By 2010, it is estimated that the number had increased to 137,000 households (Yomiuri Online, June 28, 2011).

23. For example, the Ministry of Agriculture, Fisheries, and Forestry proposed to study the possibility of using the massive amount of wooden debris generated by the March 11 disaster as fuel for biomass power generation (*Yomiuri Shinbun*, July 26, 2011).

24. Kushida (2012) gives an excellent assessment of the Fukushima crisis.

25. The others were a bill to issue deficit-covering bonds and a supplementary budget bill for FY2011 to fund earthquake reconstruction.

26. The Factory Location Law requires parties wishing to build a large-scale solar power plant to submit the plan to relevant local governments if the land on which it is built exceeds 9,000 square meters or if a facility is more than 3,000 square meters in size. The law also limits the size of a power plant to 50 percent of its land acreage (*Yomiuri Shinbun*, February 4, 2012).

27. The estimated unit prices of electrical power generation are as follows: nuclear (5.5), coal (5.75), LNG (6.45), hydro (10.75), wind (11.5), oil (13.65), photovoltaic (24.5) (author's calculations based upon data in ANRE 2010, 25). Critics point out that subsidies paid to towns that host nuclear power plants are not included in calculations of the true cost of nuclear power.

28. The term *efficiency superpower* is from Stewart and Wilczewski (2009). Support for this view is found in a report published in 2008 showing Japan used 4,500 British thermal units (BTU) per U.S. dollar of gross domestic product. In contrast, Denmark, the second most energy efficient country, used 4,845 BTUs per dollar of GDP, while the corresponding figure for the United States was 9,000 BTUs per dollar of GDP. The world's ten most energy efficient countries used 7,500 BTUs or less, while China used 35,000 BTUs per dollar of GDP (Zumbrun 2008).

29. In addition, the Ministry of the Environment predicts continued growth in Japan's environmental industry (which includes renewable energy), which, in 2008, had an estimated market size of ¥7.5 trillion and employed 1.76 million people (MOE 2010, 133).

CHAPTER 10

1. In this respect, the Korean vision reaches intentionally for a transformation that is conceptually similar to that which has occurred de facto in the Danish economy. See

our Danish Country Case Analysis report (Green Growth Leaders 2011c) for further discussion. However, Korea's specific goals, specific tools chosen, and particular obstacles differ because Korea begins from the basis of a different political configuration and resource base than Denmark. One example is the way in which Denmark's copious wind resources and particular political configuration combine to create a critical mass of popular and business support for commitment to wind energy. Korea, with a different set of resources and a different political-economic configuration, has envisioned its transformation differently and is aimed in different directions. Both represent potentially viable experiments in green growth.

2. Private communication with Korean government official, 2011.

3. Private communication with Korean government official, 2011.

CHAPTER 11

1. Energy intensity is energy consumption per unit of GDP.

2. In his investigation of the Chinese political system, Guo (2003) suggests that this form of "utilitarian legitimacy" is a powerful legacy from China's imperial era. Perry (2011) argues that this concept of utilitarian legitimacy justifies antigovernment sentiments stemming from food, housing, and other material necessities, which may in part explain why the CCP is more tolerant of protests over land and energy prices than those over religious and political freedoms. Utilitarian legitimacy also explains why the CCP places so much emphasis on sustaining high levels of economic growth, enhancing energy security, creating jobs, and controlling inflation.

3. Export industries and investment were largely responsible for the trend-breaking increase in energy intensity during the few years after China first entered the WTO. According to Kharl and Roland-Holst's research, export and investment accounted for more than 70 percent of the growth of energy consumption between 2002 and 2004 (2009, 903).

4. These statistics only account for commercial fuel consumption; rural residents in China still rely heavily on biomass and waste fuels, which account for roughly 10 percent of total energy consumption according to the IEA (2010b).

5. It is difficult to measure the total industrial output of the state-owned sector because official statistics only consider the output of wholly owned SOEs and do not treat entities in which state ownership share is less than 100 percent but greater than 50 percent as being state-owned. Many hybrid forms of ownership structures have emerged in which the state is a shareholder, including shareholding cooperative enterprises, joint-operation enterprises, limited liability corporations, or shareholding corporations whose majority share are owned by the government, public organizations, or the SOEs themselves.

6. According to the latest forecasts by the China Energy Group at Lawrence Berkeley National Laboratory, China's emissions are likely to peak between 2030 and 2035. However, this result is based on the crucial assumption that China's average GDP growth rate between 2010 and 2020 will be 7.7 percent, considerably lower than the previous ten years and in line with China's stated target, and even slower growth rates of 5.9 percent between 2020 and 2030 and 3.4 percent between 2030 and 2050 (Zhou et al. 2011, 3). This again demonstrates that compatibility between emissions reduction and

270 economic growth requires not only aggressive policies but also a much slower growth rate than what China is accustomed to.

7. For example, the province of Inner Mongolia, where the majority of China's wind resources is located, has an independent regional power grid and is not connected to the rest of China. Consumers in Inner Mongolia alone do not provide sufficient demand to digest all the wind energy, and distant demand from other parts of China cannot be satisfied with this supply due to the lack of transmission infrastructure. Thus, despite the fact that wind energy from Inner Mongolia is already cheaper than thermal electricity produced in eastern and southern China, this cheap, clean energy cannot reach consumers, and generation capacity is often forced to remain idle (Xin 2010).

8. China's highway systems are also overburdened by the transportation of coal, as well-known episodes of monster traffic congestions can attest. The 60-mile-long monster traffic jam on the Beijing-Tibet highway in the summer of 2010 was due mostly to trucks carrying coal from Inner Mongolia to the capital, and truckers report they are used to such congestion (Ni and Chua 2010; Watts 2010).

9. Recent explorations show that China has 1,275 trillion cubic feet of shale gas reserve, 12 times the size of its natural gas reserve (EIA 2011, 4). As of 2009, only 3.9 percent of China's primary energy consumption comes from natural gas (NBS 2011). If exploitation of shale gas can prove to be economical, then the share of gas in China's energy portfolio may increase given the abundance of the resource. While natural gas is still a fossil fuel and produces greenhouse gases, its carbon content is 45 percent less than that of coal (EIA 2010b, 7), and increased use of natural gas will help China lower its carbon intensity.

10. For example, in the major coal-producing province of Shanxi, restructuring has slashed the number of operating mines from 2,600 to 1,053; all mines with an annual production of less than 300,000 tons were closed, and 70 percent of the remaining mines produced more than 900,000 tons every year (Ding 2010).

CHAPTER 12

1. In 2005, Brazil's GDP per capita was US$3,326. That year, services accounted for 56.09 percent, industry for 34.86 percent, and agriculture for 9.05 percent of total GDP (Baer 2008, 405). However, counting production, transport, and commerce, agribusiness is estimated to have produced 31 percent of Brazil's GDP in 2003 and 26 percent of Brazil's total employment in 2002 (303).

2. The international cattle trade earned Brazil US$6.9 billion in 2008, with leather accounting for a quarter of the value (Greenpeace 2009, 3). In the 2000s, Brazil became the world's largest exporter of beef. Beef exports grew over 450 percent in volume and 385 percent in value from 1994 to 2005 (McAllister 2008b, 10,875). In 2008, Brazil accounted for 31 percent of the global trade in beef and 36 percent of the global trade in soybeans, and its share in each is expected to increase to 61 percent and 40 percent, respectively, by 2018 (Greenpeace 2009, 2).

3. In Brazil, given the profusion of political parties, the important policy coalitions in Congress are *bancadas*, or blocs of legislators from different parties and states, dedicated to a specific set of issues. The largest *bancadas* are the Business and Ruralist,

which have some overlapping members and share views on environmental legislation. Brazil's Congress is bicameral, with a Chamber of Deputies (lower house) composed of 513 deputies, and a Senate (upper house) composed of 81 senators.

4. Petrobras operates as a private company, but the Brazilian government holds 49 percent of the company's shares. Four of Petrobras's six biofuel distilleries are in operation, and two are experimental (Petrobras 2009).

5. The program Prorenova was announced in response to the United States' decision to allow import tariffs on Brazilian ethanol to expire on December 31, 2011.

6. McKinsey & Company estimates Brazilian *per capita* GHG emissions at 12 tons of CO_2 equivalent (tCO_2e), comparable to industrialized countries. However, "if we exclude the forestry sector, Brazilian *per capita* emissions drop to 5 tCO_2e, which would bring this country down to the level of low/moderate emitters" (2009, 5; italics in original).

In contrast to deforestation and agriculture, energy-related methane emissions are in the hundreds of gigagrams (Gg; 541 in 2005), and industrial methane emissions are in the single digits (9.2 Gg in 2005). Only waste treatment releases significant levels of methane after deforestation and agriculture: 1,743 Gg in 2005 (MCT 2010, 12). Waste treatment is not discussed in this chapter because it releases negligible quantities of all other greenhouse gases.

7. Methane gas is largely emitted from enteric fermentation and organic wastes from Brazil's roughly 200 million heads of cattle, while fire used to clear land prior to planting and nitrogen fertilizers used on crops produce nitrous oxide (McKinsey & Company 2009, 7).

8. Greenpeace is not an objective research institute, but the federal Ministry of Mines and Energy (MME) partially concurs: the MME's Energy Research Company (EPE) estimates that energy-related GHG emissions will rise from 329 $MtCO_2e$ in 2005 to 628 $MtCO_2e$ in 2020 (MME/EPE 2011, 69). While Brazil may export much of its oil in the coming years, analysts must pay attention to the integration of the presalt oil into Brazil's domestic energy matrix and to the consequences for the country's total GHG emissions.

9. In the 1970s, the air in Cubatão was so polluted that many babies born at that time had no brains (Hochstetler and Keck 2007, 192). Activists in slums that neighbored chemical factories formed an association to publicize the local pollution problem, cultivated allies among elites, and pressured the state and federal governments to act (193–194).

10. Article 225 of the 1988 Constitution decrees that "all have the right to an environment that is ecologically in equilibrium and that is available for shared use by the people, essential to a healthy quality of life, which imposes on both the government and society as a whole the duty of protecting it and preserving it for both the present and future generations" (stated in Patriota 2009, 613).

11. The law passed in part because Brazil wanted to present progress on conservation unit legislation to the World Parks Congress that year. (Author interview with Adriana Ramos of Instituto Socioambiental (ISA) on October 13, 2011.)

12. Author interview with Adriana Ramos of ISA on October 13, 2011.

13. On Stang's life and impact, see Le Breton (2008).

14. National initiatives were accompanied by state initiatives. Acre and Amazonas, Amazonian states with significant forest-dwelling populations, have adopted policies to create markets for sustainably produced forest products (Viana 2010, 37–42), and the Amazonas state payments-for-avoided-deforestation program—*Bolsa Floresta* (Forest Basket)—has recently been adopted as a national program—*Bolsa Verde* (Green Basket)—to give small farm owners incentives to keep trees standing in the Amazon (França 2011). A June 2009 meeting of the Forum of Amazonian Governors in Palmas, Tocantins culminated in a jointly signed letter sent to President Lula, "stating support for zero deforestation in the region and calling on the Brazilian government to support the creation of market-based REDD+ mechanisms" (May, Millikan, and Gebara 2011, 39).

15. These policy initiatives constitute the beginning steps of instituting a Reduction of Emissions from Deforestation and Degradation—Plus (REDD+) mechanism in Brazil. Pilot initiatives were begun between 2007 and 2009 in the Amazonian states of Mato Grosso, Pará, Acre, Amazonas, Rondônia, and Amapá. Norway donated US$110 million to the Amazon Fund in 2008 and pledged US$1 billion over ten years (May, Millikan, and Gebara 2011, 38–39).

16. As of 2001, farmers in the Amazon biome must legally set aside 80 percent of their lands for conservation. (The legal reserve requirement prior to 2001 was 50 percent.) In the Cerrado, 35 percent must be set aside, and in the Atlantic Forest and elsewhere, 20 percent. Prior to the 2000s, legal reserve requirements in the Amazon (and elsewhere) were generally ignored by landowners.

17. Due to high political party fragmentation in Brazil, parties generally do not win absolute majorities in Congress but instead must ally with other parties. The "kingmakers" are the center-right PMDB, led by ex-president and longtime senate president José Sarney. The PMDB rarely runs presidential candidates but always captures enough seats in Congress to ensure that it is a key partner in the governing coalition.

18. The Green Party is the obvious choice, but it operates almost exclusively in Rio de Janeiro—though its profile temporarily rose in 2010 when Marina Silva campaigned for president on the PV ticket.

19. These changes are limited to activities taking place within the jurisdictions of the states or municipalities that issue the licenses. When activities requiring environmental licenses cross state borders, IBAMA retains its licensing and enforcement powers.

20. State environmental agencies are often weak, politicized, and corrupt, especially in the Amazon (McAllister 2008a; Luíse 2011). In 2005, a joint sting operation carried out by the federal MP, the Federal Police, and IBAMA—known as *Operação Curupira*—ended with the arrest of over 80 people in the state of Mato Grosso for fraud and corruption in environmental licensing—including the local executive manager of IBAMA and the president of the Mato Grosso State Environmental Foundation (Brito 2009). In 2008, the former secretary of the environment for the Amazonian state of Pará and 33 other people were arrested for trafficking in illegal wood ("Ex-secretário" 2008).

21. The Belém-Brasília highway was completed in 1968, and other highways followed soon after that. In consequence, while it took about 100 hours to transport goods from Belém to São Paulo by road, by 1995 it took only half that time (Walker et al. 2009, 735).

22. The federal Northern Constitutional Fund (FNO) provides loans at subsidized interest rates, from about 1 to 4 percent. In 2006, market rates varied from 20 to
30 percent for corporations and 50 to 60 percent for individuals (Barreto et al. 2008, 22).

23. Falsification of land titles is widespread in Brazil, especially in the Amazon.

24. Forty-five percent of the 14,500 loan contracts signed in that period went to
small-scale ranchers, and 55 percent went to medium- and large-scale ranchers (Barreto et al. 2008, 22).

25. Nevertheless, some progress has been achieved in enhancing productivity
in the Amazon. Average pasture occupation by cattle in the region increased about
36 percent from 1995 to 2006 — from 0.7 to 0.96 head of cattle per hectare — partially
due, however, to the opening of newly deforested lands, which are fertilized naturally
by the burning of the forest and so can support larger herds (Barreto et al. 2008, 24).
Investments in cattle confinement and insemination technologies also increased from
the late 1990s to 2006, but fell by 2008 — due to low profitability. Indeed, a 2008 survey of four Amazonian municipalities found that technological investments resulted
in financial *losses* for ranchers, while investments in extensive herd growth produced
profits (25).

26. Illegal logging associated with expanding cattle ranches has long been a problem in the Amazon, and researchers estimated that in 2003, about 56 percent of all
Brazilian timber was produced illegally (Banerjee and Alavalapati 2009, 245).

27. Relevant NGOs include IMAZON, Imaflora, Instituto Socioambiental, The
Nature Conservancy, and the World Wildlife Fund–Brasil.

28. The possibility of creating jobs, economic growth, and tax revenues through
sustainable forestry has caught states' attention and sparked action. In 2003, the state
of Amazonas created the Maués and Rio Urubu state forests, totaling over 460,000
hectares (Agência de Florestas e Negócios Sustentáveis do Amazonas 2005). Amazonas
also has over 19 million hectares of national forests (Viana 2008, 34), and in December
2006, Governor Simão Jatene of Pará decreed the creation of four state forests, totaling
over 7.8 million hectares, in areas suffering from land conflicts between traditional
populations and encroaching ranchers (SEMA 2010). The creation of these state forests
in Pará has begun to reduce the incidence of rural violence and has slowed the expansion of cattle ranching into the protected areas (Author's interview with IMAZON
researcher, November 2011).

29. Forestry concessions may last from 20 to 40 years, and concessionaires are limited in the size and number of concessions they may hold at any one time, thus providing concessionaires with the long-term stability needed for responsible investment and
encouraging them not to waste resources. Meanwhile, some concessionaires submit
to Forest Stewardship Council labeling to improve their access to foreign markets that
require sustainability certification, and access to financing from green funds (Viana
2008, 75; Espach 2009).

30. Author's interview with ICMBio official, December 2011.

31. These concessions are in Jamari National Forest (Pará) in 2008 and in Saracá-
Taquera National Forest (Rondônia) in 2010.

32. As of 2011, the SFB was developing monitoring plans with ICMBio, IBAMA, and
INPE, but these plans have not yet been published.

274   33. Although sugarcane has been subject to a legally binding socioenvironmental zoning initiative—ZAE-Cana, or Sugarcane Agroecological Zoning (Manzatto et al. 2009)—to protect forests, reductions in legal reserves and permanent protection areas in the new Forest Code legislation may offset environmental gains from the initiative, as deforestation will be permitted on parcels of private lands where it is currently prohibited (IPEA 2011).

34. Today, most of Brazil's petroleum is produced domestically, though some light petroleum is imported from elsewhere to mix with Brazil's heavy crude in the refining process (Sennes and Narciso 2009, 33–34).

35. In the United States, the Renewable Fuel Standard (RFS1) was created by the Energy Policy Act of 2005 and expanded in the Energy Independence and Security Act (EISA) of 2007 (RFS2). Under EISA, the volume of renewable fuels required to be blended into transport fuels in the United States must rise from 9 billion gallons in 2008 to 36 billion gallons by 2022 (EPA 2011). However, RFS2 stipulates that only 15 billion gallons of biofuel blended into gasoline can be from conventional corn ethanol, so the EISA has created demand in the United States for technological innovation—and for Brazilian sugarcane-based ethanol and other biofuels from abroad. Acknowledging the need to import ethanol, on December 31, 2011, the U.S. government allowed tariffs on Brazilian ethanol imports to expire (Leahy and Pearson 2012).

36. Estimates differ across sources. BNDES and CGEE (2008, 96) estimate that sugarcane-based ethanol may avoid up to 89 percent of emissions, while corn-based ethanol varies widely. Depending on the source of energy in the production process, avoided emissions range from −30 percent (a net increase in GHG emissions) to 38 percent.

37. Rosa et al. (2009, 16) calculate that there are 90 million hectares of land in Brazil still "available for the expansion of agriculture without deforestation." However, lack of enforcement of socioenvironmental protocols in ethanol-importing countries and regions (such as the EU) has enabled Brazilian ethanol companies with environmental and labor irregularities to continue to export freely (ONG Repórter Brasil 2011, 19).

38. UNICA, founded in 1997 after Brazil deregulated sugarcane ethanol, is based in São Paulo and represents large-scale sugarcane producers. Its members "answer for more than 50 percent of all ethanol produced in Brazil and 60 percent of overall sugar production" (UNICA 2008). The organization seeks to expand the world market for sugar and ethanol and engages in lobbying on behalf of the sugarcane industry.

39. IPEA (2010b, 431) predicts that most growth in sugarcane crop areas will concentrate in the southeastern states of Minas Gerais, São Paulo, and Rio de Janeiro, and a lesser share in the more arid northeast. If strict ecological zoning policies are not enforced, sugarcane expansion risks reducing the southeast area's remaining forest cover by up to 67 percent and the northeast area's by 21 percent. (Both regions contain what remains of the Atlantic Forest.)

40. On March 18, 2011, the Brazilian meatpacking company Minerva opened a bovine fat–based biodiesel plant in the Center-West state of Goiás (*Business News Americas* March 16, 2011). Together with four other large meatpacking companies—Bertim, Independência, JBS, and Marfrig—Minerva controlled over 50 percent of Brazil's beef export market in 2007 (Greenpeace 2009, 6).

41. Biodiesel has been integrated into diesel in Brazil gradually since 2005 per Law No. 11,097/2005: 2 percent in 2005–2007, 3 percent in 2008–2012, and 5 percent starting in 2013.

42. Law No. 11,097/2005 introduced biodiesel into the Brazilian energy matrix, though BNDES Resolution No. 1,135/2004 established its Financial Assistance and Investment in Biodiesel Program (IPEA 2010a, 23). From 2005 to 2009, through its Programa Biodiesel, BNDES provided R$9.156 billion to 47 programs or actions related to biodiesel, including energy generation (R$520 million), bioelectricity (R$580 million), marketing (R$627 million), agriculture and industry (R$2.406 million), and credit for industry, commerce, and services (R$3.295 million) (32–33).

43. The baseline year is 2008. Walker's estimate does not include offsetting effects of land use intensification. When Walker introduces demand for land for sugarcane into the estimate, the total deforestation rises by 60,000 km^2 to 121,332 km^2 by 2020.

44. Provisional decrees, or *medidas provisórias*, are temporary decrees issued by Brazilian presidents that can be enacted immediately but after a time must be passed as law by Congress to remain in effect.

45. IMAZON's estimate refers only to the forests cleared in the area of the dam. It does not consider the area needed to accommodate workers and materials during construction, forests cleared to place transmission lines from the dam to electricity distribution plants, or the longer-term effects of roads, urbanization, and land grabbing by migrants to the region (Araújo et al. 2012, 8).

46. Because the Belo Monte dam is expected to create only 40,000 new jobs, the rest of the migrants will likely become loggers, farmers, and cattle ranchers (Amazon Watch 2011).

47. Researchers at IMAZON calculate that the construction of the Belo Monte dam will cause 800 km^2 of deforestation above the 2006–2009 (lower deforestation) rate over the next 20 years. If the baseline deforestation rate increases, however, to the 2000–2005 (high deforestation) rate, then IMAZON predicts that an extra 4,000 to 5,000 km^2 will be deforested (Barreto et al. 2011, 9–10).

48. As of 2009, the poverty rate in Brazil was 24.1 percent, and the GINI index of inequality was 0.55 (World Bank 2012).

CHAPTER 13

1. During this period, the peak power deficit did decline from 18 percent in 1990–1991 to 11.9 percent in 2008–2009. However, this implies that the shortage has spread over more hours in the day (Sathaye and Gupta 2010).

2. A barrier is any obstacle to reaching a potential that can be overcome by a policy, program, or measure.

3. See Sathaye, Bouille, et al. (2001) for an overview.

CHAPTER 14

1. This section draws on concepts and arguments introduced and elaborated in Nina Kelsey's forthcoming dissertation on international negotiation and domestic climate policy.

References

Acemoglu, Daron, Philippe Aghion, Leonardo Bursztyn, and David Hemous. 2009. "The Environment and Directed Technical Change." NBER Working Papers Series 15451, National Bureau of Economic Research, Cambridge, MA.

Acs, Zoltan J., and David B. Audretsch. 1988. "Innovation in Large and Small Firms: An Empirical Analysis." *American Economic Review* 78 (4): 678–690.

Agência de Florestas e Negócios Sustentáveis do Amazonas. 2005. "Grupos de Trabalho: Gestão de Florestas Estaduais." Accessed April 21, 2013. http://www.florestas.am.gov.br/programas_02.php?cod=1269.

Amazon Watch. 2011. "Stop the Belo Monte Monster Dam." Accessed April 5, 2011. http://amazonwatch.org/work/belo-monte-dam.

American Energy Innovation Council. 2010. *A Business Plan for America's Energy Future.* Washington, DC: American Energy Innovation Council.

Andersen, Jørgen G. 2002. "Valgkampen 2001: Vaelgernes politiske dagsorden." Working Paper, Det danske valgprojekt, Aalborg Universitet.

———. 2008. "Et Valg Med Paradokser: Opinionsklimaet Og Folketingsvalget 2007." *Tidsskriftet POLITIK* 11 (3): 10–26.

Andersen, Torsten, Marie D. Bertelsen, and Jørgen Rosted. 2006. *Miljøteknologiske styrkepositioner—En erhvervsanalyse af klyngedannelse.* Copenhagen: FORA. http://www.mst.dk/Publikationer/Publikationer/2006/06/87-7052-075-5.htm.

ANRE (Agency for Natural Resources and Energy). 2010. "Energy in Japan 2010." Tokyo: Ministry of Economy, Trade, and Industry.

Araújo, Elis, Heron Martins, Paulo Barreto, Mariana Vedoveto, Carlos Souza Jr., and Adalberto Veríssimo. 2012. "Reduçao de Áreas Protegidas para a Produção de Energia." Belém, Brazil: IMAZON.

Arbo-bähr, Henrik. 2010. *Samfundsstatistik 2010.* Copenhagen: Forlaget Columbus.

Arora, D. S., Sarah Busche, Shannon Cowlin, Tobias Engelmeier, Hanna Jaritz, Anelia Milbrandt, and Shannon Wang. 2010. "Indian Renewable Energy Status Report." Background Report for DIREC; NREL.

278   Arrow, Kenneth, et al. 1995. "Economic Growth, Carrying Capacity, and the Environment." *Ecological Economics* 15 (2): 91–95.

Asako Takashi. 2011. "Fears of Power Shortfalls Undimmed." Daily Yomiuri Online, September 1. Accessed September 1, 2011. www.yomiuri.co.jp/dy/business/T110831005530.htm.

ASES (American Solar Energy Society). 2008. *Defining, Estimating and Forecasting the Renewable Energy and Energy Efficiency Industries in the U.S. and in Colorado.* Boulder, CO: American Solar Energy Society, and Washington, DC: Management Information Services.

Assunção, Juliano, Clarissa C. Gandour, and Rudi Rocha. 2012. "Deforestation Slowdown in the Legal Amazon: Prices or Policies?" Working Paper, Climate Policy Initiative, Rio de Janeiro.

Azuma, Takeo, and Yoshifumi Sugita. 2011. "Kan Seeking to Leave Mark—Prime Minister Focusing on Promotion of Sustainable Energy." Daily Yomiuri Online, June 24. Accessed September 2, 2011. www.yomiuri.co.jp/dy/national/T110623005178.htm.

BACEI (Bay Area Council Economic Institute). 2010. "Global Competitiveness, China and California's Emerging Clean Energy Economy." White Paper. http://www.bayeconfor.org/media/files/pdf/CaliforniaChinaCleantech.pdf.

Badenhausen, Kurt. 2010. "The Best States for Business and Careers." *Forbes*, October 13. http://www.forbes.com/2010/10/13/best-states-for-business-business-beltway-best-states_2.html.

Baer, Werner. 2008. *The Brazilian Economy: Growth and Development.* Boulder, CO: Lynne Rienner.

Baker, Matt. 2011. Interview with Nina Kelsey. Telephone with notes, May 10.

Banco Mundial (World Bank). 2010. "Estudo de Baixo Carbono para o Brasil—Relatório de Síntese Técnica—Uso da Terra, Mudanças do Uso da Terra e Florestas." Washington, DC: World Bank.

Banerjee, Onil, and Janaki Alavalapati. 2009. "A Computable General Equilibrium Analysis of Forest Concessions in Brazil." *Forest Policy and Economics* 11: 244–252.

Barbier, Edward B. 2011. "Linking Green Stimulus, Energy Efficiency and Technological Innovation: The Need for Complementary Policies." Working Paper, Transatlantic Energy Efficiency Workshop, University of California, Berkeley. http://igov.berkeley.edu/trans/content/linking-green-stimulus-energy-efficiency-and-techno logical-innovation-need-complementary-pol.

Barkenbus, Jack, R. Jamey Menard, Burton C. English, and Kim L. Jensen. 2006. "Resource and Employment Impact of a Renewable Portfolio Standard in the Tennessee Valley Authority Region." ISSE Report 2006-01, Institute for a Secure and Sustainable Environment, University of Tennessee, Knoxville. http://web.utk.edu/~isse2006/pdf/issepubs/2006_01_renewstand.pdf.

Barreto, Paulo, Amintas Brandão Jr., Heron Martins, Daniel Silva, Carlos Souza Jr., Márcio Sales, and Tarcísio Freitosa. 2011. "Risco de Desmatamento Associado à Hidrelétrica de Belo Monte." Belém, Brazil: Instituto do Homem e Meio Ambiente da Amazônia (IMAZON).

Barreto, Paulo, Andréia Pinto, Brenda Brito, and Sanae Hayashi. 2008. "Quem é dono   279
da Amazônia? Uma análise do recadastramento de imóveis rurais." Belém, Brazil:
Instituto do Homem e Meio Ambiente da Amazônia (IMAZON).

Baumol, William J. 1972. "On Taxation and the Control of Externalities." *American
Economic Review* 62 (3): 307–322.

Bernstein, Mark, Robert Lempert, David Loughran, and David Ortiz. 2000. "The Public Benefit of California's Investments in Energy Efficiency." Report no. MR-1212.0
-CEC, RAND Corporation, March.

Bezdek, Roger D. 2009. "Green Collar Jobs in the U.S. and Colorado, Economic
Drivers for the 21st Century." Report for the American Solar Energy Society,
Boulder, CO.

Biber, Eric. 2013. "Cultivating a Green Political Landscape: Lessons for Climate
Change Policy from the Defeat of California's Proposition 23." *Vanderbilt Law Review* 66 (2): 399–462.

Bille, Lars. 2002. "Denmark." *European Journal of Political Research* 41 (3): 941–946.

BNDES (Bancion Nacional de Desenvolvimento) and CGEE (Centro de Gestão de
Estudos Técnicos). 2008. "Sugarcane-Based Bioethanol: Energy for Sustainable
Development." Rio de Janeiro: FAO, ECLAC, CGEE, BNDES. http://www.sug
arcanebioethanol.org.

Borrus, Michael, James E. Millstein, and John Zysman. 1984. "Trade and Development
in the Semiconductor Industry: Japanese Challenge and American Response." In
*American Industry in International Competition: Government Policies and Corpo-
rate Strategies*, edited by John Zysman and Laura D'Andrea Tyson, 142–248. Ithaca,
NY: Cornell University Press.

Bøss, Jakob Askou. 2011. Interview by Jakob Riiskjaer Nygård.

Bradsher, Keith. 2010a. "China Is Leading the Race to Make Renewable Energy." *New
York Times*, January 30.

———. 2010b. "To Conquer Wind Power, China Writes the Rules." *New York Times*,
December 14. http://www.nytimes.com/2010/12/15/business/global/15chinawind
.html.

Bradsher, Keith, and Matthew Wald. 2012. "A Measured Rebuttal to China Over Solar
Panels." *New York Times*, March 20.

Bragança, Daniele. 2012. "MP que Altera Tamanhos de UC's na Amazônia vai á San-
ção." *O Eco*, May 30. Accessed November 13, 2012. http://www.oeco.com.br/salada
-verde/26060-mp-que-altera-tamanho-de-ucs-na-amazonia-va-a-sancao.

Brito, Brenda. 2009. "Multas Pós-Operação Curupira no Mato Grosso." *O Estado da
Amazônia*, July 12.

Broehl, Jesse. 2004. "Colorado Voters Pass Renewable Energy Standard; Amendment
Creates First Ever Voters-Approved Renewable Energy Standard." Renewable-
EnergyAccess.com, November 3.

Brown, Stephen P. A., Kristen Hayes, Alan J. Krupnick, and Jan Mares. 2010. *Perspectives on Energy Policy and Economic Research*. Washington, DC: Resources for the
Future.

Buffa, Andrea. 2009. "Economic Development: The Missing Link in a National Clean
Energy Policy." *Apollo Alliance: Clean Energy and Good Jobs*. October 15. http://

280   apolloalliance.org/new-apollo-program/economic-development-the-missing-link
-in-a-national-clean-energy-policy091/.

Burnell, James R., Christopher Carroll, and Genevieve Young. 2008. "Colorado Mineral and Energy Industry Activities, 2007." Information Series 77, Colorado Geo-
logical Survey and Colorado Department of Natural Resources, Denver, CO.

Burtraw, Dallas, and Matt Woerman. 2012. U.S. Status on Climate Change Mitigation.
Washington, DC: Resources for the Future.

Bussolo, M., and D. O'Connor. 2001. "Clearing the Air in India: The Economics of
Climate Policy with Ancillary Benefits." Working Paper 182, OECD, Paris.

Cailliau, Marcel, José Arceluz Ogando, Richard Combescure, Theo De Waal, Vit-
torio D'Ecclesiis, Hakon Egeland, Ricardo Ferreira, Håkan Feuk, Roby Gengler,
Stine Grenaa Jensen, Kimmo Kivikko, Götz Lincke, Cesar Martinez Villar, Sam
Ridsdale, Jan Sundell, Giuseppe Tribuzi, Fernando Urquiza Ambrinos, Pekka Vile,
Bernhard Walter, William Webster, Michael Zoglauer, Anne-Malorie Geron, and
Marco Foresti. 2011. RES Integration and Market Design: Are Capacity Remunera-
tion Mechanisms Needed to Ensure Generation Adequacy. Brussels: EurElectric.

CARB (California Air Resources Board for the State of California). 2008. "Climate
Change Scoping Plan (a framework for change pursuant to AB 32)." http://www.arb
.ca.gov/cc/scopingplan/document/adopted_scoping_plan.pdf.

CBO (U.S. Congressional Budget Office). 2009a. "The Economic Effects of Legislation to Reduce Greenhouse-Gas Emissions." Pub. No. 4001, September.

———. 2009b. "Estimated Impact of the American Recovery and Reinvestment Act on
Employment and Economic Output as of September 2009." Pub. No. 4037, November.

———. 2010. "Federal Climate Change Programs: Funding History and Policy Issues."
Pub. No. 4025.

Center for American Progress. 2008. "Cap and Trade 101: What Is Cap and Trade, and
How Can We Implement It Successfully?" Center for American Progress, January 16. http://www.americanprogress.org/issues/2008/01/capandtrade101.html.

Chaffin, Joshua. 2011. "Carbon Trading: Into Thin Air." Financial Times, February 14.
http://www.ft.com/cms/s/0/368f8482-387d-11e0-959c-00144feabdco.html#axzz1
Fg6PqXVZ.

Chambers, Nick. 2010. "Brazil's 10 Millionth Ethanol Flex-Fuel Vehicle Hits the Road."
Gas2. Accessed May 19, 2012. http://gas2.org/2010/03/08/brazils-10-millionth-etha
nol-flex-fuel-vehicle-hits-the-road/.

Chang, Jae-Soon. 2009. "South Korea President Pushes Green Growth." Associated Press.

Chapple, Karen, Cynthia Kroll, T. William Lester, and Sergio Montero. 2011. "Innovation in the Green Economy: An Extension of the Regional Innovation System
Model?" Economic Development Quarterly 25: 5–25.

Chen, Yong, and Francis X. Johnson. 2008. "Sweden: Greening the Power Market in
a Context of Liberalization and Nuclear Ambivalence." In Promoting Sustainable
Electricity in Europe: Challenging the Path Dependence of Dominant Energy Systems,
edited by W. M. Lafferty and A. Ruud, 219–249. Cheltenham, UK: Edward Elgar.

Cho, Chungun. 2010. "KHNP Foremost in Nuclear Plant Operation." Korea Herald,
March 29. Accessed April 5, 2010. http://www.koreaherald.com/specialreport/
Detail.jsp?newsMLId=20100325000817.

Choi, Hyun Kyung. 2009. "Comparison and Implications on Renewable Portfolio 281 Standard (RPS) and Feed-In Tariffs for Renewable Energy." Report, Korea Institute for Industrial Economies and Trade (KIET), 26–38.

Christiansen, Alte, and Jørgen Wettestad. 2003. The EU as a Frontrunner on Greenhouse Gas Emissions Trading: How Did It Happen and Will the EU Succeed? *Climate Policy* 3 (1): 3–18.

Chung, Hyung-suk. 2011. "Green Certification for the Growth of Green Industries." *JungiShinmoon*, April 14.

CIA. 2011a. "The World Factbook: Brazil." https://www.cia.gov/library/publications/the-world-factbook/geos/br.html.

——. 2011b. "The World Factbook: China." https://www.cia.gov/library/publications/the-world-factbook/geos/ch.html.

——. 2011c. "The World Factbook: India." https://www.cia.gov/library/publications/the-world-factbook/geos/in.html.

——. 2012. "The World Factbook: India." Accessed May 2012. https://www.cia.gov/library/publications/the-world-factbook/geos/in.html.

Cogan, John F., Tobias Cwik, John B. Taylor, and Volker Wieland. 2010. "New Keynesian versus Old Keynesian Government Spending Multipliers." *Journal of Economic Dynamics and Control* 34 (3): 281–295.

CONAB (Companhia Nacional de Abastecimento). 2011. "National Data on Soybean Production." Accessed May 13, 2011. http://www.conab.gov.br/.

Cooke, Philip. 2008. "Cleantech and an Analysis of the Platform Nature of Life Sciences: Further Reflections upon Platform Policies." *European Planning Studies* 16 (3): 375–393.

Cwik, Tobias, and Volker Wieland. 2009. "Keynesian Government Spending Multipliers and Spillovers in the Euro Area." Working Paper, Center for Economic and Policy Research, Washington, DC. http://www.cepr.org/pubs/dps/DP7389.asp.asp.

Daily, Matt. 2009. "First Solar to Build Huge Chinese Solar Plant." Reuters, September 8.

Daily, Matt, Christoph Steitz, and Leonora Walet. 2011. "Special Report: Is a Solar Trade War about to Flare?" Reuters, January 17. http://uk.reuters.com/assets/print?aid=UKTRE70G2C620110117.

Daly, Herman E. 1990. "Toward Some Operational Principles of Sustainable Development." *Ecological Economics* 2 (1): 1–6.

Danish Energy Association and Energinet.dk. 2010. *Smart Grid i Danmark*. Copenhagen. http://www.danskenergi.dk/~/media/Smart_Grid/Smart_Grid_Rapport.pdf.ashx.

Danish Government. 1996. "Energi 21." Ministry of Environment and Energy. http://www.offshorecenter.dk/log/bibliotek/energi21.pdf.

——. 2009. "The Danish Business Strategy on Climate Change: Global Challenges, Danish Solutions." Brochure, Ministry of Economic and Business Affairs, Copenhagen.

——. 2010. "Grøn Vækst—Udfordringer, Muligheder Og Dilemmaer i Den Grønne Omstilling." Statsministeriet. http://www.stm.dk/multimedia/Groen_vaekst_indledning_og_sammenfatning.pdf.

282 ——. 2011. "Danish Energy Strategy 2050." Denmark: Danish Climate and Energy Ministry.

Danish Government and the Danish People's Party. 2009. "Danish Agreement on Green Growth." June 16. http://www.mim.dk/NR/rdonlyres/54887891-D450 -4CD7-B823-CD5B12C6867A/o/DanishAgreementonGreenGrowth_300909.pdf.

Danish Ministry of Climate and Energy. 2011. "Energy Strategy 2050: From Coal, Oil, and Gas to Green Energy." Policy Paper, Danish Government data/000102S. Accessed August 21.

Danko, Pete. 2011. "Cleantech Sees Big Players Investing." *Earthtechling*, February 9. http://www.earthtechling.com/2011/02/cleantech-sees-big-players-investing/.

Dashboard. 2012. "Hybrid Cars." September. Accessed October 14, 2012. http://www .hybridcars.com/news/september-2012-dashboard-53157.html.

Davidow, William. 1986. *Marketing High Technology: An Insider's View*. New York: Free Press.

Davis, Charles, and Katherine Hoffer. 2010. "Energy Development in the U.S. Rockies: A Role for Counties?" *Journal of Federalism* 40 (2): 296–311.

DEA (Danish Energy Authority). 2009. *The Danish Example*. Copenhagen: Danish Energy Authority.

——. 2010a. "Danmark Olie- Og Gasproduktion— Og Udnyttelse Af Undergrunden." Danish Energy Authority. http://www.ens.dk/Documents/Netboghandel%20-%20 publikationer/2010/Danmarks_olie_og_gasproduktion_09.pdf.

——. 2010b. *Energistatistik 2009*. Copenhagen: Danish Energy Authority. http:// www.ens.dk/da-DK/Info/TalOgKort/Statistik_og_noegletal/Aarsstatistik/Docu ments/Energistatistik_2009.pdf.

——. 2011a. "Resultatkontrakt 2011–2014—Mellem Energistyrelsen Og Klima- Og Energiministeriets Departement." Danish Energy Authority. http://www.ens. dk/Documents/Netboghandel%20-%20publikationer/2010/Resultatkontrakt%20 _2011_2014.pdf.

——. 2011b. *Energistatistik 2010*. Copenhagen: Danish Energy Authority.

Dechezleprêtre, Andre, and Matthew Glachant. 2011. "Does Foreign Environmental Policy Influence Domestic Innovation?" Working Paper, CERNA and Mines ParisTech.

De Lovinfosse, Isabelle. 2008. *How and Why Do Policies Change? A Comparison of Renewable Electricity Policies in Belgium, Denmark, Germany, the Netherlands and UK*. Berlin: Peter Lang.

De Negri, Fernanda, and Gustavo Varela Alvarenga. 2011. "A Primarização da Pauta de Exportações no Brasil: Ainda um Dilema." IPEA Radar: Tecnologia, Produção, e Comércio Exterior 13.

DeWit, Andrew. 2012. "Japan's No-Nuclear Promise Could Prove Hollow." Chinadia-logue, September 19. Accessed October 15, 2012. http://www.chinadialogue.net/ article/show/single/en/5172-Japan-s-no-nuclear-policy-could-prove-hollow-promise-.

DeWit, Andrew, and Tetsunari Iida. 2011. "The 'Power Elite' and Environmental-Energy Policy in Japan." *Asia-Pacific Journal* 9 (January 24). Accessed August 21, 2011. http://www.japanfocus.org/-andrew-dewit/3479#.

DIAP (Departamento Intersindical de Assessoria Parlamentar). 2010. "Radiografia do Novo Congresso — Legislatura 2011/2015. Brasília: Série Estudos Político — Ano V." http://www.diap.org.br/index.php/noticias/agencia-diap/15507-lancamento-radio grafia-do-novo-congresso-legislatura-2011-2015.

DiMaggio, P. 1988. "Interest and Agency in Institutional Theory." In *Institutional Patterns and Organizations: Culture and Environment*, edited by L. Zucker, 3–21. Cambridge, MA: Ballinger.

Dimitropolous, John. 2008. "Energy Productivity Improvements and the Rebound Effects: An Overview of the State of Knowledge." *Energy Policy* 35 (12): 6354–6363.

Ding, Quanli. 2010. "Shanxi meitan ziyuan zhenghe jianbing chongzu qüde zhongda jieduanxing chengguo" [Merger and reorganization of coal resources in Shanxi See important results]. *Zhongguo Guotu Ziyuan Bao* [China Land and Resources Journal], January 6.

DoE (U.S. Department of Energy). 2011a. Database of State Incentives for Renewables and Efficiency. http://www.dsireusa.org/.

——. 2011b. Energy Loan Programs Office. https://lpo.energy.gov/.

Doerr, John. 2007. "John Doerr Sees Salvation and Profit in Greentech." Lecture presented at TED Talks, Monterey, CA, March 7–10. http://www.ted.com/talks/ john_doerr_sees_salvation_and_profit_in_greentech.html.

Dollery, Paul Anthony. 2010. "Renewable Energy Use in Japan: National Policy, Critical Response and Alternative Paradigms." Master's Thesis, School of Engineering and Energy, Murdoch University.

Dong, Lilin. 2009. "Guangfu fengkuang quandi duojinggui guosheng jinbao zhouxiang" [PV industry enclosure fervor; alarm of polycrystalline silicon overcapacity is sounded]. *Jingji Guancha Bao* [The Economic Observer], August 30.

DPJ (Democratic Party of Japan). 2009. "Change of Government: The Democratic Party of Japan's Platform for Government — Putting People's Lives First." Accessed August 23, 2011. www.dpj.or.jp/english/manifesto/manifesto2009.pdf.

Dreyfuss, Robert. 2010. "The Greening of China." *The Nation*, September 2. http:// www.thenation.com/article/154483/greening-china.

Duffield, John S., and Brian Woodall. 2011. "Japan's New Basic Energy Plan." *Energy Policy* 39 (April): 3741–3749.

Duggan, Jill. 2009. "The Truth about Cap-and-Trade in Europe." World Resources Institute, November 19. http://www.wri.org/stories/2009/11/truth-about-cap-and -trade-europe.

DWIA (Danish Wind Industry Association). 2009. *Danish Wind Industry Association Annual Statistics*. Copenhagen: DWIA.

ECCJ (Energy Conservation Center, Japan). 2010a. 2009–2010 brochure. Accessed August 27, 2011. www.asiaeec-col.eccj.or.jp/brochure/pdf/eccj_2009-2010.pdf.

——. 2010b. "Top Runner Program: Developing the World's Most Energy-Efficient Appliances." Accessed August 31, 2011. http://www.asiaeec-col.eccj.or.jp/top_run ner/index.html.

Economist, The. 2012a. "Special Report: A Third Industrial Revolution." April 21–27.

——. 2012b. "Carbon Capture and Storage: A Shiny New Pipe Dream." May 12–18.

284 ——. 2013. "Dams in the Amazon: The Rights and Wrongs of Belo Monte." May 4.

Economy, Elizabeth. 2007. "The Great Leap Backward?" *Foreign Affairs* 86 (5): 38–59.

——. 2010. *The River Runs Black: The Environmental Challenge to China's Future.* 2nd ed. Ithaca, NY: Cornell University Press.

EIA (U.S. Energy Information Administration). 2008. "International Energy Annual 2006." EIA database, U.S. Department of Energy, Washington, DC.

——. 2010a. "Colorado Electricity Profile 2008 Edition." U.S. Energy Information Administration, Department of Energy, Washington, DC. http://www.eia.doe.gov/cneaf/electricity/st_profiles/colorado.html.

——. 2010b. "U.S. Carbon Dioxide Emissions in 2009: A Retrospective Review." Review, EIA, U.S. Department of Energy, Washington, DC.

——. 2011. "World Shale Gas Resources: An Initial Assessment of 14 Regions Outside the United States." Independent Statistics and Analysis from EIA, U.S. Department of Energy, Washington, DC.

ElectroIQ. 2011. "From 'Solar' to 'Technologies': What Prompted GT Solar and OPEL Solar to Change Their Names." August 30. Accessed September 6, 2011. http://www.electroiq.com/blogs/electroiq_blog/2011/08/from-solar-to-technologies-what-prompted-gt-solar-and-opel-solar-to-change-their-names.html?source=esadlfhlnal0001&lidx=1.

Energinet.dk. 2009. "Cable Action Plan, 132-150kV Grids." March.

Energy and Environment Council. 2012a. "Enerugīkankyōnikansurusentakushi" [Options on energy and the environment]. Government of Japan, June 29.

——. 2012b. "Innovative Strategy for Energy and the Environment" [Kakushin tekienerugii-kankyōseisaku]. Government of Japan, September 14. Accessed October 15, 2012. http://www.npu.go.jp/policy/policy09/index.html.

Engel, Ditlev, and Daniel M. Kammen. 2009. "Green Jobs and the Clean Energy Economy." Thought Leadership Series 04, Copenhagen Climate Council, Copenhagen. http://www.climatechange.ca.gov/eaac/documents/member_materials/Engel_and_Kammen_Green_Jobs_and_the_Clean_Energy_Economy.pdf.

Enkvist, Per-Anders, Tomas Nauclér, and Jerker Rosander. 2007. "A Cost Curve for Greenhouse Gas Reduction." *McKinsey Quarterly* 1: 35–45.

Environmental Measures in Kawasaki City. "Initiatives and Achievements of Local Governments in Japan." (No. 23) Creating a City Where "Environment" and "Economy" Go Together: Environmental Measures in Kawasaki City. http://www.city.kawasaki.jp/index_e.htm.

EPA (U.S. Environmental Protection Agency). 2005. *Acid Rain Program 2004 Progress Report: 10 Years of Achievement.* Washington, DC: U.S. Department of the Interior.

——. 2011. "Renewable Fuel Standard (RFS)." Accessed February 23, 2012. http://www.epa.gov/otaq/fuels/renewablefuels/index.htm.

EPE (Empresa de Pesquisa Energética, Ministério de Minas e Energia). 2010. *Balanço Energético Nacional 2010.* Brasília: Ministério de Minas e Energia.

Espach, Ralph. 2009. *Private Environmental Regimes in Developing Countries: Globally Sown, Locally Grown.* New York: Palgrave Macmillan.

Espinoza, Annette. 2010. "5 Arrested in Boulder Anti-Coal Protest." *Denver Post*, April 27. http://www.denverpost.com/commented/ci_14969890?source=commented.

European Commission. 2001. "Completing the Internal Energy Market." Communication from the Commission to the Council and the European Parliament, COM (2001) 125, European Commission, Brussels.

———. 2007a. "An Energy Policy for Europe." Communication to the European Parliament and the European Council, SEC (2007) 12, European Commission, Brussels.

———. 2007b. "A European Strategy Energy Technology Plan (SET-Plan)." Communication from the Commission to the Council, the European Parliament, the European Economic and Social Committee and the Committee of the Regions, COM (2007) 723, European Commission, Brussels.

———. 2009a. "A Technology Roadmap for Investing in the Development of Low Carbon Technologies (SET-Plan)." Communication from the Commission to the European Parliament, the Council, the European Economic and Social Committee and the Committee of the Regions, SEC (2009) 1295, European Commission, Brussels.

———. 2009b. "Investing in the Development of Low Carbon Technologies (SET-Plan)." Communication from the Commission to the European Parliament, the Council, the European Economic and Social Committee and the Committee of the Regions, COM (2009) 514, European Commission, Brussels.

———. 2011. "A Resource Efficient Europe—Flagship Initiative under the Europe 2020 Strategy." COM (2011) 21, January 21.

European Court of Justice. 2001. "PreussenElektra AG v. Schleswag AG." Judgment of the Court, Case C-379/98, European Union, Luxembourg.

European Greens Party. 2009. "A Green New Deal for Europe: Manifesto for the European Election Campaign 2009." Press release, European Greens Party, Brussels.

Europe's Energy Portal. 2011. "Gas and Electricity Domestic: Electricity Rates for Households." Prices and Statistics. Last modified on March 10, 2011. http://www.energy.eu/#Domestic.

Evans, Peter C. 2006. "Japan." Brookings Foreign Policy Studies Energy Security Series, Brookings Institution, Washington, DC, December. Accessed August 21, 2011. http://www.brookings.edu/fp/research/energy/2006japan.pdf.

"Ex-secretário de meio ambiente do Pará e mais 32 pessoas são denunciados por corrupção." 2008. Procuradoria da República no Pará press release, December 19. Accessed May 18, 2009. http://www.prpa.mpf.gov.br/noticias/ex-secretario-de-meio-ambiente-do-para-e-mais-32-pessoas-sao-denunciads-por-corrupcao.html.

Fackler, Martin, and Norimitsu Onishi. 2011. "In Japan, a Culture That Promotes Nuclear Dependency." New York Times, May 31. Accessed May 31, 2011. www.nytimes.com/2011/05/31/world/asia/31japan.html?pagewanted=all.

Faulin, Javier, Fernando Lera, Jesús M. Pintor, and Justo García. 2006. "The Outlook for Renewable Energy in Navarre: An Economic Profile." Energy Policy 34 (15): 2201–2216.

FERC. 2011. "Federal Energy Regulatory Commission." Accessed March 17, 2011. http://www.ferc.gov/.

Finley, Bruce. 2009. "Protestors Want Colorado to Stop 'Clowning Around' on Clean Air." Denver Post, November 19. http://www.denverpost.com/ci_13819745.

286 First Solar. 2006. "Prospectus." November 20. http://www.sec.gov/Archives/edgar/data/1274494/000095012306014305/y22319bxe424b4.htm.

Fischer, Carolyn, and Richard G. Newell. 2008. "Environmental and Technology Policies for Climate Mitigation." *Journal of Environmental Economics and Management* 55 (2): 142–162.

Florida, Richard, and Martin Kenney. 1988. "Venture Capital and High Technology Entrepreneurship." *Journal of Business Venturing* 3 (4): 301–319.

FORA. 2009. *Kortlægning Af Miljøteknologiske Virksomheder i Danmark.* Copenhagen: FORA. http://www.ecoinnovation.dk/NR/rdonlyres/AD2FD57E-DD2D-4C73-9736-171325EA529C/o/miljoeteknologisk_rapport_online.pdf.

Fox-Penner, Peter. 2010. *Smart Power: Climate Change, the Smart Grid, and the Future of Electric Utilities.* Washington, DC: Island Press.

França, Martha San Juan. 2011. "Bolsa Verde vai ajudar a evitar desmatamento." *Brasil Econômico*, September 29. Accessed February 23, 2012. http://www.brasileconomico.com.br/noticias/bolsa-verde-vai-ajudar-a-evitar-desmatamento_107515.html.

Frates, Chris, and Erin Cox. 2004. "Voters Like Tobacco Tax Poll Says Per-Pack Hike, Renewable Energy Backed Many Remain Undecided Other Amendments to Split the State's Electoral and Remove Construction Liability Limits 'Look Pretty Weak.'" *Denver Post*, October 11.

Friedman, Lisa. 2009. "A Sea Change in China's Attitude toward Carbon Capture." *New York Times*, June 22.

Friedman, Thomas L. 2007. "The Green-Collar Solution." *New York Times*, October 17. http://www.nytimes.com/2007/10/17/opinion/17friedman.html.

Frondel, Manuel, Nolan Ritter, Christoph M. Schmidt, and Colin Vance. 2009. "Economic Impacts from the Promotion of Renewable Energy Technologies: The German Experience." Ruhr Economic Papers 156, Rheinisch-Westfälisches Institut für Wirtschaftsforschung, Essen, Germany.

Gan, Lin, Gunnar S. Eskeland, Hans H. Kolshus, Harald Birkeland, Sascha van Rooijen, and Mark van Wees. 2005. *Green Electricity Market Development—Lessons from Europe and the U.S. and Implications for Norway.* Centre for International Climate and Environment Research. http://www.cicero.uio.no/media/3601.pdf.

Garud, Raghu, and Peter Karnøe. 2003. "Bricolage versus Breakthrough: Distributed and Embedded Agency in Technology Entrepreneurship." *Research Policy* 32: 277–300.

General Electric. 2010. "China Selects GE Technology Again to Support Rapid Growth in Wind Energy Sector." Press release, January 12.

George, Timothy S. 2001. *Minamata: Pollution and the Struggle for Democracy in Postwar Japan.* Cambridge, MA: Harvard University Asia Center.

Giles, Judith A., and Cara L. Williams. 2001. "Export-Led Growth: A Survey of Empirical Literature and Some Non-Causality Results. Part 1." *Journal of International Trade and Economic Development* 9 (3): 261–337.

Glaeser, Edward L. 2011. "Why Green Energy Can't Power a Job Engine." *New York Times Economix Blog*, January 18. http://economix.blogs.nytimes.com/2011/01/18/why-green-energy-cant-power-a-job-engine/.

Glantz, Aaron. 2011. "After Solyndra, a 2nd Solar Energy Firm Is Scrutinized." *New York Times*, October 16.

Gompers, Paul A., and Josh Lerner. 2001. *The Money of Invention*. Cambridge, MA: **287**
Harvard Business School Press.
Gordon, Robert J. 2000. "Does the 'New Economy' Measure Up to the Great Inven-
tions of the Past?" *Journal of Economic Perspectives* 14: 49–74.
Goulder, Lawrence H. 1995. "Environmental Taxation and the Double Dividend:
A Reader's Guide." *International Tax and Public Finance* 2 (2): 157–183. DOI:
10.1007/BF00877495.
Green, Joshua. 2009. "The Elusive Green Economy." *The Atlantic*, July/August.
http://www.theatlantic.com/magazine/archive/2009/07/the-elusive-green-econ
omy/7554/.
Green Growth Leaders. 2011a. "California State Case Analysis." White paper prepared
for the Green Growth Leaders Project in collaboration with CRESTS, May 17.
http://greengrowthleaders.org/wp-content/uploads/2010/12/From-religion-to-real
ity_December-2011.pdf.
———. 2011b. "Colorado State Case Analysis." White paper prepared for the Green
Growth Leaders Project in collaboration with CRESTS, May 17. http://green
growthleaders.org/wp-content/uploads/2010/12/From-religion-to-reality_Decem
ber-2011.pdf.
———. 2011c. "Denmark Country Case Analysis." White paper prepared for the Green
Growth Leaders Project in collaboration with CRESTS, May 17. http://greengrowth
leaders.org/wp-content/uploads/2010/12/From-religion-to-reality_December-2011.pdf.
———. 2011d. "Shaping the Green Growth Economy." White paper prepared for the
Green Growth Leaders Project in collaboration with CRESTS, May 17. http://
greengrowthleaders.org/wp-content/uploads/2010/12/From-religion-to-reality
_December-2011.pdf.
Greenpeace. 2009. "Slaughtering the Amazon." Amsterdam: Greenpeace International. Accessed June 13, 2012. http://www.greenpeace.org/usa/en/media-center/
reports/slaughtering-the-amazon/.
———. 2012. "O Carbono do Petróleo Também é Nosso." Accessed May 20, 2012. http://
www.greenpeace.org/brasil/Global/brasil/report/2011/MAPA.pdf.
Grohnheit, Poul E. 2001. "Denmark: Long-Term Planning with Different Objectives."
In *Climate Change and Power: Economic Instruments for European Electricity*, ed-
ited by Christian Vrolijk, 108–128. London: Royal Institute of International Affairs.
Grübler, Arnulf, Nebojsa Nakicenovic, and David G. Victor. 1999. "Dynamics of Energy
Technologies and Global Change." *Energy Policy* 27 (5): 247–280. DOI:10.1016/
S0301-4215(98)00067-6.
Guo, Baogang. 2003. "Political Legitimacy and China's Transition." *Journal of Chinese
Political Science* 8 (1–2): 1–25.
Hadjilambrinos, Constantine. 2000. "Understanding Technology Choice in Electric-
ity Industries: A Comparative Study of France and Denmark." *Energy Policy* 28
(15): 1111–1126.
Han, Joonkyu, and Doogul Lee. 2012. "The Drifting Alternative Energy." *Seoul Daily*,
June 7. http://www.seoul.co.kr/news/newsView.php?id=20120607005006.
Hanemann, W. Michael. 2007. "How California Came to Pass AB32, the Global
Warming Solutions Act of 2006." Working Paper 1040, Department of Agricultural
and Resource Economics, University of California, Berkeley.

288   ———. 2009. "The Role of Emission Trading in Domestic Climate Policy." *Energy Journal* 30 Special Issue (2): 73–108.

Hansen, James. 2009. "Carbon Tax and 100% Dividend vs. Tax and Trade." Testimony of James E. Hansen to the Committee on Ways and Means, United States House of Representatives, United States Congress, February 25.

Hansen, Rikke Munk. 2003. "Legislative Measures for Promotion of Renewable Energy: Wind Energy Development in Denmark as a Case Study." In *Energy Law and Sustainable Development*, edited by Adrian J. Bradbrook and Richard L. Ottinger, 115–137. Cambridge: IUCN Publications Services Unit.

Hargadon, Andrew, and Martin Kenney. 2012. "Misguided Policy? Following Venture Capital into Clean Technology." *California Management Review* 54 (2): 118–139.

Harlan, Chris. 2012. "Reports: Japan Plans for Nuclear Phaseout by 2030s." *Washington Post*, September 12.

Hausmann, Ricardo, and Cesar Hidalgo. 2010. "The Building Blocks of Economic Complexity." *Proceedings of the National Academy of Sciences* 106 (26): 10570–10575.

Hedegaard, Connie. 2010. "Europe's View on International Climate Policy Climate." Speech at the Kennedy School of Government, Harvard University, Cambridge, MA, September 30.

Helm, Dieter, Cameron Hepburn, and Richard Mash. 2004. "Time-Inconsistent Environmental Policy and Optimal Delegation." Discussion Paper 175, Department of Economics, Oxford University, January.

Herring, Horace. 2006. "Energy Efficiency—A Critical View." *Energy* 31 (1): 10–20.

Hesse, Stephen. 2012. "Japan's Nuclear Phaseout: Is It All Smoke and Mirrors?" *Japan Times*, September 23.

Heymann, Matthias. 1998. "Signs of Hubris: The Shaping of Wind Technology Styles in Germany, Denmark, and the United States." *Technology and Culture* 39 (4): 641–670.

Hidalgo, Cesar A., and Ricardo Hausmann. 2009. "The Building Blocks of Economic Complexity." *Proceedings of the National Academy of Sciences* 106 (26): 10570–10575.

Hidalgo, Cesar A., Bailey Klinger, Albert-László Barabási, and Ricardo Hausmann. 2007. "The Product Space Conditions and the Development of Nations." *Science* 317 (5837): 482–487.

Hira, Anil, and Luize Guilherme de Oliveira. 2009. "No Substitute for Oil? How Brazil Developed Its Ethanol Industry." *Energy Policy* 37: 2450–2456.

Ho, Kyungup, and Sooyong Chun. 2011. "Low Power Reserve . . . Dangers of Total Blackouts for 5 Years." *ChosunIlbo*, September 20. http://biz.chosun.com/site/data/html_dir/2011/09/20/2011092000188.html.

Hochstetler, Kathryn, and Margaret E. Keck. 2007. *Greening Brazil: Environmental Activism in State and Society*. Durham, NC: Duke University Press.

Hoerner, Andrew J., and Benoît Bosquet. 2001. "Environmental Tax Reform: The European Experience." Research Paper, Center for a Sustainable Economy, Washington, DC.

Hofstrand, Don. 2008. "Brazil's Ethanol Industry." Agricultural Marketing Resource Center. Accessed May 10, 2011. http://www.agmrc.org/renewable_energy/ethanol/brazils_ethanol_industry.cfm.

Houser, Trevor, Shashank Mohan, and Robert Heilmayr. 2009. "A Green Global Recovery? Assessing U.S. Economic Stimulus and the Prospects for International Coordination." Peterson Institute for International Economics, 2009.

Huberty, Mark, Huan Gao, Juliana Mandell, and John Zysman. 2011. *Shaping the Green Growth Economy—Executive Summary*. Prepared for the Pathways Project, University of California, Berkeley, March 31.

Huberty, Mark, and Georg Zachmann. 2011. "Green Exports and the Global Product Space: Prospects for EU Industrial Policy." Working Papers 556, Bruegel, Brussels.

Huberty, Mark, and John Zysman. 2010. "An Energy Systems Transformation: Framing Research Choices for the Climate Challenge." *Research Policy* 39 (18): 1027–1029.

Hughes, Thomas. 1962. "British Electrical Industry Lag: 1882–1888." *Technology and Culture* 3 (1): 27–44.

———. 1979. "The Electrification of America: The System Builders." *Technology and Culture* 20 (1): 124–161.

———. 1983. *Networks of Power: Electrification in Western Society, 1880–1930*. Baltimore: Johns Hopkins University Press.

Hvelplund, F. 1997. "Energy Efficiency and the Political Economy of the Danish Electricity System." In *European Electricity Systems in Transition. A Comparative Analysis of Policy and Regulation in Western Europe*, edited by Atle Midttun, 133–166. Oxford: Elsevier.

Ibsen, Christian L., and Lauge S. Poulsen. 2007. "Path Dependence and Independent Utility Regulation: The Case of Danish Energy and Telecommunications Regulation." *Scandinavian Economic History Review* 55 (1): 41–63.

ICTA (International Center for Technology Assessment). 1998. *The Real Price of Gasoline*. Washington, DC: ICTA.

IEA (International Energy Agency). 2009. "CO_2 Emissions from Combustion, Highlights." Working Paper, OECD/IEA, Paris.

———. 2010a. "2010 Key World Energy Statistics." Statistics Book, OECD/IEA.

———. 2010b. "Share of Total Primary Energy Supply in 2008, People's Republic of China." IEA Energy Statistics, Paris.

———. 2010c. *World Energy Outlook 2010 Executive Summary*. Paris: IEA.

INPE (Instituto Nacional de Pesquisas Espaciais). 2011. "Prodes Taxas Anuais de Desmatamento." Accessed May 8, 2011. http://www.obt.inpe.br/prodes/prodes_1988_2010.htm.

Integration of Variable Generation Task Force. 2009. *Accommodating High Levels of Variable Generation*. Washington, DC: North American Electricity Reliability Corporation.

Inter-American Dialogue. 2011. "Will the Belo Monte Dam's Benefits Outweigh the Costs?" *Latin America Advisor*, March 10.

IPEA (Instituto de Pesquisas Econômicas Aplicadas). 2010a. "Biocombustíveis no Brasil: Etanol e Biodiesel." *Comunicados do IPEA* 53, May 26.

———. 2010b. *Sustentabilidade Ambiental no Brasil: Biodiversidade, Economia e Bem-Estar Humano*. Brasília: IPEA.

———. 2011. "Código Florestal: Implicações do PL1876/99 nas Áreas de Reserva Legal." *Comunicados do IPEA* 96, June 8.

290   Jacobsson, Staffan, and Volkmar Lauber. 2006. "The Politics and Policy of Energy System Transformation—Explaining the German Diffusion of Renewable Energy Technology." *Energy Policy* 34 (3): 256–276.

Jakobsen, Mads Leth Felsager. 2010. "Untangling the Impact of Europeanization and Globalization on National Utility Liberalization: A Systematic Process Analysis of Two Danish Reforms." *Journal of European Public Policy* 17 (6): 891–908.

Jamasb, Tooraj, and Michael Pollitt. 2005. "Electricity Market Reform in the European Union: Review of Progress towards Liberalisation and Integration." Working Paper 05-003WP, MIT Center for Energy and Environmental Policy Research, Cambridge, MA.

Jenkins, Jesse, Ted Nordhaus, and Michael Shellenberger. 2011. *Energy Emergence, Rebound and Backfire as Emergent Phenomenon.* Oakland, CA: Breakthrough Institute. http://thebreakthrough.org/blog/Energy_Emergence.pdf.

Jin, Sang-Hyeon. 2007. "The Effectiveness of Energy Efficiency Improvements in a Developing Country: Rebound Effects of Residential Electricity in South Korea." *Energy Policy* 35 (11): 5622–5629.

Johnson, Chalmers. 1982. *MITI and the Japanese Miracle: The Growth of Industrial Policy, 1925–1975.* Stanford, CA: Stanford University Press.

Jones, Van. 2008. *The Green Collar Economy: How One Solution Can Fix Our Two Biggest Problems.* San Francisco: HarperOne.

Kamp, L., R. Smits, and C. Andriesse. 2004. "Notions on Learning Applied to Wind Turbine Development in the Netherlands and Denmark." *Energy Policy* 32 (14): 1625–1637.

Kanellos, Michael. 2010. "Intel Heads Up $3.5 Billion Green/Clean Tech Investment Fund." *Wired*, February 23. http://www.wired.com/epicenter/2010/02/intel-heads-up-35-billion-greenclean-tech-investment-fund/.

Kaplan, Steven N., and Per Strömberg. 2004. "Characteristics, Contracts, and Actions: Evidence from Venture Capitalist Analyses." *Journal of Finance* 59 (5): 2177–2210.

Karnøe, Peter, and Adam Buchhorn. 2008. "Denmark: Path Creation Dynamics and Winds of Change." In *Promoting Sustainable Electricity in Europe: Challenging the Path Dependency of Dominant Energy Systems*, 73–101. Cheltenham, UK: Edward Elgar.

Karnøe, Peter, and Raghu Garud. 2012. "Path Creation: Co-Creation of Heterogeneous Resources in the Emergence of the Danish Wind Turbine Cluster." *European Planning Studies* 20 (5): 733–752.

Katz, Michael, and Carl Shapiro. 1985. "Network Externalities, Competition, and Compatibility." *American Economic Review* 75 (3): 424–440.

———. 1986. "Technology Adoption in the Presence of Network Externalities." *Journal of Political Economy* 94 (4): 822–841.

———. 1994. "Systems Competition and Network Effects." *Journal of Economic Perspectives* 8 (2): 93–115.

Kenney, Martin. 2010. "Venture Capital Investment in the Greentech Industries: A Provocative Essay." In *Handbook of Research on Energy Entrepreneurship*, edited by R. Wüstenhagen and R. Wuebker, 214–228. Cheltenham, UK: Edward Elgar.

———. 2011a. "How Venture Capital Became a Component of the U.S. National System of Innovation." *Industrial and Corporate Change* 20 (6): 1677–1723.

———. 2011b. Interview by Nina Kelsey and Juliana Mandell. Telephone with notes, March 16.

Keohane, Nat. 2008. "What Will It Cost to Protect Ourselves from Global Warming?" Environmental Defense Fund, April 23. http://blogs.edf.org/climate411/2008/04/23/cost_of_capping_ghg/.

Kharl, Fredrich, and David Roland-Holst. 2009. "Growth and Structural Change in China's Energy Economy." *Energy* 34 (7): 894–903.

Kim, Kyung Hoon, and Hye Soon Kim. 2010. "Private Generation and Credit Rating System." *Korea Ratings Weekly* 450: 2–19.

Kim, Yong-gun, Ee-jin Kim, and Shi-won Park. 2009. "Study on the Negotiation Trends and Response on Commitments to Greenhouse Gas Emission Reduction." Korea Environment Institute (KEI) Report.

Kirsner, S. 2010. "Innovation Economy." March 14. Accessed September 6, 2011. http://www.boston.com/business/technology/articles/2010/03/14/venture_backing_may_be_scarce_for_clean_tech/.

Kitazuma, Takashi. 2008. "Japan's Renewable Energy Drive Runs Out of Steam." *Japan Times*, June 5. Accessed August 21, 2011. http://search.japantimes.co.jp/print/nb20080605d3.html.

Kivimaa, P. 2008. "Finland: Big Is Beautiful — Promoting Bioenergy in Regional Industrial Contexts." In *Promoting Sustainable Electricity in Europe: Challenging the Path Dependence of Dominant Energy Systems*, edited by W. M. Lafferty and A. Ruud, 159–188. Cheltenham, UK: Edward Elgar.

Knowles, Vince, Stefan Henningsson, Richard Youngman, and Amanda Faulkner. 2012. "Coming Clean: The Global Cleantech Innovation Index." Published by the Cleantech Group and WWF. http://info.cleantech.com/2012InnovationIndex.html.

Knox-Hayes, Janelle. 2012. "Negotiating Climate Legislation: Policy Path Dependence and Coalition Stabilization." *Regulation and Governance* 6 (4): 1–23. DOI: 10.1111/j.1748-5991.2012.01138.x.

Knudsen, J., and O. M. Larsen. 2008. "Norway: Trying to Maintain Maximal RES-E in a Petroleum-Driven Economy." In *Promoting Sustainable Electricity in Europe: Challenging the Path Dependence of Dominant Energy Systems*, edited by W. M. Lafferty and A. Ruud, 250–278. Cheltenham, UK: Edward Elgar.

Koplow, Doug, and John Dernbach. 2001. "Federal Fossil Fuel Subsidies and Greenhouse Gas Emissions: A Case Study of Increasing Transparency for Fiscal Policy." *Annual Review of Energy and Environment* 26: 361–389.

Kragh, Claus. 2012. "Eldrups Store Plan: Ville Skabe Global Vindgigant." *Mandag Morgen*, March 26.

Krugman, P. 1993. "Lessons of Massachusetts for the EMU." In *Adjustment and Growth in the European Monetary Union*, edited by Francisco Torres and Francesco Giavazzi, 241–260. Cambridge: Cambridge University Press.

———. 2009. "How Did Economists Get It So Wrong?" *New York Times Magazine*, September 2.

Krupnick, Alan J., Ian W. H. Parry, Margaret Wells, Tony Knowles, and Kristen Hayes. 2010. *Toward a New National Energy Policy*. Washington, DC: Resources for the

292   Future. http://www.rff.org/Documents/RFF-Rpt-NEPI%20Tech%20Manual_
Final.pdf.

Kushida, Kenji E. 2012. "Japan's Fukushima Nuclear Disaster: Narrative, Analysis, and
Recommendations." Shorenstein APARC Working Paper Series, Stanford University, Stanford, CA.

Lague, David. 2006. "Corruption Is Linked to Pollution in China." *New York Times*,
August 21.

Laird, Frank N., and Christoph Stefes. 2009. "The Diverging Paths of German and
United States Policies for Renewable Energy: Sources of Difference." *Energy Policy*
37: 2619–2629.

Lal, Sumir. 2006. "Can Good Economics Ever Be Good Politics? Case Study of the
Power Sector in India." Working Paper 83, World Bank, Washington, DC.

LaMonica, Martin. 2009. "Wary Green-Tech Venture Investors Shift Gears." CNET
News, November 13. http://news.cnet.com/8301-11128_3-10397440-54.html.

Lange, Julian, Edward Marram, Wei Yong, David Brown, and William Bygrave. 2011.
"Can Cleantech Sustain Green Investments?" Paper presented at the ICSB World
Conference, Stockholm, June 16–18, 2011. Accessed July 29, 2013. www.sbaer.uca
.edu/research/icsb/2011/80.doc.

La Rovere, Emilio Lèbre, André Santos Pereira, and André Felipe Simões. 2011. "Biofuels and Sustainable Energy Development in Brazil." *World Development* 39 (6):
1026–1036.

Larsen, Bjorn, and Anwar Shah. 1992. "World Fossil Fuel Subsidies and Global
Carbon Emissions." Working Paper 1002, Office of the Vice President, Develop-
ment Economics, World Bank. http://www-wds.worldbank.org/external/default/
WDSContentServer/IW3P/IB/1992/10/01/000009265_3961003153846/Rendered/
PDF/multi_page.pdf.

Larsen, Christian A., and Jørgen G. Andersen. 2009. "How New Economic Ideas
Changed the Danish Welfare State: The Case of Neoliberal Ideas and Highly Organized Social Democratic Interests." *Governance* 22 (2): 239–261.

Leahy, Joe, and Samantha Pearson. 2012. "Brazil Gives Big Sweetener for Sugar Biofuel." *Financial Times*, January 11. Accessed February 23, 2012. http://www.ft.com/
intl/cms/s/0/f16f5546-3c7f-11e1-8d38-00144feabdc0.html#axzz1nD7WRlXB.

Le Breton, Binka. 2008. *The Greatest Gift: The Courageous Life and Martyrdom of
Sister Dorothy Stang*. New York: Doubleday.

Lecar, Matt. 2011. Interview by Nina Kelsey and Juliana Mandell. Telephone with
notes, March 16.

Lee, Jonghyun. 2011. "Choi Joon Kyung 'Progress towards Realizing Electricity Price
Will Continue.'" *ChosunIlbo*, May 5. Accessed May 5, 2011. http://biz.chosun.com/
site/data/html_dir/2011/05/05/2011050500581.html.

Lee, Myung-bak. 2008. "A Great People with New Dreams." August 15. Accessed May 16,
2011. http://eng.me.go.kr/file.do?method=fileDownloader&attachSeq=2094.

Lee, Youngwan, and Sooyong Chun. 2011. "Experts Say 'Electricity Shortage of 12,200,000
kWh in Ten Years. . . . The Sole Realistic Alternative Is Nuclear." *ChosunIlbo*,
September 23. http://biz.chosun.com/site/data/html_dir/2011/09/23/2011092300234
.html.

Lehr, Ulrike, Joachim Nitsch, Marlene Kratzat, Christian Lutz, and Dietmar Edler. 2008. **293**
"Renewable Energy and Employment in Germany." *Energy Policy* 36, 1: 108–117.

Leone, Steve. 2011. "Japan Approves National Feed-In Tariff." RenewableEnergyWorld.
com, August 26. Accessed August 26, 2011. http://www.renewableenergyworld.com/
rea/news/article/2011/08/japan-approves-national-feed-in-tariff.

Lerner, Joshua. 1995. "Venture Capitalists and the Oversight of Private Firms." *Journal
of Finance* 50: 301–318.

———. 2009. *Boulevard of Broken Dreams*. Princeton, NJ: Princeton University Press.

Levi, Michael A., Elizabeth C. Economy, Shannon K. O'Neil, and Adam Segal. 2010.
*Energy Innovation: Driving Technology Competition and Cooperation among the
U.S., China, India, and Brazil*. New York: Council on Foreign Relations.

Levinson, M. 2008. *The Box: How the Shipping Container Made the World Smaller and
the World Economy Bigger*. Princeton, NJ: Princeton University Press.

Lewer, Joshua J., and Hendrik Van den Berg. 2003. "How Large Is International Trade's
Effect on Growth?" *Journal of Economic Surveys* 17 (3): 363–396.

Li, Junfeng, Pengfei Shi, and Hu Gao. 2010. "China Wind Power Outlook 2010."
Report for Global Wind Energy Council, Brussels.

Liming, Huang. 2009. "Financing Rural Renewable Energy: A Comparison between
China and India." *Renewable and Sustainable Energy Reviews* 13 (5): 1096–1103.

Lipton, Eric, and John M. Broder. 2011. "E-Mail Shows Senior Energy Official Pushed
Solyndra Loan." *New York Times*, October 8.

Liu, Yang, and Hua Huang. 2010. "Jieti dianjia lunwei zhangjia fangan?" [Has tiered
pricing turned to a rate hike?]. *Guoji Jinrong Bao* [International Finance News],
October 26.

Lovei, Laszlo, and Alastair McKechine. 2000. "The Cost of Corruption for the Poor:
The Energy Sector." World Bank Group: Private Sector and Infrastructure Network. Washington, DC: World Bank.

Lucon, Oswaldo, and José Goldemberg. 2010. "São Paulo — The 'Other' Brazil: Different Pathways on Climate Change for State and Federal Governments." *Journal of
Environment and Development* 19 (3): 335–357.

Luíse, Desiree. 2011. "Carta Verde: Corrupção é algo crônico em Secretarias do Meio Ambiente na Amazônia, diz ex-secretário." *Carta Capital*, March 17. Accessed May 15,
2011. http://www.cartacapital.com.br/carta-verde/corrupcao-e-algo-cronico-em
-secretarias-de-meio-ambiente-na-amazonia-diz-ex-secretario.

MacDonald, Lisa A., Holly Wise Bender, Eric Hurley, Sheri Donnelly, and David
Taylor. 2007. "Oil and Gas Economic Impact Analysis." Report for Colorado
Energy Research Institute, Denver, CO.

Manresa, Antonio, and Ferran Sancho. 2005. "Implementing a Double Dividend:
Recycling Ecotaxes towards Lower Labour Taxes." *Energy Policy* 33 (12): 1577–1585.

Manzatto, Celso Vainer, Eduardo Delgado Assad, Jesus Fernando Mansilla Bacca, Maria José Maroni, Sandro Eduardo Marchhausen Pereira (orgs.). 2009. "Zoneamento
Agroecológico da Cana-de-Açúcar: Expandir a Produção, Preservar a Vida, Garan-
tir o Futuro." Rio de Janeiro: EMBRAPA, MAPA.

MAPA (Ministério da Agricultura, Pecuária e Abastecimento). 2010. "Anuário
Estatístico de Agroenergia 2010." Brasília: MAPA. Accessed May 8, 2011. http://www

294   .agricultura.gov.br/arq_editor/file/Desenvolvimento_Sustentavel/Agroenergia/
anuario_agroenergia/index.html#.

Marcus, Alfred, Joel Malen, and Shmuel Ellis. 2012. "The Promise and Pitfalls of Venture Capital as an Asset Class for Clean Energy." Working Paper, Harvard University Initiative for Responsible Investment Conference: The Societal Function Implications for Responsible Investment, October 4, 2012.

Mason, Robert J. 1999. "Whither Japan's Environmental Movement: An Assessment of Its Problems and Prospects at the National Level." *Pacific Affairs* 72 (Summer): 187–207.

Mathur, Ajay. 2010. "Energy Efficiency in India: Challenges and Initiatives." Lawrence Berkeley National Laboratory Distinguished Lecture Series, Berkeley, CA.

May, Peter H., Brent Millikan, and Maria Fernanda Gebara. 2011. *The Context of REDD+ in Brazil: Drivers, Agents and Institutions.* 2nd ed. Occasional Paper 55, Center for International Forestry Research (CIFOR), Bogor, Indonesia.

McAllister, Lesley K. 2008a. *Making Law Matter: Environmental Protection and Legal Institutions in Brazil.* Stanford, CA: Stanford Law Books.

———. 2008b. "Sustainable Consumption Governance in the Amazon." *Environmental Law Reporter* 38 (12): 10873–10881.

McCurry, Justin. 2009. "Japan's New Prime Minister Promises Ambitious Greenhouse Gas Cuts." *The Guardian*, September 7. Accessed August 31, 2011. www.guardian.co.uk/environment/2009/sep/07/japan-greenhouse-gas-cuts.

McKean, Margaret A. 1981. *Environmental Protest and Citizen Politics in Japan.* Berkeley: University of California Press.

McKendrick, D. G., and G. R. Carroll. 2001. "On the Genesis of Organizational Forms: Evidence from the Market for Disk Arrays." *Organization Science* 12 (6): 661–682.

McKinsey & Company. 2009. "Pathways to a Low-Carbon Economy for Brazil." São Paulo: McKinsey & Company.

McLaren Loring, Joyce. 2007. "Wind Energy Planning in England, Wales and Denmark: Factors Influencing Project Success." *Energy Policy* 35 (4): 2648–2660.

MCT (Ministério da Ciência e Tecnologia, Brasil). 2010. *Segunda Comunicação Nacional do Brasil à Convenção-Quadro das Nações Unidas sobre Mudança do Clima—Sumário Executivo.* Brasília: Coordenação-Geral de Mudanças Globais do Clima, Ministério da Ciência e Tecnologia, República Federativa do Brasil.

Meakin, Stephanie. 1992. The Rio Earth Summit: Summary of the United Nations Conference on Environment and Development. Accessed August 29, 2011. http://dsp-psd.pwgsc.gc.ca/collectionr/lopbdp/bp/bp317e.htm#a.%20history%20of%20the%20.summit%28txt%29.

Medeiros, Rodrigo, Carlos Eduardo, Frickman Young, Helena Boniatti Pavese, and Fábio França Sílvio Araújo. 2011. *A Contribuição Econômica das Unidades de Conservação para a Economia Nacional.* Brasília: UNEP-WCMC.

Meilstrup, Per. 2010. "The Runaway Summit: The Background Story of the Danish Presidency of COP15, the UN Climate Change Conference." In *Danish Foreign Policy Yearbook 2010,* 113–135. Copenhagen: Danish Institute for International Studies.

Meilstrup, Per, Meik Wiking, Izabela Butenko-Olesen, Christian Eika Frøkiær, Sarah Pickering, and Emilie Hvidtfeldt. 2010. *Danmark Som Globalt, Grønt Vækstlaboratorium.* Copenhagen: Mondag Morgen.

Mendonca, Miguel, Stephen Lacey, and Frede Hvelplund. 2009. "Stability, Participation and Transparency in Renewable Energy Policy: Lessons from Denmark and
the United States." *Policy and Society* 27 (4): 379–398.
METI (Ministry of Economy, Trade, and Industry). 2009. "Eco-Point System for
Housing." Accessed August 31, 2011. http://www.meti.go.jp/english/press/data/2009
1215_01.html.
———. 2010. "Enerugiinikansurunenjihōkoku (2010-Nenban enerugiihakusho)" [An-
nual report on energy (energy white paper 2010 edition)]. June. Accessed August 22,
2011. http://www.enecho.meti.go.jp/topics/hakusho/2010energyhtml/index.html.
Meyer, Niels I. 2004a. "Renewable Energy Policy in Denmark." *Energy for Sustainable
Development* 8 (1): 25–35.
———. 2004b. "Development of Danish Wind Power Market." *Energy and Environment* 15 (4): 657–673.
———. 2007. "Learning from Wind Energy Policy in the EU: Lessons from Denmark,
Sweden, and Spain." *European Environment* 17 (5): 347–362.
Minard, Anne. 2010. "Colorado Seeks a Renewable Energy Peak: But Can Rocky
Mountain Power Success Be Repeated in Other Terrain?" *National Geographic*,
May 5. http://news.nationalgeographic.com/news/2010/05/100505-energy-colorado
-renewable-power/.
Ministry of Power, Government of India. Accessed 2011. http://www.powermin
.nic.in/.
Mitchell, Cynthia. 2009. "Stabilizing California's Demand: The Real Reasons Behind
the State's Energy Savings." Public Utilities Fortnightly.
Mitchell, Russ. 2007. "Behind the Green Doerr." Portfolio.com, April 16.
MKE (Ministry of Knowledge Economy). 2010a. "Amendments to the Law on Renewable Energy Development, Usage, and Dissemination on Enforcement Ordinance
and Enforcement Regulation of RPS." South Korean Government press release,
Seoul.
———. 2010b. "Foreign Smart Grid Policy and Market Research." South Korean Government Report, Seoul.
———. 2010c. "Smart Grid Fact Book." South Korean Government Report, Seoul.
———. 2010d. "Smart Grid National Roadmap." South Korean Government Report,
Seoul.
———. 2011. "Blueprint for National Greenhouse Gas Reduction." South Korean Government press release, Seoul.
MKEEID (Ministry of Knowledge Economy, Electricity Industry Division). 2010. "Development Status of the Smart Grid." South Korean Government Report, Seoul.
MME/EPE (Ministério de Minas e Energia/Empresa de Pesquisa Energética). 2011.
"Plano Decenal de Energia 2020." Brasília: MME/EPE.
MOE (Ministry of the Environment). 2010. "Annual Report on the Environment, the
Sound Material-Cycle Society and the Biodiversity in Japan." Accessed August 21,
2011. http://www.env.go.jp/en/wpaper/2010/index.html.
Moor, Andre de. 2001. "Towards a Grand Deal on Subsidies and Climate Change."
Natural Resources Forum 25 (2): 167–176.
Moore, Galen. 2011. "Cleantech-Focused Funds Take Over as General VCs
Back Off Cleantech." *Mass High Tech*, April 27. http://www.masshightech.com/

296   stories/2011/04/25/weekly12-Cleantech-focused-funds-take-over-as-general-VCs -back-off-cleantech.html.

Moreno, Blanca, and Ana Jesus Lopez. 2008. "The Effect of Renewable Energy on Employment: The Case of Asturias (Spain)." *Renewable and Sustainable Energy Reviews* 12 (3): 732–751.

Morse, Richard K., and Gang He. 2010. "The World's Greatest Coal Arbitrage: China's Coal Import Behavior and Implications for the Global Coal Market." Working Paper 94, Freeman Spogli Institute for International Studies, Stanford University, Stanford, CA.

Mufson, Steven. 2007. "Europe's Problems Color U.S. Plans to Curb Carbon Gases." *Washington Post*, April 9. http://www.washingtonpost.com/wp-dyn/content/article/2007/04/08/AR2007040800758.html.

Mulligan, Casey. 2010. "Simple Analytics and Empirics of the Government Spending Multiplier and Other 'Keynesian' Paradoxes." Working Paper 15800, National Bureau of Economic Research, Washington, DC, March.

Murota, Y., and Y. Yano. 1993. "Japan's Policy on Energy and the Environment." *Annual Review of Energy and the Environment* 18: 89–135.

NAS (U.S. National Academy of Sciences). 2010. *America's Energy Future: Technology and Transformation*. Washington, DC: National Academies Press.

———. 2011. "America's Climate Choices." National Research Council, Committee on America's Climate Choices, Washington, DC.

Nassar, André Meloni. 2009. "Brazil as an Agricultural and Agroenergy Superpower." In *Brazil as an Economic Superpower?* edited by Lael Brainard and Leonardo Martínez-Díaz, 55–80. Washington, DC: Brookings Institution.

NBS (National Bureau of Statistics of China). 2010. *China Statistical Yearbook 2010*. Beijing: China Statistics Press.

———. 2011. *China Statistical Yearbook 2011*. Beijing: China Statistics Press.

NDRC (National Development and Reform Commission of China). 2007. *China's National Climate Change Programme*. Beijing: NDRC.

———. 2011. *Zhonghuarenmingongheguo guomin jingji he shehui fazhan di shierge wunian guihua gaoyao* [The twelfth five-year guidelines of economic and social development in People's Republic of China]. Beijing: NDRC.

———. 2012. *Yeyanqi Fazhan Guihua (2011–2015)* [Shale gas development plan 2011–2015]. Fagai Nengyuan [2012] 612. Beijing: NDRC.

NEDO (New Energy and Industrial Technology Development Organization). 2000. "NEDO nijūnenshi" [NEDO's 20-year history]. Accessed August 26, 2011. www.nedo.go.jp/library/shiryou_siryouko.html.

Nef, John. 1932. *The Rise of the British Coal Industry*. London: Frank Cass.

Nemet, Gregory F., and Daniel M. Kammen. 2007. "U.S. Energy Research and Development: Declining Investment, Increasing Need, and the Feasibility of Expansion." *Energy Policy* 35 (1): 746–755.

NERC. 2011. "NERC—North American Electric Reliability Corporation." Accessed March 17. http://www.nerc.com/.

Ni, Vincent, and Baizhen Chua. 2010. "Chinese Demand for Coal Spurs 9-Day Traffic Jam on Expressway." *Business Week*, August 24.

Niez, Alexandra. 2010. "Comparative Study on Rural Electrification Policies in Emerging Economies: Keys to Successful Policies." International Energy Agency Information Paper.   297

Nordhaus, Ted, and Michael Shellenberger. 2007. *Break Through: From the Death of Environmentalism to the Politics of Possibility.* New York: Houghton Mifflin.

Nordhaus, William. 2007. "Two Centuries of Productivity Growth in Computing." *Journal of Economic History* 67 (1): 128.

———. 2010. "Designing a Friendly Space for Technological Change to Slow Global Warming." *Energy Economics* 33 (4): 665–673.

Nord Pool Spot. 2009. "Nord Pool Spot Implements Negative Price Floor in Elspot." No. 16/October. http://www.nordpoolspot.com/Message-center-container/Exchange-list/Exchange-information/No162009-Nord-Pool-Spot-implements-negative-price-floor-in-Elspot-from-October-2009-/.

Nørgaard, Niels, and Jesper Tornbjerg. 2002. "Finanslov: Sort Dag for Miljøet." *Politiken*, January 30.

North, Douglass C. 1990. *Institutions, Institutional Change, and Economic Performance.* Cambridge: Cambridge University Press.

OECD (Organization for Economic Cooperation and Development). 2009. "State Owned Enterprises in China: Reviewing the Evidence." OECD Working Group on Privatisation and Corporate Governance of State Owned Assets Occasional Paper, January 26.

OECD/IEA. 2006. "The Energy Situation in Brazil: An Overview." Paper prepared for the Standing Group on the Global Energy Dialogue, May.

———. 2010. *Interim Report of the Green Growth Strategy: Implementing Our Commitment for a Sustainable Future.* Paris: C/MIN.

Olinger, David. 2004. "Statewide Ballot Issues Amendment 37 10% by 2015: Energy Initiative would Force Colo. to Reap Renewables." *Denver Post*, October 17.

OMB. 2011. Executive Office of the President of the United States, Office of Management and Budget, Washington, DC. Usaspending.gov. http://usaspending.gov/trends.

ONG Repórter Brasil. 2011. "Brazil's Ethanol in the World: Socio-Environmental Impacts of Export Sugarcane Companies." São Paulo: ONG Repórter Brasil Biofuel Watch Center. http://www.reporterbrasil.org.br/documentos/Sucarcane2011.pdf.

Onishi, Norimitsu and Martin Fackler. 2011. "Utility Reform Eluding Japan after Nuclear Plant Disaster." *New York Times*, November 17.

Oye, Kenneth A., and James H. Maxwell. 1994. "Self-Interest and Environmental Management." *Journal of Theoretical Politics* 6 (4): 593–624.

Palmer, Karen, and Dallas Burtraw. 2005. "Cost-Effectiveness of Renewable Electricity Policies." *Energy Economics* 27 (6): 873–894.

Palmer, Karen, and Wallace E. Oates. 1995. "Tightening Environmental Standards: The Benefit-Cost or the No-Cost Paradigm." *Journal of Economic Perspectives* 9 (4): 119–132.

Park, Jong-sae, and Gil-sung Lee. 2010. "Hyundai Heavy Industries Builds America's Largest Solar Energy Plant." *ChosunIlbo*, August 11. Accessed May 5, 2011. http://biz.chosun.com/site/data/html_dir/2010/07/20/2010072001958.html.

298   Pascha, Werner. 2010. "South Korea Country Report." In *Managing the Crisis: A Comparative Assessment of Economic Governance in 14 Economies*, edited by Bertelsmann Stiftung. Gütersloh: Bertelsmann Stiftung.

Patashnik, Eric M. 2003. "After the Public Interest Prevails: The Political Sustainability of Policy Reform." *Governance* 16 (2): 203–234.

———. 2008. *Reforms at Risk: What Happens after Major Policy Changes Are Enacted.* Princeton, NJ: Princeton University Press.

Patel, Samir. 2006 "Cleantech Gets Green." *Seed Magazine*, May 3.

Patriota, Antonio de Aguiar. 2009. "An Introduction to Brazilian Environmental Law." *George Washington International Law Review* 40 (3): 611–617.

Paulson, Steven K. 2004. "List of Initiatives Certified for the November Ballot." Associated Press State and Local Wire, August 17.

PCGG (Presidential Committee on Green Growth). 2010a. "Progress Report 2008–2009." South Korean Government Report. Seoul.

———. 2010b. "Road to Green Growth." South Korean Government Report. Seoul.

———. 2012. "The 5th Green Growth Policy Implementation Review Conference." South Korean Government Report. Seoul.

Pempel, T. J. 1982. *Policy and Politics in Japan: Creative Conservatism.* Philadelphia: Temple University Press.

Perez, Carlota. 1983. "Structure Change and Assimilation of New Technologies in the Economic and Social Systems." *Futures* 15 (5): 357–375.

———. 2002. *Technological Revolutions and Financial Capital: The Dynamics of Bubbles and Golden Ages.* Cheltenham, UK: Edward Elgar.

Perry, Elizabeth J. 2011. "Challenging the Mandate of Heaven: Popular Protest in Modern China." *Critical Asian Studies* 33 (2): 163–180.

Petrobras. 2009. "Perfil." Accessed February 12, 2012. http://www.petrobras.com.br/pt/quem-somos/perfil/.

Pew Environment Group. 2012. *Who's Winning the Clean Energy Race? 2011 Edition.* www.PewTrusts.org/CleanEnergy.

Pfund, Nancy, and Ben Healey. 2011. *What Would Jefferson Do? The Historical Role of Federal Subsidies in Shaping America's Energy Future.* Double Bottom Line Investors. http://www.dblinvestors.com/documents/What-Would-Jefferson-Do-Final-Version.pdf.

Phadke, Amol, Ranjit Bharvirkar, and Jagmeet Khangura. 2011. "Reassessing Wind Energy Potentials for India: Economic and Policy Implications." LBNL-5077E, Lawrence Berkeley National Laboratory, Berkeley, CA.

Pierson, Paul. 2000. "Increasing Returns, Path Dependence, and the Study of Politics." *American Political Science Review* 94 (2): 251–267.

Plant, Tom. 2011. Interview by Nina Kelsey. Telephone with notes, May 12.

Pooley, Eric. 2010. *The Climate War: True Believers, Power Brokers, and the Fight to Save the Earth.* New York: Hyperion.

Porac, Joseph F., Howard Thomas, Fiona Wilson, Douglas Paton, and Alaina Kanfer. 1995. "Rivalry and the Industry Model of Scottish Knitwear Producers." *Administrative Science Quarterly* 40: 203–229.

Porter, Michael, and Claas van der Linde. 1995. "Toward a New Conception of Environment-Competitiveness Relationship." *Journal of Economic Perspectives* 9 (4): 97–118.

Prabhakar, Arati. 2011. Interview by Nina Kelsey and Juliana Mandell. Telephone with notes, March 29.

PricewaterhouseCoopers LLP. 2012. "Cleantech MoneyTree Report: Q2." August 20. Accessed September 26, 2012. https://www.pwcmoneytree.com/MTPublic/ns/moneytree/filesource/exhibits/Cleantech%20MoneyTree%20Q2%202012.pdf.

Purdy, Penelope. 2004. "Amendment 37 Voters Get Their Say on Energy Ballot Measure Sets Renewables Standard." *Denver Post*, October 10.

Rai, Varun, David Victor, and Mark Thurber. 2009. "Carbon Capture and Storage at Scale: Lessons from the Growth of Analogous Energy Technologies." *Energy Policy* 38 (8): 4089–4098.

Randolph, Sean. 2011. Interview by Nina Kelsey and Juliana Mandell. Telephone with notes, March 8.

RATB (Recovery Accountability and Transparency Board). 2011. "Track the Money." www.recovery.gov.

Reddy, Shravya. 2010. "Protest Against Fuel Subsidies Cutback—Test of Leadership for Indian Government." *Switchboard National Resources Defense Council Staff Blog*, July 8. http://switchboard.nrdc.org/blogs/sreddy/protest_against_fuel_subsidies.html.

Redman, Elizabeth. 2011. "Shifts in the Cleantech Investment Landscape." Reuters, April 13. http://www.reuters.com/article/2011/04/13/idUS74705167920110413.

Regeringen, Venstre, Dansk Folkeparti, Enhedslisten, and Det Konservative Folkepart. 2012. "Aftale—mellem regeringen (Socialdemokraterne, Det Radikale Venstre, Socialistisk Folkeparti) og Venstre, Dansk Folkeparti, Enhedslisten, og Det Konservative Forlkeparti—Om den danske energipolitik 2012–2020." Danish Ministry for Climate, Energy and Building. http://kemin.dk/Documents/Presse/2012/Energiaftale/Aftale%2022-03-2012%20FINAL.doc.pdf.

Reich, Michael R. 1984. "Mobilizing for Environmental Policy in Italy and Japan." *Comparative Politics* 16 (July): 379–402.

Reuters. 2010. "Venture Beat's Best and Worst of Cleantech in 2010." December 29. http://www.reuters.com/article/2010/12/29/idUS120422778120101229.

RGGVY.gov (Government of India). 2011. "Scheme for Rural Electricity Infrastructure and Household Electrification." Accessed October 2011. http://www.rggvy.gov.in/rggvy/rggvyportal/index.html.

Ritter, Bill. 2010. "Colorado's New Energy Economy." *Forbes*, May 27. http://www.forbes.com/2010/05/26/clean-energy-wind-technology-colorado.html.

Roland-Holst, David. 2008. "Energy Efficiency, Innovation, and Job Creation in California." Research Papers on Energy, Resources, and Economic Sustainability, University of California, Berkeley.

Romer, Christina. 2011. "What Do We Know about the Effects of Fiscal Policy? Separating Evidence from Ideology." Mimeo, November 7.

Romer, Christina, and Jared Bernstein. 2009. "The Job Impacts of the American Recovery and Reinvestment Plan." Office of the President-Elect, Washington, DC.

Roney, J. Matthew. 2010. "Eco-Policy Indicators: Solar Power." Data from the Earth Policy Institute. Accessed August 31, 2011. www.earth-policy.org/indicators/C47.

Rosa, Luiz Pinguelli, Christiano Pires de Campos, and Maria Silvia Muylaert de Araujo. 2009. "Biofuel Contribution to Mitigate Fossil Fuel CO_2 Emissions:

300

Comparing Sugar Cane Ethanol in Brazil with Corn Ethanol and Discussing Land Use for Food Production and Deforestation." *Journal of Renewable and Sustainable Energy* 1 (033111): 1–21.

Rosenfeld, Arthur H., and Patrick K. McAulliffe. David W. Hafemeister (ed.). 2008. "Opportunities in the Building Sector." *Physics of Sustainable Energy: Using Energy Efficiently and Producing it Renewably* 1044: 3–14.

Rosenfeld, Arthur H., with Deborah Poskanzer. 2009. "A Graph Is Worth a Thousand Gigawatt-Hours: How California Came to Lead the United States in Energy Efficiency." *Innovations* 4: 57–79.

Rosenthal, Elisabeth. 2010. "Portugal Gives Itself a Clean-Energy Makeover." *New York Times Green Blog*, August 9. http://www.nytimes.com/2010/08/10/science/earth/10portugal.html?pagewanted=all&_r=0.

Rosted, Jørgen. 2012. Interview by Jakob Riiskjaer Nygård.

Rüdiger, Mogens. 2011. *Energy Moving Forward*. Copenhagen: DONG Energy.

Ruef, Martin, and Kelly Patterson. 2009. "Credit and Classification: The Impact of Industry Boundaries in 19th Century America." *Administrative Science Quarterly* 54: 486–520.

Russo, Michael V. 2001. "Institutions, Exchange Relations, and the Emergence of New Fields: Regulatory Policies and Independent Power Production in America, 1978–1992." *Administrative Science Quarterly* 46 (1): 57–86.

Ryall, Julian. 2009. "New Japanese PM Pledges Deep Greenhouse Gas Cuts." *The Telegraph*, September 7. Accessed August 31, 2011. www.telegraph.co.uk/earth/earthnews/6148559/New-Japanese-PM-pledges-deep-greenhouse-gas-cuts.html.

Ryu, Hyun-jung. 2011. "Samsung Builds Green Industrial Complex in Saemangum. . . . 7 Trillion Won Investment." *ChosunIlbo*, April 27. Accessed May 5, 2011. http://biz.chosun.com/site/data/html_dir/2011/04/27/2011042701470.html.

Sargsyan, Gevorg, Mikul Bhatia, Sudeshna Ghosh Banerjee, Krishnan Raghunathan, and Ruchi Soni. 2010. "Unleashing the Potential of Renewable Energy in India." Energy Sector Management Assistance Program, South Asia Energy Unit Sustainable Development Department, World Bank.

Sathaye, Jayant. 2011. "India's Energy Efficiency and Renewable Energy Potential: Policies and Programs." Berkeley–India Joint Leadership on Energy and Environment (BIJLEE), Lawrence Berkeley National Laboratory, Berkeley, CA, October.

Sathaye, Jayant, Daniel Bouille, et al. 2001. "Barriers, Opportunities, and Market Potential of Technologies and Practices." In *Climate Change Mitigation*, edited by B. Metz, O. Davidson, and R. Swart. Cambridge: Cambridge University Press for the Intergovernmental Panel on Climate Change.

Sathaye, Jayant A., Stephane de la Rue du Can, Maithili Iyer, Michael A. McNeil, Klaas Jan Kramer, Joyashree Roy, Moumita Roy, and Shreya Roy Chowdhury. 2011. "Strategies for Low Carbon Growth in India: Industry and Non-Residential Sectors." Formal Report, Lawrence Berkeley National Laboratory, Berkeley, CA.

Sathaye, Jayant, and Arjun Gupta. 2010. "Eliminating Electricity Deficit through Energy Efficiency in India." Formal Report, Lawrence Berkeley National Laboratory, Berkeley, CA.

Sathaye, Jayant, P. R. Shukla, and N. H. Ravindranath. 2006. "Climate Change, Sustainable Development and India: Global and National Concerns." *Current Science* 90 (3): 314–325.

Schepelmann, Philip, Martin Stock, Thorsen Kosta, Ralf Schüle, and Oscar Ruetter. 2009. *A Green New Deal for Europe.* Green New Deal Papers Series Vol. 1. Brussels: Green European Foundation.

Schipper, Lee, and Michael Grubb. 2000. "On the Rebound? Feedback between Energy Intensities and Energy Uses in IEA Countries." *Energy Policy* 28 (6–7): 367–388.

Schmalensee, Richard. 2012, "Evaluating Policies to Increase Electricity Generation from Renewable Energy." *Review of Environmental Economics and Policy* 6 (1): 45–64.

Schmid, Gisel. 2011. "The Development of Renewable Energy Power in India: Which Policies Have Been Effective?" Working Paper Series 11103, University of Geneva.

Schmidt, Jake, and Aaron Haifly. 2012. "Delivering on Renewable Energy Around the World: How Do Key Countries Stack Up?" Natural Resources Defense Council Report.

Schreurs, Miranda, and Yves Tiberghien. 2007. "Multi-Level Reinforcement: Explaining European Union Leadership in Climate Change Mitigation." *Global Environmental Politics* 7 (4): 19–46.

Scott, Mark. 2010. "GE, Vestas Fall Behind in China's 'Tough' Wind Market." *New York Times*, May 14.

Scott, Michael J., Joseph M. Roop, Robert W. Schultz, David M. Anderson, and Katherine A. Cort. 2008. "The Impact of DOE Building Technology Energy Efficiency Programs on U.S. Employment, Income, and Investment." *Energy Economics* 30 (5): 2283–2301.

SEMA (Secretaria de Estado de Meio Ambiente do Pará). 2010. "Unidades de Conservação Federais, Estaduais, e Municipais do Estado do Pará." Last modified September 7, 2010. Accessed March 3, 2012. http://www.sema.pa.gov.br/interna .php?idconteudocoluna=4625.

SEMI, PV Group, and CPIA. 2011. "2011 Zhongguoguangfuchanyefazhanbaogao" [2011 Report of China's photovoltaic industry]. Changzhou, China: China PV Industry Association.

Sennes, Ricardo Ubiraci, and Thais Narciso. 2009. "Brazil as an International Energy Player." In *Brazil as an Economic Superpower?* edited by Lael Brainard and Leonardo Martínez-Díaz, 17–54. Washington, DC: Brookings Institution.

Seroa da Motta, Ronaldo. 2011. "A Política Nacional sobre Mudança do Clima: Aspectos Regulatórios e de Governança." In *Mudança do Clima no Brasil: Aspectos Econômicos, Sociais, e Regulatórios*, edited by Ronaldo Seroa da Motta, Jorge Hargrave, Gustavo Luedemann, and Maria Bernadete Sarmiento Gutierrez, 31–42. Brasília: IPEA.

SFB (Serviço Florestal Brasileiro). 2011. *Relatório de Gestão de 2010.* Brasília: Ministério do Meio Ambiente, Serviço Florestal Brasileiro.

———. 2012. "Duas Florestas Nacionais Abrigam Concessão Florestal." Accessed March 4, 2012. http://www.sfb.gov.br/concessoes-florestais/florestas-sob-concessao/ duas-florestas-nacionais-abrigam-concessao-florestal.

302   Sharan, Suni. 2010. "The Green Jobs Myth." *Washington Post*, February 26. http://
www.washingtonpost.com/wp-dyn/content/article/2010/02/25/AR2010022503945
.html.

Shiel, Patrick, Nick Jeffers, and Mark Dyar. 2011. "Energy Conservation Measures in
Japan." Paper presented at the Atlantic Energy Efficiency Workshop, Berkeley, CA,
February 11.

Sieferle, Rolf Peter. 2001. *The Subterranean Forest Energy Systems and the Industrial
Revolution*. Cambridge, MA: White Horse Press.

Singh, Anoop. 2006. "Power Sector Reform in India: Current Issues and Prospects."
Energy Policy 34 (16): 2480–2490.

Smil, Vaclav. 2011. "Global Energy: The Latest Infatuations." *American Scientist* 99:
212–219.

Smith, Kirk R. 2000. "National Burden of Disease in India from Indoor Air Pollution."
Proceedings of the National Academy of Sciences 97 (24): 13286–13293.

Solarbuzz. 2011. "Solarbuzz Reports World Solar Photovoltaic Market Grew to 18.2
Gigawatts in 2010, Up 139% Y/Y." Accessed September 6, 2011. http://solarbuzz
.com/our-research/recent-findings/solarbuzz-reports-world-solar-photovoltaic
-market-grew-182-gigawatts-20.

Song, Victoria. 2011. "The Economics of Conservation." *American Chamber of Commerce in Japan Journal* 48 (August): 28–31.

S.O.S. Mata Atlântica. 2011. "A Mata Atlântica." Accessed December 19, 2012. http://
www.sosma.org.br/nossa-causa/a-mata-atlantica/.

Sovacool, Benjamin K., Hans H. Lindboe, and Ole Odgaard. 2008. "Is the Danish Wind
Energy Model Replicable for Other Countries?" *Electricity Journal* 21 (2): 27–38.

Spongenberg, Helena. 2011. "Nordic Countries Are Greening Their Economy More
Than Ever." *Does Sustainability Pay?* http://www.norden.org/en/analys-norden/
tema/does-sustainability-pay.

Stalley, Phillip. 2010. *Foreign Firms, Investment, and Environmental Regulation in the
People's Republic of China*. Stanford, CA: Stanford University Press.

Stanton, Chris. 2010. "Russia Threatens 'Asian Premium.'" *The National*, February 13.
Accessed August 22, 2011. http://www.thenational.ae/business/energy/russia-threat
ens-asian-premium.

State Electricity Regulatory Commission of China. 2011. *Dianli Jianguan Niandu
Baogao 2010* [Annual report of power industry 2010]. Beijing: SERC.

State Grid Corporation of China. 2010. *Guojia Dianwang Lanwa Fazhan Baipishu*
[State Grid white paper on green development]. Beijing: State Grid.

Stavins, Robert N. 2003. "Market-Based Environmental Policies: What Can We
Learn from U.S. Experience (and Related Research)?" KSG Working Paper
RWP03-031.

Stern, Nicholas, ed. 2006. *Stern Review on the Economics of Climate Change*. HM
Treasury.

Stewart, Devin T., and Warren Wilczewski. 2009. "How Japan Became an Efficiency
Superpower." *Policy Innovations*, February 3. Accessed April 18, 2013. http://www
.policyinnovations.org/ideas/briefings/data/000102.

Stinchcombe, Arthur L. 1965. "Social Structure and Organizations." In *Handbook of
Organizations*, edited by J. G. March. Chicago: Rand McNally.

Streeck, Wolfgang, and Kathleen Thelen. 2005. *Beyond Continuity: Institutional Change in Advanced Political Economies.* New York: Oxford University Press.

Suchman, M. C., and M. L. Cahill. 1996. "The Hired-Gun as Facilitator: The Case of Lawyers in Silicon Valley." *Law and Social Inquiry* 21 (3): 679–712.

Sudarshan, Anant, and James L. Sweeney. 2008. "Deconstructing the 'Rosenfeld Curve.'" Working Paper, Precourt Energy Efficiency Center.

"Superpower: Lessons for U.S. Energy Policy under Obama." *Policy Innovations*, February 3. Accessed August 21, 2011. http://www.policyinnovations.org/ideas/briefings/data/000102S.

Sweeney, James L. 2002. *The California Electricity Crisis.* Stanford, CA: Hoover Institution Press.

Szamosszegi, A., and C. Kyle. 2011. "An Analysis of State-Owned Enterprises and State Capitalism in China." Prepared for the U.S.–China Economic and Security Review Commission, Washington, DC, October 26.

TemaNord. 2007. *The Nordic Energy Market and Environment.* Nordic Council of Ministers.

TMG (Tokyo Metropolitan Government). 2011. "Principal Policies of the Tokyo Metropolitan Government." Accessed October 18, 2012. www.metro.tokyo.jp/ENGLISH/PROFILE/IMG/2012_en_39-55.pdf.

Toke, Dave. 2002. "Wind Power in UK and Denmark: Can Rational Choice Help Explain Different Outcomes?" *Environmental Politics* 11 (4): 83–100.

Toke, Dave, Sylvia Breukers, and Maarten Wolsink. 2008. "Wind Power Deployment Outcomes: How Can We Account for the Differences?" *Renewable and Sustainable Energy Reviews* 12 (4): 1129–1147.

Troesken, Werner. 1996. *Why Regulate Utilities? The New Institutional Economics and the Chicago Gas Industry, 1849–1924.* Ann Arbor: University of Michigan Press.

Tyebjee, Tyzoon T., and Albert V. Bruno. 1984. "A Model of Venture Capitalist Investment Activity." *Management Science* 30: 1051–1066.

UNEP (United Nations Environment Programme). 2009. "Global Green New Deal—An Update for the G20 Pittsburgh Summit."

UNESCAP (United Nations Economic and Social Commission for Asia and the Pacific). 2010. "Low Carbon Development Path for Asia and the Pacific: Challenges and Opportunities to the Energy Sector." ESCAP Energy Resources Development Series no. 41, United Nations, Thailand.

UNICA (Brazilian Sugar Cane Industry Association). 2008. "About Us—Mission." Accessed April 21, 2013. http://english.unica.com.br/quemSomos/texto/show.asp?txtCode={A888C6A1-9315-4050-B6B9-FC40D6320DF1}.

United Green Parties for Europe. 2009. "A Green New Deal for Europe: Manifesto for European Election Campaign." Manifesto presented at Black Sea Greens Conference, Sevastopol, Ukraine. http://europeangreens.eu/fileadmin/logos/pdf/manifesto_EUROPEAN_GREENS.pdf.

Unruh, Gregory. 2000. "Understanding Carbon Lock-In." *Energy Policy* 28 (12): 817–830.

———. 2002. "Escaping Carbon Lock-In." *Energy Policy* 30 (4): 317–325.

Urpelainen, Johannes. 2012. "How Do Electoral Competition and Special Interests Shape the Stringency of Renewable Energy Standards?" *Environmental Economics and Policy Studies* 14: 23–34.

304   Usami, Toru. 2004. "Economy Specific Research and Introduction of Successful Results of New / Renewable Energy Technology Development and Demonstration." Presentation to the 23rd Meeting of the Expert Group on New and Renewable Energy Technologies, Christchurch, New Zealand, November 10–13. Accessed August 25, 2011. http://www.docstoc.com/docs/43584290/Economy-Specific-Research-and-Introduction-of-Successful-Results-of.

van Ark, Bart, Robert Inklaar, and Robert McGuckin. 2002. *Changing Gear: Productivity, ICT, and Services: Europe and the United States*. Research Memorandum GD-60, Growth and Development Center, University of Groningen.

Vestergaard, Frede. 2006. "Foghs 180-Graders Vending." *Weekendavisen*.

Viana, Virgílio. 2008. *As florestas e o desenvolvimento sustentável na Amazônia*. Manaus: Editora Valer.

——. 2010. *Sustainable Development in Practice: Lessons Learned from Amazonas*. London: International Institute for Environment and Development.

Victor, David. 2011. *Global Warming Gridlock*. Cambridge: Cambridge University Press.

Victor, David, Joshua House, and Sarah Joy. 2005. "A Madisonian Approach to Climate Policy." *Science* 309 (5742): 1820–1821.

Vidal, John. 2010. "Cancún Climate Change Summit: Japan Refuses to Extend Kyoto Protocol." *The Guardian*, December 1. Accessed August 31, 2011. www.guardian.co.uk/environment/2010/dec/01/cancun-climate-change-summit-japan-kyoto.

Vlasic, Bill, and Matthew Wald. 2012. "Stalled Clean Energy Loan Program Feels Solyndra's Chill." *New York Times*, March 12.

von Burg, U., and M. Kenney. 2000. "There at the Beginning: Venture Capital and the Creation of the Local Area Networking Industry." *Research Policy* 29 (9): 1135–1155.

Wagner, Marcus. 2003. "The Porter Hypothesis Revisited: A Literature Review of Theoretical Models and Empirical Tests." Report, Center for Sustainability Management, University of Lueneberg, Germany. http://129.3.20.41/eps/pe/papers/0407/0407014.pdf.

Walker, Robert. 2011. "The Impact of Brazilian Biofuel Production on Amazônia." *Annals of the Association of American Geographers* 101 (4): 929–938.

Walker, Robert, John Browder, Eugenio Arima, Cynthia Simmons, Ritaumaria Pereira, Marcellus Caldas, Ricardo Shirota, and Sergio de Zen. 2009. "Ranching and the New Global Range: Amazônia in the 21st Century." *Geoforum* 40: 732–745.

Walsh, Bryan. 2010. "Prop 23 Is Defeated." *Time*, December 9. http://www.time.com/time/specials/packages/article/0,28804,2035319_2034098_2034140,00.html.

Wang, Tao, and Jim Watson. 2008. "China's Carbon Emissions and International Trade: Implications for Post-2012 Policy." *Climate Policy* 8 (6): 577–587.

Warde, Paul. 2007. *Energy Consumption in England and Wales, 1560–2004*. Naples: Consiglio Nazionale della Ricerche.

Watanabe, Chihiro. 1995. "Identification of the Role of Renewable Energy—A View from Japan's Challenge: The New Sunshine Program." *Renewable Energy* 6 (3): 237–274.

Watts, Jonathan. 2010. "China's Mega-Jams Show the True Cost of Coal." *Guardian Environment Blog*, August 25.

WCED. 1987. *Report of the World Commission on Environment and Development: Our Common Future.* New York: United Nations.

Weitzman, Martin. 1974. "Prices vs. Quantities." *Review of Economic Studies* 41 (4): 477–491.

Wen, Jiabao. 2011. "Zhengfu gongzuo baogao" [Report on government's work]. Presentation at the 4th Plenary Session of the 11th National People's Congress, Beijing.

Whitmore, Chris. 2011. "First Solar Completes 238 MW German Manufacturing Facility." PVTech, February 17. Accessed September 6, 2011. http://www.pv-tech.org/news/first_solar_completes_238mw_german_manufacturing_facility.

Williams, James H., Andrew DeBenedictis, Rebecca Ghanadan, Amber Mahone, Jack Moore, William Morrow, Snuller Price, and Margaret S. Torn. 2012. "The Technology Path to Deep Greenhouse Gas Emissions Cuts by 2050: The Pivotal Role of Electricity." *Science* 335: 53–59.

Woody, Todd. 2010. "China Snaps Up California Solar Market." *New York Times Green Blog,* January 14. http://green.blogs.nytimes.com/2010/01/14/china-snaps-up-california-solar-market/#more-38129.

World Bank. 1992. *World Development Report 1992.* New York: Oxford University Press.

———. 2012. "World Development Indicators." Accessed November 14, 2012. http://data.worldbank.org/country/brazil.

World Energy Council. 2010. *2010 Survey of Energy Resources.* London: World Energy Council.

Wüstenhagen, R., and T. Teppo. 2006. "Do Venture Capitalists Really Invest in Good Industries? Risk-Return Perceptions and Path Dependence in the Emerging European Energy VC Market." *International Journal of Technology Management* 34 (1/2): 63–87.

Xin, Yang. 2010. "Fengdian weihe 'songbuchu'?" [Why can't wind power be sent out?]. *China Daily,* April 6.

Xinhua. 2010. "Energy Reduction Policies Cause Unexpected Diesel Shortage in China." *Global Times,* November 7.

———. 2011a. "Sinovel Becomes World's No. 2 Wind Turbine Maker." *China Daily,* April 7.

———. 2011b. "China Drafting New Rules for Small Wind Farm Projects." *China Daily,* April 11.

Yang, Yongping, Xiyan Guo, and Ningling Wang. 2010. "Power Generation from Pulverized Coal in China." *Energy* 35 (11): 4336–4338.

Zachmann, Georg. 2011. "Is European Climate Policy the New CAP?" Bruegel Policy Brief 2011/01, Bruegel, Brussels.

Zachmann, Georg, Michael Holtermann, Jörg Radeke, Mimi Tam, Mark Huberty, Dmytro Naumenko, and Anta Ndoy. 2012. "The Great Transformation: Decarbonizing Europe's Energy and Transport Systems." Blueprint 16, Bruegel, Brussels, February 2.

Zhang, Chao. 2010. "Fengdian quanhai: Touzi huanyan zhong de xinyilun channeng guosheng?" [Wind power's ocean enclosure: Another round of over capacity in an investment feast?]. *Caijing Guojia Zhoukan* [Economy and Nation Weekly], April 23.

306   Zhang, Yi. 2010. "Xibu zuida tegaoya dianli tieta jidi luohu liangjiang xinqu" [Largest ultra-high-voltage transmission tower construction facility comes to the new zone of Chongqing]. *Renminwang Chongqing Shichuang* [People's Daily Network Chongqing], December 1.

Zhou, Nan. 2010. "Wen Jiabao: Baozhang nengyuan gongji anquan, zhichi jingji shehui fazhan" [Wen Jiabao: Ensure energy supply, support social and economic development]. *Xinhua*, April 22.

Zhou, Nan, David Fridley, Michael McNeil, Nina Zheng, Jing Ke, and Mark Levine. 2011. "China's Energy and Carbon Emissions Outlook to 2050." LBNL-4472E, Lawrence Berkeley National Laboratory, Berkeley, CA.

Zhou, Nan, Mark D. Levine, and Lynn Price. 2010. "Overview of Current Energy Policies in China." *Energy Policy* 30 (11): 6439–6352.

Zichal, Heather. 2010. "Expanding Safe and Responsible Energy Production." *The White House Blog*, March 8. http://www.whitehouse.gov/blog/2011/03/08/expanding-safe-and-responsible-energy-production.

Zider, Robert. 1998. "How Venture Capital Works." *Harvard Business Review* 76 (6): 131–139.

Zumbrun, Joshua. 2008. "The Most Energy-Efficient Countries." *Forbes*, July 7. Accessed September 3, 2011. www.forbes.com/2008/07/03/energy-efficiency-japan-biz-energy_cx_jz_0707efficiency_countries.html.

Zysman, John. 1983. *Governments, Markets, and Growth*. Ithaca, NY: Cornell University Press.

———. 1994. "How Institutions Create Historically Rooted Trajectories of Growth." *Industrial and Corporate Change* 3 (1): 243–283.

Zysman, John, and Mark Huberty. 2010a. "An Energy System Transformation: Framing Research Choices for the Climate Challenge." *Research Policy* 38 (9): 1027–2029.

———. 2010b. "Governments, Markets, and Green Growth: Energy Systems Transformation for Sustainable Prosperity." Working Paper 192, Berkeley Roundtable on the International Economy, University of California, Berkeley. http://brie.berkeley.edu/publications/WP192.pdf..

Contributors

EDITORS

John Zysman: John Zysman is a professor of political science at the University of California, Berkeley, where he is also codirector of the Berkeley Roundtable on the International Economy and cofounder of the Center for Research in Energy Systems Transformation. He is also a councilor for the Mandag Morgen Green Growth Leaders forum. Professor Zysman has served on a variety of public and private boards and as a consultant to governments and companies in Europe, Asia, and the United States, including the director's advisory board of Lawrence Livermore National Laboratory and the industrial advisory board of Los Alamos National Laboratory. He received his B.A. at Harvard and his Ph.D. at MIT.

Mark Huberty: Mark Huberty is a research associate at the Berkeley Roundtable on the International Economy and a visiting fellow at Bruegel. Mr. Huberty has received several notable awards, including the 2010–2011 Fulbright-Schuman fellowship at the European Union and the 2010–2013 STAR fellowship from the U.S. Environmental Protection Agency. Prior to his academic work, Mr. Huberty consulted in the United States and India with the international consultancy Accenture. He has degrees in chemistry from Harvey Mudd College and in European politics and in international economics from the Johns Hopkins University School of Advanced International Studies.

Benjamin Allen: Ben Allen is a Ph.D. candidate in political science at the University of California, Berkeley. His doctoral dissertation focuses on the politics of nature conservation in Brazil.

Crystal Chang: Crystal Chang is an instructor of political science at the University of California, Berkeley. Chang received her Ph.D. in political science from the University of California, Berkeley. She holds an MPIA degree in international management from the Graduate School of International Relations and Pacific Studies at the University of California, San Diego, and a B.A. in international relations from Stanford University.

Irene Choi: Irene Choi is a recent graduate of the University of California, Berkeley, where she served as an undergraduate research apprentice. Her work was prepared in close supervision by Nina Kelsey, Crystal Chang, and the Presidential Green Growth Commission of Korea. Choi is currently interning with the Korean Green Growth Commission.

Huan Gao: Huan Gao is a former researcher at BRIE and is now employed in local economic planning in Canada. Ms. Gao holds an M.A. from the University of California, Berkeley.

Andrew Hargadon: Andrew Hargadon serves as the Charles J. Soderquist Chair in Entrepreneurship and a professor of technology management at the Graduate School of Management at the University of California, Davis. Professor Hargadon is also a senior fellow at the Kauffman Foundation.

Nina Kelsey: Nina Kelsey is a Ph.D. candidate in the Department of Political Science at the University of California, Berkeley, where she focuses on international climate negotiations and green growth. Prior to entering the program, Nina worked for five years as a management strategy consultant for firms specializing in high-technology and telecommunications. She has a B.S. in molecular, cellular, and developmental biology, with a concentration in neuroscience from Yale University.

Martin Kenney: Martin Kenney is a professor of human and community development at the University of California, Davis, and senior project director at the Berkeley Roundtable on the International Economy.

Alice Madden: Alice Madden serves as the Writh Chair in Sustainable and Community Development at the University of Colorado Denver School of Public Affairs. She is a former Colorado state representative and majority leader, and she was Governor Ritter's climate change advisor and deputy chief of staff. Representative Madden is currently a senior fellow on climate change at the Center for American Progress.

Juliana Mandell: Juliana Mandell studied political science at the University of California, Berkeley, and she is currently a researcher at the Berkeley Roundtable on the International Economy.

Jakob Riisjkaer Nygård: Jakob Riisjkaer Nygård is working toward his M.Sc. in political science at the University of Copenhagen. Currently he is a trainee in the European Parliament with the S&D group working specifically with the Committee on Industry, Research and Energy. He worked as a researcher at the Berkeley Roundtable on the International Economy at the University of California, Berkeley.

Sean Randolph: Sean Randolph is president of the Bay Area Council Economic Institute. He is the former president and CEO of the Bay Area Economic Forum, and he previously served as director of international trade for the state of California. He has held numerous advisory positions in public and private sector endeavors, including time in the U.S. State Department, as special adviser for policy in the Bureau of East Asian and Pacific Affairs, and as the deputy assistant secretary of energy for international affairs, where he managed nuclear nonproliferation, energy research, and global oil and gas issues.

Jayant Sathaye: Dr. Jayant Sathaye is a group leader for international energy studies at Lawrence Berkeley Labs, and co-CLA for the Sustainable Development and Mitigation chapter of WG III of the IPCC Fourth Assessment.

Brian Woodall: Brian Woodall is an associate professor, associate chair, and director of graduate programs at the Sam Nunn School of International Affairs, Georgia Tech. Dr. Woodall has taught at the University of California at Irvine and at Harvard University. His research focus is comparative politics, with an emphasis on Japan and East Asia, international relations, and political economy.

Index

Italic page numbers indicate material in tables or figures.

tance to transmission lines, 146. *See also* consumers/citizens

QCells, 123, 258n13
Qinhuangdao, China, 201

radioactive waste, 167, 183, 252, 261n2
RadioPulse, 177
Rajiv Gandhi Grameen Vidyutikaran Yojana Act (2005; India), 241
ranching (Brazil), 214–216
R&D investment: by California, 134; by electricity sector, 31; by European Union, 113; and ICT boom, 56; by Japan, 156; by Korea, 175–176, 186; public vs. private, 57; research priorities, 261n5; research/regulation virtuous circle, 132; technology policy must support, 20
Rasmussen, Anders Fogh ("Fogh"), 95–96, 98
Rasmussen, Lars Løkke, 95
rebound effects, 53
recession (2008–2009): as emissions reduction tool, 45–46; green stimulus in response to, 49–50, 144, 172; and potential Eurozone dissolution, 265n19, 265n22; and timing of European Commission white paper, 264n9
REDD+ (Reduction of Emissions from Deforestation and Degradation–Plus; Brazil), 272n15
regulatory policy, 20, 57, 127
Remote Village Electrification Project (India), 242
renewable energy: average vs. marginal cost of, 259n5; intermittency issues, 29–30; possibilities for India, 235–238. *See also* hydroelectric power; solar energy; wind energy
Renewable Energy Directive (EU), 111, 114
renewable portfolio standards (RPS). *See* RPS (renewable portfolio standards)
Republican Party (U.S.), 142–143, 145, 146
research. *See* R&D investment
resilience, 40
Resources for the Future, 265–266n1
responsiveness, 40

retrofitting: buildings, 52; power plants, 145; systems, 15, 17, 58
retrofitting jobs, 17, 52
RFS1 and RFS2 (Renewable Fuel Standards; U.S.), 274n35
Risø, Denmark, 91
Ritter, Bill, 141, 144, 146
River Law (Japan), 165
river restoration, 171–172, 179, 182–183, 186
Rokkasho reprocessing plant, 168
Roland-Holst, David, 52, 269n3 (chap. 11)
rolling blackouts, 164, 230–231, 235
"Rooftop Program," 158
Rosted, Jørgen, 103
Rousseff, Dilma, 213–214, 224–225
RPS (renewable portfolio standards): in California, 134; in Colorado, 141–143, 145; in India, 238; in Japan, 160, 162; in Korea, 174
Russia, 117, 119, 159
Russo, Michael V., 63

Samsung, 178
Sancho, Ferran, 48
Sarney, José, 210
scalability of new ventures, 69–71
Schipper, Lee, 53
Schumpterian creative destruction, 60–61, 64
Scotland, 121
Seager, Ashley, 266n3 (chap. 9)
SEE ("supply with energy efficiency") scenario, 234–235
SELCO India, 237
self-sustaining processes: as appropriate goals, 19–20; Denmark's green growth policy, 100; requirements for, 148
semiconductors, 12
sequestration, 200, 205, 257n5, 258n14
SERCs (state electricity regulatory commissions; India), 240–241
SET-Plan, 111, 120
SFB (Brazilian Forest Service), 217, 273n32
Shah, Anwar, 47
shale, 126, 193, 255, 270n9
Sharan, Suni, 51
Shellenberger, Michael, 46, 53, 56